Representative
English Novelists:
Defoe to Conrad

———

Representative English Novelists: Defoe to Conrad

by

BRUCE McCULLOUGH

Professor of English
New York University

HARPER & ROW, PUBLISHERS

NEW YORK, EVANSTON, AND LONDON

Contents

Preface

My purpose in this book is not to trace the history of the English
novel in its many lines of development but to subject a limited number of representative novels to a more searching scrutiny than would
be possible in a general survey. Although there are many approaches
to the criticism of fiction and many diverse interests to be taken into
account, the purpose of any critic worthy of the name is to contribute
to a full understanding of the work occupying his attention. For a
thing so natural and so seemingly easy of comprehension as a novel,
the aid of the critic may seem to be unnecessary. It is possible, however, to enjoy a work of art and yet miss much of the artist's intention. And the fact that the novel has become one of the most natural
of literary forms does not signify that it is always the most intelligible
to the general reader. In fact, its very flexibility has given rise to a
formidable multiplication of methods and types of structure. Intelligent appreciation of the best in music, in painting, or in sculpture,
is hardly possible without study and training. Similarly a full appreciation of the art of fiction is the product of experienced reading
and reflection. To respond thoroughly to the stimulus of a great
novel is to go through something of the experience of the author in
writing it. Such a response requires not only sensibility and perception but also some knowledge of the author's craft and of the creative
process.

Henry James, who had cause to be exasperated by the inability
of readers to grasp his intentions, once promised his brother William
in an ironic outburst to write a novel for him on the "two-and-two-
make-four system" which would render it comprehensible and on
which so much "awful truck" was being produced. Few novels of
distinction, it is hardly necessary to observe, have been the products
of such a formula. Much of what is of the highest importance in a

novel is there by implication only; to perceive it the reader must be able not merely to follow the general drift of the narrative but to discern the complex of emotions and ideas from which it has originated. Here the critic can be of service if he possesses the knowledge, the sympathy, and the perception necessary to his task. Although he cannot expect to have all the knowledge, the breadth of sympathy, and the understanding required by such a far-ranging task of interpretation, he derives encouragement from the hope that his familiarity with novels and his experience in dealing with them can be made serviceable to the young student and the general reader.

One soon learns to distrust the critic who employs an endless stream of superlatives and finds genius lurking under every bush. The true love of literature is not fostered by such ready-made enthusiasm. One learns to value a book not from being given a certificate of its merit but by being shown how to get at the secret of its power. The critic's function in this respect is to help the reader gain an understanding of the conditions under which the author has worked and by which his impulses and intentions have been shaped. Like other problems, the problem of technique is to be considered not as a thing in itself but as a natural element in the equipment of the artist, closely related to his sensibilities and his point of view.

In dealing with these selected novels extending from a work of Defoe to one of Conrad and embodying widely divergent points of view, I have tried to meet each novelist on his own ground and never to condemn without first seeking to understand. I have made an effort to examine each novel from its germinating point in the mind and circumstances of the author and thus to see the different aspects of the book in their natural organic unity. I have sought to avoid repetition by placing emphasis in each chapter upon some significant feature of the novelist's art not elsewhere in this book treated with equal thoroughness. Finally, I have endeavored to trace, in some degree at least, the processes of change in fictional art which have been quietly taking place underneath the diversities of individual temperament and practice. In such changes, reflecting the complex of forces in a growing civilization, can be discerned the fundamental relation of literature to life.

In the preparation of this book I have been helped by many writers, to some of whom references will be found in the text and in footnotes. I should like to acknowledge particular indebtedness to Percy Lubbock's *The Craft of Fiction* (1921), E. M. Forster's *Aspects of the Novel* (1927), Edwin Muir's *The Structure of the Novel* (1929), Joseph Warren Beach's *The Twentieth Century Novel* (1932), and Ernest A. Baker's *The History of the English Novel,* 10 vols. (1924–1939).

Thanks of a more personal nature are due to Professor Louis Cazamian, who helped me to formulate the initial plan of the book. I am grateful to Professors Matthew W. Black and Walter MacKellar for reading portions of my manuscript and helping me with valuable suggestions, and to Dr. John Fisher for compiling the index. I have the deepest sense of obligation to Professor Homer A. Watt, who has helped me generously not only by reading sections of the manuscript and making suggestions but also by his kind encouragement throughout the progress of my work.

B. M.

CHAPTER I

The Conquest of Realistic Incident

DANIEL DEFOE

The author of *Robinson Crusoe* probably never paused in his labor to reflect that he might some day be hailed as one of the chief founders of the English novel. In all likelihood he was more concerned with the simple and immediate necessity of pleasing his readers than with useless speculations upon the future course of English fiction. There was nothing extraordinary about recounting the adventures of a man forced to live alone upon an uninhabited island. To give a faithful account of the career of a successful pirate, to tell the plain story of a woman the circumstances of whose life should lead her into bigamy, theft, and prostitution, was to do what others had done before. And what could be more natural in relating the life history of a famous courtesan than to do so in her own words? The secret once mastered, there was no limit to the possibilities of such dramatic impersonation as long as one could muster up enough detailed knowledge to achieve the appearance of validity. Castaway, adventuress, or pirate—it was all the same to Defoe. So he might assume the role of a young Englishman participating in a series of military campaigns, or write an account of London during the Plague of 1664–65 as if he had been present and an eyewitness of its many horrors.

Ostensibly there was nothing new in this trick of writing fiction as if it were fact. Mrs. Aphra Behn had frequently called her stories "histories." She had claimed to have been an eyewitness of many of the incidents set forth in *The History of the Royal Slave*. During the Restoration period and earlier, the practice of disguising fiction as fact and fact as fiction had become more and more general. Secret histories, spurious memoirs, *romans à clef*, chronicles of scandalous gossip, took the place of fanciful and lighthearted romance. A growing taste for credibility was inevitable in an age which was turning in every way less imaginative and more literal and controversial in its attitude to the problems of life. Writers felt in the change a greater need for clarity and avoidance of improbability. The old-fashioned and improbable romance was no longer quite the thing.

In giving his fiction to the public in the form of travel book, biography, or make-believe history, Defoe was not departing from the prevailing fashion. His originality consisted not in the form into which his novels were cast but in the fact that he did completely and effectively what his predecessors had only halfheartedly feigned to do. He invented a technique of circumstantial narration which enabled him to secure an unparalleled appearance of credibility and validity in the depiction of wholly imaginary events. By prolonged consistency in point of view, explicit concentration upon the focal point of his narrative, and extreme care and economy in the handling of details, he was able to create the appearance of lifelike reality and to destroy once for all the flimsiness and superficiality which, with the loss of the imaginative attitude of the Elizabethans, had come to be the chief stumbling block of the fiction writer. His imagination was nourished upon the outer manifestation of human activity, which he presented in scenes of remarkable energy and solidity.

In pretending to break completely with the literary tradition of fiction Defoe was actually giving to fiction the impetus of a new starting point. He was establishing it upon a new foundation of realism more in accord with the needs and tastes of the time. Pretending that his stories were the authentic records of actual personages, he concealed his invention so well, and his skill in deception was so great, that for a long time the *Memoirs of a Cavalier* was accepted as an actual military journal. *A Journal of the Plague Year* was likewise thought to have come from the pen of an eyewitness of the events described. *Roxana,* according to its preface, was different from the ordinary chronicle of scandal in that its foundation was laid in truth of fact; it was not a story but a history. In the preface to *Moll Flanders* the author sought to lure his readers into an acceptance of the actuality of the central personage by complaining that the world was so taken up with novels and romances that a private history in which the names had to be concealed was in danger of not being taken for genuine.

Why did Defoe go to such lengths to conceal from his readers the extent of his invention? Why did he, good journalist that he was, reject all claim to literary originality, and pose as the simple chronicler of out-of-the-way scenes and events? Moreover, why, in setting forth such extraordinary adventures as life in a plague-stricken city or on a lonely island, in tracing such out-of-the-way careers as belonged to pirates and highwaymen—why, in dealing with the unusual, did he avoid all appearance of the unusual? Why did he reject all ornament and subtlety and set forth his most striking subjects in the atmosphere of everyday reality?

The answers to these queries may be looked for in the temper of the age, as has been suggested, in the author's temperament, in his experience as political writer and journalist, and in the fact that fiction, as commonly understood, had come to be held in low esteem by the mass of middle-class readers, to whom its artificial gallantry and cynical idealization of vice were offensive and its affected, high-flown sentiment and pose hardly comprehensible. Defoe's renunciation of the outward forms of literary pretense, and his subordination of all aims to the single contrivance of making his stories lifelike by a circumstantial narration of details carefully marshaled to resemble the truth, have frequently been denoted as lying. To give it such a name and to treat it as a personal idiosyncrasy or perversity of the writer is to ignore his great astuteness in so shrewdly diagnosing the taste of his reading public both in its insatiable curiosity for facts and in its impatience with the threadbare conventions of romantic fiction.

For more than two centuries before the time of Defoe prose fiction had not succeeded in establishing itself in England as a leading literary form. Its failure was due in a measure to the excessive concern which it had for ingenuity of form, to its inability to bear the load of romantic and fantastical extravagancies heaped upon it by Sidney and Lyly. The romantic and chivalric world reflected in the *Morte d'Arthur*, when it was first printed in 1485, was already a world of the past. Later in the bustling years of the Renaissance, poetry and drama became the outstanding forms of literary expression. Until well into the seventeenth century the theatre served as the most important means of popular entertainment. The romance, in verse or prose, had fallen from the place of importance which it held in the Middle Ages. It became more limited in its appeal, a sort of pretty toy for the delectation of people of leisure and culture. *Euphues*, by John Lyly, was such a gem of courtly language and rarified sentiment, and even more remarkable was the *Arcadia*, written by Sir Philip Sidney for the pleasure of his sister, the Countess of Pembroke. It is a highly intricate tale of chivalry and love in a setting and atmosphere exquisitely pastoral. Enamored princes in disguise pay court to lovely princesses who have been temporarily reduced by circumstances to the simple and carefree life of shepherd maidens. Adventures ranging from the most sanguinary fighting to the most poetic love-making are depicted in a style delicately embroidered and bestrewn with jeweled figures of speech, and so perfectly interwoven are the maze of incidents that the reader can only marvel at the ingenuity of the author in evolving order out of such seemingly utter perplexity.

Nevertheless, remarkable as the *Arcadia* was in intricacy of pattern and sense of color and in the strength of its poetic conception, it represented a fantastic game rather than an effort to mirror contemporary reality. Realism began to appear in cony-catching pamphlets describing the activities of rogues. Thomas Nashe showed in *The Unfortunate Traveller* that stirring material for fiction could be found in the real life of camp and tavern. Thomas Deloney, a silk weaver, depicted the careers of fellow tradesmen and opened up in the material of domestic fiction a homely sphere which the romancer felt to be beneath his notice. In general, however, the gulf between fiction and contemporary life remained unbridged.

The romance failed on the one hand to mirror the contemporary scene and on the other to throw any new light upon the face of experience.

In time a change did come. Change is the law of life, and so of literature. The worldly fervor and passion of the Renaissance must bow before the thwarting will of the Reformation. The rich humanity and splendor of Shakespeare's world must cool into a world of religious and political controversy. The resultant growing cleavage between courtly circles and Puritans was marked by a change of manners. Romanticism began to wear a mask and to mock at itself and at virtue. Wit usurped the place of fancy, and sentiment lost the purity of its tone and became tainted with insincerity and sensuality. Little wonder that the Puritans grew to look upon the novel as the work of the devil to be held in abhorrence. Moreover, there was arising a new section of public taste neither courtly nor wholly Puritan, represented by the growing mass of uncultivated readers of the lower and middle classes. Such readers did not have the experience or training to appreciate the urbane gallantries and fopperies of Restoration fiction. Thus, as a result of various factors, fiction came to be scorned as something childish and trivial, or condemned for its licentiousness and impurity.

Obviously the appetite for romance, or something like it, was not dead. Because of her excesses and indecencies the novel had caused barriers of prejudice to be raised up against herself. Contaminated and disreputable, she was disowned even by her own practitioners, who sought to appease their readers by the appearance of sobriety and utility based upon fact. So it was that Defoe, by concealing the purely imaginary character of his stories and disguising them as the records of actual lives, was read by many well-meaning people who would have hesitated to waste their time or endanger their souls by reading romances. By writing in a direct, plain style in place of the slightly formal style still current among literary men, by adopting a tone of gravity and earnest morality in place of the former flippancy and cynicism, and by creating for his readers the convincing illusion of being present at the scene of action instead of indulging in the childish make-believe of his predecessors, Defoe widened and rendered more universal the appeal of fiction and established it anew upon a solid basis of dignity and popular approval.

The highest triumphs in literature are not won by technical dexterity. It was to something more than skill that Defoe owed his greatest success. *Robinson Crusoe* has been one of the most widely read books in the world. Its phenomenal success sets it apart as the book with which its author's name is most generally identified. Thousands upon thousands have read it to whom its successors, equally deserving in workmanship, have remained unknown. The explanation of this superiority of appeal does not lie in greater skill as much as in a happier combination of circumstances working together in a way which the author did not contrive, and producing an effect which he did not wholly foresee. In no other instance did he hit upon a theme so inherently attractive and so pregnant with suggestiveness. It was man's struggle against nature set forth in bare and simple terms and in a clear and vivid picture in which there was nothing to confuse or obscure the single dramatic issue. The island setting, itself stimulating to the imagination, was, moreover, admirably adapted to the theme and the drama of its enactment. It is worthy of note also that to no one of Defoe's subjects was his method of circumstantial narration better suited. What the hero *did* to maintain his life upon the island was the essential story and the central core of the drama. Even this harmony of theme and setting and narrative medium was not everything working in the author's favor. A curious blending of impressions, half familiar and half unfamiliar, was effected by the homely and familiar treatment of a romantic and far-distant scene. Crusoe behaved like a good Englishman. He did what anyone would have done—anyone blessed with ordinary courage and skill, if we assume it possible under such conditions to keep one's sanity. It was the island and the lonely situation which transformed the story from prosaic fact to potent fancy. It was not only what was said but what was implied. The chill of loneliness, the sense of freedom from interference, the opportunity to work out one's own salvation with the tools at his disposal—such a combination of the homely and the unusual it was that gave the fillip to the reader's imagination and served as a corrective sauce to the dry manner and evenness of tone of the author. Never again was he to strike just this happy combination of factors. He might in his subsequent books depict emotion more revealingly; he might show more sustained constructive power and employ a more sprightly style. He might in a number of ways here and there surpass the earlier book, but nothing could take the place of Crusoe and his wonderful island. When we think of the careers of Moll and Roxana and Singleton, we can readily understand why.

The art of Defoe may be said to consist primarily in simplification. Whatever is not necessary to the making of a thread of consistent narrative has little place in it. The person best fitted to act as reporter of such an extended series of happenings is the person most directly involved in them. This is particularly the case if the events are to be presented as they have occurred, a fact which is attested by the premium placed upon firsthand evidence in any court of law. It would seem that, in adopting the method of putting his story into the mouth of the chief character, Defoe was following the logic of necessity. He was, in any case, employing the only method well suited to his trick of authentication by means of excessive detail. Undoubtedly a circumstantial narration of events in the third person would lose something of the air of authority and naturalness which the presence of the first person singular gives to it.

His method once established, Defoe apparently found it adequate to his needs. He used it with almost equal effectiveness in dealing with a variety of subjects. It is true that his subjects were all similar in that they involved the careers of adventurous men or women. Whatever superiority one of his fictions might have over another was due to the subject more than to his treatment of it. A *Journal of the Plague Year*, dealing as it did with striking scenes, such as the burial of the dead at night under the light of torches, was particularly effective in its graphic power. *The Fortunate Mistress* came the nearest to having a symmetrical plot of any of the novels. It also contained at least one situation conducive to the production and dramatic portrayal of emotion of a somewhat complex character. Probably, however, Defoe did not concern himself much with the niceties of execution. Whether he realized that his method could not be pushed too far or relied upon for a great variety of effects, or whether he simply ignored aspects of his subjects lying beyond a certain range, cannot be fully determined. It must be remembered that he wrote rapidly and turned out during his lifetime an enormous amount of copy. His life had already been long and fruitful before he wrote *Robinson Crusoe*. With the tremendous success attending the new venture, he could not reasonably be expected to trouble himself greatly about fine points of psychology or nuances of feeling. Such refinements were for the formal fiction in the cultivated literary tradition, which he had fortunately not been bred up to. They represented the artificiality and insincerity which, as a writer of popular literature for the sober middle-class reader, he naturally would wish to avoid.

Moll Flanders

Probably no one of Defoe's novels provides better material for the study of his method than *The Fortunes and Misfortunes of Moll Flanders*. Though less picturesque than *Robinson Crusoe*, it contains more of the stuff of human relations, in which respect it also surpasses *The Fortunate Mistress* and *Captain Singleton*. Moll, though she preys upon it, comes closer to ordinary society than any of the other characters. Her story raises a number of problems for the author. She goes through various stages of prosperity and also of shame and misfortune. She figures variously as respected wife and mother, as semi-respectable mistress, and as thief, prostitute, and convict. Her life history is set before us from childhood to old age.

Mr. Ernest A. Baker[1] has pointed out that the Elizabethan writers of fiction had only a vague notion of what a novel should be. They did not know "whether the main object was the story or the moral, the incidents or the picture of life." They had also to learn at what point to begin and how to bring the story to an end. What aspects of the story material should be emphasized and what were the effects properly to be sought? There would be new problems arising later, but any sensible novelist could proceed without trying to do everything at once. There would never be an ideal solution for all the problems, and time would pass and progress be made before

[1] *The History of the English Novel: the Elizabethan Age and After*, London, 1929, p. 14.

the simplest of them could be clearly comprehended and defined. In the meantime fiction had to be one thing or another. Experimentation as to what it can best be has not yet ceased.

Although Defoe did not tackle many of the problems confronting the fiction writer, he at least had a working conception of his task. He provides a convenient point at which to begin the study of the novel because, though he lacks much which has now come to be regarded as essential to the novelist, he brings together the best of what went before him. He provides an excellent example of what can be done with a few tools effectively used. Narration is the only tool which he uses with full effect. The shortcomings of his method can be realized more completely when the work of his successors is examined. For the present it is more essential to attend to what, with the limiting factors of his personality, his time, and his method, he did manage to achieve. He is withal the first English novelist who can properly be called modern.

The complete title of *Moll Flanders* is *The Fortunes and Misfortunes of the Famous Moll Flanders, who was born in Newgate, and during a Life of continued Variety, for Threescore years, beside her Childhood, was Twelve years a Whore, Five Times a Wife (whereof once to her own Brother), Twelve years a Thief, Eight years a Transported Felon in Virginia, at last grew Rich, lived Honest, and died a Penitent. Written from her own Memorandums.* The criminal part of the story predominates in the novel. It is pointed out in the preface, however, that a moral benefit may be derived from reading a record of debauchery. While promising a variety of adventures which are likely to be shocking, the author reassures the more timid of his readers by a forecast of repentance and eventual success. Sensational material leading on to forbidden ground combined with improvement for the reader and gratification of his taste for moral edification provide an unfailing formula for popular appeal. The title of the novel, as well as its preface, shows that Defoe wrote definitely with his reading public in mind and knew how to appraise its tastes.

He takes an impersonal view of his subject rather than a personal one. A woman's career it is, not her character. There is no close connection between her character and her actions. Despite the perfunctory effort to give moral weight to Moll's acts, they are, in the main, as essentially unmoral as the basketmaking of Crusoe. They spring from external necessity rather than from moral disposition. It would be wrong, however, to infer that Defoe makes a careful study of the effect of environment upon character. Not much attention is given to the underlying sources of conduct. This is another way of saying that the subject matter of the novel is the activity of the main character for its own sake. The singular way in which she escapes the corroding and disintegrating effects of a life of crime is evidence that her creator was little concerned with the problem of her development. Moll always retains a resourceful nature, which a life of crime seems to sharpen rather than dull. When in Newgate prison, she says of herself that she became thoroughly degenerate as a result of the horrible influences of the place. In reality, however, her enterprising nature is displayed with all her accustomed zeal when she discovers that one of her earlier husbands is also an inmate of the prison.

The practice of taking a personage from low life for his central character has led to the classification of Defoe as a picaresque novelist. Although he followed certain of the picaresque conventions, his treatment as a whole was markedly different. The picaresque novel was developed principally in Spain and France, where its origin was associated with the satirical reaction against the pastoral and heroic romances. A humble character, usually employed as a servant and possibly driven to petty cheating or thieving by the narrowness of his circumstances, was given the place of importance in the story which in the romance had been occupied ordinarily by a person of high degree and heroic character. In place of the heroic exploits of the romantic hero, the picaresque romance concerned itself with the petty and often ridiculous doings of a servant. Ridicule was cast not only upon the rogue servant but also upon his master, or succession of masters. The rogue served as the center of action and connecting link between the different adventures, but frequently the subject lay rather beyond the rogue himself in the satirical representation of manners. The tone was gaily satirical rather than sober and sympathetic. Although the rogue might be in some measure a victim, he was usually depicted as glorying in his roguery. The reader could find pleasure in his tricks to cheat others without sympathizing with him personally.

Defoe's inspiration did not come by way of comic reaction to the poetic. His concern with the old romances was merely to avoid their artificial unreality and sense of improbability. He was closer in spirit to the criminal biographies of his day than to the ironical and socially motivated picaresque novels of France and Spain. These accounts of famous criminals appealed to much the same instincts in the reader as the police news of the modern newspaper. The picaresque novel, though it often fell to pandering to the gross desire for sensation, showed, in its finer manifestations, a more intellectual attitude. There was in it a relish of experience and a sense of maturity which came from a detached contemplation of man's frailty and folly, rather than the almost exclusive absorption in the affair of the moment which is characteristic of Defoe.

Moll is a sympathetic figure, never ridiculous. She tells her story soberly and earnestly, not in the mocking manner of the picaresque hero. She does not wantonly rejoice in her rogueries. Her creator concentrates so intently upon his subject that the atmosphere of his story seems almost painfully unrelaxed as compared with the genial mood and episodic manner of the picaresque novel. Nobody ever has time to enjoy an inn fire or listen to a story in one of Defoe's novels. Perhaps the nearest that any of his characters ever come to sheer enjoyment is Crusoe at dinner with his island family:

> It would have made a stoic smile to have seen me and my little family sit down to dinner. There was my majesty, the prince and lord of the whole island; I had the lives of all my subjects at my absolute command. I could hang, draw, give liberty, and take it away; and no rebels among all my subjects.
>
> Then to see how like a king I dined, too, all alone, attended by my servants. Poll, as if he had been my favorite, was the only person permitted to talk to me. My dog, who was now grown very old and crazy, and had no species to multiply his kind upon, sat always at my right hand, and two cats, one on one side the table, and one on the other, expecting now and then a bit from my hand, as a mark of special favor.

Even here, Crusoe is not giving himself up wholeheartedly to the pleasure of the moment but is pointing out how God has treated him mercifully. And he goes on immediately to explain that the two cats were not the ones that he had taken from the boat: "They were both of them dead, and had been interred near my habitation, by my own hand. But one of them having multiplied by I know not what kind of creature, these were two which I had preserved tame, whereas the rest run wild in the woods, and became indeed troublesome to me at last; for they would often come into my house, and plunder me too, till at last I was obliged to shoot them, and did kill a great many; at length, they left me."

This passage will serve to show how far is Defoe's tone from the ironic mood of picaresque fiction. Defoe, on the whole, performed a humbler function than that of the picaresque novelist and appealed to a less complex mental attitude. In general, he appears as the simple recorder without *arrière-pensée*, other than to point a moral now and then, although there is doubtless irony in the reference to the relation of a king to his subjects in the passage quoted. His moral attitude is usually conventional. It does not render his treatment more complex but serves as a superficial gloss. Sometimes he is definitely satirical, but the more literal tone prevails. In avoiding complexity he gains in unity and consistency.

Moll takes a simple but recognizably human attitude toward the problems of her life. What she does is credible and consistent and always expressive of her unflagging energy and resourcefulness. The background of society in which she moves is indistinct when compared to the work of Scott or Thackeray. There is, however, a more recognizable background than in the romances, and Moll alone against the law acquires a certain vividness of outline. Defoe's impassiveness enables him to escape the danger of sentimentalizing his heroine as the victim of society. Her superficial moral protests in regard to her own guilt are so many sops to the reader, which were no doubt necessary at the time. They are now so meaningless that the baldness of her narrative is hardly affected by them. For the author to have made her more sensitive would have been to destroy the credibility of his heroine. It would have given a different kind of value to the subject and required a different treatment.

In addressing itself to the taste for the marvelous, the romance had not been bound by the necessity of consistency. The narrator's irresponsibility might extend to every important feature of his story. The behavior of the hero might be improbable or impossible, the attendant circumstances lacking in plausibility, and the setting have only a fanciful reality. The great weakness of fiction, Defoe must have felt, was its failure to evoke an illusion of actuality. His choice of the chronicle form showed that for him the most important element in fiction was its factual consistency. In so choosing he helped to establish the conception of the novelist as historian and provided a valuable lesson in documentation, which Swift and Richardson were soon to utilize. Fielding and Scott, in turn, enlarged the tradition of the novel as history and created the novel of manners.

Defoe does not recount with equal fullness everything that happens to Moll. He devotes only ten pages to her childhood and thirty-four pages to her seduction and first marriage. The five years of married life coming immediately afterwards are disposed of in a paragraph. The part of her life most vivid in the presentation is probably her career as a thief. In the more or less respectable portion of her life the most memorable events are her early seduction, her discovery that she is married to her half brother, her unusual relationship with the man at Bath whose mistress she eventually becomes, and her clever postponing of one marriage while she disposes of a child which is the unwelcome product of another. The five years of tranquil married life coming just before she turns thief do not have any interest for her chronicler. He can describe her marriages and thefts because they provide material easily caught in action. As the settled routine of a contented married woman cannot be dealt with effectively in the same manner, it receives less attention than the more adventurous episodes.

We get no such sense of a densely populated world in Defoe's novels as in the pages of Fielding or Scott. The concentration upon a single figure leaves the surrounding circumstances dim. Our attention is centered not only upon one character but upon a circumscribed area of her personality as well. Moll is always intent upon the problem immediately confronting her. What to do next is her sole concern. Instead of pausing to enjoy the relaxation that might be expected to follow the completion of an enterprise, she gives the impression of turning quickly to something else. She spends no time in useless regret or in pining for what is not. She does not change appreciably with time but is the same Moll in prosperity and in misfortune, in youth and in age. One gets no impression that her childhood is rich in dreams or her age in memories. In short, she comes fully to life only in her actions; in her reflections and feelings she is only a faint echo of her creator. We should know her better if we saw more particularly into her intentions, or if her feelings were more genuinely a part of her.

The method made so peculiarly his own by Defoe became for him something of a tyrant—a consuming dragon that could live only on facts. He had to find expression for his material in a process of explicit action. The result was to imprison the characters in the web of circumstance. Somehow they were infected by their creator's habit of incessant toil, or they could not escape the effects of the steady accumulation of mallet strokes that served to pound their beings into shape. Their lives never came, in a personal sense, to any proper flowering. Growing in a soil that was spiritually barren, they were soon enclosed in the struggle for existence. The game itself excited the author and served equally to absorb his puppets. Moll knew little enough of the happy irresponsibility of youth. Her life was lacking in the factors making for a full personality. Viewed in such a light, she remains rather mechanical and flat. She does not go through the normal fluctuations of mood. One gets from her no definite sense of the intangibility of emotion, in which reflection and feeling, hope and disappointment, faith and skepticism, may all have a share. She gives no impression of a completely rounded life, enriched by the process of living and the accumulation of time.

In tracing the development of a literary form we are in danger of assuming that art follows regular processes of development and that, as in science, the blunders of one generation can be rectified by the superior learning of the next. Such an attitude is founded upon a false assumption that art, like science, is always groping its way nearer to demonstrable truth. Science advances independently of the individual scientist. On the other hand art, which is more than mere technique, is the record of an experience. The validity of a work of art depends upon the success with which it gives expression to a widely felt experience. It cannot be supplanted by subsequent expression of subsequently felt experience. A naïve science possesses only historical and humanistic interest for later generations. A naïve art, on the other hand, does not necessarily lose its vitality. Although there is development in technique, the freshness with which an artist looks at life and catches the wonder of an experience is not subject to laws of progressive development. A self-conscious craftsman may be master of all the tricks of his trade and yet repel us by his expert manipulation of material without any personally felt emotion.

Accordingly it is not necessary to make excuses for Defoe's limitations. It is more important that he gave expression to the widely cherished emotions of his age and class than that he should have possessed a different kind of sensibility or have been more interested in the dramatic possibilities of his material. His service to fiction was to bring it down to earth and plant its feet squarely on the ground. In *Moll Flanders* he was recording the life of a criminal. It was in her acts that she was a criminal and it was natural for her delineator, with his journalistic background, to find his subject in such aspects of his material as were commonly written about. The form in which he set forth the problem of a woman leading the life of a criminal in the London of his time was a likely, if not an inevitable, one.

What is interesting to us as readers of a later age is to apprehend as fully as we can what the novel under scrutiny essentially is. It cannot be for us exactly what it was for its first readers. It was written to meet needs and satisfy tastes that are not ours today. Subsequent modifications of the art of fiction and changes of attitude toward the problems with which the book deals make it a different thing for us from what it was to the eighteenth-century reader. By throwing light upon a past age and helping to mark a stage in the development of an art form, it thus acquires an interest and significance which it did not originally have.

Considered in relation to later developments, it does not, for one thing, convey an adequate sense of social atmosphere. Moll's life is too much isolated from that of her fellow creatures, even from that of her fellow criminals. Also it is deficient in the sense of place. The presence of London is not felt as it is in *A Tale of Two Cities*, or as Paris is felt to permeate *The Ambassadors,* of Henry James. Such a lack of atmosphere is the natural result of Moll's being so little aware of her surroundings. We can hardly call it a deficiency in the novel, however, since it was not necessary to the author's purpose and did not figure therein. When the hero of *The Ambassadors* goes to Paris from his home in Massachusetts, it is an essential element in the situation that the charm of the foreign city shall be a factor in the determination of his course of action.

Equally marked in the novel is the lack of a sense of genuine development. The narrow functioning of the heroine's consciousness deprives the action of a high degree of unity. Aristotle defines plot as the "synthesis of the particular incidents which give form or being to the tragedy as a whole." He says further that the unity of a plot does not consist in having one man as a hero. Moll seems to live from day to day or from episode to episode. She retains no impressions of the past, to speak of, and there is not much to bind the different parts of her life together. The lack of close relationship between her actions and her character also militates against the effect of dramatic development.

The sense of isolation of the main character is intensified by the failure of the secondary characters to stand out distinctly. Compare the family with which Moll lived as a young girl with any family group of Jane Austen or Scott. The string of husbands, for the most part, leave but shadowy impressions. Not much of a picture is given of the underworld in which the heroine was forced to live. In other words, Defoe's novels are notably deficient in exterior or framing action, such as the background of public events in a novel of Scott, or the general social scene in *Vanity Fair.* Even such background as is represented by the stagecoaches and inns of Fielding is not to be found in *Moll Flanders.*

These various limitations indicate that the novel belongs to a low order of artistic expression, being historical and expository rather than lyrical or dramatic. It does not express as much or address itself to as many channels of feeling and experience as it is possible for a novel to do. Flaubert, for example, thought about Emma Bovary and the effect to be produced by his presentation of her in a way quite unlike Defoe's thought of his heroine. There was a fundamental difference between the two experiences of life which the two novelists wished to express. Flaubert's vision was of a different order and what he had to convey was as different as his procedure was unlike that of the earlier writer. To Flaubert the *facts* associated with his heroine were charged with particular meaning. Moll's career was for her creator a much simpler phenomenon. His art did not consist in sifting the facts, in selecting and rejecting, and in presenting such aspects of his heroine's consciousness of her world as would be necessary to convey an important truth about her whole epoch. Whereas Defoe could present a series of episodes designed simply to make the central figure plausible and interesting, Flaubert had to evoke an image and place it in relation with a particular community. He had to work out an adjustment between various aspects of his problem and order his heroine's behavior in accordance with a complex set of requirements.

The earlier novelist, needless to say, did not see his subject as the realization of a woman's life rendered significant in terms of her epoch. Although Flaubert's theme was bigger than his heroine, it could be rendered only through her. It was the essence of his subject that she should be what she was. No such weight was placed upon Moll. Little was required of her except to be the moving center of a series of plausible incidents. Being her own narrator, she could not, even if Defoe had so desired, employ the double vision of Flaubert, by which he was able to show Emma Bovary to the reader as she appeared to herself and also in her creator's more penetrating view of her.

The story of a woman's life told in the first person suggests something intensely personal. Defoe, however, was no Charlotte Brontë. Although Moll's story is something in the nature of a confession, it has little of the quality of a *personal* confession. As has already been indicated, it is the personal element in her account of herself that is most perfunctory and unreal. It is the practical aspect of her life which has appealed to Defoe. She tells her story with commendable frankness, under her disguise, and without pose or self-consciousness. She does not offend by subjective wailings, as a more modern Moll might have done.

The absence of a sense of perspective is particularly to be noted in the handling of the time element. Presumably the heroine tells her story in her old age with most of her life far behind her. In reality the record does not seem to bear out such a supposition. She is far enough from the event under scrutiny to relate it dispassionately and not far enough for its outlines to have become hazy in her memory. Richardson was soon to discover the value of letters written, as he said, "to the *moment,* while the heart is agitated by hopes and fears, or events undecided." Had Moll, in fact, written the account of her life in her old age, it would hardly have been as it is. On the other hand, had she written it as a diary from day to day, it would certainly have been very different. The method followed is arbitrary and does violence to the truth in that it does not reflect a definite impression from any clearly recognizable point of view in time. Neither the obscuring effect of distance nor the intensifying effect of nearness can be felt.

The point of view, or the points of view, from which a story is told is an important consideration for the novelist, as can be seen in novels all the way from Richardson to the present day. Defoe's choice of autobiography was made in the interest of the support and credibility of his narrative. His minutely circumstantial manner of narration had the effect of seeming to place the narrator close to the events related. Unfortunately it also reduced the means of securing light and shade and of varying the tension in accordance with the need for dramatic verisimilitude. More attention to the time element in the point of view would have helped to remedy these defects.

Defoe, then, to summarize, is not a fully equipped novelist. There is not much intimation in his pages of the rich procession of characters soon to appear in the novels of Fielding and Scott. He is also deficient in drama. Situations that cry for dramatic handling are coldly narrated by Moll with a few ineffective side remarks about her feelings. Although the narration of action is the novelist's chief stock in trade, he differs considerably from the later novelist of adventure, a fact which does not necessarily make him inferior to his more sophisticated descendants. He rarely employs incidents felt to be thrilling in themselves and he does not build up his situation so as to arouse a keen degree of suspense. He does not employ

the various forms of dramatic heightening of the tension by combining picturesque setting with unusual and exciting action. Some
exceptions to this are to be found, particularly in *Robinson Crusoe*
and *A Journal of the Plague Year,* but, in general, his quest for
verisimilitude leads him to seek for the usual rather than the thrilling. It must be admitted, however, that his simplicity is not always
without design. It is part of his art that the stories which he tells,
being presumably accounts of actual people, should appear to be
artless. Moreover, simplicity and freedom from self-consciousness
are qualities still worthy of esteem in the novel of adventure, which
to retain its atmosphere of heartiness and vigor and irresponsibility
must not be made to bear too heavy a load of artifice and intrigue.
I do not mean to suggest that Defoe is a writer of novels of adventure. On the whole, the lives which his characters lead seem to be
prosaic rather than adventurous, if we consider their own responses
to what confronts them. They keep themselves so firmly in hand
and pay such unbroken attention to the duty of the moment that
they have little heed for the world which to the adventurous soul
beckons from beyond the horizon. Being wrecked upon an uninhabited island is unquestionably an adventure, but to a Robinson
Crusoe it becomes mainly a practical problem of survival.

Not much has been said here about the plot of *Moll Flanders.*
Plotting involves care in working out the progression of events. It
requires attention to the causal relationship between one event and
another. It necessitates the presentation of a character with a due
regard to his motives as well as to his circumstances. The motivation
of character in a Defoe novel is considered only generally and
mostly from the outside. Only the resulting action is seen in its
particularity. The interlocking between action and character which
a complete and unified presentation of Moll's life would require, a
logical rather than a factual consistency of events, is lacking from
the novel.

The contribution of Defoe to the growth of the novel in England
was, for all his limitations, very important. He rescued fiction from
the narrowing artificiality of the Restoration romancers and pseudo-
realists. By breaking with the taste for elegance characteristic of
the prose of his time and writing in the idiom of the people, he

succeeded in establishing the novel upon a broad basis of popular approval and marked an important step in the democratization of letters. He showed the extraordinary force and cogency of realism as applied to factual detail. He had a remarkable faculty for minute narrative, which, even if it went unnecessarily far, was admirably well suited to the taste of the readers of his day. He lifted popular literature to the dignity and seriousness of humane letters; and, by the precision of his realism, he destroyed the vague indefiniteness of intention out of which the writers of fiction had been unable to grope their way. The novel was no longer to be a confused by-product of other forms of literature but could now exist in its own right. The ground was cleared for Richardson and the host of novelists who were to follow.

CHAPTER II

$\mathcal{T}_{he}$ $\mathcal{N}_{ovel}$ of $\mathcal{S}_{entiment}$

SAMUEL RICHARDSON

The aspect of Defoe that I have been most desirous of emphasizing is the vitality of his depiction of incident. It is in his capacity to set forth people in action that he is most original. The world in which his characters move is, with some exceptions, not much more than a featureless stage for their exploits. The world of their inner life, what we are permitted to see of it, is even less arresting, and of little account to us in forming an impression of them. Moll Flanders is not a person of strongly marked traits, either of the inner or the outer variety. She is not a *character* in the sense that Squire Western is one, or Walter Shandy. To compare her with Jane Eyre, or even with Clarissa Harlowe, is to perceive how completely she is without the self-consciousness or inner activity which is the distinguishing mark of a complete personality. Defoe may be designated as a novelist of incident and Richardson, who found his chief inspiration in Puritan sentimentalism, as a novelist of sentiment.

Defoe's main object in employing the method of putting his story into the mouth of his chief character was to secure authority for the events and an air of plausibility. Richardson's method of telling his story in a series of letters was similar in that it gave him the advantages of personal narration and freed him from the necessity of assuming the role of author. It provided him a greater opportunity for variety than the autobiographical framework but, as a medium for telling a story of much complexity, it was unwieldy and difficult to manage.

The casual manner in which Defoe had slipped from journalism into the writing of fiction was a sign of the way in which the novel was soon to attract many distinguished pens and become a much more important vehicle of literary expression than it had been in the past. Richardson, Fielding, Smollett, Sterne, and Mrs. Radcliffe, to name the leaders, turned to fiction and won for it a great extension of popularity, while for themselves they achieved a more lasting distinction than had been won by any novelist in the age just prior to Defoe.

Twenty years after the appearance of *Robinson Crusoe*, Samuel Richardson, a man of about fifty and a well-established printer in London, was asked by two of his friends to put together a small volume of letters to serve as models for poorly educated people. The proposal pleased him and he accepted it readily. The period to which he belonged has since come to be designated as the golden age of letter writing in England, and he shared in the disposition of the time to express itself in letters. Moreover, he probably derived pleasure from admonishing and instructing others. Such a tendency, besides being reflected in his novels, can be felt in his account of the way he began his humble venture into authorship: "Will it be any harm, said I, in a piece you want to be written so low, if we should instruct them how they should think and act in common cases, as well as indite? They were the more urgent with me to begin the little volume for this hint."

These letters eventually appeared as *Familiar Letters on Important Occasions*. They dealt with a variety of situations such as anyone might at some time or other have to face. How to reply to a proposal of marriage, how to avoid lending money, how to deal with an undutiful son, and how to dun a tenant behind in his rent are characteristic subjects. Some of the letters are recommendations to service; some offer consolation to persons in distress; others are descriptions of life in London such as might be written by a visitor to her friends at home. One of the model letters purports to be from a father to his daughter, who is in service, upon the occasion of her

being threatened by improper attentions from her master. The father advises her to leave her place at once and is soon gratified by her obedience to his commands. The important thing for us about this interchange of letters is that it contained the germ of *Pamela,* of which *Clarissa* was to be an elaboration with the circumstances changed.

The servant girl robbed of her virtue by her master was certainly not a strikingly original subject. Richardson had once heard of an affair in which a girl so situated had held her own against her master and had eventually won him to an honorable marriage. It occurred to him that the story of a young girl in such a situation could be told in a series of fictitious letters. The idea was carried out in *Pamela,* with the result that the author became quickly famous and was encouraged to go on with other similar stories. The book of model letters, which started it all, was put aside and not completed until after the publication of *Pamela.*

Clarissa, or the History of a Young Lady was first published in 1747–48 in seven volumes, about a quarter of a century after the appearance of *Moll Flanders.* Although *Clarissa* contains in the neighborhood of a million words and is seven or eight times as long as Defoe's novel, it covers less than a year in the life of its heroine as compared with the lifetime of Moll. Such a marked difference of treatment will be found upon examination to correspond to differences of various kinds. Defoe's active mind and adventurous life provided him with an abundance of material. Richardson's life was by comparison uneventful and his world restricted. Telling a story by the circuitous method of a voluminous correspondence would not have suited Defoe. His picture of the tangible world of events needed a simpler means of presentation. Had Richardson, however, been compelled to tell his story autobiographically and retrospectively, he would have soon come to the end of his matter. Not having anything like the diversity of material of Defoe for his imagination to work upon, he hit upon a method which enabled him to build up a world, even though an artificial one, out of the domestic doings and polite social rounds of his characters.

It is not simply a world of gossip and tea-drinking. The background is only slightly sketched, the main interest being concen-

trated upon the emotional life of the heroine. The issues at stake are vital to the person directly concerned, and Richardson manages to spread the contagion of emotional disturbance in which his chief characters move. In *Pamela* the problem is whether a man will succeed in debauching his servant or whether she will be able to withstand his attacks and win him to an honorable marriage. In *Clarissa* an intelligent and high-spirited young woman becomes so circumstanced between a false lover on the one side and a misled and stupidly tyrannical family on the other that she falls into her lover's power and dies as a result of his mistreatment. Here the issue rises above mere decorum and also above the problem of family authority.

In *Sir Charles Grandison* the plot turns upon which of two girls the hero will marry. Will it be Harriet Byron, a young woman of great charm, whom Sir Charles has saved from an attempted abduction, or will it be Clementina della Porretta, an exquisite young Italian of noble birth? Sir Charles, who always turns up at the right moment, like the hero of an adventure story, has saved Clementina's brother from being assassinated, as a result of which he is received into the family on terms of such friendliness that he teaches the young lady English. She falls in love with him, of course, and so does Miss Byron afterwards when he rescues her. The first obligation of Sir Charles is to the Italian girl, whose heart he has won unintentionally before having any knowledge of Miss Byron. The fate of the English girl thus hangs in the balance while the issue of the love match with Clementina is being decided.

The deciding point of this dilemma is the difference of religion between the two people; the hero is saved for Miss Byron when Clementina decides to renounce her love in the interest of her religion. The reader of the interminable negotiations between Sir Charles and the Porretta family may gain the uncomfortable impression that the heart of the hero beats rather too much in accord with the demands of propriety. For him to have given so much of his heart to Miss Byron while he was still under obligation elsewhere seems to be out of harmony with his otherwise perfect control of himself. His punctilious wooing of one girl while he apparently preferred another does not please the reader as much as it seems to

have pleased his friends. We are inclined to wish that Clementina had not been so grateful for his favors and to suspect that for all his protestations he did not care very much for her.

The first novel of Richardson was entitled *Pamela, or Virtue Rewarded,* and the author did not fail to reward his heroine. The fact that Clarissa was not so rewarded in a material way was due, no doubt, to the nature of the subject, although the criticism of *Pamela* may have caused the author to be on his guard against such a solution. In *Sir Charles Grandison,* however, he had a subject in which he could pile up rewards and pay compliments all around, the greater proportion of the praise being bestowed upon the hero.

It is not often that we are privileged to meet such a man. Clementina and Miss Byron were only two of half a dozen women who, in the course of the story, were eating their hearts out for him. He made a point of caring more for his own ideas of right and wrong than for the opinions of the world. He disapproved of dueling and refused to accept challenges despite his phenomenal skill with the sword. He refused to dock the tails of his horses. So independent was he that he was not afraid to dine earlier than the fashionable hour. Regardless of his bad opinion of it, the world threw itself at his feet, covering him with compliments. One feels, indeed, that, in the mind of Richardson, Miss Byron's chief reason for being meritorious was to fit her for being mated to such a prodigy.

Of the three principal characters in *Sir Charles Grandison,* Clementina is most likely to win our sympathy. Her misfortunes shield her from our dislike; her inability to control her heart is a form of human weakness. She is not a pattern of propriety. But in the case of the other two there is surely some vulgarity in the display of so much virtue. One is likely to feel that ladies and gentlemen take things more for granted. To let one's mind dwell perpetually upon another's inferiority would be offensive. To keep constantly in mind the excellence of a fellow creature, on the other hand, comes unpleasantly near to priggishness and the snobbishness of virtue.

Miss Byron's self-congratulatory attitude at the time of her marriage makes her appear not a little ridiculous. We can excuse her somewhat upon the grounds that in our own century the social status of women has improved and marriage is not made the occasion of so much ceremony. There is also the point to be taken into account that Richardson is using her to set forth the many superior qualities of his hero. Everything that Sir Charles does draws new cries of wonder and delight from her. While showing his friends through Grandison Hall he obliges them with a song, in which he manages to convey a neat compliment to his Harriet. She gives the following account of the scene to her grandmother:

How did our friends look upon one another, as the excellent man proceeded! I was astonished. It was happy I sat between my aunt and Lucy! They each took one of my hands. Tears of joy ran down my cheeks. Every one's eyes congratulated me. Every tongue but mine, encored him. I was speechless. Again he obliged us. I thought at the time, I had a foretaste of the joys of heaven! How sweet is the incense of praise from a husband; that husband a good man; my surrounding friends enjoying it! How will you, madam, rejoice in such an instance of love so pure, and so grateful! Long, long may it be, for the sake of his Harriet, his and her friends, for the world's sake, before his native skies reclaim him!

He approached me with tender modesty; as if abashed by the applause he met with. But seeing me affected, he was concerned. I withdrew with my aunt and Lucy. He followed me. I then threw myself into his arms; and, had speech been lent me, would have offered him the fervent vows of a heart overflowing with love and gratitude.

Lady Grandison was happy to have such a husband. A more impartial scrutiny of the man, however, is likely to convince the reader that Richardson has made his last novel like his early book of model letters. Sir Charles and Miss Byron are model characters to an extent that is not true of Pamela or Clarissa. Sir Charles moves through his genteel paces with too clocklike a precision to convey the impression of a living being. The simplest process of living requires a certain amount of resistance between the living organism and its environing conditions. Complete and uniform harmony between the two could hardly result in emotion or the sense of experience. Pamela's conduct does not conform wholly to her code of behavior. There is resistance between her awakened love and the path of duty and safety. Clarissa's struggle is a real one. The clash of forces between which she is caught cannot be calculated to a nicety. Her will may triumph over circumstances but the circumstances remain to plague her.

By comparison with Clarissa, Sir Charles is the spoiled darling of circumstance. The stage is always arranged for him to display himself to advantage. He has such complete mastery over every corner and crevice of his moral and social milieu that he can walk the tightrope of an intricate courtship as faultlessly as a spider spins its web. It is apparently nothing to a man of his tact and diplomacy to be in the situation of being loved simultaneously by two equally desirable women. Tom Jones could not have maintained such a position without committing some act of folly. Nevil Beauchamp, of *Beauchamp's Career,* by George Meredith, did love two women, though not simultaneously. He blundered and lost both of them. But in his blunders and in what would have been the folly of Tom there was more of human truth and feeling than in the delicately poised considerateness of Sir Charles.

Richardson, like Bunyan and Defoe, was a product of Puritan culture. His writing, like Bunyan's, represents strife between the forces of good and of evil. The vices which he depicts reflect the vanity and irresponsibility of the old aristocratic order, whereas his virtues are the virtues of the prudent and God-fearing lower and middle classes. *Clarissa* was intended to teach a lesson of obedience to children and of moderation and intelligence to parents in their handling of the marriage problem. In its more than two thousand pages only one thing matters greatly. Will vice, in the person of Lovelace, triumph over virtue, in the person of Clarissa, and, if so, what will be the ultimate result? If the author, in depicting the struggle, has the air of being shocked by the iniquities of the passing aristocratic order and at the same time of being dazzled by its brilliance, he is probably being true to the middle-class spirit of his age. There is much that is naïve as well as vulgar in his moral and also in his social attitude. His morality is not so just as Bunyan's and his picture of the Puritan conscience not so clear of the dross of worldliness. The sin entering his purlieus does not arouse emotions of unmixed abhorrence. A stray spirit has slipped unawares into this well-tended, formal moral garden. Lovelace's flouting of the law contains in it the element of *escape* from rigid decorum. Changed somewhat, he will reappear as the villain in Gothic fiction and will even leave his mark upon the romantic rebel of a later generation.

Clarissa

The title page of Richardson's novel runs as follows: *Clarissa. Or, The History of a Young Lady: Comprehending The most important Concerns of Private Life. And particularly shewing, The Distresses that may attend the Misconduct Both of Parents and Children, In Relation to Marriage. Published by the Editor of Pamela.*

Although the amount of action in *Clarissa* is not great, it would require many pages of summary to give a full account of the intricate pattern of motive and cross-motive, of comment and cross-comment, through which the comparatively simple action unfolds. The heroine is a young woman in her late teens who is a member of a well-to-do country family. The family circle, which is important since the novel deals primarily with a domestic situation, consists of Clarissa's father and mother, an older sister Arabella, and a brother James, who, as the only male heir, seems to regard himself as the virtual head of the house. There are also two uncles and an aunt, who take part in the deliberations by which the affairs of the family are conducted. No important step seems ever to be taken by the family without solemn meetings and consultations of the members.

Up to the opening of the story Clarissa has been a dutiful daughter, the delight of her parents and uncles. Her grandfather, now deceased, has, perhaps too fondly, distinguished her beyond the other children in his will. Thus, through no fault of her own, she, the general favorite, has incurred the enmity of her brother and sister. James sees in the popularity of his sister a threat to his ambition to gain a peerage, particularly as his uncles show signs of making her their principal heir. Arabella, already envious because Clarissa is so much admired, is stung to malicious fury when her supposed suitor, Mr. Lovelace, joins the throng of the younger girl's admirers.

It soon becomes clear to the reader of this novel that Richardson is not proceeding by a simple recording of events in the order of their occurrence and that a more complex method is being followed than the letter form makes necessary. The author is engaged in showing that a variety of factors are at work in shaping the situation of his heroine. A just estimate of this situation is necessary in order to understand the true significance of what is to follow. Accordingly we are given glimpses into the past life of the family. We learn how Lovelace has disappointed Arabella and has more than once been a thorn in the side of James. Lovelace, we discover, has been careless of his reputation in dealing with women and has thus put a weapon against himself in the hand of his enemy. No alliance could be more repugnant to James than one between his sister and Lovelace. It might result in her receiving a large share of the family fortune and in Lovelace winning the title so much coveted by himself.

Wishing to prevent the match and being a man of violent temper, he plays upon his mother's fear of a possible duel. Arabella's malicious envy makes her his willing tool. Accustomed to act with the willfulness of a pampered son, he manages to bind the other members of the family to his own cause against Lovelace and to stampede them into the belief that the only way to save Clarissa from marrying the disapproved suitor is to force her into a hasty union with someone else. The harsh measures which they take to carry out their views, and the fact that the suitor proposed is particularly objectionable to the sensitive young girl, cause her to resist, as any girl of spirit might do, their unreasonable demands.

It would require much space to trace step by step the process by which Clarissa is betrayed. The behavior of her family plays into the hands of Lovelace, giving him the opening he needs. Skilled in the subjection of feminine hearts, he takes advantage of his opportunity and manages, by devious and artful means, to trick Clarissa into going away with him. To her family her departure looks like a willful elopement and act of defiance. Actually the girl is the victim of a clever stratagem.

Lovelace is such an artificial creation that it is not always easy to take him seriously. He is a compound of romantic and aristocratic conventions, derived mainly from the heroic drama and sentimental tragedy of the late seventeenth and early eighteenth centuries. His egotism, his bravado, and his cynical libertinism are all qualities common enough in Restoration drama. Designed by Richardson to be shocking to the Puritan mind and sober middle-class spirit of his time, he now seems, by reason of his extravagant artificiality, to be less shocking than preposterous. He is not a distinct literary type, like the wit of Restoration comedy, for example, but a somewhat crudely fashioned composite figure, interesting not so much for what he is as for what he represents of the changing spirit of the age.

Being extravagantly proud of his conquests, he is aroused to extraordinary efforts when, in attempting to win Clarissa, he encounters difficulty. Nothing will satisfy him but to gain from her an acknowledgment of his power. Failing this, he can satisfy his pride only by breaking her pride and humbling her, as he also wishes to humble her family. Surfeited with easy conquests, he takes greater pleasure in the chase that proves to be difficult. He delights in matching his wits against the proud reserve of Clarissa and, having her in his power, takes pleasure in tormenting her.

One of the difficulties for Richardson in his situation is to make it appear plausible that his heroine does not escape from her captor. We are not altogether satisfied with the explanation that to run away *from* Lovelace after having just run away *with* him would put her in a ridiculous light, although it must be admitted that fear of public opinion would have been a powerful incentive normally. It does not, however, seem to be worthy of Clarissa, in the light of her later behavior. We must remember, of course, that to return would have been to accept the detestable Solmes. Moreover, it was only gradually that Clarissa learned how completely she had been deceived. Then she made every effort to escape, but it was too late.

When Lovelace first got Clarissa into his power he may not have intended to go to such length. Afterwards his inability to break her will drove him on. His admiration of her grew but his perversity would not allow him to do the only obviously proper and sensible thing. It was something new to him to be despised by his intended victim and laughed at by his accomplices. His attitude was full of contradictions—a compound of love, pride, desire for revenge, and delight in stratagem. In a letter to his friend Belford, he says: "I am mad with love, fired by revenge, puzzled with my own devices, my invention is my curse, my pride my punishment."

His eventual triumph over Clarissa was achieved in such a fashion that it could not satisfy his pride but became rather a thing to be remembered with shame. It was an important part of the author's purpose to emphasize the element of retribution. We soon see Lovelace on the rack of a terrible remorse with his pride damaged by the refusal of Clarissa to have anything further to do with him. The remainder of the novel is the account of his retribution, of Clarissa's illness and death and burial, with the sorrowing of her friends and the bitter suffering of her relatives, who have been too late in forgiving her. Lovelace, the prime instrument in her fate, is killed in a duel by Colonel Morden, cousin of the dead girl. Others who have contributed to her suffering are punished. The author is determined to let no one off.

It is clear from this outline that *Clarissa* is a different kind of story from *Moll Flanders*. Like Defoe, Richardson provides a patient accumulation of details, but he does it in a different manner. He turns the searchlight of his scrutiny back and forth over a limited area and peers into it from different angles, showing a multitude of motives playing about and through the life of a young girl. The feelings of Moll Flanders hardly count in our sense of what she is. The feelings of Clarissa, however, are important. She is aware of herself in relation to others. In reading her letters we perceive that, like other people, she is not the same person to everybody. Yet she is always recognizably Clarissa.

The device of telling his story in letters written by the chief participants and by others deeply concerned in what was going on was of great service to Richardson. It provided him with a natural and immediately recognizable source of authority. It had the merit of placing the novelist completely outside his story, making him essentially a dramatist rather than a narrator. He could show events in the course of their happening and while yet undecided in their outcome. Sometimes he reminded his readers of the advantages of his method, unmindful perhaps that such reminders served to suggest the author behind the scenes. Belford, after being appointed executor of Clarissa's will, writes to Lovelace about his anticipated pleasure in going through her papers: "How *much more* lively and affecting, for that reason, must her style be, her mind tortured by the pangs of uncertainty (the events then hidden in the womb of fate), *than* the dry narrative, unanimated style of a person relating difficulties and dangers surmounted; the relater perfectly at ease; and if himself unmoved by his own story, not likely greatly to affect the reader."

The letter form provides the novelist not only with the objectivity of the dramatist but also with his multiple point of view. The story of Clarissa is set forth from four principal sources of information. Clarissa's own version of what happens to her is the most important one. Next to hers is that of Lovelace, who, being the aggressor, is aware of much that is necessarily veiled from the heroine. His account of what goes on behind the scenes throws added light upon the actions of Clarissa and casts into sharper relief her forbearing and courageous conduct. Anna Howe, as the friend and confidante of the heroine, and John Belford, acting in a similar relationship to Lovelace, are rendered practically necessary to the novelist by the letter convention. Clarissa, alienated from her family, must have a sympathetic recipient for her outpourings, and such dark schemes as those of Lovelace can be confided only to a friend and crony.

Miss Howe serves the author in a variety of ways. She is an ardent friend to whom Clarissa can lay bare the shameful secrets of her captivity. She is the one person whose view of what is happening is most complete. It is from her that one is able to round up most of the essential factors in the situation. She knows the truth about Clarissa's actions; she understands the extent of Lovelace's villainy; and she knows what is going on among the Harlowes. With Clarissa, she contributes to the sum of feminine intelligence and independence which is being championed in the novel. She is something of a foil to the heroine, representing the feminine character in its more practical and down-to-earth aspect as opposed to the almost faultless and ideal portrait of Clarissa.

Belford, like Miss Howe, is a functional character. After being the confidant of Lovelace he becomes the friend of Clarissa and executor of her will. He thus provides a means of picturing the declining days of both of the principal characters. His repentance and reform can be traced to Clarissa's influence, and his ministering to her during her last hours sharpens the punishment of Lovelace, who has forfeited his right to be near her.

These four correspondents write the letters forming the main stream of the narrative. No one of them could have told it all without the loss of dramatic edge and color. Miss Howe is, of the four, the least involved in the action and the least often present at the scenes which she describes. As a result she is more of a mere reporter than the others, and her letters are less moving than theirs. Even so, they are less impersonal in tone than the account given by Moll Flanders of her own past actions. They are touched by anxiety for Clarissa and indignation against Lovelace and the Harlowes. The letters of the two principal personages, coming side by side as they frequently do and dealing with the same incidents in such different tones, bring the characters of the two into vivid contrast, sharpen the sense of struggle, and produce sometimes an effect of irony.

There are many other correspondents, each one contributing his or her minor note to the elaborate and slowly unfolding drama. One remembers, for example, the father's stilted anger at his daughter's insubordination, as he considers it, the brother's malice, the sister's petty spitefulness, the mother's timidity before her family, Uncle John's pomposity, Uncle Anthony's nastiness, the prosy didacticism of Lord M. These are things that help to fill out the dark background of the lovely Clarissa, making appear more inevitable the failure of reconciliation. Smollett, working more discursively than Richardson, was afterwards, in *Humphry Clinker,* to make a more effective use of letters to bring out oddities of temper and contrasting points of view. Richardson's purpose was different. He had little interest in his minor characters apart from their relationship to the situation of his heroine.

One important aspect of *Clarissa* is that it shows people acting under the pressure of a social code, particularly with regard to the family. Family discipline was then much more severe than now, it being the general opinion of domestic moralists that though parents had a right to command obedience from their children, they were not expected to force a dutiful daughter into marriage with an unwelcome suitor. In other words, a daughter had the right, theoretically, to refuse a man chosen for her, but she did not have the right to choose one for herself, except with her parents' consent. These matters are dealt with interestingly by Mr. Alan Dugald McKillop,[1] who points out that *Clarissa* "represents a testing of the principles of the conduct-books in terms of living personalities acting within the framework of society." Some of the things in the novel which throw light upon eighteenth-century family life are "the authority of the father, the subservience of the mother, the predominant position of the elder brother, the heroine's attitude toward her parents, particularly her feeling that their severity cannot nullify her duty toward them."

Richardson is enough of a moralist and Puritan precisian to interest himself in such matters. He states specifically in the title of *Clarissa* that his novel shows "the distresses that may attend the misconduct both of parents and children in relation to marriage." It is misconduct for Clarissa to keep up her correspondence with Lovelace when her parents disapprove, and it is also wrong for them to attempt to force her into marriage with Solmes. Doubtless the author is opposed to granting daughters much freedom. Sir Charles Grandison, whose judgment is held up as impeccable, deals sternly with the skittishness of his sister Charlotte in regard to her marriage. As an enthusiastic friend of women and unconscious artist, however, Richardson builds up such a good case for his heroine and so overloads the scales in her favor that his criticism seems to be directed mainly at her family. No doubt he intends it as a lesson that, if so prudent and well-meaning a person as Clarissa gets into trouble, it is all the more clear that young ladies should be careful. Nevertheless, as a warning against disobedience the novel is something of a boomerang. Unintentionally, perhaps, the author rises above his moral intention. For all its admonitory stuffiness and haggling morality, there sounds from the novel a genuine human cry. In her distress Clarissa achieves a quality of dignity that Richardson does not elsewhere impart to his characters. The penalty paid by her is

[1] *Samuel Richardson: Printer and Novelist,* Chapel Hill, 1936, pp. 134–135.

so much out of proportion to her offense that she becomes a figure of tragedy rather than a mere object lesson.

The fact that nearly everybody expected Clarissa to marry Lovelace and that many readers urged the author thus to patch up the affair may be taken as a commentary upon what the eighteenth-century world expected of women in the way of submission to masculine oppressiveness. Although such submission would have been in accord with the sentimental spirit of the time, Richardson held his ground. Clarissa was deeply wounded. Her pride was greatly mortified, as she said, but not *sufficiently* mortified to submit to the man she most abhorred. Was she to *creep* to her violator and be thankful for his poor justice? Her sequestering of herself from the world is evidence of the seriousness with which she viewed the break with her parents; it also reveals in a general way how great was the force of public opinion in her world. Her refusal, in such circumstances, to accept the vulgar conventional compromise of a belated marriage was, in reality, a more eloquent protest against a common form of injustice than was generally realized.

The general sentimental desire for a reconciliation between Clarissa and her betrayer carries with it the implication that some of the finer points of the heroine's character were missed by contemporary readers. Even while taking a high view of this aspect of her behavior, Richardson showed himself in other respects to be thoroughly a man of his time. He evidently admired his heroine for remaining devoted to her father despite his cruelty. She says that she would prefer death to the sight of her father kneeling to her.

Some people, it would appear, even in Richardson's time, took a less rigid view of the duty owed to parents. In *Tom Jones*, Fielding deals comically with the attempt of a domineering father to force his daughter into a marriage distasteful to her. It is instructive to compare the behavior of Sophia Western, Fielding's heroine, with that of Clarissa. Nobody would accuse Sophia of being disrespectful to her father. Yet she ran away from home without much misgiving or heart searching. She acted more naturally and less self-consciously than Clarissa. One reason for this difference of treatment was the fact that Fielding dealt broadly with events, the act of his heroine being conceived in relation with other equally important matters. Richardson, on the other hand, made Clarissa's act the axis of his long, slow-moving story, thus giving it a weight that exaggerated it almost out of the bounds of common credibility. His keeping his mind fixed upon his heroine and viewing everything else in relationship to her dilemma served to produce an effect of distortion. It is unnatural to find oneself in a world so much dominated by one major interest and in which so little that is casual or unpremeditated ever happens. Nevertheless, for the most part, the spell holds. The narrative is at once more tense and more tenuous than the composed atmosphere of *Tom Jones*. At its best *Clarissa* is tragic, but it is not possible to maintain the tension of tragedy through hundreds and hundreds of pages. The sense of emotional disturbance is maintained so well, however, that to put down the book is to feel the shock of renewed contact with a normal world.

If *Moll Flanders* produces an effective illusion in the sphere of action, *Clarissa* carries the illusion over into the realm of feeling. It deals with a single vital affair in the life of an individual. It is more unified than *Moll Flanders*, being expressive not simply of a general will to survive, but of particular responses to a given situation of persons involved in a specific relationship. Clarissa stands high in the estimation of her friends, and her situation is of a kind certain to cause misunderstandings and produce violent reactions for or against her. Nobody can be indifferent. Susceptibilities of various kinds are aroused. Her relatives feel themselves disgraced and outraged. Pity and indignation and shocked bewilderment are felt by Miss Howe. The heroine herself is the prey of numerous alarms, anxieties, and regrets. When she is accused by her faithful friend of failing to elicit a direct proposal from Lovelace because of an excess of modesty, she replies that she has not acted wholly from maidenly niceness, or from apprehension, but has followed the impulses of her heart and the principles implanted there. It is this connection between action and feeling that distinguishes the work of Richardson from most earlier English fiction.

The author of *Clarissa*, no less than Defoe, employed a circumstantial method of narration. Letters provided as substantial a form of documentation as journal or memoir and had the added advantage of bringing the reader nearer to the events described. There was an important difference between the two methods in the fact that, whereas the autobiographical record stood without supplementary authority, each one of the letter writers could give only a limited view of the situation in hand. Clarissa, unlike Moll, was engaged in relating events so close at hand that the accompanying emotional state was reflected in the narration. Moreover, she was limited in her knowledge in a way that Moll was not. Cut off from her family and friends, deceived by the man who should have been her protector, hanging suspended in a web of events not yet brought to a decisive issue—she could write only what she knew. Had her letters failed to reflect her circumscribed condition, they would have failed in their most important function. It is precisely because they were written from a sharply delimited point of view that they evoke a distinct sense of the writer's personality. Others could supply additional information, and from the blended picture the heroine would emerge as a distinct individual, affected by and affecting others.

To accomplish this effect Richardson developed a method more elaborately detailed than Defoe's. Only by going through the many pages of *Clarissa* or *Sir Charles Grandison* can one appreciate to the full the author's scrupulous regard for fact. Any reader of *Clarissa* in an unabridged edition is certain to be struck by the extraordinary attention to detail. Much of what occurs is made the theme of more than one correspondent. We learn of the violation of the heroine from Lovelace, but the full force of this occurrence comes later from Clarissa's own pen. Fielding made comment upon the action a recognized part of the novelist's business, something to which the autobiographical form was not well adapted. Letters, however, provided a natural medium for comment. Clarissa, for example, sends Miss Howe a letter in which she has something to say, quite naturally, about her captor Lovelace. Miss Howe replies with comments upon what has been written. This letter falls into the hands of a servant who copies part of it for Lovelace, who, in turn, writes about the incident to Belford and makes his own comments about what he has thus learned.

How much more complex Richardson's method is than Defoe's can be seen by a comparison of Lovelace with Robinson Crusoe. Both men are involved in a series of actions, one in adapting himself to his island home and the other in endless intrigue. In one case the interest is derived largely from the action itself; in the other the action is interesting for another reason. Our interest in what Lovelace does is conditioned by our concern for its effect upon Clarissa. Crusoe's motives are comparatively simple and constant. Lovelace, on the other hand, is interested not only in his plots but also in their effect upon Clarissa. Her reactions are shown as they occur and also as they are anticipated by Lovelace. He gives us also immediate and retrospective views of her, while she deals with events both at close range and afterwards reflectively. There are also the comments of Miss Howe, who forms her impressions of what is going on from a distance but in the light of her close friendship with Clarissa. In short, the behavior of the heroine is subject to the judgment of various people favorably or unfavorably disposed toward her.

As a result of this gradually enlarged familiarity we grow into a knowledge of the subject, which is due to no one angle of treatment but to a multitude of impressions gained in various ways. As in life, we form our own opinion and are not told what to think. After the death of Clarissa, Miss Howe, at the request of Belford, writes a long letter describing the character of her friend. This direct eulogy does not add any vividness or color to the image we have already gained. It is clear that Richardson's dramatic rendering of his subject is the only thing that counts.

The patient suffering of Clarissa and her death, just before a possible reconciliation, are matters treated by the author with his accustomed thoroughness. Later novelists will eventually bring such scenes into disrepute, but here the handling of death is not without its dignity and restraint. The virtue of Clarissa and the respect in which she is held are the things insisted upon, not the mere harrowing details of pain and grief. Several days before her death Clarissa orders her coffin sent up to her room. It is tastefully ornamented and bears upon its lid verses from the Bible appropriate to the occasion. She leaves letters sealed with black wax for Miss Howe,

Lovelace, and the members of her family, to be delivered to them after her death. As the hearse bearing her body from London draws near home, the church bell is tolled nearby. The intense grief of the family is described as six maidens from the neighborhood reverently carry the coffin into the house.

Violation of maidenly innocence is not an uncommon occurrence in eighteenth-century fiction. Clarissa, however, is far from being a casual victim of a casual encounter. It is not her victimization itself that counts for the novelist so much as her resistance to the ordeal imposed upon her. Too sensitive in her pride to bow to the will of Lovelace, when he offers reparation, and too strict in her principles to adapt herself to the changed world into which her misfortune throws her, she resigns herself to death. Cut off from normal social contacts and denied free communication with her family, discovering in the midst of her alienation the perfidy of her supposed protector and subjected to his cruel treatment, she is greatly in need of consolation and friendship. What can be more natural than for her to confide in Miss Howe? The record of her suffering and the consciousness of self into which she is plunged by her injured pride and her separation from her friends—these are the things that particularly count in the novel.

We may call *Clarissa* a novel of sentiment and recognize at the same time that it is not particularly sentimental, as sentimentality later came to be understood. It is a study of violence done to a temperament formulated upon the moral concepts of a highly sensitive and somewhat romanticized Puritan conscience. It is not a record of adventure or a picture of manners. Clarissa is not a typical or representative young lady of her time in the sense that Squire Western, of *Tom Jones,* is a typical country squire. It is not the eighteenth-century *sentiments* in the novel that we remember but something more dramatic and living, not the didacticism of the author but the personality of his heroine. It is the cumulative force of masterly handling of innumerable small details that makes the novel what it is. The connection between action and feeling finding dramatic expression in the character of Clarissa makes her not just a character but a personality.

CHAPTER III

The Novel of Manners

HENRY FIELDING

If Defoe succeeded in establishing prose fiction upon the plane of human activity and Richardson upon the plane of sensibility, making a start toward the novel of personality, Fielding gave to it an enlarged significance and authority by adding to action and sensibility the general background of manners. His wide acquaintance with literature and his apprenticeship to the drama aided him in working out for the novel a new type of structure, derived largely from the methods of the epic and the drama. The new form enlarged the novelist's capacity to deal with life in its various manifestations; it could be put to a greater variety of uses than the specialized narrative method of Defoe, and was superior in adaptability to the epistolary method of Richardson.

Richardson undoubtedly influenced his fellow novelists greatly by teaching them how to deal with the emotional reactions of their characters, but he did not succeed in establishing the letter form as a lasting method. It was too artificial and too easily productive of improbabilities and absurdities. Fielding provided the method which was to be the most generally followed throughout the next century. He brought fiction back into the older current of literary tradition, thus enabling it to profit from the usages of epic, romance, and drama. He gave a new range and suppleness to it and made it possible for the capable novelist to combine grace with vigor, delicacy of treatment with range of observation and documentary authority, sympathetic feeling with searching analysis. By placing his chief actors not in a social vacuum but in their normal relation to the surrounding world of men and women, he was able to produce a picture of manners much richer in quality and more extended in scope than had yet appeared in English fiction.

Moll Flanders deals with only a small fragment of society and gives only glimpses of the underworld to which the heroine belongs. In *Clarissa* no attempt is made to include the world surrounding the Harlowes. When the author sends Anna Howe to a ball, he is concerned only about her agitated feelings in the presence of Lovelace. Richardson's method excludes attention to the bustling life of inns or other places of public assembly; it does not provide incidental personages to fill up the background and create an impression of a world outside the pressing concerns of his main drama. He moves in this direction, it is true, in *Sir Charles Grandison,* and Smollett and Miss Burney are to show, before much time has passed, that letters can be excellently adapted to the broad depiction of manners.

Such a world is supplied by the innkeepers and their wives and servants, the doctors and lawyers and other persons, more or less anonymous, encountered everywhere in *Tom Jones.* The minor characters of *Clarissa* do not so serve to represent the world outside. Mr. Brand is not a typical clergyman but a stupid pedant, whose blunder in a delicate mission destroys Clarissa's last chance of a reconciliation with her parents. The doctor who takes care of her in her illness is merely an attendant physician and one more witness of her heroism under trial. Fielding, like Molière and Shakespeare, shows us that servants can be as interesting as their masters. The servants in the Harlowe family, however, are little more than compliant tools of those who employ them.

Fielding did not adopt the autobiographical pose of Defoe or the epistolary method of Richardson. Instead of making the shallow pretense that he was writing an authentic history, he did not disguise the fact that he was writing a novel. He openly adopted the storyteller's time-honored convention of knowing everything about his characters and their affairs. This convention, commonly known as the omniscient point of view, solves a multitude of difficulties for the novelist but brings, in turn, its own problems, as we shall see later. Richardson was hampered by the necessity of devising plausible occasions for letter writing, as a result of which he was inclined to keep his heroine away from her family and friends. The more he tried to extend the range of his novel, the more he had to resort to clumsy and laborious devices to get all his material into the form of correspondence.

Wishing to keep clear of the confused improbabilities of romance, Defoe adopted the point of view of the chief participant in the action. He thus sacrificed range and depth in the interest of simplicity and verisimilitude. Richardson was superior to Defoe in handling the time element and in securing an impression of immediacy, but his method of relating everything from a point close at hand produced a maze of details sometimes difficult to traverse.

For dealing with an extended subject, the omniscient point of view is greatly superior to the methods of Defoe and Richardson. The omniscient novelist can employ a variety of methods. He can summarize, interpret, or explain in any way he likes. He can, upon occasion, limit his omniscience and represent events with no more light thrown upon them than is shed by the characters themselves. In other words, such a novelist can shift back and forth between narration and a more purely dramatic form of representation.

In addition to adopting the omniscient point of view, Fielding reveals himself as a distinct personality by addressing comments to the reader. Such intrusion of an author into his story has the effect of placing the reader at a greater distance from the events. It is an offense against art, for a novelist, so long as he is wholly an artist, speaks *through* his characters and not *about* them. There are, of course, different ways in which to deal with one's characters. The author can simply employ the third person and write without personally intervening between his characters and his reader. He may go further and break into his presentation with comments of his own. It is this personal intrusion that is most damaging to the illusion. Such comments are usually put by Fielding into the introductory sections reserved for them.

As a commentator, the author of *Tom Jones* keeps within the comic tone of his novel. He does not preach too much and is not too grave. He is clearly on the side of virtue without being a prig. He moves easily through a wide range of comedy without becoming tiresomely facetious. His style is graceful and fluent without being shoddy or bombastic. His confidential manner of expatiating upon his subject brings the reader into an attitude of sympathetic responsiveness. It was this tone of openhearted laughter that was to become characteristic of the English novel.

It was Fielding, more than anyone else, who gave to the novel in England the structural principles, the subject matter, and the tone that enabled it to grow into a dominant literary form. Defoe, though he did not write in the picaresque vein, dealt mainly with low life. Richardson seemed to find it impossible to write a novel without basing it upon the stock situation of an abduction. Fielding showed more originality in turning whatever form he used to his own particular needs. In *Jonathan Wild* he made a criminal biography serve as a philosophical satire upon human folly and hypocrisy. *Joseph Andrews,* begun as a burlesque of *Pamela,* grew into a mirthful record of adventures on the road. *Tom Jones* had no specific model but was worked out in accordance with a plan devised by the author from his knowledge of epic and drama and romance. It proved to be the most ample framework for the depiction of English life that any novelist had yet been able to provide. In no one of the novels, *Amelia* included, did Fielding repeat himself.

The History of Tom Jones, a Foundling

Fielding began his career as a novelist by an attempt to define the kind of writing upon which he was engaged. In the preface to *Joseph Andrews* he likened his work to a comic romance or comic epic poem in prose. The term *romance* was at that time so universally applied to prose fiction that it was difficult for him to avoid it, although it had, in his view, the disadvantage of being associated in the public mind with the outmoded pastoral and heroic romances of France, such as *Clélie* and *Le Grand Cyrus.* Consequently he preferred to call his novel a prose epic. There was no reason, he considered, why a piece of writing containing so many of the qualities of an epic should not be called an epic rather than a romance, from which it differed so greatly.

Romances were out of favor in Fielding's time. There had been much anti-romantic fiction, particularly in France and Spain, where the picaresque novel and various comic and satirical novels had flourished, the most famous of all such works being *Don Quixote*. Both *Joseph Andrews* and *Tom Jones* are anti-romantic in temper; they both contain elements of burlesque of the high-flown and heroic. Not wishing to have his novels confused with the artificial romances familiar to the public, Fielding begins *Joseph Andrews* with a preface in which he explains his idea of romance as being a comic epic in prose, which he defines as follows:

> Now a comic romance is a comic epic-poem in prose; differing from comedy, as the serious epic from tragedy: its action being more extended and comprehensive; containing a much larger circle of incidents, and introducing a greater variety of characters. It differs from the serious romance in its fable and action, in this; that as in the one these are grave and solemn, so in the other they are light and ridiculous: It differs in its characters, by introducing persons of inferior rank, and consequently, of inferior manners, whereas the grave romance sets the highest before us; lastly, in its sentiments and diction; by preserving the ludicrous instead of the sublime.

Elsewhere Fielding likens his work to that of the biographer and the historian, being careful to distinguish it, however, from that of the mere chronicler. His aim is not simply to record events but to deal with essential, underlying truths. His concern is to paint manners, not men. He reveals the tendency of his age to think in terms of abstractions by saying at the beginning of *Tom Jones* that he intends to write about human nature. In short, his conception of the novel is that it should be a broad and representative picture of mankind rather than a study of individual lives. It is comic and satirical in spirit and purpose, and markedly more democratic than the fiction of the seventeenth century. The author suspects, in fact, that many readers will consider his material too common and vulgar for their taste, which has been formed upon the elegant romances.

Fielding's characters are for the most part types, with typical reactions. The impulsiveness of Squire Western is the impulsiveness of any violent and undisciplined man of his class. After we have become well acquainted with Tom, we always know what to expect of him. We know that his ardent nature will continue to get him into trouble. We are not surprised when he is generous to an enemy, when he drinks too much, or when he gets into a scrape because of his imprudence. But beyond his instinctive generosity and affectionateness, beyond the overflow of youthful ardor and animal urgency, what kind of a man is he?

Viewed simply as an individual, he is not a striking figure. He is not capable of feeling in the degree that his situation might lead us to expect. To compare him with the central figure of *Jude the Obscure* or with Paul Morel, of *Sons and Lovers,* is to make his deficiency in sensibility all the more striking. It is not surprising that his relation to Sophia never affects the reader as does the attraction between Paul Emanuel and Lucy Snowe, in Charlotte Brontë's *Villette,* or the fascination of Clym Yeobright by Eustacia Vye, in *The Return of the Native.* It is important in *Villette* that the starving heart of Lucy should be quickened into vibrant life by the kindly warmth of M. Emanuel's love. Clym's passion for Eustacia is the axis upon which revolves the question of his own, his mother's, and Eustacia's fate. Their ill-fated attachment is the point of friction out of which there grows a discord that swallows up three lives.

No such weight is attached to the tender feeling of Tom for Sophia. His love for her is only one of several relationships, each one of which contributes to the total impression of manners. His susceptibility to Molly, his association with Squire Western, his shielding of Black George, his devotion to Mr. Allworthy, his hatred of sham, and generosity to distress—all these things contribute to our view of him and of the world in which he moves.

What might have been, in less capable hands, a sentimental account of how a gallant but misjudged young man finally won the lady of his choice becomes in Fielding's handling something far more substantial. Tom is not merely the titular hero of a love story. He is a ward, a pupil, a companion, a young man on the highroad. He is, in fact, eager and impulsive youth plunging forward with rash impetuosity into the perils of life. Sophia, too, is not just a girl in love. She is an occasion of dispute between her father and her aunt.

To Lady Bellaston she is a rival to be disposed of, to Blifil a prize to be schemed for, and to Tom an object of adoration. She is plucky as well as beautiful, loving but not blind. Her relation to her father and to Tom places her, so to speak, in the position of a symbol of feminine devotion and feminine sensibility in a world of greedy and appropriative masculinity.

It is not that either Tom or Sophia is an abstraction, but rather that their story becomes so involved in secondary concerns that it serves to represent a whole society. The moral and social fabric of their world is exposed in the dilemma by which they are first separated. As a foundling Tom can hardly aspire to the squire's daughter, although he may be on friendly terms with the squire. Western looks upon his scrape with Molly as a fit subject for laughter, but he is enraged that his own daughter should be, as he seems to think, the object of a similar interest. In wishing to marry his daughter to Blifil, he is concerned chiefly with the convenient joining of estates. Sophia's aunt has different ambitions for her, but neither aunt nor father approves such a suitor as Tom. In placing her affections upon Tom, Sophia shows the strength of her feelings and a disregard of social barriers natural to youth. Her instinctive dislike of Blifil is a safer guide to conduct than the material considerations of her father.

Tom's career serves as a lesson in the value of generosity and disinterestedness and also in the need for prudence. He does not guard himself against the misrepresentation and slander of those who expect to profit by his downfall. His mistakes, which are used so effectively against him, stop short of being fatal. It is not surprising that the machinations of his secret enemy should finally come to light. Having regained the favor of Allworthy, now disclosed to be his uncle, and with Squire Western on his side, Tom can hardly fail to win Sophia. He could hardly have failed to do so in any case. It was necessary for Fielding to rescue his hero. The manner in which he was to do so he kept concealed, but he was working toward that end from the beginning. A violent or tragic solution would have been out of harmony with the spirit in which the events were conceived. Although Tom is far from being the ideal hero of romance, he is equally not a villain. His faults do not lie deep, and he shines by comparison with most of his associates.

Sophia's defiance of her father and flight from home are acts of simple courage on the part of a girl subjected to harsh and unreasonable treatment. She is not a figure of tragedy, and her disobedience is not earth shaking in its consequences. Although it causes some family squabbles, it sets in motion no such train of disaster as the less forthright disobedience of Clarissa. For Lord Fellamar to have succeeded in his design against her would have been to visit upon her a fate wholly out of keeping with the simplicity of her role. Her role, which is to fall in love with the hero, is a less weighty one than Clarissa's, and she plays it with less self-consciousness. She is engagingly frank without being censorious and is spirited but not inflexible. Although her trials are many, she does not complain. Her father's violent fluctuations of fondness and rage distress her; her love for Tom brings her mortification. His behavior repeatedly puts her love to the test and wounds her all the more in the defenseless state in which her flight from home has placed her.

If I have seemed to make light of Tom and Sophia, it is because I wish to point out that their development is not what has interested Fielding. Tom is essentially the same person at the end of the story that he was before his estrangement from Allworthy. Sophia goes through no great crisis. She reveals her love as truly and as charmingly while under her father's roof as she does in the stress of her later conflict. Fielding is not engaged in tracing the personal development of hero and heroine. Their story is incidental to a larger picture of manners, in which respect the hero is more important to the author's purpose than the heroine. As a traveling hero, Tom enables the author to describe scenes in the country, later on the road to London, and finally in London. It happens that Sophia also goes to London, and it is to be noted that Fielding's hero is less constantly on the move than such a character as Roderick Random.

As a picture of manners *Tom Jones* contains an abundance of characters and incidents. The characters are of the first importance. Whereas Defoe's chief concern is with what his characters do, the first consideration of Fielding is what his characters are. In every novel there must be some kind of balance between the incidents and the characters. The novelist who succeeds in presenting his material in an essentially dramatic form, as in *Emma* or *The Return of the Native*, effects such a close union between the two that they can hardly be dissociated. Incident in such a novel is, as Henry James says, "the illustration of character" and character is "the determination of incident." Such a balance is not always the aim of the novelist. He may allow incident to dominate over character, as in *Treasure Island*, or he may make the revelation of character his main objective, as in the case of *Vanity Fair*.

In *Tom Jones* the balance is on the side of character. Incidents are illustrative, and the plot has been devised arbitrarily as a means of holding the characters in place. The germ of the action does not appear in the early scenes, as in *Pride and Prejudice*. Although present from the beginning in the mind of the author, it is withheld from the reader, who, as a result of this concealment, can see only retrospectively the full meaning of many of the early scenes. But it is only with reference to the final outcome of events that the reader is kept in the dark. He does not have to wait till the end to know that Blifil is thoroughly untrustworthy. In fact, the reader does not have to wait until the mystery of Tom's birth is solved and the treachery of his enemies laid bare to know what is essentially true of the characters. These things cap the climax and round out the pattern of events but do not add essentially to our knowledge of the characters, who have been wonderfully transparent all along. Fielding's purpose has been to exhibit them, and he has succeeded.

In working out the scheme of action in which his characters were to be displayed, Fielding followed the structural principles of the epic as they were understood in his time. Aristotle had said that the story of the epic should be constructed on dramatic principles with everything in it turning about a single action, whole and organically perfect. The organic unity thus specified is far from being the accidental unity of the chronicle. The picaresque hero, for example, serves as a connecting thread for a more or less random series of adventures. It is not possible to say of such adventures that they are essential to the main action, for there is no single main action but a series of actions casually related by having happened to a single person. In *Tom Jones* there is a main action and the structure of the story is anything but loose and rambling. No character of importance is allowed to drop out of the story. Except for the story told by the Man on the Hill, there is no incident that does not contribute to the development of the plot or the revelation of character. Even this episode reveals character and the general state of manners. Blifil's releasing of Sophia's bird gives us a glimpse of his hypocritical meanness and of Tom's natural generosity. It helps us to understand why she should distrust one and prefer the other of the two boys. Tom's affair with Molly is not just something casual, as a character of Smollett might engage in. It makes him, for a time, less likely to respond to Sophia's suddenly awakened interest in him. It contributes to Allworthy's alteration of attitude toward him. It intensifies the hostility of Squire Western to his interest in Sophia. It complicates the state of mind of Sophia herself, and contributes to the picture of manners in the light it throws upon the Seagrim family and in the moral reactions of Allworthy and Western.

It would be easy to multiply instances of Fielding's skill in weaving seemingly trivial occurrences into the main design. There is, for example, that affair of the muff which Sophia gives to her maid but retrieves from her upon hearing of Tom's interest in it. This behavior of Sophia, when Tom learns of it, does not help him to put all thoughts of her out of his mind, as he has been trying to do. The muff, in fact, becomes something of a talisman for the two lovers. Sophia clings to it while at the harpsichord; it interferes with her playing, and her father tosses it angrily into the fire. Her eagerness to recover it gives Tom fresh evidence of her feelings. Not long afterwards Sophia, having treasured the muff in the interval, runs away to London to escape being forced into marriage with Blifil. Stopping one night at an inn on the journey thither, she learns that Tom is passing the night in the same hostelry. The pleasure of seeing him is denied her, however, for it turns out that Tom is in the company of Mrs. Waters, and Sophia learns anew of his too great susceptibility to feminine charms. She departs precipitately after having given orders for her muff to be placed on his empty bed, where, tumbled onto the floor in the morning, it electrifies him into a state of agonized self-reproach.

Of the eighteen books into which *Tom Jones* is divided, the first six deal with Tom in the home of Allworthy in Somersetshire. Then we leave the domestic circle and through the next six books follow the hero on the road to London. In the last six books we are in London, where the change of scene not only suits the growing complication of intrigue but makes possible the introduction of human nature as seen under the veneer of more sophisticated manners. Altogether we are given a picture ranging from the rustic manners of the country, through the varied types encountered on the road, to the affectations of town life.

Fielding knows too well the value of selection and dramatic elaboration to follow a simple chronological method. In the first six books, while laying the foundations and establishing the situation of his story, he employs narrative summary with dramatic scenes interspersed to bring out salient features. He is thus able to cover somewhat more than twenty years in six books, whereas in the next twelve books he covers only about thirty-eight days. This great difference in scale of treatment is due to the fact that at the point when Tom has to leave home the author shifts from the manner of the epic to one that is more essentially dramatic. The first third of the novel is illustrative and expository. It introduces most of the characters, establishes the relationships between them, and leads up to a crisis in the situation of the hero: his loss of favor with his protector and his departure from home. With the situation thus established, Tom's enemies in the ascendancy, and Squire Western clamoring for a marriage between his daughter and Blifil, the action gathers momentum and never pauses until the end. After a quick succession of adventures on the road, the complications reach in London a point of extreme intricacy, for the solution of which the plans have been skillfully laid. The solution is attended by reversals of fortune in the best Aristotelian tradition. Tom is discovered to be the nephew of Allworthy and enters into the happiness for which he has been marked. He passes from ill fortune to good, and Blifil from good to ill. This discovery and reversal tend to render the end of the novel more definitely conclusive than a mere breaking off of adventures. It satisfies the Aristotelian definition of an end being something which comes after something else but which does not in turn lead to any further succession of adventures. The situation which prevails throughout the novel is so completely changed at the close that there is nothing else to happen. What might happen afterwards would belong to a new and different story.

Much of what happens in the latter part of the novel makes the reader think of a "well-made" play, of something cleverly manipulated rather than inevitable. The Nightingale episode seems to have been put in to provide a means for showing Tom in a good light and raising up a champion for him in Mrs. Miller. The plot of Lady Bellaston and Lord Fellamar, with the accidental intervention of Fitzpatrick, is a temporary stacking of the cards against Tom so as to punish him for his folly and provide also a trap for ensnaring Blifil. The young widow's unexpected proposal, a bolt out of the blue for Tom no less than for the reader, serves to show Sophia the state of her feelings and to weigh the balance in favor of the hero at a time when he greatly needs it. Jenny Jones is a fitting agent for helping to disclose the secret of Tom's birth. Many other persons contribute in one way or another to the solution of the plot, which is made to seem probable despite its intricacy and many surprising revelations.

It is made to seem plausible, but it does not conform to the inner logic of necessity. Just as the plot is dominated by the purpose of revealing character, so is this depiction of character dominated by the still larger aim of setting forth human nature. Thus, as I have pointed out in dealing with the hero and heroine, the characters exist for us not so much for the interest we take in their affairs as for the way in which they serve as indexes of the moral and social values of their world. The individual is not the pivot of the story. His affairs are not elevated to a point of such dignity. The English novel will have to wait for a hundred years or so before taking up seriously the problem of individual destiny.

Here the point of view is that of a spectator of the human scene who judges what he sees without entering far into the interests of any of the participants. We do not identify ourselves with any of the characters except in the most superficial way. Even our feeling for Sophia is the more or less patronizing sympathy that we bestow upon a child without sharing its anxiety or entering into its hopes.

In other words, the author has not penetrated deeply enough into her consciousness to render such things evident.

The characters, no less than the plot, have to be considered with regard to their places in Fielding's general scheme. They do not all function in the same way but may make their chief contribution to the plot, to the atmosphere, or to the theme. Of these the least colorful characters are those belonging principally to the plot. Such are Dowling, Northerton, Mrs. Fitzpatrick, Arabella Hunt, and Jenny Jones. Nightingale, Lady Bellaston, and Lord Fellamar are also plot characters, but their functions are broadened somewhat by their contribution to the atmosphere of life in London. Square and Thwackum contribute principally to the author's development of his theme. They represent attitudes that are held up to ridicule and seem hardly to be real men. Blifil, a plot character, serves also to convey a moral. As a portrait he suffers, like Square and Thwackum, from being conceived in general terms. A foil to the hero, he is prudent where Tom is imprudent, selfish where his rival is generous, cunning and sly where the other is open and trustful. His villainy, like Allworthy's goodness, is too uniform to seem altogether human. Blifil is intended to represent the corruptness of heart by which human nature is debased, whereas Allworthy represents the goodness of heart conducive to a sound humanity.

The purpose of Fielding being to exhibit human nature, his most expressive characters are the ones most richly endowed with natural impulses. Most of the personages in the novel, whether great or small, possess a greater amount of character than their roles in the plot require. They come to life in more ways than the minor characters of Richardson. They possess an excess of vitality, which enriches the novel as a document of manners. Had Fielding's intention been like Richardson's to depict a particular case, this excess might well have served to blur the main intention. As it is, however, it gives life and color to the novel. The hero is a spectator of the scenes through which he moves as well as an actor in them. These scenes are infused with the zestful humor in which the author looks at life, and his ironic, though not unsympathetic, point of view provides a philosophical unity for the novel not less essential to it than the unity of the hero's actions. The hero is himself subservient to the

social surroundings from which he gains experience. Whatever
change there is in him is due to the maturing of his judgment in
the light of such experience rather than to any deeply felt experience
itself.

It is in their exhibition of human nature that the characters of
Tom Jones are most notable. Fielding does not view their doings
simply in relation to a necessary sequence of events. Many of the
acts recorded give rise to concomitant actions, which, though expressive of the natures of those involved, are not necessary to what
will follow. A foundling in the bed of Mr. Allworthy gives rise
naturally to a lot of gossip. The immediate reverberations of the
mystery have little bearing upon the outcome of events. Had the
author been writing a mystery story he could have veiled it all in
complete silence. But he is dealing with human nature, and Mrs.
Deborah Wilkins is a human being as well as a servant. Accordingly
we are granted the spectacle of Mrs. Wilkins and her matronly
friend scrutinizing the characters of several young girls in an endeavor to find a likely mother for the infant. Suspicion lights on
Jenny Jones. She confesses, and Mr. Allworthy, a magistrate, pun-
ishes her by giving her a lecture upon chastity. She has once been the
servant of a schoolmaster by the name of Partridge and, having also
been his pupil, has occasioned some jealousy on the part of his wife.
By a process of natural ramification, the appearance of a foundling
in Mr. Allworthy's home becomes the means of showing traits of
character in several people. Mr. Allworthy's simple goodness, Deborah's servility and malicious curiosity, Partridge's vanity, and his
wife's jealousy are all exposed. Bridget's behavior on this occasion
is veiled in mystery and Jenny's is also somewhat unaccountable.
Since they are each playing a part which, as Fielding conceives his
story, must be concealed from the reader, we have to wait until the
secret of Tom's birth has come to light to understand the meaning
of their actions. The other characters are under no such constraint.

Subsequently the novel is rich in scenes designed for the exposure
of human foibles. The marriage of Captain Blifil and Bridget is
shown in all its sordidness of motive. The captain marries her for
her expectations and dies while dreaming of the wealth he is to in-
herit. By thus dying he regains the affection of his wife, who sets

forth her devotion in a laudatory but not too truthful epitaph. Molly Seagrim's appearance in church in the discarded finery of Sophia so arouses the envy of the women of the parish that a battle takes place in the churchyard after the service. Mr. Allworthy, believing himself near death, calls the members of his household around him and explains to them the terms of his will. Square and Thwackum, treated quite liberally, are dissatisfied with the amount of their legacies. The housekeeper is displeased because she is not remembered in a special legacy but is placed with the other servants. Blifil indulges in a false exhibition of grief. Only Tom, who might reasonably have had greater expectations, is truly and disinterestedly sympathetic.

Fielding's method of enriching his narrative with adventures by the way is illustrated in the journey to London. Having decided to go to sea, Tom sets out for Bristol, loses his way, and stops at an inn in company with a Quaker, who is vexed because his daughter has eloped with a poor man. The chance arrival of a company of soldiers causes Tom to join as a volunteer. Getting into a dispute, he receives a blow on the head, for which he is attended by a pretentious humbug of a physician who would make as much of his wound as possible. His assailant escapes and the company of soldiers departs, leaving him behind. While recuperating he makes the acquaintance of Partridge, now a barber, who, for reasons of his own, joins Tom upon his expedition. One night they stop at the home of a man known as the Man of the Hill, whom they have the good fortune to rescue from robbers. During the night their host entertains them with an account of his adventures, a rather long story, which is itself interrupted by Partridge's account of a farmer boy who lost a mare and of the trial of a man accused of stealing it. Early the next morning Tom comes upon a ruffian in the act of tying a woman to a tree. He rescues her and has the satisfaction of discovering that her assailant is Ensign Northerton, who had given him the unavenged blow a few days before. Northerton escapes a second time, and Tom accompanies the woman he has rescued to an inn at Upton, where the condition of her attire causes her to be taken for a prostitute. This supposition leads to a fight, in which Tom, the woman, and Partridge take sides against the innkeeper, his wife, and their maidservant. Order is restored by the arrival of a small party of soldiers, one of whom identifies the woman who has been the occasion of the fracas as being Captain Waters' lady.

In the events that follow there is a swift succession of ludicrous situations. Mrs. Waters dines with Tom and lures him into spending the night with her. A Mr. Fitzpatrick arrives looking for his wife. Following a false clue, he breaks in upon Mrs. Waters and Tom and thus causes a disturbance that enables the real Mrs. Fitzpatrick to elude her pursuer. During the night Sophia arrives with her maid and learns that Tom is also in the inn. Surprised to find that she has been the subject of gossip and learning that Tom is with Mrs. Waters, she departs before daybreak and is soon joined on the road by Mrs. Fitzpatrick, who proves to be her cousin. Western arrives at the inn too late to intercept his daughter, and Mr. Fitzpatrick, knowing the squire, takes him to the room of Mrs. Waters, under a mistaken impression that *she* is Sophia.

When order has been restored out of the ensuing confusion, nobody has much cause to be pleased with the events of the night. The pleasant little affair with Tom that Mrs. Waters has promised herself is speedily ended. The squire is furious at missing his daughter while finding new evidence of her weakness for Jones. Sophia, we know, is in distress at what she has discovered, and Tom is unhappy in having given her such an excellent reason to run away from him.

It would be easy to multiply instances of Fielding's ability to set forth his characters in their characteristic foibles. There is the scene of Black George's debate with his conscience, of Partridge at the theatre, of Sophia preparing to brave the dangers of the road. There is the scene of Western being taken to task by his sister, who believes that she knows better than he how to manage Sophia. Not a scene in which the squire appears fails to catch the infection of his passionate, undisciplined nature. It is in the portrait of this man of impulse with his drinking, his coarse language, and his excitability that Fielding's art rises to its greatest power.

CHAPTER IV

The Picaresque Novel

TOBIAS GEORGE SMOLLETT

The term *picaresque* comes from *pícaro*, the Spanish word for rogue or knave. Thus in its origin the picaresque romance was a rogue romance, and it doubtless came into existence as a protest against the tendency of romancers to deal with heroic and poetically conceived themes. Accordingly it developed a tradition of satirical realism, dealt with what was low and ridiculous, and often burlesqued the more tender emotions. The picaresque hero, although conceived in a different spirit and engaged in exploits of a different character, is recognizably a modern derivative of the knight-errant of the age of Chivalry.

It is important to note that the hero of such a romance is not a serious criminal or a villain. His rascality is set forth in light, humorous terms, his wrongdoing being attributable, it would seem, to his evil circumstances as much as to himself. When his circumstances improve, he may cease to be an offender. In any case his motives are not scrutinized closely.

They are not scrutinized closely because the interest of the author is in the shifts of his hero to maintain himself rather than in the man himself, and more particularly the attention is centered upon the world through which the adventurer moves. Being a man who lives by his wits, the picaresque hero is an opportunist who makes what he can of the affair of the moment without having a more definite goal than the natural desire to get on in the world and improve his position. He is usually a more happy-go-lucky kind of person than we are accustomed to meet in Defoe's novels, and his adventures take place in an atmosphere of greater freedom than we associate with the unremitting diligence of a Defoe character.

The broad intention of the author and the fact that the central character passes lightly from one adventure to another without being deeply affected result in a type of story that is not greatly unified. The single adventure is the unit of such a form rather than the situation as a whole. Indeed a picaresque novel is likely to be a series of stories threaded together rather than a single story. Separate episodes may be added or withdrawn without seriously affecting the whole.

Being easily adaptable to various uses, such a form is attractive to writers with matter at their disposal but without training or experience in literary method. It can be extended indefinitely to include miscellaneous adventures centered about a character similar to the picaresque hero only in his roving disposition. It can manage even to get along without a human being for hero, as, for example, *Chrysal, or the Adventures of a Guinea,* by Charles Johnstone, and *The History of Pompey the Little,* a story by Francis Coventry, in which a lap dog is the central character.

The original model of Spanish novels of roguery is *Lazarillo de Tormes,* of uncertain authorship, published in Spain in 1554. Its hero, the son of a thieving miller and none too honest mother, rises from obscurity to comparative prosperity through serving a series of more or less dishonest masters and learns from hard experience how to shift for himself. His first master is a blind beggar, who treats him brutally and from whom he pilfers everything that he can. From one of his masters, a miserly clergyman, he has, by ingenious devices, to steal food to keep from starving. His cleverness in outwitting his master is highly amusing and reveals, at the same time, how rapid has been his progress in trickery. Other of his masters are a destitute but proud gentleman making a desperate effort to preserve his respectability, and a seller of indulgences, who knows how to beguile the pious by the working of sham miracles. Lazarillo, although he tells his own story, reveals nothing of himself that is deeply personal and arouses little compassion in the reader for his sufferings. The interest awakened is in his circumstances and in the shifts to which he is put in combating them. Equally absorbing is the picture of the world around him in the satirical portraits of his masters, which he manages to make particularly effective by the artlessness and seeming naïvete of his recital.

One of the most famous novels to be written in the tradition of Spanish picaresque romance is *Gil Blas*. It was written in the early eighteenth century (1715–35), more than a century and a half after *Lazarillo*. Though its setting is in Spain, its author, Alain-René Lesage, was a Frenchman. The hero, who tells his own story, is the child of poor parents. Aided by his uncle, he sets out from home as a young man of seventeen or thereabouts to attend the University of Salamanca. Before he has gone far on his journey he has been cheated of his mule and has fallen in with a band of robbers, by whom he is detained. Now begins an adventurous career for him, in the course of which he goes not to the University but to Valladolid, Burgos, Madrid, Valencia, Toledo, and to other places as well. He serves, among others, a quack physician, becomes a valet, sees something of the life of theatrical folk, has various affairs with women, becomes the favorite of an archbishop, the confidant of a duke, and eventually rises to the confidential service of a minister of state.

Lesage follows the usage of the pastoral romance in allowing people whom the hero encounters in his travels to recount their own adventures, even though such episodes may have no bearing upon the main story. Gil Blas is not a person of much depth or delicacy of feeling. He thus satisfies all the better, perhaps, the requirements of such a novel. Not being sensitive he recovers quickly from reverses of fortune and is always ready for a new adventure. The personality of the hero counts for less than the picture of manners for which his career serves as the framework. Like *Tom Jones, Gil Blas* is a great gallery of portraits; Lesage, like Fielding, is skilled in the art of revealing men in their exterior manifestations of speech, gesture, and other habits of behavior.

The Adventures of Roderick Random

When Tobias George Smollett took *Gil Blas* as the model for *Roderick Random*, his first novel, which appeared in 1748, he explained that while following the plan of the earlier novel he was changing the point of view and treatment in accordance with his own views. In his hands the gay and ironic romance of roguery began to lose the attitude of humorous detachment characteristic of Lesage and to acquire instead a tone that was at once sentimental, severe, and censorious. A passage from the preface will serve to illustrate this change:

The disgraces of Gil Blas are, for the most part, such as rather excite mirth than compassion: he himself laughs at them; and his transitions from distress to happiness, or at least ease, are so sudden, that neither the reader has time to pity him, nor himself to be acquainted with affliction. This conduct, in my opinion, not only deviates from probability, but prevents that generous indignation which ought to animate the reader against the sordid and vicious disposition of the world.

I have attempted to represent modest merit struggling with every difficulty to which a friendless orphan is exposed, from his own want of experience, as well as from the selfishness, envy, malice, and base indifference of mankind.

Smollett approached the problem of writing fiction in a less complex attitude of mind than was characteristic of Fielding. In *Tom Jones* there is unity of situation, of theme, and of tone not to be found in *Roderick Random*. Whereas Fielding, like Lesage, is capable of a sustained comic point of view, Smollett mingles romantic and farcical elements that do not blend properly. In *Ferdinand Count Fathom*, a novel that is both sentimental and cynical, there are romantic elements anticipatory of the Gothicism of Walpole.

As compared with the dramatic conception of *Tom Jones*, the method followed in *Roderick Random* is simplicity itself. The subject of Fielding's novel is presented in such a manner that the end comes not merely as a happy turn in a succession of events but as the final illumination of the theme. The veil of secrecy having been torn away, Blifil's deceit stands forth in all its ugliness. The result is the product of careful calculation, in which the separate incidents and the various characters are all made to contribute to the central purpose.

Smollett does not know so well as his fellow novelist how to make incident contribute to the revelation of character. In his novels, adventure is likely to be adventure, exciting or amusing on its own account. Characters seem to be animated bits of surface behavior. They are less variable than Fielding's characters and do not show as many sides of their natures. They are also less responsible for their actions and not so clearly fitted into a recognizable social arrangement.

Roderick, unlike Tom, moves through a world in which he has no very secure place. Except for a notable period of a few weeks, Tom is always under the protection of Mr. Allworthy. Roderick, like a picaresque character, has to fend for himself. His world is less compact than Tom's and his progress through it does not follow any very strict observance of the laws of probability. The chief function of the hero seems to be to pass from one adventure to another without succumbing to any of the accidents that befall him. He has even less sensibility than characterizes Fielding's hero, who has at least consistency of feeling. Roderick shows resentment for injuries and not much else. A piece of machinery with stock responses, his sufferings have little effect upon the reader. His flatly conventional feeling for Narcissa is in no way revealing of his character.

Although an adequate summary of the novel would require several pages, a brief outline will suffice to indicate that it records a casual succession of events rather than a consistent or logical development. The death of his mother and the disappearance of his father leave young Roderick at the mercy of an indifferent grandfather, hostile cousins, and a brutal schoolmaster. From this unhappy state of affairs he is rescued by his uncle Tom Bowling, lieutenant of a man-of-war, and is sent to the university. His uncle's support failing him after a time, he becomes assistant to an apothecary and, after about three years at the university, he sets out for London, accompanied by Strap, a former schoolmate and now a barber's assistant, whom he chances to encounter.

Their journey to London is crowded with ludicrous adventures. At one inn they are frightened by a robber, at another by a recruiting sergeant who talks in his sleep, at still another by a raven and a white-bearded old man. Part of the way they travel in a wagon in which their fellow passengers are as droll a set of persons as one could wish for. One night, while they are traveling with this company, Strap, who is always committing blunders, gets into the wrong room and the wrong bed. As a result of this misadventure, Roderick has to fight a duel with a Captain Weazel, in which he uses a spit for want of a sword. Later, on the road, when a highwayman is thought to be approaching, the captain hides under his wife's skirts.

In London, after being fleeced in a game of cards and tricked into lending money to a chance acquaintance, Roderick passes an examination qualifying him for the position of surgeon's assistant in the navy. He can obtain no appointment, however, and, being in need of money, he secures a place as assistant to an apothecary, which position he eventually loses from having learned too much about the affairs of his master's household. Alone and friendless, for Strap has now gone abroad as a gentleman's valet, Roderick secures cheap lodgings and soon discovers that one of the other lodgers is Miss Williams, a woman whom he has once, while ignorant of her true character, been on the point of making his wife. She is, in fact, an adventuress, who has now been reduced by illness and want to a state of great wretchedness. He treats her kindly, and she tells him the story of her life.

At this point an accident to the hero brings about a complete change of scene. He is caught by a press gang, placed on board a man-of-war (of course it is the ship on which his uncle had served), and is appointed surgeon's third mate. The description of life on shipboard is the most vivid and absorbing part of the novel. Between the bullying brute of a captain and the ignorant surgeon, who soon has special reasons for hating and fearing him, Roderick finds his existence a daily torture.

The only alleviation for him is his friendship for the other two surgeon's mates, who never turn against him. The sick are made to work when they can hardly stand. His friend Thomson jumps overboard in an attempt to end his life. Roderick is accused as a spy and is left bound on deck during an engagement. Later he nearly dies of a fever.

His return to England is accompanied by violence equal to that of his departure. The ship, after having run aground, is deserted by captain and crew, and Roderick makes his way among the other deserters at his pistol's point. He has a standing quarrel with Crampley, now the captain, and no sooner do they reach land than he offers to fight him. For this act of folly he is punished by being treacherously knocked down, stripped of his valuables, and left lying senseless on the ground.

This not too happy home-coming marks the beginning of a new series of adventures. Our luckless hero does not return to London but becomes a servant to an eccentric maiden lady, something of a blue stocking, from whom he conceals his identity and past experiences. He falls in love with her niece Narcissa, whom he one day chances to rescue from the unwelcome attentions of a neighboring squire. Having thus made an enemy, he runs away, only to stumble upon a place frequented by smugglers. Being thought by them to be a revenue agent, he is captured and carried to France.

There he sees his uncle, who is surprised to learn from him that Captain Oakum is still alive. It was because of a duel with Captain Oakum, supposedly fatal, that Lieutenant Bowling had left the service and had kept away from England. Roderick's next adventure is to fall in with a Scottish priest, with whom he travels for a time and by whom he is robbed. Then he enlists in a Picardy regiment and goes to war. At Rheims he happens upon his old friend Strap, who procures his discharge from the army and supplies him with money to set himself up as a gentleman.

The remainder of the novel is taken up mainly with a satirical picture of the world of fashion and with fruitless attempts of Roderick to marry advantageously. In London he joins the wits at the coffeehouses, visits the theatre, and devotes himself to Melinda, a reigning beauty, to whom he proposes marriage. Being reduced to the necessity of pawning his sword, he manages to get new clothes, and, while paying court to an heiress at Bath, he sees Narcissa again and learns that Miss Williams has become her maid. Now he turns his attention to Narcissa, but his courtship is soon interrupted by his being put into debtor's prison. His uncle, now the captain of a merchant ship, comes to his rescue and takes him and Strap on a voyage to South America, where Roderick discovers his father, still living and now grown comfortably rich. It is hardly necessary to add that the hero and Narcissa are married with his father's approval, that the elder Random purchases his paternal estate in Scotland, and that Miss Williams becomes the wife of Strap.

Throughout all this Smollett's aim is to provide a variety of objects for satirical delineation and to record an interesting series of actions. The picture of manners lacks the depth, range, and continuity of *Tom Jones*. The author looks at mankind satirically but without a definite philosophy. He does not construct his story in terms of a complete social situation, nor does he organize it according to the principles of drama. The plot has the appearance of having been improvised. We hardly know what to expect of the hero. Presented at first as a guileless rustic who is only less simple than Strap, Roderick is yet cunning enough to conceal his knowledge of French from his employer Lavement in the hope that he may thus learn something that can be turned to his advantage.

Usually Roderick moves according to the whim of fortune. His loss of his uncle's support comes as the result of a duel. His loss of his position with the apothecary in London turns upon the narrow chance of his entering by mistake the bedroom of his master's daughter at the moment she is expecting someone else. His going to sea is the result of seizure by a press gang. His rescue of Narcissa from the squire provides him with an opportunity to declare his love and also gives him a reason for quitting the neighborhood. His accidental discovery of the place haunted by smugglers causes him to be transported to France.

If you are fashioning a novel upon the tradition of picaresque fiction and spicing it with a romantic turn of events, you can cause a surgeon's second mate to jump overboard and be rescued by a former schoolfellow who has become the master of a Rhode Island schooner. You can land your hero in France and have him at once come upon one of the two men there that it is important for him to encounter—in this case his uncle and former benefactor. When it is time for another change of scene, and you wish to return to England, you can rub the lamp and a genie will appear in the form of Strap, a stupid fellow but wonderfully supplied with money and devotion to bestow upon his undeserving idol. You can see to it that the woman whom your hero had once befriended reappears as the maid of the woman he has since come to love. You can, if you wish, bring your novel to a happy conclusion by conjuring up from the fabulous land of South America a father rich enough to make all reasonable dreams come true and thus enable your hero, no longer a friendless orphan, to shine before his friends and to triumph over his enemies.

In such a novel unity and consistency are sacrificed in the interest of diversity. The author does not linger long enough for a situation to grow complex. The nearest exception to this relentlessness of pace is the time spent on shipboard, where the characters are held together in an enforced association. Even here the captain and the surgeon are not completely credible human beings. They are not given an opportunity to reveal many sides of their characters. We see Captain Oakum only as the brutal, domineering master of his ship, and we see him only with his subordinates. Squire Western, on the other hand, is shown in several relationships. He is affectionate and domineering with his daughter, on terms of hearty and jovial fellowship with his neighbor Allworthy, and suspicious and resentful of his sister's interference. We see him deep in his cups, egging on a timid suitor with coarse words and gestures, losing all other concerns in the excitement of a fox hunt, and doting on his granddaughter.

Smollett does not look at his characters with such thoroughness. He dwells upon physical traits and superficial manifestations of temperament and produces a picture of society somewhat similar to the view of a tourist. A tourist looks for things that are picturesque or different from what he has known. There is something of this tendency in Smollett's fastening upon what is odd, fantastic, or whimsical. Many of the people encountered by Roderick have a touch of the grotesque in them. His employer, Mr. Crab, the surgeon, is described as follows:

This member of the faculty was aged fifty, about five feet high, and ten round the belly; his face was capacious as a full moon, and much of the complexion of a mulberry; his nose, resembling a powder-horn, was swelled to an enormous size, and studded all over with carbuncles; and his little grey eyes reflected the rays in such an oblique mannner, that, while he looked a person full in the face, one would have imagined he was admiring the buckle of his shoe.

Such exaggeration of purely physical traits seems rather pointless. It suggests that the author is ill-natured rather than humorous. Comic exaggeration is more effective when applied to oddities of temperament, such as are illustrated by Commodore Trunnion, the retired mariner of *Peregrine Pickle,* who lives on land as if he were in a ship at sea. He keeps the guests waiting while he rides to his wedding, tacking his horse from left to right and back again down the narrow road in the manner of a sailing vessel, because he is travelling against the wind. He introduces his wife into his household, which is managed as if it were on a ship, and insists upon her sleeping in a hammock, with results that can easily be conjectured.

Such satirical delineation of people is reminiscent of the Jonsonian comedy of humors. Jonson presents his characters as stereotyped manifestations of some dominant trait. Smollett also follows the practice of setting forth his characters in terms of a single dominant trait or ruling passion. Jonson, however, having a logical mind, a sense of dramatic situation, and inventive power, conceives his matter, his plot, and his characters all together and functioning in unison. In addition, his characters are conceived in more distinct moral terms than are those of Smollett, in whose novel there is little connection between the plot and the moral intention.

Although packed with action, *Roderick Random* is not primarily a story of adventure. In a novel of adventure the exploits of the hero are of the first importance. A knight goes on a quest, the attainment of which beckons the reader on. The novel of adventure needs something of this primitive curiosity. It needs a goal, or something to be accomplished. It needs, above all, a hero with an adventurous spirit. Such a spirit is to be encountered in the world of Scott, where a young man setting out on a journey arouses a sense of expectancy never associated with the doings of Roderick.

In *Ferdinand Count Fathom* an attempt is made to remedy this deficiency by the introduction of scenes in which the interest is not in any purpose of satire or character delineation. Instead the author attempts to build up an atmosphere of foreboding and to arouse interest in the incident itself. One such occasion is provided when Fathom one dark night loses his way in a wood that is reported to be infested by robbers. He seeks refuge in a lonely cottage and retires for the night, only to find, to his horror, that not only has he been locked in his room but that there is concealed in it, under some straw, the body of a man who has been put to death only a short while before. Immediately scenting danger, he has the presence of mind to undress the bleeding corpse and place it in his bed. Let what follows be told in the author's own words:

Then he extinguished the light, took possession of the place from whence the body had been removed, and, holding a pistol ready cocked in each hand, waited for the sequel with that determined purpose which is often the immediate production of despair. About midnight he heard the sound of feet ascending the ladder; the door was softly opened; he saw the shadow of two men stalking towards the bed, a dark lanthorn being unshrouded, directed their aim to the supposed sleeper, and he that held it thrust a poinard to his heart; the force of the blow made a compression on the chest, and a sort of groan issued from the wind-pipe of the defunct; the stroke was repeated, without producing a repetition of the note, so that the assassins concluded the work was effectually done, and retired for the present with a design to return and rifle the deceased at their leisure.

CHAPTER V

The Comic Novel

LAURENCE STERNE

Laurence Sterne, the author of *Tristram Shandy* and *A Sentimental Journey*, showed that it was possible to write fiction without following any of the styles then in vogue. In comparison with such a novelist as Fielding, he seemed to follow no fixed plan. Instead of bowing to the established rules he ridiculed them by making his method of procedure, like so much of his subject matter, a theme for extravagant satire. His search for oddity, both in material and in method, led him to do not what was expected but what was unexpected, to cultivate surprise at every turn. Although such cultivation of whimsicality and of the personal note might, in a less agile writer, have resulted in boredom, Sterne succeeded in arousing an extraordinary amount of interest both in his books and in himself.

The novel had not outgrown its seventeenth-century formalism. The art of *Tom Jones* was based upon the formal art of the classic drama. Furthermore, the achievements of Sterne's predecessors were not easily to be repeated. To the factual consistency of Defoe's method, Richardson added an elaborate moral formula. To follow adequately in the path of Fielding, one needed the training of a dramatist. Even Smollett's rambling narratives were the work of an unusually vigorous person whose shrewdness and relish it would not have been easy to match.

Sterne was not qualified by experience or temperament to emulate any of these novelists, even had he wished to do so. He had neither the industry of Defoe, the patience of Richardson, the vigor of Smollett, nor the broad training and disciplined mind of Fielding. It was not to these writers that the author of *Tristram Shandy* looked for inspiration but to less traditional novelists like Cervantes and Rabelais, in whose work he found elements of absurdity and extravagance akin to his own whimsicality.

Although he was a clergyman, Sterne did not cultivate the sobriety of manner expected of men in his position. He greatly disliked any kind of pomposity or primness. Quite possibly he rebelled against his role and had as a result an exaggerated tendency to kick over the traces, and accordingly to violate the usages accepted by most novelists as their ritual. He did not adopt the tone of the conventional moralist or satirist. If he was humorous or pathetic or ironic, it was not according to any clearly recognizable policy. He did not follow the usual course of tracing his hero's career from birth through childhood to marriage; indeed he seemed almost to ignore the novelist's primary requirement to tell a story. He was unconventional both in his choice of material and in the manner of its presentation. A family circle was not something new in English fiction, but never had there been one presented with such bizarre treatment of the situations commonly associated with family life as in *Tristram Shandy.*

It should not be assumed, however, that Sterne's sole intention as a novelist was to fly in the face of convention. Underneath his mask of drollery was a serious purpose to produce something more natural than the conventional novelists had produced. Defoe's naturalness in dealing with action did not extend to the feelings of his characters. Richardson's naturalness in conveying emotional reactions was combined with formalism in dealing with moral problems. Fielding was inclined to let intellectual concepts get between him and his characters. Sterne went further than the others in stripping his characterization of secondary concerns. Not having to be fitted into an arbitrary moral scheme or to support a weighty intellectual thesis, his characters were free to follow the mood of the moment and to exhibit in their behavior things too fleeting and irrelevant to catch the attention of the serious moralist. It was this interest of Sterne in the small, evanescent, personal aspects of life rather than in abstractly conceived problems that made his fiction different from that of his contemporaries. His effort to render these minute shiftings of the feelings and the complex interplay of personalities upon one another caused him to produce a type of writing pointing forward to the later psychological novel and making him closer in spirit to our age than was either Richardson or Fielding.

The Life and Opinions of Tristram Shandy, Gentleman

Tristram Shandy first appeared in nine small volumes between the years 1759 and 1767. Owing to its individuality of method, it does not fall readily into any of the types of novels then current. Its plot is loose and episodic, but it is not the looseness of the picaresque novel, and its material is not picaresque in character. Its appeal to the emotions is different from Richardson's, and its humorous treatment of character is unlike Fielding's. It is a novel of humors rather than of manners. Least of all does it resemble a novel of action. Its closest affinity is with such comic and burlesque romances as *Gargantua* and *Pantagruel,* by François Rabelais.

Although it purports to be the history of a family, it is far from being a conventional record of the usual concerns of family life. The first son, Bobby, is hardly mentioned until we learn that he is dead. He exists apparently only for the purpose of dying and affording his father and other members of the household an opportunity to discuss his death. Tristram, who acts as narrator, has to tell, for the most part, of events that happened before his birth or before he was old enough to know what was going on. His real importance is to provide his father with an object of anxiety and care. Like other fathers, Mr. Shandy is not without illusions about how to provide for his offspring and make certain of his happiness and success. Never was a man more doomed to disappointment and more in need of a sustaining philosophy, for an unparalleled series of misfortunes upset his precious plans at every important turn of his son's life.

Compared with other novels of the period, the number of characters in *Tristram Shandy* is limited. In addition to Mr. Shandy and

Tristram, there are only Uncle Toby, Mrs. Shandy, the parson, the family doctor, a few friends, and the servants, if one omits the travels of young Tristram into France. An important personage in the later books is the Widow Wadman, who so nearly succeeds in her plan to marry Uncle Toby.

There is an occasion when Trim, the faithful servitor of Uncle Toby, is unable to recite the Fifth Commandment without beginning at the first and taking them in order. Mr. Shandy does not have much faith in the value of knowledge that rests upon such a bare mechanism of learning. In like manner Sterne distrusts whatever is mechanical. He warns his readers that he will not follow a set plan. He will not be like the muleteer who drives from Rome to Loretto without looking to either side of the road. He berates the critics who judge by rule and compass, and pictures himself in Yorick as a man of quick sympathies who is given to scattering gibes and jests without regard to the consequences. In particular he dislikes the affectation of gravity in people, which he declares is a hypocritical device to gain credit for more sense and knowledge than one actually possesses. With such a man of whim, such an inveterate and indiscreet jester, as author, we need not be surprised to find the world of *Tristram Shandy* a topsy-turvy one.

Not only is the world of Shandy Hall a topsy-turvy one, but everything about the novel fails to conform to the usual method of procedure. Tristram is not the central character or the one most conversant with the action. Most of what he narrates must have been learned by him at some period outside the time limits of the novel. We do not altogether identify the narrator with the infant about whose birth and early training the household revolves. It is a little disconcerting to us, or would be in a less disconcerting book, when the narrator suddenly stops giving an account of his uncle's campaigns and begins to tell of his own travels in France. The Tristram that we know is far too young for such adventures.

The night when Tristram is born is a time of extraordinary confusion, even for Shandy Hall. Among other things no less out of place at such a time, Trim reads a sermon and Dr. Slop, in a hurry to open his bag of obstetrical instruments, cuts his thumb. The effect of having a person yet unborn recite in great detail the events leading up to his own birth and describe the mad goings-on in Shandy Hall on that memorable evening is unquestionably droll. But, apart from this advantage, the choice of Tristram as narrator had for Sterne a number of advantages. The fact that the narrator is a member of the family gives to the chronicle an air of intimacy. His interest in his father and uncle comes to us as something bred of long familiarity. Moreover, there is an advantage in the narrator being himself outside the events that he records. The delicacy with which Uncle Toby is depicted, for example, could hardly have re¬ sulted from the slapdash method of a narrator absorbed in his own affairs, like Roderick Random.

By setting up as narrator one who belonged to the family circle and who was at the same time detached from it, Sterne achieved a more personal effect than any other novelist of his time had achieved. The autobiographical heroes and heroines of Defoe and Smollett, having to record a series of incidents, had little attention to devote to anything else. Usually in the autobiographical novel the chief character acted as narrator, but in *Tristram Shandy* there was no clearly defined line of action and no single dominant character. Neither Mr. Shandy nor his brother could have served in this capacity without doing violence to his position in the novel. They needed to be rendered from the outside if they were to retain the simplicity so essential to our belief in them. Even Richardson was less personal in the effect he created than was Sterne. Clarissa lived in a state of crisis that narrowed the range of her susceptibility. Tristram, as narrator, had nothing to occupy his attention presumably but the members of the household to whom he could devote himself unreservedly, recording their changes of mood and their slightest flickerings of impulse. It may be objected that Tristram, as narrator, is not an actual person but only a disguise for Sterne, who adopts what is essentially an omniscient point of view toward his material. Actually the author fuses the personal and the omniscient points of view by dwelling not upon the inner activity of his char- acters but upon the external manifestations of feeling which serve to reveal them as people are revealed in life.

Take, for example, the remark of Mrs. Shandy that she would like to look through the keyhole at Uncle Toby's courting of the

Widow Wadman, out of *curiosity*. Mr. Shandy, always quick to speak, insinuates that it is not curiosity but something else which moves her. Immediately his conscience smites him for what he has said. At the moment the two are walking along the road, and the scene is described as follows:

My mother was then conjugally swinging with her left arm twisted under his right, in such wise, that the inside of her hand rested upon the back of his —— she raised her fingers, and let them fall —— it could scarce be called a tap; or if it was a tap —— 'twould have puzzled a casuist to say, whether 'twas a tap of remonstrance, or a tap of confession: my father, who was all sensibilities from head to foot, class'd it right —— Conscience redoubled her blow —— he turn'd his face suddenly the other way, and my mother supposing his body was about to turn with it in order to move homewards, by a cross movement of her right leg, keeping her left as its centre, brought herself so far in front, that as he turned his head, he met her eye —— Confusion again! he saw a thousand reasons to wipe out the reproach, and as many to reproach himself ——

One advantage that Sterne derived from his transference of authorship was freedom from the tendency to be self-conscious. For an artist who worked for minute effects, the danger of slipping into affectation was serious. As long as he preserved the simplicity of his shadowy narrator he was safe. Sometimes he went too far and coarsened the effect by laying on too much stress. The story of the death of Le Fever throws into clear relief the compassionate heart of Uncle Toby as it shows him sitting by the bed of the dying soldier, engrossed in plans for nursing him back to health. But the effect is marred at the end by a style that attracts too much attention to itself and incidentally to the narrator: "Nature instantly ebb'd again, —— the film returned to its place, —— the pulse fluttered —— stopp'd —— went on —— throb'd —— stopp'd again —— moved —— stopp'd —— shall I go on? —— No."

Such scenes lend themselves more readily to overemphasis than humorous situations, which require an air of spontaneity. *A Sentimental Journey*, which contains more of the pathetic and relatively less of the humorous than *Tristram Shandy*, gives the impression of being more studied in method. One possible reason for this difference is the fact that *A Sentimental Journey* was written ostensibly by Yorick, who was such a thin disguise for Sterne that it did not veil him from the reader. Having gained a reputation for himself as a wit and a man of sensibility, he could not easily forget what was expected of him. If he cut a caper or shed a tear, the world was there to be convinced that he was a gay fellow or that he had a tender heart. Happily in *Tristram Shandy* he could hide more or less under the cloak of Tristram. It made it all the better that Yorick, who was generally known to be modelled upon Sterne, was only a minor character uninvolved in the role of narration.

As we never see Tristram in the process of becoming an adult or of forming an attitude toward his parents, it does not surprise us to find him dealing with them without personal bias. Although his uncle is an amiable innocent, his mother a simpleton, and his father a pedantic theorist who is the dupe of the most absurd hypotheses, Tristram writes of them without malice and without apparent irony. Seemingly he is unaware of the extent of their absurdity. Although the novel opens with a lament by Tristram that his parents have not been in everything considerate of his welfare, Sterne leaves for a later generation of novelists serious attention to the theme of parental responsibility. The success of *Tristram Shandy* depends to a greater degree than is perhaps generally realized upon the lightness and delicacy and simplicity maintained by the narrator in relating it.

It was already a time-honored custom for a novel to begin with an account of the birth of the hero. Usually a few pages sufficed to project the newly born child to a point in life where it was possible for him to think and act for himself. Sterne did not follow the usual course. The father of Tristram, instead of dying or being sent to prison, instead of being too poor to provide for his son or too rich to get along amicably with him, did not do any of the self-abnegative things that it was customary for fathers to do as a means of launching their sons upon careers of their own. Although Mr. Shandy had no intention of being the hero of his son's novel, he virtually did become so, sharing the role with his brother. The story of Tristram's birth, which readers doubtless expected would be followed by the story of his life, became so much intermingled with associated matter that the child actually was not born until well along in the third volume. The only justification for calling him the hero is the fact that he is so designated in the title and the more important fact that his birth, christening, and early development occupy so much attention. As a child Tristram is simply a puppet, the object of his father's plans and of Susannah's care.

Behind the apparent confusion of *Tristram Shandy* there was a genuine desire to produce an effect of naturalness. The author carefully avoided anything mechanical. Not only did he keep his style supple but he continually introduced unforeseen breaks in his narrative. These sudden shifts and digressions, thrown in apparently at random but actually according to careful planning, had the effect of giving to the progress of the story a sense of freedom from control more truly characteristic of life than the steady progress and regularity of a *Tom Jones* or a *Clarissa*. The principle of organization that guided Sterne was derived from the *Essay concerning Human Understanding*, by John Locke. A little attention to this book will serve to reveal how it was utilized in the writing of *Tristram Shandy*.

According to Locke there are no innate ideas. The mind at birth is likened to a *tabula rasa*, a smoothed tablet, upon which characters are written by experience. Knowledge arises ultimately from sense perception. Sensation gives rise to simple ideas and subsequently ideas of growing complexity are built up out of the combination of sensations and from the interplay between sensation and reflection. Such an assumption places great responsibility upon education, since, according to it, the growth of the mind depends almost entirely upon impressions received from the external world. In *Some Thoughts concerning Education* Locke suggests that nine men out of ten are what they are as a result of their education. A very slight impression upon the tender mind of the child has important and lasting consequences. A gentle application of force at one point in its course may cause the waters of a river to flow in a different channel. Similarly, Locke continues, "I imagine the minds of children as easily turned this or that way, as water itself." In such an assertion we find the reason why Mr. Shandy takes so much pains in bringing up Tristram and why he is so eager to have only what he considers to be beneficial influences brought to bear upon his child.

Locke uses the term *idea* not as it was used by Plato and not in the sense of modern psychology, but in a broad sense that includes all the objects of the understanding. Consequently when he speaks of the association of ideas he is really referring to things which are associated in the mind. One chapter of the *Essay concerning Human Understanding* contains the following passage:

Some of our ideas have a natural correspondence and connection one with another: it is the office and excellency of our reason to trace these, and hold them together in that union and correspondence which is founded in their peculiar beings. Besides this, there is another connection of ideas wholly owing to chance or custom: ideas, that in themselves are not all of kin, come to be so united in some men's minds, that it is very hard to separate them; they always keep in company, and the one no sooner at any time comes into the understanding, but its associate appears with it; and if they are more than two, which are thus united, the whole gang, always inseparable, show themselves together.

Locke deals with association only incidentally, his main concern with it being to explain or account for aberrations from ordered thinking. One example cited is that of a young man who learned to dance in a room where there was an old trunk. "The idea of this remarkable piece of household-stuff had so mixed itself with the turns and steps of all his dances, that though in that chamber he could dance excellently well, yet it was only whilst that trunk was there; nor could he perform well in any other place, unless that or some other trunk had its due position in the room." It would not be surprising if such an example as this suggested to Sterne the use of queer and ridiculous cases of association. Much of the humor of *Tristram Shandy* has its origin in some grotesque juxtaposition of things. Take, for example, the following interchange:

We'll go, brother Toby, said my father, whilst dinner is coddling —— to the abby of Saint Germain, if it be only to see these bodies, of which monsieur Seguier has given such a recommendation. —— I'll go see any body; quoth my uncle Toby; for he was all compliance through every step of the journey —— Defend me! said my father —— they are all mummies —— Then one need not shave; quoth my uncle Toby —— Shave! no —— cried my father —— 'twill be more like relations to go with our beards on ——

William James, in his *Principles of Psychology*, cites an instance of looking at his clock and then finding himself thinking of a resolution in the United States Senate dealing with legal-tender notes. The chain of association leads from the clock to the man who has repaired it. He suggests the jeweler's shop, which, in turn, revives the memory of some shirt studs purchased there. They lead to thought of the recent decline in the value of gold and accordingly to the Senate resolution about paper money.

The psychologist has various ways to account for this tendency of thoughts to awaken other thoughts which have been recently associated with them or which are habitual associates. The basic factor seems to be that the two things have been active together or in close succession. Another important point is that one tends to think of what interests him. When Mr. Shandy, in discussing the question of time and duration, happens to mention a succession of ideas which follow each other in train, Uncle Toby, whose consuming interest is military history, immediately thinks of a train of artillery. At another time Mr. Shandy, who has learned about the injury to his son's nose, asks his brother if ever a man has received so many lashes. Toby replies that the most he ever saw given was to a grenadier in Mackay's regiment.

In addition to such possibilities of humor the principle of the association of ideas provides Sterne with a means of revealing people through their dominant interests. Take, for example, the occasion when the news of Bobby's death is received by the servants. Susannah can think only of a green satin dress belonging to her mistress, a dress which she has doubtless been coveting and which may now be given to her since Mrs. Shandy will go into mourning. The kitchenmaid, who has been ill, is led to think gratifyingly that she has escaped death. Obadiah thinks of the work of stubbing the Ox-moor. The expense of Bobby's travels has interfered with the project of clearing and fencing in this neglected tract of land; now that he is dead the work on the Ox-moor can be put into execution. Trim, who is naturally loquacious and who has seen death on the battle-field, is moved to make a speech. His mind is never far from his master, and he soon thinks of how Captain Shandy will grieve for the boy.

The scene in which these personal interests and idiosyncrasies are revealed is a brilliant piece of comedy, in which death and the pettiness of life are brought into close conjunction. Each character is preoccupied with his or her own concerns and only secondarily with the news of Bobby's death. It is a different kind of portraiture from the straightforward narrative of Defoe or Smollett. It does not remind us of Richardson or Fielding, for it is not a link in a chain of larger issues, and it is more concerned with presenting a picture than an interpretation of life. Sterne is more unreservedly an artist and less of a moralist than the others. His aim is to exhibit his characters and create a series of impressions. Elsewhere he shows us Mr. Shandy staggering under the knowledge of the injury done to his son's nose, groping for his breeches on the night of Tristram's unlucky baptism, or striving desperately to drive home the point of an argument. We become familiar with his oddities and have him presented to us in details of gesture and movement, but there is not much analysis of him.

A cursory survey of eighteenth-century novels reveals the fact that a large proportion of them, if we are to believe their titles, are adventures, histories, or memoirs. *Tristram Shandy,* however, is a story not of "adventures" but of "opinions." It does not deal, like *Tom Jones* or *Roderick Random,* with a world crowded with life and activity. Mr. Shandy and his brother have both retired and their contact with the world is quite limited. Even the small world in which they live is not presented with any sense of completeness. What continuity there is in the novel is not in the setting or the action but in the characters.

Stories of adventure are likely to follow a temporal sequence, since one act must follow another and no single individual can be involved in a multiplicity of actions at one time. A man's opinions, however, do not follow one another according to any regular sequence. For one to live in his mind is not to live simply in the present because in the mind the present and the past are fused.

In *Swann's Way,* by Marcel Proust, the author tells how the taste of a morsel of cake soaked in tea brings back to him childhood memories of Combray and fills him with exquisite pleasure. The key that unlocked the door of the past for him was not a conscious

effort to remember but an accidental revival of the taste of
madeleine dipped in tea like that which his Aunt Léonie had given
him many years before at Combray on Sunday mornings. A remembered odor, a gesture, a musical phrase, in other circumstances, may
serve to revive the past and the emotions associated with it. The
renewed sensation brings back not only the original incident but a
vast structure of memories. Referring to the moment in which he
drank the tea, Proust says: "In that moment all the flowers in our
garden and in M. Swann's park, and the water lilies on the Vivonne,
and the good people of the village and their little dwellings and the
church and all Combray and its surroundings, taking shape and
solidity, came into being, both town and gardens, from my cup of
tea."

The general title of Proust's series of novels is *A la Recherche du
Temps perdu*, which signifies an attempt to recapture the past. In
his handling of time and of individual consciousness Sterne makes
a beginning of what Proust does so brilliantly. In *Tristram Shandy*
there is a merging of present and past time. Uncle Toby and Trim
spend much of their time living over the excitement of their military
campaigns. Anything that reminds them of those stirring days is
likely to arouse emotions in them associated with their past lives,
as when Mr. Shandy's disappointment over the name "Tristram"
causes Uncle Toby to say that had his name been Alexander, he
could have done no more at Namur than his duty.

This tendency of the past to obtrude itself upon the present is
responsible for much of the shifting of time in *Tristram Shandy*. The
characters are shown to be living in a present in which the past has
its place. It is because they have something to remember and interests which can be aroused that the working of association has
the power to lead them off on various paths of digression. Moreover,
the fact that each character has his own fund of consciousness, his
own pronounced interest and point of view, makes possible the complex interplay of personality in which the novel abounds. Emphasis
upon the individual mind means emphasis upon the individual point
of view. The humor of the irrelevant and the significance of the
small and fleeting become apparent when we consider that whether
a thing is great or small, relevant or irrelevant, depends very much

upon the point of view from which it is seen. As Virginia Woolf says, "We must consult our own minds before we can say what is the comparative importance of a cathedral, of a donkey, and of a girl with a green satin purse." This truth, important for the writing of fiction, was more clearly understood by Sterne than by other eighteenth-century novelists.

The point of view of *Tristram Shandy* is more personal than that of *Tom Jones*. At the same time Sterne does not write about himself directly. He puts something of himself in Mr. Shandy, in Uncle Toby, in Yorick, and in Tristram. He limits the point of view of the omniscient storyteller by blending it with that of an individual, and shows that he recognizes the value of indirectness. Although Tristram writes in the first person he writes not about himself primarily but others, and he prefers to present them in their words, gestures, and actions, as they might appear to any onlooker. "Our minds," says the author, "shine not through the body, but are wrapt up in a dark covering of uncrystallized flesh and blood; so that, if we would come to the specific characters of them, we must go some other way to work." He who would draw a man's character is thus put to various expedients, and Tristram decides that a good way to draw his uncle's character is from his hobbyhorse.

Conceiving of consciousness not as a light from within illuminating the external world but as a photographic plate upon which objects were represented, Locke believed that the objects of perception consisted of separate sensations or impressions. One who came into contact with a physical object experienced sensations which were conveyed by the nerves from the sense organs to the brain. What the mind perceived was not the object itself but a series of isolated sensations produced by the object. Accordingly there was a difference, in Locke's view, between "mental truth" and "real truth." Such a theory of knowledge placed great emphasis upon the senses.

In concerning himself as he did with the physical expression of emotion and with the relation between appearance and reality, Sterne was being a good disciple of Locke. *Tristram Shandy* and *A Sentimental Journey* contain many scenes in which careful attention is paid to the tone of the voice, to gesture, or to the description of some bodily movement. Mr. Shandy's restlessness and Uncle Toby's composure are shown in their bodily movements as well as in their speech. The way in which a man puts down his hat or takes it up, according to Mr. Shandy, is expressive of his character. Trim drops his hat once in just the right manner to cause Susannah to burst into tears.

Despite his artificiality, Sterne brought a new touch of nature to the novel. He paid more attention to the element of time than Richardson, and achieved a more noteworthy impression of immediacy. He employed various devices, such as Uncle Toby's smoking of his pipe, to arouse a sense of the passing of time. The dashes strewn through his writing break up the sentences and help to produce the effect of deliberateness and of the pauses characteristic of actual speech. His sentiment, unlike Richardson's, is not tinged with didacticism. Incongruities are everywhere in the novel, both in the way in which the characters clash and in the basic dualism of life as it is depicted. Humor acts as a balancing agent by which, in the words of Coleridge, "the finite great is brought into identity with the little, or the little with the finite great."

This linking of the great and the little, of the sublime and the ridiculous, occurs repeatedly. Man is depicted as a compound of wisdom and folly, a creature of inconsistency, "languishing under wounds, which he has the power to heal! —— his whole life a contradiction to his knowledge!" Mr. Shandy spends years working on a system of education for Tristram, all the while totally neglecting him. The boy for whom such elaborate plans are made is meanwhile the victim of a series of ridiculous and preventable mischances. So many elements, of trivial and of serious import, come together in the christening of Tristram that life itself seems to have been transformed into farce. The whole story of Uncle Toby and the Widow Wadman is an excellent illustration of the humor of looking at life and love from widely opposite points of view. Mr. Shandy is even driven to lament that some other provision has not been made "for continuing the race of so great, so exalted and godlike a Being as man."

Much of the humor of *Tristram Shandy* arises from the dramatic contrast of the two brothers. Each one in riding his hobby unintentionally vexes the other, but Mr. Shandy is the more harassed of the two. His consuming passion is for theorizing, and neither his wife nor his brother has any intellectual curiosity. Consequently his craving for a sympathetic audience is always being left unsatisfied. Mrs. Shandy's readiness to assent to any proposition without comprehending it is a continual source of vexation to him.

Apart from being so very much absorbed in his hobby of military history and maneuvers, Uncle Toby is a simple, unassuming man, naïve in comparison with his brother, but always wise in his feelings. He is sorry to hear the devil cursed and has not the heart to retaliate upon a fly. He and his brother are foils to each other and represent different aspects of human nature. Hazlitt says of him: "My Uncle Toby is one of the finest compliments ever paid to human nature. He is the most unoffending of God's creatures; or, as the French express it, *un tel petit bon homme!* Of his bowling-green, his sieges, and his amours, who would say or think anything amiss!"

CHAPTER VI

The Gothic Romance

Thus far, in tracing the development of the novel from Defoe onward, I have had few occasions to deal with romance except to take note of the anti-romantic tendencies of certain of the novelists. In order to get a better understanding of this antipathy to romance in the eighteenth century, let us make a brief examination of some of its origins. In the latter part of the seventeenth century, particularly after the Revolution of 1688, certain political and cultural changes came into English life, bringing a sense of relief from the insecurity and strain of the period of civil war and making possible an increased spirit of tolerance. By comparison with what had gone before, the eighteenth century was a time of growing enlightenment.

Scientific progress led to a new conception of nature and to emancipation from the superstitious beliefs of the past. The fear of secular learning, which had characterized the Middle Ages, was replaced by an attitude which looked upon Newton and Locke as the prophets of a new era, in which nature and reason, supplanting the supernatural, were to be the guiding lights. Instead of being a "dim vast vale of tears" suffering under God's wrath, the world, according to the new faith, was a place of harmony and law, which Pope characterized in the following terms:

> All nature is but art, unknown to thee;
> All chance, direction, which thou canst not see;

All discord, harmony not understood;
All partial evil, universal good.

An age that made a religion out of reason could be expected to look with disfavor upon the confusion and disorder of former centuries and to regard the Middle Ages as a barbarous and uncivilized period.

The taste now was for order and regularity rather than for the mysterious and heroic, for practical virtue rather than theological speculation. The crisp, precise couplets of Pope displaced in popularity the more elaborate verse forms and extravagant conceits of the so-called metaphysical poets. A simple and direct prose style took the place of the long, involved sentences of earlier prose. The fiction of the period was lacking in the spirit of adventure and in the picturesque and passionate. Life on a lonely island was for Robinson Crusoe a rather sober and matter-of-fact proceeding.

This change in temper can be detected in the Restoration period in the declining popularity of the older dramatists and in the preference shown then for Ben Jonson over Shakespeare. John Evelyn remarked in his *Diary*, after seeing a performance of *Hamlet*, that the old plays were beginning to cause disgust, and Pepys called *A Midsummer Night's Dream* a "most insipid, ridiculous play."

Addison referred to the cathedral at Siena as a masterpiece of Gothic architecture, and also expressed the belief that the people who had gone to so much expense in the erection of barbarous buildings of that type might have produced "miracles of architecture . . . had they only been instructed in the right way." Saint Mark's Church, in Venice, was pronounced by one traveler to be "in wretched taste both inside and out," and by another to have nothing to recommend it but its great antiquity and vast riches.

Eventually these old buildings, which had been treated so contemptuously and with so little understanding, came to be treasured as relics of a past age. Remote times and regions and the customs of other peoples became objects of interest, valued for the very reason that they were unfamiliar. A new spirit of inquiry and adventurousness found inspiration in the heroic spirit and the mysteriousness of the Middle Ages.

The novels of the period reflected, for the most part, a world devoid of poetry. *Clarissa* never managed to escape entirely from an atmosphere of caution and calculation. *Tom Jones* did not plumb the depths of sensibility but played out its drama of good and evil on a plane of practical sanity and wisdom. Sterne likewise did not attempt to enthrall the reader. He went further than Fielding in ridiculing intellectual and moral pedantry, and made game of the world of good sense, setting up sensibility rather than sense as a principle of behavior. In thus looking to sentiment for guidance, and in refusing to employ the novel as an instrument of instruction, he took a step forward on the road toward romance.

The development of the Romantic movement in the eighteenth century was an extremely complex phenomenon, covering several decades and spreading over western Europe. It was related to industrial, social, political, intellectual, and literary changes. It was a form of protest against the stereotyped, or against the tendency of life and society to harden into fixed forms of custom, privilege, convention, and established authority. It was a state of intellectual ferment that wrought profound changes, figuring in the French Revolution and incidentally producing stories about old ghost-haunted castles. It was a manifestation of the recurring contention between the forces of stability and the forces of change. On the one side were ranged tradition, propriety, restraint, authority, and experience; on the other side was the restless, inquiring spirit of mankind— impatient of restraint, hating tyranny, seeking liberty and progress toward the fulfillment of its dream of perfection.

Such a revolutionary change of traditional forms of thinking could not be accomplished in a brief period. A sense of the mysterious is not something to be acquired by pretending. *The Castle of Otranto*, published in 1764, represents the attempt of a man of reason to indulge in a fancy for mystery. Horace Walpole, the author, was a dilettante and man of wit, better fitted, as Walter Raleigh has pointed out, to be the parodist of Gothic fiction than its inaugurator. Having purchased a small property at Twickenham to serve him as a retreat, he decided to make a little Gothic castle out of his house and thereafter spent several years converting it into a villa in a fantastic stucco-Gothic style and storing it with bric-a-brac. By reason of these architectural experiments, his little estate, which he christened Strawberry Hill, soon became a famous show place. *The Castle of Otranto* was explained by its author as "an attempt to blend the two kinds of romance, the ancient and the modern." It was an effort to combine greater freedom of invention than was admitted in the modern novel with greater truth to nature than had characterized the old romances.

Having been drawn to his task by his interest in medieval architecture, Walpole gave a prominent place in his story to the castle which served as its setting. The action, which supposedly takes place at some time during the Crusades, has to do with the usurpation of a principality, a prophecy, and retribution. The chief ingredients of the story are crime and violence and, most of all, supernatural visitations. The specter of Alfonso, victim of the initial crime, returns to haunt the grandson of his murderer. It manifests itself first by a helmet, then by a sword, and later by a foot and a hand. In accordance with the terms of the prophecy, these spectral fragments are all greatly enlarged. Eventually the complete specter appears. Medieval coloring is provided in the feudal society, the tyrannical prince, knights in armor home from the Crusades, a hermit, and particularly by the castle itself with its cloisters and arched vaults, its old doors and winding passageways. One of the most exciting incidents in the story is the escape of the heroine from the lord of the castle through a trap door with a secret lock.

The supernatural elements are set forth with such violence and crudity that they seem ridiculous rather than impressive. Details that should be veiled in semi-darkness are presented in full light. The marvels fall plump into an atmosphere in which they are so jarringly out of place that they seem preposterous rather than terrifying. The portrait of Manfred's grandfather, at a critical point in the story, utters a sigh and heaves its breast. Afterwards it quits its panel and descends to the floor, "with a grave and melancholy air." A statue bleeds at the nose. The helmet with which the wonders begin is far from being impressive in proportion to its huge size. Though spectral in character, it is corporeal enough to have broken through the courtyard and pierced an arched vault below. The stagiest of stage effects could not be worse than the claps of thunder and the moonlight, which are turned on and off at will. Such inventions do not represent a true liberation of the powers of fancy. They do not express the mysterious forces of nature and can neither excite wonder nor gain credence.

Thirteen years after the appearance of *Otranto,* Clara Reeve published a story admittedly of the same species. She criticized Walpole, however, for not having kept more strictly within the limits of probability, and tried, in *The Old English Baron,* to refine the supernatural element and present it in terms acceptable to the imagination. Scott, writing at the height of the Romantic period, said that the fault of Walpole lay in his excessive demands upon the reader's credulity. Not too much acceptance of wonder could be expected even in the most fanciful mind. Although there may have been a time when every enchantment was believed in with a thrill, that time had long passed.

The second edition of *The Castle of Otranto* bore the subtitle *A Gothic Story.* Clara Reeve followed suit by calling her novel *The Old English Baron, a Gothic Story.* The term "Gothic" was then, as we have seen, practically synonymous with barbarous. It was applied generally to things that we would now call medieval. Thus in calling his story Gothic, Walpole was, in effect, calling it a rude medieval story and was doubtless seeking extenuation for it as something not to be taken too seriously or judged by the strict standards of classical art. His use of the term being taken up by others, the new type of novel became generally known as Gothic.

Now that the principles of Gothic art and architecture have come to be more thoroughly understood and appreciated, the use of the term as applied to fiction can be regarded only as inappropriate and misleading. The novels commonly called *Gothic* are neither Gothic in style nor medieval in spirit. Their supernaturalism is not a true expression of the love of the marvelous, such as characterized the popular imagination during the Middle Ages. Their medievalism is almost non-existent, particularly in Mrs. Radcliffe's novels, which are colored by eighteenth-century sentiment and reflect little sense of history.

One of the most important pieces of Gothic machinery is the castle with its paraphernalia of feudal customs. No matter what the time of the story, this castle is almost certain to be old and in need of repairs. It is usually haunted by ghosts of its former inhabitants. The lord of the castle is usually a gloomy, mysterious person, passionate and often villainous, a type of character derived in part from the Elizabethan revenge tragedy. There is, of course, a romantic young hero, the missing heir of so many of Scott's novels, and a sensitive, delicate heroine. Characteristic situations are crimes of ambition leading to usurpation, with eventual restoration of the true heir; imprisonment in dungeons; incestuous love; pacts with the devil and various manifestations of the black arts.

The purpose of Gothic fiction caused it to deteriorate quickly into crude sensationalism. An early example of such crudity and coarseness was *The Monk* (1795), by Matthew Gregory Lewis. This notorious novel, written under German influence, contains a criminal monk, a legendary ghost, a child forced into conventual vows, an evil spirit disguised as a woman, scenes of temptation and of torture. *Melmoth, the Wanderer* (1820), a long novel containing several interwoven tales, by Charles Robert Maturin, makes use of various legends and is rich in gruesome effects produced with greater artistry and more attention to the power of suggestion in instilling terror than was usual in such novels. The central situation is that of a man who has sold his soul to the devil in return for the gifts of a prolonged life and other superhuman powers. The gift of long life becomes a curse, and the victim of the pact tries vainly to evade the consequences of his evil bargain. *Frankenstein* (1818), by Mary W. Shelley, is an interesting and unusual story dealing with the horrors attendant upon the creation of a man-made monster endowed with life and human attributes.

Terrorism in a large variety of forms is to be found in Victorian fiction, in the work of Dickens, Collins, Reade, not to mention a host of less important novelists. An interesting development of Gothicism was instituted by Edward Bulwer-Lytton, who sought to give the novel of terror an intellectual or scientific justification. Examples of this type of fiction are *A Strange Story* (1862), which deals with mesmerism and a search for an elixir of life, and *Zanoni* (1842), in which the principal characters are two surviving members of a secret brotherhood who possess knowledge placing them above the ordinary passions and limitations of mankind. These men, who are vaguely allegorical in character, have lived for somewhat more than five thousand years before the opening of the story, one as a contemplative old man and the other as an active and less detached young man. *The Haunted and the Haunters, or the House and the Brain* (1859) is a short story in which the strange influences at work in a haunted house are traced to a mechanical contrivance containing a clear liquid, a compass, and other properties, which have been left in a secret room. Some very interesting later examples of stories reflecting the appeal of science to the imagination are the fantasies of Mr. H. G. Wells, of which *The Time Machine* (1895), *The Island of Dr. Moreau* (1896), and *The War of the Worlds* (1898) are noteworthy.

MRS. ANN RADCLIFFE

Mrs. Radcliffe, the novelist who is most definitely identified with the rise of the Gothic novel in England, was born in 1764, the year in which *The Castle of Otranto* was published. By the time she was thirty she had achieved fame for herself and popularity for the new type of fiction. So great was her success and so quickly was it achieved that it could hardly have been possible except under favorable conditions. The widespread change of taste that was taking place during the later half of the eighteenth century was preparing a public for her. Her success was due to her appeal to the romantic temper of the age and to the fact that she mingled pleasing effects with her fear-provoking materials. By exercising restraint she kept her novels from becoming offensive or ridiculous.

Unlike most of the novelists who followed her venture into the realm of mystery and terror, Mrs. Radcliffe did not strive too openly to be sensational. She did not call her stories Gothic, at least in their titles, but simply romances. The first one was *The Castles of Athlin and Dunbayne: a Highland story*, which appeared in 1789. Then came *A Sicilian Romance* (1790), *The Romance of the Forest* (1791), *The Mysteries of Udolpho: a Romance* (1794), and *The Italian, or the Confessional of the Black Penitent* (1797). Of these, *Udolpho* and *The Italian* are generally conceded to be the best, the latter being more effective dramatically in situations of terror and the former more pleasing in its atmosphere. Of the two, *The Mysteries of Udolpho* is the only one now easily accessible to the general reader.

The Mysteries of Udolpho

The Mysteries of Udolpho is closely related to the novel of sentiment. The heroine, Emily St. Aubert, is a young lady of extreme sensibility who loses her parents and falls into a situation of great distress. She resembles one of Richardson's heroines in her courage in the midst of danger, but a more romantic turn is given to her adventures. Much more attention is devoted to atmosphere than in the novels of Richardson and to making the action harmonize with the setting. Emily is the persecuted maiden of the typical sentimental novel of the time, but the scope of her sensibility is enlarged while the scope of her action is restricted. She is not so much an acting agent as a sensitive instrument for registering the fluctuations of fear and distress to which she is subjected.

The change of tone between *Clarissa* and *Udolpho* is quite marked. In one novel there are clear-cut moral issues and in the other vague threats and fears of dimly hinted dangers. The setting of the one is neutral; that of the other colored by an atmosphere of dark, gloomy forests, lonely mountain roads, castles falling into ruin. Whereas the relation between Clarissa and Lovelace is sharply delineated, that between Emily and Valancourt is shrouded in mystery and confused by misunderstanding. When it is time for the two lovers to be reunited, the difficulties which have been contrived to keep them apart are summarily disposed of. In short, to move from one novel to the other is to pass from orderly precision and clarity to a sense of remoteness and obscurity, from moral didacticism to fancifully drawn pictures of nature in its romantic aspects.

To accomplish such a change of emphasis Mrs. Radcliffe placed more reliance upon emotional suggestion than the earlier novelists had done. She made greater use of setting and blended it with action so as to make one support the other and create singleness of effect. The situations in which Emily becomes involved make her more fearful of her surroundings, while her surroundings increase her tension and cause her fears to be exaggerated.

Atmosphere is always being drawn upon to contribute its share to the effect. The reader soon grows accustomed to the gypsies, smugglers, *condottieri,* old chests, instruments of torture, which serve as the backdrops of the theatre. Monks sing chants at midnight; lamps burn blue, presumably when spirits are close at hand; a goblet filled with poisoned wine bursts as it is being lifted to the lips. Papers bearing secrets have to be destroyed in compliance with a dying father's wishes. Emily, as befits a heroine of romance, writes verses and plays upon the lute. At La Voisin's cottage she hears upon awakening "the matin bell of a distant convent, the faint murmur of the sea waves, the song of birds, and the far-off low of cattle."

Being a romantic heroine, she is less resourceful than Sophia Western. When circumstances get the better of her or take her too completely by surprise, she has still the resource of swooning. Mrs. Radcliffe takes no liberties with her heroine as Fielding does with his. Emily can swoon with decorum, whereas she could not conceivably fall from a horse into the arms of a gouty innkeeper and have her skirts disarranged, with a consequent shock to her modesty. It is not such vulgar difficulties that agitate her but accidents more befitting a heroine of romance. While she is yet with her parents amid the quiet surroundings of her country home, mysteries begin to envelop her. A sonnet is left in one of her favorite retreats by an unknown admirer. Her mother's bracelet, containing a miniature of herself, disappears. Her lute is taken during her absence, played within her hearing, and afterwards returned to its place. Though a more unshrinking maiden might have been expected to bear up under the realization of what was, after all, flattering to her, Emily became alarmed and apprehensive.

There could not be anything very sinister in such occurrences. They seemed, however, to come from a single source and to be directed at her by someone acting in secret. The knowledge that something was being withheld from her was disquieting. This situation illustrates an important aspect of the narrative method being followed. Incidents, like details of setting, are used for the purpose of suggestion. Not everything is told but only enough to arouse curiosity without satisfying it. The incidents thus take on an imaginative coloring and a passing importance out of proportion to their actual magnitude. Sometimes the reader is kept waiting through many pages for an explanation of what has been withheld.

There is an occasion, for example, when Montoni begins to explain to his guests something in regard to a former owner of Udolpho. At a pause in his speaking, a mysterious voice is heard to repeat his last words. When the voice is heard again a few minutes later, the company is startled and Montoni refuses to continue his recital. On another occasion, while he is urging Emily to sign away her rights to her aunt's estates, some of his words are repeated, and groans seem to rise from the chamber underneath. Later it is found that these sounds have come from a prisoner who has discovered a secret passage, built wholly within the thick castle walls, which enables him to draw near and hear the conversations of Montoni and his guests. Being in love with Emily, the prisoner has taken this method of attempting to frighten Montoni by repeating some of his words after him. The discovery of this captive also serves to explain a number of other occurrences that have frightened and bewildered the heroine.

Emily's escape from Udolpho is an exploit made possible by the cleverness and daring of Ludovico, a servant, who is in love with her maid. As they are returning to France by ship a storm forces them to land, by which accident the heroine becomes a visitor of Count de Villefort and his family at Château-le-Blanc.

This place, no less than Udolpho, seems to be the abode of ghosts. So firmly convinced are the servants that the north wing of the castle is haunted that there is almost no keeping them. Stout-hearted Ludovico offers to spend the night in the supposedly haunted place in order to disprove the rumors. The scene in which, provided with food and a sword, he sits alone at midnight, stirring the fire and reading a blood-curdling old tale of a situation not unlike his own, is one of the most thrilling in the novel. On the next morning, to the amazement of everyone, he has completely disappeared. No trace of him remains. The room is still in order and the door through which he might have departed is locked securely from the inside.

Not long afterwards the Count and a small party are traveling in the Pyrenees. On a stormy night they stop for shelter at an old watchtower, which is inhabited apparently by hunters. While the thunder peals above, Blanche, the Count's daughter, becomes accidentally separated from the other members of the party and overhears the supposed hunters, who are in reality outlaws, plotting to take the lives of the innocent travelers.

At this point Ludovico turns up providentially and helps them to escape. His disappearance from the castle is now accounted for by the fact that the outlaws, having discovered him there, have taken him away through a secret passage in order to keep up the fiction that the place was haunted. The vaults underneath the castle, connected by an underground passage to the sea, have been used by the outlaws as a place to hide their plunder. They have been responsible for the unaccountable sights and sounds by which the servants have been frightened, and they have also circulated reports that the north wing of the castle was haunted, in order to make it safe for their operations.

Every mystery story appeals to a variety of interests. It may stimulate the reader's sense of the mysterious, arouse his emotions, or simply provoke his curiosity about things not inherently mysterious. Although the three kinds of appeal may be combined in the same story, there was an attempt in early Gothic fiction to deal imaginatively with elements of mystery and terror. In Victorian melodrama the emphasis was upon the emotional element, and in the later detective story it was upon the element of simple curiosity. Of these three stages in the development of the same general impulse, the Gothic novel was at once the most naïve and the most pretentious. Crude as it now appears, it had the advantage, for its time, of possessing a fresh appeal. In Victorian melodrama, where the interest was chiefly emotional, a great variety of stock devices were employed to provoke pity for someone in distress. The detective story as now practiced makes very slight appeal to the emotions. The intricate methods of crime detection have been turned into a game, in which the equipment of the modern laboratory and the trained technique of the scientific investigator are utilized. A type of fiction that in the eighteenth century represented an attempt to liberate the imagination has gradually been transformed into something almost as rational as a crossword puzzle.

The element of the supernatural in "Wandering Willie's Tale," by Scott, is so well combined with the natural that the reader experiences no shock in passing from imagined to actual experience. Ordinarily, however, the early Gothic novelists did not succeed in fusing their supernaturalism with their materials of ordinary life. They either set it forth as tricks and fantasies meaning nothing to the imagination or pointed out that what had seemed to be inexplicable was really something quite natural. Both methods failed to give a human meaning to the supernatural, for one explained nothing and the other destroyed everything. Mrs. Radcliffe devoted much space and artistry to working up superstitious terror after which she demonstrated that the weird occurrences had been produced by natural causes. After being tricked a few times in this way, the reader is not likely to be as susceptible to strange sights and sounds as is the heroine.

The Lyrical Ballads, by Wordsworth and Coleridge, is a collection of poems some of which deal with supernatural incidents and some with ordinary life. Coleridge explains in *Biographia Literaria* that in dealing with his supernatural materials, in such a poem as *The Rime of the Ancient Mariner,* he has sought to give dramatic truth to the emotions that "would naturally accompany such situations, supposing them real." He has wished to bestow upon his supernatural characters "a human interest and a semblance of truth sufficient to procure for these shadows of imagination that willing suspension of disbelief for the moment, which constitutes poetic faith." Between them, in short, Wordsworth and Coleridge wished to awaken their readers to a sense of the strangeness underlying reality, one by dealing with familiar situations in a way to show their inexhaustible loveliness and the other by giving human interest to subjects outside of ordinary experience. Neither Walpole nor Mrs. Radcliffe succeeded in joining the world of imagination and the world of fact. The former sacrificed credibility to strangeness and the latter strangeness to credibility.

Burke, in his treatise *Of the Sublime and Beautiful* (1756), says that our sense of the sublime is founded on fear. Pain and danger when too near, he admits, are terrible, but at a distance, as when we have the idea without the actuality, they are delightful. Anything that contributes to make a thing more terrible contributes to its power over us. Consequently, according to Burke, vacuity, darkness, solitude, and silence contribute to sublimity or grandeur. The vastness of the starry heavens arouses our astonishment and awe. Great strength, like that of a storm which makes us feel our littleness by comparison, intensifies our sense of awe.

Beauty is considered by Burke to be founded on pleasure. Beautiful things are not things of great strength, or vastness, or darkness and gloom. On the contrary, they are light and delicate. The things that arouse our sense of loveliness are the softer virtues. Beauty, according to this theory, does not consist in proportion, or fitness, or perfection. Beauty in women, says Burke, "almost always carries with it an idea of weakness and imperfection. Women are very sensible of this, for which reason they learn to lisp, to totter in their walk, to counterfeit weakness, and even sickness. . . . Beauty in distress is much the most affecting beauty."

Probably few modern critics would accept Burke's definition of beauty or his assertion that the sense of the sublime is always founded on fear. His theories are not without interest, however, particularly to readers of Mrs. Radcliffe's novels, which may be considered, in fact, as attempts to evoke images of the sublime and the beautiful. The heroines represent "beauty in distress" and the general effect apparently sought for is what Burke has characterized as "a sort of delightful horror, a sort of tranquillity tinged with terror." Lavish use has been made of the darkness and obscurity and vagueness which, according to Burke, serve to make an object more terrible. This deliberate use of suggestive obscurity both in narration and in description is the quality that most clearly distinguishes Mrs. Radcliffe's work from that of earlier novelists of the century.

$\mathcal{T}_{he}$ $\mathcal{N}_{ovel\ of}$ $\mathcal{C}_{haracter}$

JANE AUSTEN

The last quarter of the eighteenth century was not without signifi-cance in the history of prose fiction. It saw a great increase in the production and popular consumption of novels. Propagandists intro-duced new themes in the clash of social and political theories. Gothicists introduced new materials and experimented with a type of intrigue different from that of the domestic novel. In various ways fictional art was being gradually extended.

It was being extended, however, without growing appreciably in power or in technical resourcefulness. The achievements of Richard-son and Fielding had come with too little heralding and had been too broad in their implications to be at once assimilated. Fielding's intention was too comprehensive to be understood in full and Sterne's delicate emotionalism did not run into any perceptible single channel. The ironic detachment of the former and the light-hearted indifference to practical considerations of the latter caused both to be frequently misunderstood. The letter form of Richardson was widely adopted, and his morality and sentiment were imitated. But the patient and remorseless adding of fact to fact in the slow evocation of a tensely dramatic situation, the minute shaping of emotion until it should express a personality, the placing in juxta-position of several angles of vision out of which combined scrutiny there should grow a larger and more complete truthfulness—these were things beyond the power of simple imitation.

For the most part, indeed, the novelists of the period did not show themselves capable of handling the new technique with power or originality. *Evelina,* by Fanny Burney, and *Castle Rackrent,* by Maria Edgeworth, reveal what could be done by talented writers. These two novels are notable exceptions of naturalness in an age of artifice. Most novelists of the period were incapable of such fidelity to actual life. They sought subjects with a special appeal and set them forth in an artificial manner. Stock characters endowed with ready-made sentiments, preposterous situations, unblushing propagandism, inflated and ornamental language, incredible or unrecognizable motives—such ingredients were what was commonly relied upon by the minor novelists of the late eighteenth century. Simplicity and naturalness were such rare qualities that their presence in a novel would probably have been interpreted by some reviewers as a deficiency in grace and distinction. In seeking the spectacular the muse of fiction failed for a time to see the beauty lying at her feet. While Wordsworth was bringing to poetry a new sense of the dignity and worth of familiar experience and of simple, unadorned language, the novel was in need of a similar service.

What was needed was a novelist who could see that it was not the business of the artist to address himself solely to the rational faculties of his readers nor, on the other hand, to turn romance into a charting of emotional storm and stress. Rather it should be the purpose of the artist to address the whole man and to address him through the medium of his story, not forgetting that truth so perceived should appeal to the experience of the reader as well as to his feelings. Such a novelist would understand that a novel was neither a demonstration in logic nor a mechanical touching off of stock emotional responses.

Jane Austen was such a novelist. At the age of fifteen or thereabouts she showed how well she understood the absurdities of the sentimental novel by her parody of fiction types in *Love and Freindship.* Throughout her life the inconsistencies, contradictions, and pretensions of romance, as they then flourished in the novel, never failed to awaken her sense of the ridiculous. Following hints from some of her friends and admirers, who failed to discern the true quality of her work, she once drew up a plan for a novel embodying such suggestions as she had received. As a compendium of the faults of the romantic novel—such faults as she was careful to avoid—it provides us with a key to her conception of the novelist's function.

In this projected story the heroine, like the heroine of romance, is endowed with every grace of mind and person except ordinary common sense. Her cheeks are plump and her eyes dark. She excels in music, is accomplished in modern languages, and can converse elegantly. The story opens with an irrelevant account of the heroine's father, a clergyman, the recital of whose adventures is to take up the greater part of a volume. Eventually the novelist arrives at her main story, and misfortunes follow thick upon misfortunes. The scene shifts frequently. The heroine is always being carried away and rescued. Finally the father dies, leaving his daughter in despair. Then the hero, who has been held back by an excess of reserve, overcomes his scruples and arrives in time to save her. All their misunderstandings are cleared away and nothing stands in the way of their happiness.

No such person as this innocent beauty ever plays the role of heroine in one of Jane Austen's novels. Catherine Morland, in *Northanger Abbey,* has formed her taste and judgment upon artificial romances, but when she gets out into the world she soon learns that such books are not safe guides to conduct. The dilemmas of actual life, she finds, do not bear much resemblance to those suffered by the heroine of romance, who, no matter what her terrors, rarely has to undergo genuine embarrassment or humiliation.

Marianne Dashwood, one of the two sisters who occupy the center of the stage in *Sense and Sensibility,* is a young lady with the exaggerated sensibility of the romantic heroine of the period. She admires picturesque scenery and has all the illusions about love characteristic of her kind. When she falls in love too unguardedly and is subsequently jilted, she nurses her grief and suffers the pangs of outraged sensibility until the discovery that her sister is stoically enduring a similar trial encourages her to control herself.

Here we have the author's commentary upon the much-prized

[margin note: THAS NOBIG SAVAGE ISN'T SO NOBLE]

sensibility of the time. Marianne's impulsiveness and inexperience are in reality dangerous and bring her ultimately not happiness but pain and humiliation. She is deceived by her enthusiasm into a too ready acceptance of appearances and has to adjust herself to stubborn and unpleasant facts. She escapes the heroic perils of romance to fall into a dilemma that could confront anyone; she has to learn the simple truth that understanding and experience as well as impulse have a legitimate part to play in the direction of our lives.

Although the other novels of Miss Austen are not directed explicitly at the caprices of romantic fiction, they are all shaped by the desire to render life simply and veraciously. Each one of them is by implication a rebuke to pretentiousness in art. In attempting to extend the range of their writing, novelists had come near to destroying the spontaneity and naturalness and, accordingly, the vitality of their work. For all their faults Jane Austen had a simple remedy—to avoid writing about what lay outside the range of her imagination and experience.

A simple enough prescription but not an easy one for a romantically inclined generation to heed! It meant a sacrifice of nearly everything most prized by the authors of popular fiction. It meant that a novelist had so to control and direct his material as to avoid the necessity of writing about people or places with which he had no familiarity, or about themes for which he could muster up no sympathy. Wild flights of fancy, feigned emotions, display of whatever kind, were banned. Mrs. Radcliffe's beloved mountains, the extraordinary dilemmas of her heroines, and other such romantic devices were things which did not fall within the range of Miss Austen's experience or sympathetic understanding and were accordingly not to be relied upon.

[margin note: MISS MARCHIv IN OF F. ELIZABETH MR. DARCY]

Thus her novels deal only with such life as the author knew personally. *Pride and Prejudice* tells the story of some love affairs in a family in which there are several daughters and a mother with a decided propensity to matchmaking. Unfortunately she is so wanting in tact and understanding that instead of being a help to her children she is a hindrance and a source of humiliation, particularly to Elizabeth, an alert and high-spirited girl, who cannot easily bear to see her family looked down upon. How Mr. Darcy, after offending her, rises to the occasion and overcomes his reluctance to enter her family provides a natural but fascinating conflict in which Elizabeth plays her role brilliantly but without any of the airs of a heroine of romance.

The situation in *Mansfield Park* is that of timid young girl suddenly thrust into the difficult position of having to live with wealthy and not altogether sympathetic relatives. Here is the author's most complete picture of a family group: a considerate but reserved father, a weak and self-absorbed mother, an officious and selfish aunt, shallow and vain daughters, a teasing elder son and a a sympathetic younger one. Naturally the heart of the shy little visitor turns to the young cousin who befriends her, and in the course of the novel we see her gradually grow from her lowly position to that of one whose merit is recognized and esteemed.

Persuasion recounts the circumstances of one who years before has been induced to give up the man she loved. She has not ceased to care for him, however, and now, with her youth gone and her beauty somewhat faded, she has to be a silent witness of his search among her friends for one to fill the place that she has once renounced but would now gladly win back. A quiet though tremulous story and one that glows unwontedly in the final triumph of renewed avowals!

Emma

Although each one of Jane Austen's novels possesses some claim to distinction, probably no more brilliant example of structural felicity can be found among them than *Emma*. Nowhere else does the author reveal more conspicuously her ability to work within a narrow compass without awkwardness or constraint. The reader is not taken on a tour of society. The theater of events is limited to the neighborhood of a village near London and the time consumed is approximately a year. There is no character whose life cannot be said to have some bearing upon the life of the central character, and it is in the interplay between this personage and the others who dwell in her small world that the theme of the novel finds its dramatic expression.

Emma Woodhouse is a young lady who lives with her father in

a spacious home in Highbury, a sizable village sixteen miles from London. The death of her mother many years before, the early marriage of her sister Isabella, and the inactivity of her father, an affectionate, fussy old gentleman, have combined to make her mistress of the house at an early age. Her relationship with her governess, who has continued to live with her since her childhood, has for a long time ceased to be that of pupil and teacher. The first twenty years of her life have been passed in a manner unusually free from restraint.

The marriage of her governess, Miss Taylor, to Mr. Weston leaves a gap in her life, which she attempts to fill by forming a friendship with Harriet Smith, a young girl of unknown parentage and no social position. With lofty disregard of logic, Emma assumes that Harriet's prospects in life are brighter because of this connection with herself and looks forward complacently to helping the girl to an advantageous marriage. She never has the satisfaction of realizing her ambition in this regard. What begins as an innocent display of vanity and busybodyness leads Emma from one mistake of judgment to another until she becomes deeply involved in situations which both frighten and humiliate her.

One of her best friends is Mr. Knightley, the brother of her sister's husband and a resident of the neighborhood. He is somewhat older than Emma and has known her since her girlhood. She looks upon him almost as if he were a big brother and has never thought of him in the light of a possible suitor. He is the only one to express disapproval of this project in regard to Harriet, for Mrs. Weston has relinquished her place in the family and Mr. Woodhouse never seriously questions his daughter's acts as long as they do not endanger his own comfort or peace of mind. As for Harriet, she is flattered by the attention of so important a person and is led into building up unjustified hopes for herself from the new association.

Emma's first error is her assumption that she can bring about a match between Harriet and Mr. Elton, the vicar of Highbury. His excessive interest in her portrait sketch of Harriet she interprets as a tribute to her subject rather than flattery of herself. She does not think of him being presumptuous enough to aspire to her own hand. Accordingly when Harriet receives an offer of marriage from a young farmer whom she likes and would gladly enough accept, Emma persuades her to reject the proposal and hints at a more brilliant match with Elton. The outcome of this blunder is a brilliantly prepared-for scene in which the vicar offends Emma by proposing to her and is himself angered by her disclosure that she considers Harriet a suitable match for him.

After this unexpected *contretemps,* doubly distressing to Emma for its possible effect upon Harriet, the visit of Frank Churchill to the Westons is a particularly welcome distraction. Churchill is the son of Mr. Weston by an earlier marriage. Since his mother's death he has been living with an uncle and aunt and has taken their name. Now upon the occasion of his father's second marriage he is expected to pay a visit of respect to his stepmother. To Emma the anticipated visit is a matter of more than ordinary interest. Having long regarded Mrs. Weston somewhat as her own property, she now unconsciously extends her sense of proprietorship to the stepson. In any case, his former visits to the neighborhood have been rare enough to make of him an object of curiosity. Accordingly her imagination sets to work upon him and, before his arrival, casts him in the role of a possible admirer of herself.

While thus working up a predisposition in favor of Churchill and fancying herself in a degree of intimacy with him not warranted by the accidental character of their relationship, she continues to hold, with hardly more justification, an unfavorable view of her friend Jane Fairfax. Just why she has never been able to like Jane she can hardly explain to herself, except that she finds her reserved. Possibly her antagonism is due to the fact that everybody has always expected them to be friends. Whatever the reason, they have never been drawn to each other, and Emma, being naturally of a frank disposition, dislikes the necessity of pretending an affability that she does not feel. Of recent years she has been spared that necessity by Jane's absence from Highbury.

Jane Fairfax is the niece of Miss Bates, who lives with her mother in rather cramped circumstances. The parents of Jane having died when she was quite young, she would have had to live with her grandmother and aunt had it not been for the kindness of one of the friends of her father. Colonel Campbell took her into his family, made her the companion of his daughter, and educated her. Miss Campbell has recently been married and Jane is now paying a visit to her relatives in Highbury, preparatory, one would suppose, to securing a position somewhere as governess in order to support herself.

As a matter of fact, she is secretly engaged to Frank Churchill. The concealment, made necessary by the disapproving attitude of Mrs. Churchill, places Jane in a false position and naturally is repugnant to her. Her scruples having been overridden by the reckless optimism of her suitor, she now finds herself in an extremely difficult position.

It is her presence in Highbury and not his father's marriage that has caused the visit of Churchill. Wishing to see his fiancée often without having his secret suspected, he falls into the device of affecting an interest in Emma to conceal his real attachment. The victim of his unbecoming conduct is herself partly to blame. She meets his affectation of candor in regard to Miss Fairfax with a frank revelation of her own biased attitude. Her unfounded and rude assumption that Jane is in love with the husband of the former Miss Campbell doubtless arouses Churchill's sense of fun and helps to spur him on to a duel of wits, in which, unknown to his opponent, he enjoys all the advantages. Emma is fittingly punished for her overconfidence by finding herself wrong in all her conjectures. Having before led Harriet into an act of folly, she now finds herself taking the role of dupe.

Her faults are not of a kind to destroy our liking for her. She is never petty or malicious and is quick to feel penitence for the injuries to others resulting from her heedlessness. Although her pride may be wounded, her greatest suffering is not for herself. Her habitual quickness to shield her father and her genuine regret at Box Hill for her cutting words to Miss Bates are proof that she is not without feeling. When the truth of Churchill's engagement becomes known, her chagrin for the injury done to herself is not as keen as her feeling of culpability in regard to Jane. She has believed Jane capable of harboring the emotions of an illicit love affair and has laughed at what she supposed to be a guilty secret.

She has played into the hands of Churchill and has had the tables turned on her. She who has been accustomed to rule has been led blindfolded through a maze without even knowing that the bandages were on her eyes.

But the sharpest blow is yet to fall and, fittingly, it is reserved for the hand of Harriet to administer it. Harriet has been taught to fancy herself in love with Elton only to learn of his engagement to Miss Hawkins. Subsequently Emma encourages her to believe in the possibility of a match with Churchill, only to be faced with the necessity of acquainting her with his engagement to Miss Fairfax. It is at this point that Emma's plans for her friend break down completely. A misunderstanding has led to Harriet's fixing her mind upon Knightley rather than Churchill, and circumstances have encouraged her to continue in her misconception.

Harriet's facility in fancying herself in love, now that it involves Knightley, is no longer agreeable to Emma. She does not like for anyone to have designs upon him, and it is a hundred times worse if there are any justifiable grounds for such hope. The reason for her agitation, she suddenly realizes, is that she herself loves him. Her protégée, it now appears, is her rival. A few weeks before the girl had had the charm of artlessness and modesty; now she speaks with unperturbed assurance of marrying no less a man than Mr. Knightley. Emma has taught her to value herself, and now she carries her presumption to these preposterous heights.

Such is the outcome for Emma of all her fine plans. Knightley has been right about Elton; he has been right in his surmises about Churchill and Jane; he has been right in thinking that Harriet ought to marry Robert Martin. It now appears to the repentant heroine that her folly may bring unhappiness to Knightley. Such an incurable simpleton as Harriet cannot make him happy. That he should be in danger of being entrapped is the outcome, Emma believes, of her own contriving. Without intending it, she has made Harriet an object of pity to him. In whatever light she looks at her behavior she has to convict herself of folly. The moral, as in the greatest comedy, is embedded in the heart of the story. Emma had laughed at the strictures of Knightley, but she does not laugh when confronted by the results of her own conduct.

The reader of *Emma* soon makes the discovery that he is dealing with something different from the clumsy makeshifts of so much eighteenth-century fiction. Here is a novelist who is content to be simply a *novelist,* to let her story stand on its own merit without seeking justification for it in an imposing theme or an ostentatious moral. Her business, she understands, is to get firm hold of her subject and set it forth with scrupulous regard to its truth. Her problem is to bring together the proper materials and fashion them into an expressive whole.

This direct and unassuming attitude toward her task results in a conception of the novel more pleasing to modern taste than the larger and more confused aims of her predecessors. She is not morally pretentious like Richardson, facetious like Sterne, or artificial like Mrs. Radcliffe. She does not go about her business in the weighty and mock-solemn manner of Fielding. She is neither prim on the one side nor jocular on the other. Her nature is a happy blend of sympathy, understanding, and good humor. Her art, which reflects a similar balance of qualities, manages to extract much of what is admirable in eighteenth-century fiction while avoiding its excesses and inequalities. *Emma* surpasses *Tom Jones* in ease and naturalness. It challenges comparison with *Clarissa* for skillful elaboration of a theme dominated by a single character. Emma's role is not like that of the traveling hero of picaresque fiction; it is as essential as is the role of Clarissa. At the same time the minor characters in *Emma* are greatly superior to Richardson's.

Clarissa does not escape a sense of artificiality and strain in the central situation. *Tom Jones,* though more natural, leaves an impression of a somewhat arbitrary sequence of adventures. It leaves, in fact, a twofold impression of freedom and necessity, or, more explicitly, of looseness and arbitrariness. There is on the one hand a great fund of behavior that seems to spring up from nothing and to lead to nothing, being only pictorial and illustrative in intent. There is another order of behavior that always leads to important consequences. In short, the historian of manners is sometimes uppermost while at other times the dramatist is in evidence. At still other times it is the philosophizing moralist who has to be taken into account.

One does not read *Emma* with any such sense of a multiplicity of aims. So well has the author fused her properties that the situation, the characters, and the theme all seem to be one. It would have been easy to divulge more about this or that character. But to what purpose? We know enough to understand them in relation to one another. What we know about them is what is needed to enable us to appreciate their behavior. At the same time so skillfully are they presented that we are not concerned with the limitation of our knowledge. They are for us complete individuals functioning normally, Mr. Woodhouse being, for example, a very limited person but complete in his way. It would be possible for the author to show us more of the humors of Highbury society, or to multiply incidents and entangle the heroine in a more intricate network of intrigue. To do so, however, might be to destroy the equilibrium of the story. Too much mystery would spoil the tone of comedy, and too much of the prosing of Mr. Woodhouse or of the confused loquaciousness of Miss Bates would take the edge off the drama.

It was probably fortunate that Jane Austen was without intellectual pretensions. Being neither educationist, moralist, nor revolutionary, she had no axe to grind and could devote herself to essentials. She did not waste her powers upon such derivative issues as the analysis of problems of conduct or the punishment of delinquent characters. She did not, like so many of her forbears, contrive plots in order to show off the idiosyncrasies of her characters. Although a writer of less poise might have been tempted to exploit an unusual gift for satirical portraiture, she allowed nothing, particularly in her more mature work, to interfere with the symmetry of her novels. Her balance and economy and self-restraint enabled her to achieve a fusion of materials which the novelist of manners had hitherto failed to attain.

The earlier novelist of manners had been primarily concerned with the general aspects of character. From the point of view of an individual's development an act is more significant in its inception than in its translation into external fact. From the point of view of society in general, only the completed act counts. Intent upon a representative picture of society, the novelist of manners had been in the habit of dealing with action in its performance and only incidentally or analytically with its origination. The individual being thus cut off from the true springs of his conduct was of less vital interest in himself than in his contribution to general truth.

Naturally the possibilities of such a character were limited. His depth was soon plumbed and, since there was a limit to the effectiveness of repetition, the author had to base his appeal upon the variety rather than the subtlety of his characters. His problem was to find a dramatic center for a subject that was not in its nature dramatic.

Indeed it is not surprising that novels like *Tom Jones* should have failed to be wholly dramatic. Characters whose actions are regulated by a purpose which largely ignores the individual's needs in the interest of a larger view cannot be truly dramatic. The absence of a close connection between what is done and why it is done results in actions being set forth as things in themselves. Just as the characters are typical members of their class or station so are their actions typical of human nature. The characters possess fixed attributes and their actions are marked by fixed tendencies.

Such acts seem to have been made to order. They are stamped with the marks of weakness or strength, of folly or wisdom, and are immediately recognizable for what they are. As such they fail to suggest the complexity of actual experience. In life we are not often aware of the general significance of what we see. We are not always able to see to the bottom of every man's motive or to recognize the significance of every act. We would not find it easy, even if it were desirable, to read every man's character at a glance and judge his every act. Fiction in which such simple and immediate judgment is possible does not picture reality as it is. It sacrifices the particular in the interest of the general. It shows men following definite lines of action without making sufficient allowance for the unforeseen and unforeseeable, the shadowy and only half-formulated nature of their intentions.

Jane Austen had little of the eighteenth-century taste for generalization. Furthermore, she was too disdainful of pretension to venture into unfamiliar realms of thought. She did not employ the novel as a means of attracting attention to herself. She employed the omniscient point of view circumspectly and without giving the impression of personally intruding in her story. She managed for the most part to create the effect of leaving her characters to themselves, not exhibiting them like so many puppets but arranging situations in which they could reveal themselves for better or worse. She could introduce explanatory passages without detracting from the total effect of objectivity. What she did, in effect, was to turn the novel from its pursuit of general problems to a closer union with the art of the drama. In an age of theorizing she wisely eschewed philosophy and turned her attention to her characters.

This change of emphasis at a time when fiction was so much occupied with weighty problems or with the picturesque and overwrought was not universally appreciated. There was certainly no attempt in *Emma* to follow the whims of fashion. The author went counter to the taste of the time in seeking neither to embellish her country setting nor to cast ridicule upon its society. Her theme—the perils of vanity—was not made the occasion for unalloyed distress or for unalloyed laughter. The plight of the heroine was amusing but its meaning was not measured by the laughter it might provoke. The characters did not fit into the conventional patterns of eighteenth-century satire. Some were ridiculous and at the same time likable; others were admirable though touched with absurdity. The Eltons were disagreeable without being monstrous, and Harriet was a goose for whom one could feel some compassion.

It goes without saying that Jane Austen did not attempt to trace motives to their ultimate sources. Nevertheless, the reader of *Emma* was in contact with reality at more points than the reader of *Clarissa* had been. The characters were held together by currents of feeling of which they were not wholly aware. The obstacles between the heroine's aims and their fulfillment were not the contrivances of a villain but the outgrowth of her nature and her surroundings. Life was pictured as a process of adjustment and readjustment. The characters followed ends of their own without perceiving clearly what it was that impelled them. Knightley's ill opinion of Churchill was in part the outgrowth of jealousy. Emma could take Churchill's seeming defection lightly because, without knowing it, she held Knightley in reserve. Harriet retained her feeling for Martin while fancying herself in love with Elton and subsequently with Knightley.

Jane was thrown into such a state of distress by her false position among her friends that she came near to breaking her engagement.

The earlier novelists would have found little to attract them in such acts as these. Their interest was not general but particular. Sometimes they were almost invisible threads holding the drama together and becoming more apparent with the progress of the story. Taken altogether, they brought a variety of lights to play upon the characters and revealed new and unexpected traits. Such a form of treatment brought a deeper significance to the casual interplay between individuals in their daily life than had been characteristic of eighteenth-century portraiture.

Closely allied to the balance in the work of Jane Austen is her detachment. Smollett made the novel a means of venting his spleen, and Richardson made himself the outright champion of certain of his characters. The author of *Emma* is not aloof. There is abundant evidence of her relish and sympathetic understanding of the life depicted. She enters into the lives of her characters but never to the point of identifying herself with any of them. Knightley, to whom she is well disposed, does not escape her irony, and Emma, her favorite, is shown to be more than a little ridiculous. How much more complex the author's attitude is than that of simple approbation or disapprobation is revealed in her treatment of Harriet, who for all her silliness never quite forfeits our sympathy. Miss Bates is tiresome enough, in all conscience, but her goodheartedness shines through all her wilderness of speech. The most thoroughly disagreeable character, Mrs. Elton, is allowed to continue in the enjoyment of her vulgar self-esteem without rebuke or correction. The author realized, no doubt, that a strict meting out of rewards and punishments bore little resemblance to life and had no justification in art.

This detachment of the author enables the reader to gain a more lifelike impression of the characters than would be possible otherwise. The novelist who repeatedly and directly reveals what he thinks of his characters makes it nearly impossible for the reader to arrive at an independent impression. Although art is not a demonstration, the novelist who keeps a pointer in hand is in danger of making it appear so. Miss Austen prefers to let us see for ourselves, and what we see for ourselves will always have for us an appeal that is denied to the most eloquent exposition.

We see, for example, that Emma is mistaken about Harriet; that she does not understand Churchill; and that she does not understand herself. We see in the desire of the Westons to have Frank marry Emma a manifestation of the interest in matchmaking that rules Emma. We see everywhere throughout the novel situations arising which are rich in comic and sometimes ironic import. There is the perturbation with which Mrs. Weston tells Emma of Churchill's engagement, the hesitant manner in which Knightley breaks the news of Harriet's engagement, the astonishment of Emma when she learns of Harriet's feelings about Knightley. These scenes and others like them arise naturally in the course of the story. They illustrate the fact that the effectiveness of a scene depends largely upon the way in which it has been prepared for.

One of the noteworthy scenes is the visit of John Knightley and his wife and the talk about family affairs. Afterwards comes the visit to the Westons leading to Elton's proposal. One is likely to remember the preparation for the ball and Mr. Woodhouse's doubts upon the subject. Most famous of all the scenes, probably, is the one recording the visit to Box Hill. No scene in the novel brings into play a larger number of undercurrents. What had promised to be a very pleasant outing turned, without apparent cause, into a day of wretchedness for more than one member of the party. There was cause enough under the surface for the want of harmony that characterized the occasion. What appeared as a flirtation between Churchill and Emma served to cover a crisis in the situation between Churchill and Jane. Knightley was bewildered, and Emma was in a state of irritation and dissatisfaction with herself. Each member of the party took home a different impression of the day, for each one had only an imperfect comprehension of what was going on between the others. The complicated interplay of motives, which revealed while it confused the characters, serves as an illustration of the author's admirable control of her material.

To say that *Emma* deals with the perils of vanity is to use a phrase more applicable to the romances than to the work of Miss Austen. Emma's perils are not those of Mrs. Radcliffe's Emily. In the atmosphere of Highbury the worst that can happen to the heroine is that she may lose Mr. Knightley. It is not the dangers confronting her but her character that interests us. There is nothing extraordinary in her officiousness. It is such a manifestation of egoism as any bright young woman in Emma's position might conceivably be guilty of. It is combined with estimable traits in such a way that the total effect is to provoke our sympathy. In any case, the absence of perfection is not likely to be lamented by any reader who is familiar with the faultless heroine of the period.

Emma is not a romantic story of dangers surmounted. It is a portrayal of a small group of people, which, limited as it is, provides ample scope for the depiction of life as it was lived in a corner of England more than a hundred years ago. In it we find love and affection, envy, pride, good sense, folly, imprudence. No great show is made of good or of evil. No black villainy darkens the page. Virtue does not go on parade. Emma's devotion to her father is as unconscious as it is deep-rooted. Mrs. Elton's spitefulness is mean and silly, in keeping with her shallowness. That everything should be set forth lightly and humorously does not lessen its fidelity to life or detract from its profound significance. The mirror which the author holds up to nature provides an image of truth.

CHAPTER VIII

The Historical Romance

Sir Walter Scott

The two greatest novelists in Britain between Fielding and
Dickens were Jane Austen and Sir Walter Scott. Rarely do two
eminent writers belonging to the same period have so little in common. *Waverley* appeared in the same year as *Mansfield Park.*
Two years later came the publication of *Emma* and *Old Mortality,*
and *Persuasion* coincided with *The Heart of Midlothian.* Thus fate
ruled that the fame of Jane Austen should be linked with that of
a man whose genius was, in many respects, in direct contrast with
her own.

While Jane Austen was restricting herself to a narrow circle of
characters and incidents such as she knew by experience, Scott was
enlarging the scope of the novel in a way undreamed of by his
predecessors. While she was perfecting her craft in a way hardly
to be surpassed for more than half a century, he was falling back
upon the stock devices of conventional romantic intrigue. While one
was leaving upon every turn of her narrative the mark of her deft
and delicate hand, the other was bringing to the novel a richness
and profusion of character and humor such as it had never known.
One saw her material coolly and calmly in a spirit of unruffled
irony; the other could work at his best only under the stimulus of
his enthusiasm. The contagion of sentiment that Scott managed to
communicate to his readers was his wand of enchantment.

It was the special forte of Jane Austen to show that the hackneyed materials of domestic fiction could be wrought into a more expressive pattern and made to glow afresh with animation and sentiment. She cultivated her garden intensively, making it bloom not in profusion but with a new grace and exquisiteness. It was the business of Scott not to refine but to invigorate and expand. He broke new ground and showed how the novel could be made to minister to the great and growing demand for romance and adventure. He extended the boundaries of fiction, pushing it into new areas of time and place. He infected it with his enthusiasm, his keen interest in diversity, his spirit of tolerance, and his humanity. He did much to liberate the novel from the social and moral prejudices of the preceding century. In his work, prose fiction caught a larger and bolder spirit and began to reflect something of the hearty eagerness and curiosity of Elizabethan times. It ceased to be didactic in tone and took upon itself the epic qualities of objectivity and universality. It awakened, particularly in Scotland, old and slumbering loyalties and stimulated in man the sense of belonging to an interlocking civilization held together by innumerable bonds of interest and sentiment.

Whereas the author of *Emma* restored sanity and reasonableness to the novel by going counter to the prevailing taste for romanticism, Scott humanized romanticism without sacrificing the spirit of poetry. He restored to fiction the heroic and adventurous spirit that it had lost. He broke the distinction that had grown up between romance and the novel. To the comedy and realism and humor of Fielding and his school, he joined such themes as had formerly been the province of the minstrel and the poet. Romance came naturally to him. He was not self-conscious about it like Mrs. Radcliffe, and he did not make the mistake made by the Gothic novelists of being too fanciful or grossly extravagant. He was never for long out of touch with everyday reality. His romances were ballasted with men and manners, which, no matter of what century, were recognizable as belonging to a world of actuality.

When Scott produced *Waverly* in 1814 he was no literary novice. He had already shown in his poetry that he could write exciting narrative and make effective use of Highland scenery. He had drawn romantic and chivalrous lore from much reading in the literatures of Germany, France, Spain, and Italy. He was familiar with Shakespeare and Spenser, and had read widely in balladry, memoirs, history, and accounts of travel. Young Waverley, we are told, particularly relished the pages of Froissart. The verse romances showed the influences of Gothic romances, ballads, and romances of chivalry.

Although far more indulgent to the caprices of romance than Miss Austen, Scott showed in *Waverley* that he was no out-and-out romantic. He poked fun, in the opening pages of the novel, at the characteristic properties of the Radcliffian romance, the German horror story, the sentimental novel, and the novel of fashionable life. He wished to avoid the banalities alike of the romances and of the paint and powder school. His purpose, according to his own confession, was to throw the force of his narrative upon the characters rather than upon the properties of romance.

A number of circumstances had caused him to turn, for the time, from the Middle Ages to more recent times in Scotland. The writing of *The Lady of the Lake* had served to stimulate his interest in the Highlands. Moreover, the success of Maria Edgeworth in her novels of Irish life had encouraged him to hope that he might acquaint English readers with the characteristics of his own countrymen and thereby help to bring about a greater degree of sympathy and understanding between the two peoples. There was an additional incentive to write of recent times in Scotland, rather than of the Middle Ages, in the failure of *Queenhoo Hall* to arouse much interest. *Queenhoo Hall* was a story of the fifteenth century by Joseph Strutt, an antiquarian, who had left it unfinished at his death. Scott provided it with a conclusion and got it ready for publication. He was disappointed by its lack of success, which he attributed to its too liberal display of antiquarian knowledge and also to a lack of interest on the part of the public in the Middle Ages.

Waverley, the full title of which is *Waverley, or 'Tis Sixty Years Since*, dealt with the attempt to restore the Stuart line in 1745. Scott was here dealing with events still alive in the memory of many whose parents or grandparents had been engaged in them. *Guy Mannering*, his second novel, dealt with a more recent period, and *The Antiquary* with a period more recent still. In the advertisement to *The*

Antiquary, Scott wrote: "The present Work completes a series of fictitious narratives, intended to illustrate the manners of Scotland at three different periods. *Waverley* embraced the age of our fathers, *Guy Mannering* that of our own youth, and *The Antiquary* refers to the last ten years of the eighteenth century." In fact, seven of his first nine novels dealt with Scotland in the eighteenth century. The remaining two went back to the preceding century but kept to happenings in Scotland. It was only when the author began to fear that he might exhaust the appetite of his readers for stories dealing with Scotland that he turned elsewhere for a subject and, in the interest of novelty, wrote the tale of chivalry that had been his youthful ambition. The success of *Ivanhoe,* which dealt with England in the twelfth century, made unnecessary any further anxiety about his capacity to hold his readers. Thereafter he could feel assured of interest in whatever subject he might put his hand to.

As Scott conceived it, the historical novel was similar to the novel of manners. He wished to provide such a complete picture of the times he presented that the reader would have the impression of living in the midst of the events depicted. For this purpose, verisimilitude, he rightly considered, was more essential than historical accuracy. He did not confuse his aim with that of the historian. A presentation of the recoverable facts of the past, he realized, could not in itself create an illusion for the reader of being present at the scene described. Although the historian may have a variety of aims, his chief purpose must be to elucidate those factors in the past, an understanding of which will be of some use to succeeding generations. His method of direct presentation of material leaves the reader conscious that he is reading about a world not his own. Scott wished to translate such a knowledge of the past into what would amount to a personal experience. He worked for an imaginative reconstruction which would create in the reader the sense of belonging, for the time being, to the world of great issues and great adventures which was being depicted. To do this the author created situations in themselves fictitious, of which the historical characters and incidents served only as the background. This way of dealing with history allowed the past to speak for itself.

For his depiction of manners Scott turned to such novelists as

Fielding and Smollett and to the older tradition of comedy. He sprinkled his pages lavishly with flavorful characters ranging from the absurdly outlandish to the romantically picturesque. Dandie Dinmont, Meg Merrilies, Jonathan Oldbuck, Andrew Fairservice, Nicol Jarvie, Isaac of York serve to illustrate his resourcefulness in characterization; the list could be multiplied many times. One encounters, amid the profusion, clownish rustics, faithful servitors, cheats, vagabonds, respectable tradesmen, officials, and a hundred and one others. A reader of the early nineteenth century would have had to go back to Shakespeare to find elsewhere in British literature such abundance and variety.

He would have had to go back to Shakespeare likewise to find such color and bustle and humanity. There was nothing in eighteenth-century fiction to correspond with the naturalness and vitality of the picture of the Scottish peasantry. Devoid as he was of the class spirit and the condescension of the English novelists, Scott saw his humble characters not as comic clowns or as foils to the more gently born but as men and women in their own right. He did not philosophize about the dignity of the common man; his sympathy was not a matter of theory. It was indeed the absence of the rationalizing, classifying tendency that set his realism apart most distinctly from that of his forbears in the preceding century.

Accordingly Scott's eccentrics are rarely if ever the plain caricatures to be encountered in the pages of Smollett. Dominie Sampson, of *Guy Mannering,* may be a ridiculous pedant but there is nothing ridiculous in his devotion to the Bertram family. Balzac was commended by Henry James for his attention to the *conditions* of his creatures, for his evocation of the medium in which they lived. Scott deserves to have a share in this tribute. Being the products of observation and experience, his characters bear traces of their surroundings. They are not the scarcely identified, rootless creatures who help to make up the procession in so many early novels—characters soon forgotten because they hardly belong to a world that the reader's imagination can grasp.

A man with a sense of history, Scott sees his characters in relation to a period in time. He also sees them as belonging to a particular locality and as manifesting the peculiarities of people in that locality

Of more importance, he sees them not as isolated specimens in a social vacuum but as bound to one another by ties of blood, of country, of religion, or of some other tradition helping to control their destinies. They belong to a world in which they have been nurtured and in which they have a place. If George Eliot surpassed her predecessors in relating her characters to their conscious aims and aspirations, Scott was superior to earlier novelists in dealing with the instinctive, communal aspects of life. Andrew Fairservice, of *Rob Roy, is such a scoundrelly* servant as might be encountered in one of Fielding's novels but is, in addition, a man with religious and national prejudices characteristic of his time. Dandie Dinmont, a humble Border farmer, in *Guy Mannering,* has been drawn with a power and command of feeling equal to the portrayal of Squire Western and superior to it in range. There is more suppleness of imagination and more instinctive sympathy in Scott's grasp of character than in Fielding's more intellectual approach.

Most early fiction had been episodic like the picaresque novel or it had followed an arbitrary course of intrigue as in *Tom Jones.* In the romantic fiction of Mrs. Radcliffe and her followers, the course of intrigue had grown increasingly artificial. Scott, though usually careless in working out his plots, was less artificial than most novelists of his time. He did not dispense with intrigue but he managed to give it greater credibility. His characters were beset by such difficulties as they might reasonably be expected to encounter. His villains were not the stock figures of Gothicism but were such rogues and rascals as flourished during the times depicted. The background of public events was, for the most part, blended skillfully and easily with the purely fictitious matter. The onrush of affairs, springing from natural causes in the political background, served to give a sense of direction and momentum to the narrative.

In the central love-intrigue Scott was usually at his conventional worst. He adopted the hero and heroine of the sentimental novel and generally found little in the situation to stimulate him to originality. He was usually content to treat love as a matter of chivalrous etiquette or, with his humbler characters, to touch upon the lighter and more humorous aspects of courtship. Nevertheless, his woodenness in such matters is less offensive than the overwrought emotionalism of such a writer as Lytton, in whose work there is often an unhappy mixture of so-called love interest with the sterner stuff of political intrigue and warfare.

There are, of course, various ways of putting history into fiction. Some novelists, like Tolstoy, look for the underlying factors in social evolution, and some for more obvious and immediate lessons. Others may find their chief delight in the atmosphere of knight-errantry, or they may turn to the crime-stained pages of history for tales of mystery and terror. Kingsley finds in the historical novel an opportunity for religious polemics, and Pater makes it serve his aestheticism. Dickens characteristically selects subjects that will serve his penchant for thrilling mysteries and also enable him to champion the cause of the oppressed. In *Barnaby Rudge* he attacks the evils of religious bigotry and in *A Tale of Two Cities* the tyranny of the old monarchic regime in France. Thus we see that, by his treatment of material, the historical novelist reflects himself and his age as well as the subject of his story.

In this respect Scott has often been criticized for the lack of depth and complexity in his reading of the past. He was not a man of pronounced moral earnestness, nor was he introspective or speculative or mystical. The loss in sensitiveness is counterbalanced, however, by a gain in objectivity. It is not easy to perceive how he could have succeeded so well without the impartiality, the poise, the dislike of controversy, the unfailing zest that went along with his generous and ready sympathy. Wordsworth, Coleridge, Carlyle, Byron, each possessed, in some respects, greater intensity or greater complexity of feeling. But which one of them, had he been gifted with equal powers of narration, could have produced a long series of romances with an equally sustained charm? Which one of them could have produced so much with so little an effect of monotony?

There is no satisfactory way of explaining personality. Whatever his merits, a man rarely rises above the peculiar limitations of his age. The graceful gentlemen of the Age of Reason had their faults, and the Romantics had theirs. If Scott lacked the sensibility of the more thoroughgoing Romantics, he also lacked their egoism and occasional confusion. If he lacked their ecstasy, he also lacked their morbid self-absorption.

He had his own kind of fervor and, goodness knows, he had imagination. It was not the ecstasy of one who

> on honey-dew hath fed,
> And drunk the milk of Paradise.

If his flights of fancy did not convey him to such savage and enchanted places as the land of Xanadu, it was to more habitable regions. Fielding's young men had traveled usually in stagecoaches or on foot, and had seldom been in danger of a worse adventure than that of encountering the familiar figure of a highwayman or of having their heads broken in a tavern brawl. Scott sent his young men on more perilous journeys into regions less well policed than the England of Fielding's day and capable of providing a greater variety of incident. Their characteristic mode of travel was on horseback, often unaccompanied and sometimes in disguise. The heroes of *Guy Mannering* and *The Antiquary* came into possession of their rightful names only after much adventuring. Wilfred of Ivanhoe returned from Palestine disguised as the Disinherited Knight. The missions upon which they, and the other young men of Scott, journeyed were many and various; the perils which they encountered were correspondingly abundant. The undaunted spirit which never deserted them was the spirit of the knight, tempered by Scott's own modesty. It was gallant and resolute and resourceful without excessive swagger.

Their adventures were neither the prosaic and half-ridiculous exploits of a Roderick Random nor the fantastic waking dreams of an Ancient Mariner. They combined an interest in the familiar with a feeling for the picturesque. Whereas the imagination of Scott was broad enough to include attention to the practical aspects of life, it was too daring to be ruled by narrow considerations of order and utility. It produced, in the historical novels, a feast containing something for almost every taste. The effect was enlivened by humor and wit and was further enriched and softened by the pleasing blend of mirth and sentiment in the author and the light shed by his kindness and loving sympathy.

Scott's devotion to history was genuine. He did not allow an interest in specific causes to color his pictures of past times with the passions and prejudices of his own age. He did not, like Ainsworth, look into history for the materials of melodrama. Nor did he, like Dickens, look for ancient wrongs that could be fashioned into modern pleas for reform. His romanticism never took the form of symbolism and political bias characteristic of Hugo. His mind was filled with memories and associations, and, in the case of Scotland, with affections and regrets. Consequently his novels were not reconstructions of the raw materials of history, like *The Last Days of Pompeii,* but more spontaneous growths of a closer fidelity to nature. They were products not so much of conscious artifice as of a teeming fancy, which, if sometimes impetuous and clumsy in its inventions, was rarely false to the essential reality.

His love of the past for its own sake prevented him from turning it into propaganda for any cause, either literary, political, social, or religious. He let it speak for itself and recaptured in his attitude something of the reverence, the curiosity, and the zest that had been reflected in the older historical traditions of the epic, the romance, and the ballad or folk tale.

The epic element is manifest in the regard for great events and great personages, and in the view of the past as a heritage to be esteemed and celebrated. In looking back upon the former glories of his race and in taking a heroic view of man's fortitude and loyalty to community ideals, Scott reflects an attitude of respect for tradition. His interest in the ceremony and ritual of church and court recalls the epic's fondness for important ceremonies. Like the chronicle plays of Shakespeare, the Waverley novels spring, in some measure at least, from patriotic feelings and display an interest in the pomp and stir of momentous affairs.

Closely associated with this heroic world is the more homely element of folk imagination which colored Scott's reading of the past and which came to him, partly no doubt, from his interest in ballads and legends. He took his themes sometimes from old stories and personal reminiscences reflecting the superstition, the stoicism, and the resigned fatalism of the folk mind. "Wandering Willie's Tale," in *Redgauntlet,* is an example of his superiority to the conventional

Gothicist in dealing with the element of superstitious terror in the mind of the peasant. *The Bride of Lammermoor* is a tragedy reflecting the ballad conception of blind, illogical fate.

The influence of the romance was particularly great upon the cast of Scott's mind and upon the shape which he gave to his material. The Middle Ages was his favorite period in history, and feudal society with its knightly personages and ideals was peculiarly attractive to him. In dealing with Scotland in the two previous centuries he wrote mainly as the realistic portraitist with romantic materials intermingled, but in such a novel as *Ivanhoe* he could allow his liking for the color and pageantry of the Middle Ages to have full sway. Chivalry provided him with an attitude of mind and a type of adventure. The knightly hero bore himself as valiantly as his ancestor in the medieval romance and could be trusted to come as safely through his dangers. He bore a charmed life, in fact, and when, upon occasion, he was wounded, a maiden was likely to be on hand to nurse him quickly back to health.

As was natural for a man of his temperament, Scott saw history as a series of events. He did not go as far as Dumas in reducing it to a rapid and absorbing current of narrative. His story, though important, was not everything. He did not reduce his material to a single stream of consistent narrative but introduced characters and incidents not strictly necessary or developed them to an extent out of proportion to their importance. Not every thread of narrative was successfully woven into the main fabric, the purpose of the author being not simply to provide an absorbing flow of narrative but to give a broad and varied picture of manners as well.

This balancing of the central story with an accompaniment of incidental matter was, in effect, a balancing of romance with its opposite. The major trend of the narrative was likely to be conceived in a romantic mood to which the minor divagations contributed a more homely and comic strain. In the novels of the Middle Ages there was more of a tendency for the minor personages themselves to contribute to the general atmosphere of romance. Nevertheless, even in such romantic novels as *Ivanhoe* and *The Fair Maid of Perth* there was a goodly proportion of humor and common sense in the background.

Old Mortality

Old Mortality, which is one of the more purely historical of the romances, deals with an uprising of the Scotch Covenanters following the assassination of the archbishop of St. Andrews by a small band of fanatics during the reign of Charles II. The more extreme Presbyterians were dissatisfied because the king had failed to observe the stipulations of the Solemn League and Covenant, a treaty for the preservation of the reformed church in Scotland. They felt that Charles had not been sufficiently grateful for their help in restoring him to his throne, and they looked upon Archbishop Sharpe, primate of Scotland, as a persecutor and traitor to their cause. The uprising followed the violent measures taken by the government as a result of the assassination.

The two most important historical portraits are of the leaders on each side of the struggle. One is the royalist leader, John Grahame of Claverhouse, who, Scott felt, had been dealt with unfairly by history. As he is here portrayed, there is an effort to weigh the scales more evenly. Claverhouse is depicted as a compound of cruelty and nobility. As Colonel of the Royal Life Guards and member of the Privy Council of Scotland, he is merciless in performing what he considers to be his public duty. He is a stern, daring, and brilliant military leader, a graceful gentleman among his friends, generous to those he admires, and acting from a high sense of duty to his sovereign.

Though a less pleasing image of a man, the portrait of the leader of the Covenanters exhibits a more powerful aspect of Scott's character drawing. John Balfour of Burley is the most striking figure in the novel. He is a terrible fanatic, daring, shrewd, unscrupulous. One of the chief participants in the murder of the archbishop, he is in other ways directly responsible for the uprising. Religious passion and prejudice take in him the form of self-torture and semi-madness. Hatred of one's enemies and desire for vengeance could hardly go further. He stoops to the foulest methods of obtaining his ends; yet he never loses his wild dignity. In the more satirical and less imaginative fiction of the eighteenth century, he would almost surely have been made to seem ridiculous or grotesque or purely fanciful.

Following his usual practice, Scott takes a fictitious character for his hero. Henry Morton, a moderate Presbyterian with little sympathy for the extremists, has more than one reason for wishing to keep aloof from the impending civil strife. He has no faith in violence as a method of settling disputes and does not trust the sincerity of the leaders of the insurgents. Furthermore, he is in love with Edith Bellenden, whose grandmother, Lady Margaret Bellenden, is a staunch supporter of the Stuarts.

It is one of Scott's favorite situations to confront the hero with the necessity of making a choice between irreconcilable loyalties. The conflict between love and duty, or between affection and principle, is an old theme in tragedy and romance. Morton has such a choice forced upon him. His uncle, the Laird of Milnwood, with whom he is living (his parents being dead), is too miserly to deal with him with any liberality. To make matters worse, the young man has fallen in love with a young woman of higher station than himself; he has, moreover, in Lord Evandale, a powerful and wealthy rival.

Having little hope of success in his suit and wishing to escape the torment of being near the girl he loves, Morton thinks of going abroad, if he can gain his uncle's consent, to seek his fortune as a soldier. Such is his state of mind at the beginning of the story, when, on May 5, 1679, he attends a sports festival and wins the prize for being the best marksman. On the way home from the festival he encounters John Balfour of Burley, a man who once saved his father's life. Knowing Burley to be in danger from the authorities but ignorant of the fact that he has helped to murder Archbishop Sharpe, Morton gives him shelter for the night. He is consequently arrested and brought before Claverhouse. A quick sentence of death follows, from which he is saved only by the intervention of his rival, Evandale. Then, when the insurgents win the first engagement, he escapes with a few other prisoners.

The purpose of the author in these early scenes is to contrive a situation that will drive the hero to support the cause of the insurgents in spite of his lack of complete sympathy with it. Accordingly Morton must be induced to shelter Burley and thus appear friendly to the Covenanters. He must be led to believe that Edith is fickle and accordingly be suffering from jealousy when he is questioned by Claverhouse. His audacity, which is nothing more than his naturally independent spirit heightened by jealousy and the insolence of his captors, looks to Claverhouse like calculating design. The result is that, almost before he has time to realize it, Morton finds himself being dealt with as an open enemy of the state. It is not surprising for him to accept the challenge of such tyranny and oppression when the opportunity arises. In doing so he alienates his friends on the other side. Edith, whose love is deeper than he suspects, is greatly shocked by his act. His joining the cause of her enemies seems to her to be a wanton betrayal of her affection. Accordingly there is established a situation not uncommon in romantic fiction: a misunderstanding between lovers, rival suitors, conflict between love and some other passion, inclination, or necessity.

There is a smaller amount of pure adventure in *Old Mortality* than is usual with Scott. Public events hold the center of the stage; most of the novel is directly concerned with giving an account of the military struggle and a description of the leading participants. Of intrigue there is bound to be a certain amount, though it plays here an unimpressive role. With the uprising crushed and Morton banished to Holland for his punishment, there is a break of about ten years in the narrative, which is resumed with the reappearance of the hero in Scotland early in the reign of William III.

The remainder of the story is little more than a conventional winding up of the love element. Believed by his friends to be dead, the hero, having returned secretly to his native country, learns that Edith, though still unwed and still clinging to his memory, is on the point at last of rewarding Evandale's devotion. Morton heroically resolves not to interfere and, to further their happiness, attempts to recover a deed, the loss of which has served to impoverish Lady Margaret and her granddaughter. Learning by chance that Evandale is in grave danger, he makes an effort to save him but fails through no fault of his own. As Evandale dies he joins the hands of the two lovers. All barriers have now been swept away.

Having adopted Fielding's conception of the novel as a picture of manners, Scott is confronted, as Fielding was, with the problem of making the drama and the picture of manners work in harmony. Fielding saw the problem and achieved a working, if artificial, solution of it. Scott, possessed of less patience and skill, is content to let his story hang together as it will. He sees the separate episodes more distinctly than the whole design. In the ability to arouse interest, to provoke curiosity and suspense, to produce a multitude of living figures, to evoke the atmosphere of other times and places, to stimulate imagination and sentiment, to bring into play the clash of human foibles, prejudices, attachments—such things Scott can do with astonishing ease and fertility of invention. His best art is the art that conceals itself. His best effects come unheralded and seemingly unsought. The talk, of which there is such an abundance in the novels of Scottish life, is a wonderfully faithful record of living speech. It is rich in flashes of fancy, sudden bursts of feeling, oddities of humor. So effortlessly does it flow and so unassuming is it at its best that the unwary reader may fail to realize that he is in the presence of great art, as Partridge, beguiled by the naturalness of Garrick in the role of Hamlet, was unaware that he was in the presence of great acting.

It is when Scott comes to fit the different parts of his invention together that he shows a less masterly hand. A certain amount of intrigue is necessary in his view of the novel; accordingly he provides it, taking it not too seriously but not without relish. His tendency to rely upon his ability to improvise frequently causes him to strain credulity or to resort to a conventional solution of his problem. He employs freely such stock situations as Fielding was inclined to treat half in the spirit of burlesque. Forced misunderstandings, mistaken identities, disguises, long-lost heirs, sudden deaths, miraculous escapes, mysterious disappearances, stolen wills —such contrivances are familiar to the reader of Scott. He probably did not write a single full-length novel in which he did not resort to one or more stock tricks.

There is, for example, a stolen deed in *Old Mortality.* To further his schemes, Burley secures the deed to Lady Bellenden's property and establishes her kinsman Basil Olifant in her place. A letter sent by Morton from Holland and never delivered causes him to assume that Edith has married Evandale. Only in a romance would a lover be so easily convinced, and in a romance important letters habitually are lost. The failure of a message to be delivered has fatal consequences in one instance, for Lord Evandale would have been warned in time if Goose Gibbie had had the wit to deliver his message, or Lady Margaret the good sense to receive it. There is irony in this incident, however, for it is the memory of her previous humiliation at the hands of the messenger that prevents Lady Margaret from admitting him. Thus the end of the novel is linked with the opening scene, and a man's fate rests upon the blunder of a drunken half-wit and the pride of a silly woman.

Another situation that strains credulity is the scene in which Morton overhears the interview between Edith and Evandale and, being seen by the overwrought girl, is mistaken for a ghost. It is a crucial scene in which the chief participants are represented as being keyed up almost to the breaking point. Probably most readers do not find it effective in the way intended. So flimsy and farfetched is it, so palpably contrived, that the effect can hardly be other than humorous.

One of the romantic conventions made use of by Scott is the uniform chivalry of the rival suitors in their dealings with each other. So perfectly does it function at all times that the veriest schoolboy must feel it to be somewhat mechanical. It begins in the opening scene and continues to the end. At the shooting match Morton offers to exchange horses with Evandale. They have to fire at the target while riding at a gallop, and Morton is the better mounted of the two. When Morton is about to be shot, at Claverhouse's order, Evandale intercedes. This debt Morton wipes clean by saving his rival in battle. When the uprising fails, Evandale again intercedes in behalf of Morton, who tries finally to repay him by renunciation of his claim to Edith. It all follows a very neat formula. Years of waiting do not quench the ardent devotion of the two suitors, and the girl remains true through thick and thin to her first love.

It is pretty but it leaves the reader cold. There is nothing revealing in Morton's attachment. His feeling for Edith is not conveyed with anything like the truth and insight displayed by Jane Austen in the handling of Emma and Knightley. Upon the rare occasions when

Scott's two young people meet, they speak in the conventional language of a decorous age. " 'I have taken a strange step, Mr. Morton—a step that perhaps may expose me to censure in your eyes— But I have long permitted you to use the language of friendship—perhaps I might say more—too long to leave you when the world seems to have left you.' "

Worse even than.such polite jargon is the parade of pasteboard emotion resulting from Scott's attempt to lift his formalism to a higher key. When she learns that Morton has joined the insurgents, Edith exclaims: " 'I will tear him from my heart, if my life-blood should ebb in the effort!' " Having resolved to give up all claims to Edith, Morton repressed his emotions "with an agony which thrilled his every nerve."

The artificiality of the central characters contributes to the awkwardness of Scott's construction. The center of interest and the central focus of the action do not coincide. The conflict between Burley and Claverhouse, or the general conflict for which they serve as the rallying points, transcends in interest and intensity the rivalry between Morton and Evandale. Consequently there is a loss of interest after the close of the insurrection.

In *Emma*, and also in *Tom Jones*, the situation of the hero and heroine is interwoven with the main situation. In *Old Mortality* the story of the two lovers is handled in such a manner that it appears trivial and mechanical in comparison with the general situation. The hero is a rather colorless young man, who is represented to be a person of commanding personality capable of becoming overnight a wise and resourceful military leader. The author briefly explains that "Henry Morton was one of those gifted characters, which possess a force of talent unsuspected by the owner himself"—unsuspected, it may be added, by the reader as well.

Such unexpected transformations do not daunt the romancer. He may even prefer them to the less spectacular course of nature. It is not an easy thing in nature to produce a rabbit. The conditions that make rabbits possible must be complied with. The commonest object in nature must follow the laws of its being. A sleight-of-hand performer, however, can pull a rabbit out of his hat, and a romancer can pull whatever he needs out of the hat of coincidence. He does not trouble himself about the hundred and one considerations that a strict adherence to the logic of causality would entail. Morton has hardly landed in Holland before an old friend of his father turns up to warn him of the dangers he must avoid. When he returns to Scotland it is to fall plump into circumstances connecting him with the past.

In the dominion of romance the laws of probability are not strictly enforced. It is a place where the reader can escape the tyranny of prosaic routine. He can enjoy the sensation of adventure without being the prey of anxiety. His apprehension is relieved by a sense of security. The hero lives dangerously but untroubled by fear. However much the odds may seem to be against him, his courage never deserts him, and time will nearly always find him triumphant.

It is not in such matters as these, however, that the greatness of Scott consists. He is one of those massive figures the excellence of whose work cannot be expressed in a formula. The weakness of his heroes and the conventionality of much of his treatment should not blind us to those things in his novels which are neither weak nor conventional. Compare his painting of manners, in its warmth and color and variety, its prodigious multiplicity of detail, with that of any eighteenth-century novelist. Consider his range, the naturalness and strength of his humor, his sanity in an age of sensibility, his remarkable sense of the dramatic contrasts in scenes drawn from the past. In what other novelist before him does one find such a flow of simple eloquence and unstudied speech, or such feeling for people of humble rank, like Bessie Maclure, in *Old Mortality?*

Compare the fertility of invention and the far-flung pageantry of *Ivanhoe* with the stiff artificiality of the Gothic romances. What eighteenth-century writer of fiction, one may ask, could have matched "The Two Drovers" or "Wandering Willie's Tale"? It is in such writing that the genius of Scott finds its truest expression, and in such novels as *The Heart of Midlothian,* with its portrait of Jeanie Deans, and *Guy Mannering,* with its portrait of Dandie Dinmont. A novel unusually rich in characters and in scenes of country life is *The Antiquary,* in which there are Jonathan Oldbuck, the Antiquary, Saunders Mucklebackit, the fisherman, and his mother, Elspeth of the Craigburnfoot. In this novel, too, is Edie Ochiltree, a mendicant, who has been called the most Shakespearean figure outside Shakespeare.

Being a novel about a grim subject, *Old Mortality* lacks the geniality of *The Antiquary*. It is not without its human side, however; relief from the stress of religious fanaticism is found in such characters as Cuddie Headrigg, Jenny Dennison, and Niel Blane, the innkeeper. Jenny serves as a foil to Edith Bellenden, and, in general, the prosaic world in the background is never long out of view. The cool detachment of Claverhouse stands out against the fervent enthusiasm of the Covenanters.

It is in the picture of these Scottish Puritans that *Old Mortality* is most memorable. One may quickly forget the trials of the heroine, but he will be likely to remember some of the battle scenes, Mucklewrath preaching, Burley alone with his torments, or Macbriar submitting to torture. There is a quality of imagination in these scenes not to be found in eighteenth-century portraits. Even Cuddie, Morton's devoted attendant, a shrewd fellow under his appearance of clownishness, is not without his moments of heroism. He never fails his master, and his faithfulness is all the more to be admired for the nonchalant spirit that seems to prompt it.

Prose fiction in the eighteenth century had always been looked upon with a certain amount of condescension. Scott's great popularity and prestige did much to establish the novel as a literary form of the first rank. In no novelist before Scott had there been such breadth of observation combined with such precision in the handling of details. In the work of no novelist before him had there been so much imagination and sympathy and the sense of a world inhabited by such a great diversity of men and women. Scott, according to Louis Maigron, in *Le Roman historique,* was the father of the realistic novel, for it was the historical romances which provided Balzac with the model for his novel of manners. "The novel of Balzac," says Maigron, "is only the novel of Walter Scott emptied of its archaic substance and filled with modern material."

CHAPTER IX

The Comedy of Character

CHARLES DICKENS

In the hands of Scott the novel won for itself the accolade of critical approval and at the same time rose to a new level of popular favor. One effect of this growth in popularity was an increasing tendency for the novelist to be influenced by his desire to please the public. As the moving pictures of today must succeed at the box office, so did the novel begin to feel the pressure of the publisher's desire for profits. Scott, who found novel writing a profitable occupation, was eager to please his readers and sensitive to a falling-off of receipts. In the words of one of his detractors, he turned the writing of novels into a trade.

Other men have used their talents to make money, and Scott, at any rate, did not stoop willfully to cheapen his profession. His novels were too high in price for him to reach the wide circle of readers that a less costly form of publication was soon to make possible. Moreover, he was too well schooled in the culture of the previous century to indulge in the crude and counterfeit forms of appeal of such popular romancers as Ainsworth and Lytton. Naturally well balanced, he viewed his popularity with equanimity and did not take his position too seriously.

With Charles Dickens the case was different. He had missed the benefit of a comfortable upbringing and had suffered in childhood from various humiliating experiences. Under the circumstances of his early life, it is not surprising that his success, coming so suddenly and in such quantity, should go somewhat to his head. How could a man so young and of so excitable a temperament be expected to withstand the flattery of such success?

Dickens would probably have found it difficult to imitate Scott in concealing his authorship. He had too much relish for his position. Probably he needed the stimulus of popular acclaim. He liked to read aloud from his work to a circle of friends. There was not a little of the actor in him and, like the actor, he was highly conscious of his audience. Finally, indeed, he took to the platform and read scenes from his novels before large audiences, impersonating the characters as he read. In this way he brought to himself the evidence of his hold upon the public. He entered without reserve into the feelings of his auditors, his readiness to laugh or cry with them being an important factor in his success as a novelist.

Like Defoe and Richardson, Dickens came to the novel from a background which was not particularly literary. Even after becoming a prominent novelist he is said not to have bought many books; his library consisted chiefly of volumes presented to him by admiring authors and publishers. In *David Copperfield* he pays tribute to a small number of books read in childhood, which must have influenced him greatly. Among them are *The Vicar of Wakefield, Robinson Crusoe, Don Quixote, The Arabian Nights,* and the principal novels of Smollett. As a young man he read sensational fiction, and he went to the theater considerably at a time when there was much melodrama and farce on the stage. He had a keen interest in private theatricals, once acting in *Every Man in His Humor.* Anyone familiar with the three writers cannot fail to see resemblances between the work of Dickens and that of Smollett and Jonson. It is possible to find additional influences in the humor and sentiment of Irving, in the farcical sketches of Theodore Hook, and in Pierce Egan's pictures of cockney life. Generally speaking, the literature that influenced *Pickwick Papers* was a literature of high spirits and breezy jocularity, filled with odd characters and ludicrous adventures.

More important to Dickens probably than such literary influences were the materials drawn from his experience and his faculty for sensing the popular taste. He brought new scenes and characters into the novel and discovered romance in obscure corners of London. He did not follow any particular model but appropriated and combined materials and methods of other novelists to suit his fancy. He joined sensationalism with domestic comedy, humor with horror, broad comedy with the sentimental idyll. He drew what he wanted from each of the dominant types of fiction and gave his own stamp to it. His conception of the novel was nurtured upon the traditions of the novel of manners, the novel of sentiment, and the horror story.

Let us consider first the element of horror. The novels abound in mysterious occurrences and nefarious plots against the innocent. *Bleak House* reveals that the author was no unworthy disciple of Mrs. Radcliffe and could greatly excel her in ingenuity and theatrical effectiveness. He could create an atmosphere of foreboding and terror, and provide a remarkable variety of turns and surprises. His villains are full of evil designs and, when eventually trapped, are ready to burst with hatred and vengefulness. Although ghosts and haunted houses have given way, for the most part, to more recherché sources of terror, there are plenty of graveyards and a great variety of deaths. In one novel a house tumbles down and buries a scoundrelly blackmailer; in another a man dies of spontaneous combustion; a blow on the head with a convict's leg iron disposes of Mrs. Gargery; Sydney Carton is number twenty-three at one day's performance of the guillotine.

Sentiment had been an important ingredient of the novel since the days of Richardson. In the novel of purpose the sufferings of the poor and destitute were depicted as a means of arousing readers to a sense of evil and injustice in the social order. For the Gothicist the persecuted heroine was a ready-made object of sympathy. Similar combinations occur in the work of Dickens. He shows, for example, the suffering which may result from the failure of an institution to minister properly to its charges. The fault may lie in the institution itself, as in the machinery of the civil service or of the courts, or it may lie in the viciousness and greed of the administrators. An oft-recurring situation is that of a child subjected to cruelty or suffering from the indifference and neglect of society. Innocent people are often persecuted for no clear reason except the malicious pleasure of those who torment them. Quilp's treatment of his wife, in *The Old Curiosity Shop,* is an example.

Probably no other English writer has surpassed Dickens in the capacity to rouse the emotions. The change in emotional temper between his age and ours has resulted in a weakening of this basis of his popularity. Few writers have rung more changes upon the theme of death. He treated it melodramatically, humorously, sentimentally, religiously, poetically. He made it the occasion of mystery. Sometimes he carefully set the stage for it and let the victim expire, as it were, to the strains of the violin.

Although the direct assault upon the emotions added greatly to his popularity, it was a dangerous gift, liable to overreach itself. Great art, in the long run, must not take the short cut. Obvious means lead to obvious effects. A more delicate and more lasting impression, which approximates more nearly the effect of life upon us, requires a less direct method of expression. One reason why the humor of Dickens is more uniformly engaging than his sentiment is that it springs more directly and spontaneously from his delight in life. Those emotions that are most closely associated with his humor partake of this relish and share in its spontaneity. Such emotions find their truest expression not in words but in attitudes, which are evident without being obtrusive. Thus in their simple goodheartedness and unstudied kindly feelings for each other the characters are possessed of a grace and charm which desert them in moments of crisis. Similarly the characters conceived in the spirit of comedy are likely to touch us more than those whose roles are highly charged with emotion. If there are any unheard melodies in *David Copperfield* played

Not to the sensual ear, but, more endeared,

they come from Betsy Trotwood and Peggotty, not from such overwrought creatures as Rosa Dartle or Emily.

Of the three strains of humor, sentiment, and sensational intrigue in Dickens, it was humor that was most important. He became increasingly skilled in the handling of mystery and intrigue, as witness

Great Expectations and *Edwin Drood*, but this ability was not the most worth while of his gifts. Others could do comparable things and, in any case, such writing was of an artificial kind. His sentiment was not so easily imitated; among his contemporaries it was held in as high esteem as his humor. But it was in the humorous portrayal of character that he was most original and universal. His exuberant and whimsical fancy enabled him to catch the idiosyncrasies and grotesque features of mankind in a manner unparalleled among his fellow novelists. Although a taste for the ridiculous, for "monkey tricks," for ludicrous and eccentric turns of character, is by no means limited to the English, as witness the world-wide popularity of Charlie Chaplin, it is none the less true that the English temper is particularly receptive to such an appeal.

It was the comedy of character that Dickens displayed, not manners but mannerisms. He did not depict a society. His characters show little evidence of being controlled by a sense of their surroundings. They are not held in check by a fear of ridicule. The behavior of the humorously conceived characters seems to originate from a fixed point which nothing short of a catastrophe can appreciably affect. This impression of fixity can be attributed to the tendency of the author to exhibit surface peculiarities rather than underlying motives, and to the absence of a definite or wholly credible background. There is a tremendous amount of animation in a Dickens novel and a curious sense of unreality in the background. The characters do not have the appearance, like Scott's, of belonging to a past or of partaking in a common inheritance of culture. They have no stake, to speak of, in the issues of their time. There is not much of an impression of relationship between them and life in general, unless, as in *A Tale of Two Cities*, the theme of the novel requires it. Probably the most important unifying force that Dickens made use of was the affections of the family circle. Such a stage was adequate for Jane Austen but not for him. He habitually introduced issues into his novels which lay outside the range of family jurisdiction.

He introduced serious and far-reaching issues without sufficient explanation or sufficiently illuminating treatment to make their significance clear. He so oversimplified social and psychological problems as to raise doubts as to the seriousness of his aim or the depth of his comprehension. His motives, in fact, along with his methods, were mixed. The result was an unusual degree of heterogeneity in his work.

Although his creation of character owed something to the comedy of humors, in which each character was represented by a single dominant trait, he did not employ the method with the singleness of aim of Jonson. The comedy of humors was predominantly satirical in purpose. Jonson followed a rational plan and avoided what he regarded as romantic improprieties of structure, wishing, in fact, to draw comedy away from its allegiance to romanticism. He was a master of dramatic exposition capable of developing a situation in the tone of his comic conception of character. There was no such expressive unity in the work of Dickens. He conceived only a portion of his characters in the spirit of comedy and only a portion of his comic characters in the spirit of satire. Thus we find side by side in the same novel conventionally normal people, eccentric drolls who are likeable, and other unusual characters who are disagreeable. Each type required different treatment. Humor and satire had to yield here and there to a more nearly realistic treatment. Actually Dickens was conventional and sentimental rather than realistic in dealing with his normal characters. In the development of situations he relied both upon the casualness of picaresque fiction and the intricacy of the tale of intrigue.

Smollett, loose as his constructions were, produced more of an effect of unity because he kept closer to a single method. His leading character dominated the scene to a greater extent than was usual in a novel of Dickens, and accordingly there was less in the way of distraction from the central situation. The purpose of Smollett, being predominantly satirical, contributed to uniformity of impression.

Dickens, of course, went far beyond Smollett in what he attempted. He was too ardent a student of the theater to ignore the value of a multiplicity of details pointing to a common objective. Sometimes he achieved a noteworthy symmetry. A *Christmas Carol* marches steadily to its conclusion, which, according to its formula, is particularly effective. The tone is well sustained and admirably keyed to the theme. *Bleak House* and *A Tale of Two Cities* show the effect of unity of atmosphere. *Hard Times* is built with some success around one idea. *Great Expectations* develops a situation with less interruption and more consistency than usual.

Despite such exceptions it is none the less true that Dickens' novels lack unity. No novel can produce a single dominant impression unless the parts unite in creating it. When the parts are more vivid or significant in themselves than in any value they convey upon one another, there is a failure of unity in the direction of looseness. What we have is not a single experience, or a single impression that can be summed up in a few words, but a succession of impressions, such, for example, as in *Pickwick Papers* or *Martin Chuzzlewit*. When, on the other hand, the parts are forced into an association that does not arise from their own dynamic relations with one another, there is a failure of unity, because true unity is a living quality that cannot arise from what is arbitrary or accidental. What is accidental cannot be universal. It may arouse surprise but it cannot gratify expectation. It is deficient in vitality, for the life of an organism depends ultimately upon the harmony between its center and its component parts. Although the inward spring of life is not itself visible, its presence can be detected by outward manifestations. Accordingly if there is not reciprocal action between the central design of a novel and its parts the result is not an organism but a mechanism. The design does not operate from within but is superimposed from without. The simplest organism contains within itself an active ingredient contributing to the vitality of its parts, but the most intricate machine contains no such ingredient. Wheels move within wheels and puppets perform in intricate figures. If it were not for the author behind the scenes providing the motive power, they would fall into a lifeless heap.

Dickens' novels are most truly alive when there is least interference with the characters by the imposition of design. In *Pickwick Papers* many of the adventures express the characters by a kind of comic contradiction. Winkle, the reputed sportsman, cannot fire a gun without endangering himself and his friends. Pickwick, the best-intentioned of men, is continually becoming the object of suspicion. Such a harmony between character and incident, a harmony that works by perversity and contradiction, gives vitality to the separate episodes but is not adequate for the novel as a whole.

The later novels are nearly all complicated in design. They mingle what is comic with what is serious and sometimes professedly tragic. The formulas of comedy and farce are combined with various other formulas drawn from the "thriller" and from didactic and sentimental fiction. Virtue triumphs over villainy; lowly characters reveal that in sensibility and affection they have no superiors; hard hearts are melted; the neglected child grows into the competent and much-prized woman. The most persistent formula is that of an optimistic sentimentalism. The scheme of things is remolded nearer to the heart's desire. Cinderella turns up in various guises. A society pictured as having stupid or corrupt officers of justice and unwieldy courts paradoxically manages to bring confusion to scoundrels and happiness and success to the deserving. The courts cannot insure legal justice but the author, working behind the scenes, cannot fail to obtain poetic justice.

That any kind of formula can be detected indicates the operation of a preconceived plan. Some kind of plan, of course, is necessary to a novelist, the important point being how it functions. Dickens was inclined to base his plan upon a situation conceived with regard to its effectiveness. Of the inception of *The Old Curiosity Shop* he writes: "I had it always in my fancy to surround the lonely figure of the child with grotesque and wild, but not impossible companions, and to gather about her innocent face and pure intentions, associates as strange and uncongenial as the grim objects that are about her bed when her history is first foreshadowed." Here we have a formula for a story which can be made sentimental, romantic, and humorous. The problem that the author raises for himself is not "What light can I throw upon experience?" but "To what advantage can I turn my situation?" Let us, in justice, assume that he wishes to make his readers feel more acutely the sufferings of children. Even so, the effect of pathos is sought through a series of heart-rending situations not necessarily true in essential respects to the characters involved.

Concerning *Great Expectations* we have the following excerpt from a letter to a friend of the author: "You will not have to complain of the want of humour as in the *Tale of Two Cities.* I have made the opening, I hope, in its general effect exceedingly droll. I have put a child and a good-natured foolish man, in relations that seem to me very funny." Here again the author is thinking of the effect. He apparently accepts the criticism of *A Tale of Two Cities,* although one would think that a novel about the French Revolution might have been allowed to be serious.

Although Scott could be clumsy and farfetched, he usually gave an air of naturalness to happenings. His errors sprang from haste and carelessness rather than from defects of taste or judgment. The faults of Dickens were more deeply ingrained. His exaggerated desire to astonish and thrill led him into artificiality. His sense of the ludicrous helped him more in the depiction of character than in the selection of themes or the manipulation of events. Possibly the simplification that marked his rendering of character led him to seek a compensating complexity in action.

A writer who bows to the whims of the public may end by expressing the conventional prejudices and aspirations of the public. Dickens was such a writer. It was his glory and his weakness. Popular acclaim was his standard of success. The will of the public was his law. He molded it and it in turn molded him. A devotee of the theater, he saw his novels as a series of stage effects. Issuing them in parts, he could watch their effect month by month and alter them to suit his readers without regard to their inner logic. Serial publication also led to false emphasis and to a multiplicity of incident, for each number had to have a climactic happening. Thus, in various ways and for various reasons, Dickens cultivated the externalities of his art while he neglected the problem of inward synthesis.

David Copperfield

David Copperfield began to appear serially in 1849 when Dickens was in the middle of his career. It has always been one of the best-liked and most famous of the novels. It contains magnificently drawn portraits, situations evocative of pity, and exciting and mysterious action. Its comparative simplicity may be attributed to the fact that it was written to a large extent out of boyhood memories.

The fact, too, that it was told in the first person must have had a restraining effect upon the author, who had to remember, particularly in the early scenes, that his customary jocularity was not in keeping with the youthfulness and simplicity of his narrator.

The most autobiographical of Dickens' novels, it occupies the position in his works taken by *Pendennis* in Thackeray's. As in *Pendennis*, the interest lies not so much in the hero as in what passes under his eyes. Pen is more of a young man of the world than David, and his escapades smack more of reality. Following his tendency to deal with the outward show of things, Dickens makes no thorough study of individual problems even when the individual is himself. *Great Expectations*, which resembles *David Copperfield* in being told in the first person, attempts to depict the working of pride in a well-meaning young man who is suddenly taken from humble circumstances and placed upon the road to becoming a gentleman. The resulting conflict between pride in his new circumstances and loyalty to his humble companions is not very interestingly drawn. Pip's disillusionment and eventual conquest of himself rather follow the storybook formula.

It is when he is least concerned with problems that Dickens is most to be relied upon. There is, to be sure, a kind of nature-versus-art philosophy running through his work, an offshoot of the popularization of eighteenth-century primitivism. Whether consciously or not, his gospel of kindness is based upon certain assumptions with regard to the influence of feeling in determining behavior. In line with his theory, his good characters are instinctively good-natured and generous. They evince the primary virtues and are responsive to the claims of fellowship. In the opposite class are those in whom the natural affections have suffered atrophy or extinction. They are selfish, avaricious, and hypocritical. Anything that checks the spontaneous flow of benevolence, according to this conception, is harmful. Institutions, even when not run by corrupt or self-seeking officials, represent a mechanical and impersonal form of behavior and are deficient in sympathy. Such a theory reveals a distrust of science and of scientific method; it places more reliance upon the chance operation of individual benevolence than upon rational cooperation between men. When applied to social problems, it is certain to lead to perplexity and contradiction. *Hard Times,* for example, attacks the ruthless impersonality of *laissez faire;* yet the gospel of humanitarianism of which Dickens is the apostle rests upon a policy of non-interference with the free play of generous sentiments and individual agency. In other words, Dickens both advocates and condemns non-interference of government.

The meaning of *David Copperfield* is to be found in the general philosophy of the author rather than in any specific theme. The career of the hero leads to nothing in particular, beyond his success and happiness. He is less an end than a means, through whom we get to know Micawber, the Peggottys, and the rest of the characters. Miss Trotwood once makes a little speech to David, which, though it bears no particular relationship to anything, may be taken as the keynote of the novel: "Never be mean in anything; never be false; never be cruel." The characters are like the vices and virtues of a morality. Steerforth is mean and false and cruel, and so, in their ways, are Littimer and Uriah Heep. One meets death by drowning and the others land in prison, where they can continue to practice their hypocrisy. David is never base, and with him, in this regard, can be put most of the other characters. It is better to be duped than to dupe, Dickens would say, and he enforces the moral by seeing that the chief duper is himself trapped in the end.

The gospel of kindness, to which I have referred, permeates the novel. Mr. Dick is saved from the wretchedness of life in an institution by the generous sympathy of Miss Trotwood. Though a lunatic, he brings about an understanding between Doctor Strong and his wife, his simple, warm heart succeeding where a better head might have failed. Martha is reclaimed from her life of shame not by any agency of society but by the sympathy of Mr. Peggotty. Emily is saved from the worst effects of her misstep by the unwavering love of her uncle. Mrs. Gummidge forgets her own wretchedness in her sympathy for Mr. Peggotty. Traddles has an inexhaustible fund of good will, which brings happiness to one forgets how many needy sisters-in-law. David gives up trying to change his impossible little wife, realizing the unkindness of his efforts.

Everywhere we encounter the domestic affections. There is Mrs. Micawber's touching devotion to her husband and Micawber's pleasure in meeting old friends. Mrs. Steerforth loves her son above everything. With Agnes Wickfield filial devotion is almost a religion. David and Peggotty and Miss Trotwood form a close circle of friendship. Death provides some of the most affecting scenes. Peggotty tells David of his mother's last hours; David breaks the news of her son's death to Mrs. Steerforth. Barkis dies as the tide goes out, and Betsy Trotwood follows her husband to his grave, despite his treatment of her and her long separation from him. Most elaborately staged of all such scenes is the slow fading of Dora.

The author of *David Copperfield* does not exactly live up to his title and give us a personal history of his hero. In his early affections, his school experiences, and his fear of Murdstone, David stands out vividly. But after his fortunes take a turn for the better, he gradually ceases to command our sympathy. As the pampered ward of his great-aunt he is no longer the object of our solicitude. Having relinquished the appeal of pathos, the author never afterwards succeeds in investing his hero with a comparable degree of interest. There is, of course, the love affair with Dora and the initiation of the couple into housekeeping, but the jocular tone in which the episode is related rather tends to cast ridicule upon the object of David's raptures and, unintentionally, to reveal him in a somewhat priggish light. Afterwards it is as a link between the episodes and a reporter of what comes under his notice that he chiefly concerns us.

Even in the childhood portrait Dickens reveals his tendency to work with externals. We are given an account of David's surroundings and circumstances but not such a realization of a child's point of view as in Jane Eyre or Maggie Tulliver. It is as if the author has pieced together fragments of memory that do not coalesce into a complete individual. Having no definite dramatic intention with regard to his hero, Dickens is under no necessity of building up a fully rounded character. His situation rather than his character is of primary concern. The sensitiveness of young Jude, in *Jude the Obscure,* is an important factor throughout his life. The sensitiveness of young Copperfield possesses sentimental rather than dramatic or psychological significance. It belongs to his situation rather than to his character. There is hardly anything of consequence in his character that the author keeps steadily in view, except the conventional heroic traits.

Sometimes Dickens mars the consistency of his portrait by failure to keep within the child's point of view. There are, for example, David's swagger in his love affair with little Emily, his frequent references to Peggotty's buttons, his remark about her way of pronouncing Ham's name, and his commentary upon the stray sheep seen through the church doorway. Such things are likely to remind us of the novelist behind the scenes.

The world of Dickens' fantasy is more like a topsy-turvydom than like any known region of reality or romance. It lacks the definite attributes of the realm of romance, which, despite its strangeness to us, is not strange to its inhabitants. The heroes of *Quentin Durward* and *Ivanhoe* are thoroughly familiar with the codes under which they dwell; they know how to perform in the roles assigned to them. The harmony between them and their surroundings gives plausibility to their actions. David Copperfield belongs to no such definite background. Compare, for example, the insubstantiality of his connection with Spenlow and Jorkins with the exploits of Ivanhoe. Or compare his beginnings as a writer with the early literary activity of Pendennis.

David cannot fit smoothly into his background because it is largely nonexistent. His world is lacking in definiteness of outline. It has no true center. It is not a world of business, of society, or of anything in particular. There is not much distinction between background and foreground. Matters of minor importance are treated as if they were of major importance. The result is often a succession of scenes not essentially related to each other. Take, for example, the story of Micawber's indebtedness. When David is sent with some books to a bookseller, the transaction is described as follows:

The keeper of this bookstall, who lived in a little house behind it, used to get tipsy every night, and to be violently scolded by his wife every morning. More than once, when I went there early, I had audience of him in a turn-up bedstead, with a cut in his forehead or a black eye, bearing witness to his excesses over-night (I am afraid he was quarrelsome in his drink), and he with a shaking hand, endeavouring to find the needful shillings in one or other of the pockets of his clothes, which lay upon the floor, while his wife, with a baby in her arms and her shoes down at heel, never left off rating him. Sometimes he had lost his money, and then he would ask me to call again; but his wife had always got some—had taken his, I dare say, while he was drunk—and secretly completed the bargain on the stairs, as we went down together.

This passage illustrates Dickens' tendency to become absorbed in one thing at a time. The personal habits of the bookseller can have little bearing upon Micawber's difficulties. Dickens, however, is interested in the strange ménage, and that is enough. Thackeray would handle the detail so as to make it contribute to the general effect. Scott or Fielding would be likely to make the man's behavior more truly representative of his class or status. With Dickens he remains isolated and bizarre.

The failure to provide an adequate role for his hero and a plausible and continuous background leaves Dickens without a genuine basis for the movement of his narrative. Scott finds a motive for *Old Mortality* in historical events, and Miss Austen finds one for *Emma* in a woman's character. Dickens starts with a situation which does not appear to be controlled by any very definite intention. Not having an initial situation of sufficient germinating power to keep up momentum of itself, and not following a normal sequence of cause and effect, he is forced to be on the lookout for new and unforeseen situations as he proceeds. When all else fails he can always fall back upon the familiar contrivance of coincidence, which he employs repeatedly. It is a device more suitable to romance than to the more matter-of-fact atmosphere of *David Copperfield.*

Dickens, in fact, proceeds by a series of surprises rather than by a natural process of development from within. Miss Trotwood's strange behavior at the time of David's birth is not consistent with what we later learn of her. Murdstone makes a surprisingly easy conquest of Mrs. Copperfield. Uriah Heep is astute in the way he gains power over Mr. Wickfield but remarkably unwary in the way he loses his advantage. Micawber is the essence of incompetence in practical affairs, yet he tracks down Heep with what appears to be weeks of patient and cunning investigation. Steerforth, who has never shown any unusual weakness for women, seduces a young woman who is the close friend of his old schoolfellow, without even the excuse of passion to justify his folly. Emily, having been brought up in an atmosphere of rigid propriety in which sexual irregularity is looked upon as worse than death, elopes with a man whom she fails to trust even at the time of her departure with him, as can be seen from her letter to her uncle.

Striking situations are Dickens' most obvious means of securing climactic effect. Emily's elopement is a double blow to David because of his initial responsibility for the culprit and his great admiration for him. Effect is piled upon effect in the drowning of Steerforth. There is a storm to begin with. Then the scene of his drowning is the scene of his earlier treachery, his body being thrown on a part of the shore where David and Emily have played as children. Ham, made reckless by the loss of Emily, gives his life in a gallant but vain attempt at rescue. To round off the episode, Emily is on the point of sailing for Australia while ignorant of the fate of her two lovers, and Mrs. Steerforth has to be told of her son's death.

Everyone likes to see a villain caught in the net of his own villainy. Such a situation must appeal to the most primitive sense of justice. The criminal nearly always leaves some clue for the benefit of those whose business it is to catch him. Otherwise the chase might become unmanageable. Uriah Heep is so indiscreet as to burn an incriminating document without destroying the charred paper on which the ink is still legible. Micawber may have no fitness for the task of uncovering Heep's villainy, but from the point of view of the romancer he is just the man for it. No one could find greater satisfaction in the role, would make more of a mystery of it, or preside at the final unmasking with a more magnificent flourish. Furthermore, this service to his friends enables him to justify his existence and prepares him for the reward which needy and deserving characters in a Dickens novel usually receive before the last adieus. Mr. Dick, be it noted, justifies the good opinion of his patroness by what he does for the Strongs.

Since David is the narrator of a story that is largely about other people, he has to do a good deal of moving about. The method is often cumbersome and sometimes it makes the hero appear intrusive. He overhears the shrill interview between Rosa Dartle and Emily and is present at the meeting between Mr. Peggotty and his niece. One of the worst of such scenes is the *éclaircissement* between Doctor and Mrs. Strong, which, bad enough in itself, is made worse by the presence of spectators and the declamatory manner of the wife:

> She had her arms around the Doctor's neck, and he leant his head down over her, mingling his grey hairs with her dark brown tresses.
>
> "Oh, hold me to your heart, my husband! Never cast me out! Do not think or speak of disparity between us, for there is none, except in all my many imperfections. Every succeeding year I have known this better, as I have esteemed you more and more. Oh, take me to your heart, my husband, for my love was founded on a rock, and it endures!"

It is characteristic of Dickensian optimism that it should take a hopeful view of this marriage between an elderly man and a young woman.

Possibly I have dwelt too long upon some of the less important aspects of Dickens. We must not, in his case, rely too much upon conventional standards. Little discrimination is required to discern his frequent lapses of taste, his exploitation of the feelings, his excessive use of the paraphernalia of plot, his various irrelevancies. For a more just appraisal of his work, however, we should turn to his comedy. Many of his faults, in fact, arise from his desire to be more than a comedian.

I use the term without any sense of disparagement. It is in his command of laughter that Dickens is most worthy of praise and most in need of analysis. It is easy enough to see that his characters are laughable but it is not so easy to explain why. Why we laugh and what effect laughter has upon us is not easily explainable. Meredith's assertion that "the test of true comedy is that it shall awaken thoughtful laughter" implies that there are different kinds of laughter and places a restriction upon comedy. We must of course not confuse comedy with the laughable or think that everything tending to provoke laughter is comic. Nevertheless, it is not nec· essarily true that laughter is in itself thoughtful. The situations in *David Copperfield* that move us to laughter do not usually incline us much to reflection, and it must be admitted that Dickens is a comic writer. There is something in the nature of laughter, in fact, that breaks the chain of reflection or analysis. Laughter has a way of bringing us up short, of landing us in a void, and, at the same time, of disarming us. It does not introduce problems but disposes of them, leaving us in no state of mind for anxiety about consequences. When we have laughed at Micawber we do not consider what an annoyance he must have been to his family and his friends. It is true, of course, that great satirists, like Swift, jab something into our minds while they make us laugh. Dickens, too, often brought something home to his readers by his ridicule. Nevertheless the tendency of the reader is to laugh and pass on to the next item; similarly the tendency of the critic has been to praise the humor rather than to probe for explanations.

Henri Bergson, in his essay *Laughter,* propounds a theory of the comic which takes inelasticity of mind or body as the starting point of the laughable. A comic character, according to this theory, is one who fails to adapt himself to a situation, like the victim of a practical joke or an absent-minded person. Continued failure in adaptation leads to a permanent lack of adjustment. An eccentric person is one whose failure to comply with the social ideal has become habitual. "Any individual," says Bergson, "is comic who automatically goes his own way without troubling himself about getting into touch with the rest of his fellow beings." The fear of ridicule engendered by laughter acts as a restraining influence upon such indifference to the will of the majority. Bergson could easily have found examples for many points in his argument in the characters of Dickens. They reflect the tendency to behave like automatons. Micawber goes his own way, seemingly unaware of his absurdity in the eyes of others. For him to be so aware would spoil him; he would then be likely to become either a tiresome clown or an equally tiresome penitent. His continued blindness to his faults enables him to go on being ridiculous.

Probably Dickens had no definite theory of comedy. A novelist who would have his characters resemble human beings must have, of course, some knowledge of human behavior. Individuals, we know, resemble one another in varying degrees. What we expect of one depends upon what we know of many. We cannot predict to a certainty what any one will do in a given circumstance. The law of averages provides us with a measure of expectation, but the behavior of one individual cannot be expected to conform exactly to an average of many individuals. Even if it did, the comic writer would not be interested in such an average character. A story in which all the characters did everything that could be normally expected of them would be neither a comedy nor a tragedy. The tragic character breaks the law in one way and the comic character in another. In each case there is a deviation from the established code.

The deviation of a comic character differs from that of a tragic character in being of less serious consequence and less provocative of sympathy. The reason for the inactivity of our sympathy, which in tragedy is active, may be attributed to the nature of laughter and also to the character of our relationship with the victim. Laughter, though it may be aroused by what is ugly and despicable, is in itself agreeable. The pleasure may be associated with the act of perception in which the laughter originates or it may have, and probably often does have, a more complex significance. Laughter soothes ruffled feelings and helps us to maintain a serene temper in the midst of harassing circumstances. It relieves the tension of pent-up emotion and, in Freud's view, provides a release of psychic energy which would be disturbing and disquieting if not discharged.

Although in its simpler manifestations laughter is doubtless often consciously malicious and expressive of the desire to chastise, it is not necessarily associated with conscious or active malice. Our lack of sympathy can be attributed to the limited nature of our perception. The laughable aspect of a thing may be quite limited; nevertheless, at the time of our laughter it is this partial view that absorbs our attention. Tragedy enlarges our vision, focuses it upon a particular object, and brings us into close range with suffering; comedy sees not the personal problem in behavior but the reflection of human nature in general. Tragedy asks for our sympathy in a particular case; comedy makes light of suffering, shows it as deserved, or ignores it. The comic character is completely comic only so long as we keep him and his misfortunes outside the range of our sympathy. In the presence of an actual victim we hide our smiles or curb our laughter, admitting thus that we recognize it to be cruel. The comic writer frees us from such constraint and enables us to laugh unreservedly at the various forms of folly and evil without fear of giving offense.

Whereas romance clothes the world in beauty, and tragedy shows it as heroic, at least in intention, comedy looks at its ugliness and deformity. Romance provides us with something to admire, comedy with something to condemn. In a comic situation our expectations are broken by a sudden drop into what is ignoble or ridiculous. Bergson finds the source of this descent in the struggle between matter and form. Micawber, for example, is a man in whom form has triumphed over matter. He can walk, talk, gesticulate, and wear clothes, but he is all outward manifestation. There is no depth in him and no sensibility. His feelings are a part of his masquerade. He is a colossal fool whose folly serves to cut him off from his fellows and enables him to turn life into a continual frolic, untroubled by a thousand cares that would crush him if he were capable of grasping his true situation.

To say that he is without sensibility is not to say that such a man in actual circumstances would escape all suffering. It is rather to point out that as a comic character he is freed from the prosaic consequences of his behavior. We laugh at his absurdity rather than feel sorry for his suffering because his absurdity is evident and his suffering is not.

In tragedy, according to Hegel, the individual must bow to the world outside himself. The harmony which is produced is produced at the expense of the tragic character. In comedy, on the other hand, the laws of the outside world are held in suspension for the benefit of the individual. Thus the completely comic character can be comic to himself as well as to others because he escapes the bitterness of disappointment which would normally be the product of his failure. Falstaff, says A. C. Bradley, makes us happy and at ease because he is happy and at ease. Thus humor enables us to escape for a time the strain of living. Seeing the world as a place of iron necessity, tragedy is inclined to strain out what is irrelevant and incidental. It keeps what is absurd out of view as being distracting. Comedy, on the other hand, not ruled by such necessity in the world outside the comic character, strains out what is of serious consequence and turns everything into absurdity. It thrives upon irrelevance.

Micawber's life is a continual series of fluctuations between dignity of attitude and indignity of circumstances. He makes high-flown speeches which get out of hand before he can round them off with the proper oratorical flourish. When his water is turned off, he soothes the injury to his pride by referring to "the momentary laceration of a wounded spirit, made sensitive by a recent collision with the Minion of Power." He makes up for the dinginess and drabness of his actual situation by the opulence of his imagination. However mean and ignoble may be the shifts to which he is put, in his talk his career becomes a thing of splendid possibilities. His wife is, no less than he, absurdly out of touch with actuality. Her method of attacking the problem of her husband's future is to make appraisals of his situation and prospects in which the lucidity of her manner is equaled only by the fantasticality of her material. Micawber, the shiftless and improvident, is in his fancy a man of resourcefulness and foresight. The contrast in Mrs. Micawber is between an appearance of logic and a point of view no less enchantingly romantic than her husband's.

Comic contrasts and ludicrous situations of various kinds are to be found everywhere in the novel. A waiter at a country inn serves David a generous dinner and consumes the greater part of it himself. David falls in love with a girl who, he is indignant to learn, has been punished for turning her toes in. He worships the eldest Miss Larkins, who rewards him by marrying Mr. Chestle, a hop grower. Barkis woos Peggotty by cryptic messages delivered through David and apparently without the use of a superfluous word. Dora shows her aptitude for housekeeping by buying a barrel of oysters. Mr. Omer, an undertaker, is afraid to inquire about his friends when they are ill for fear of shocking them.

In a review of *Our Mutual Friend* in 1865, Henry James characterized Dickens as being "a great observer and a great humorist" but "nothing of a philosopher." He was a novelist who knew *men* but not *man*. For the truly great novelist, we are told, "there are no oddities, for him there is nothing outside of humanity." Essentially the same criticism was repeated almost twenty years later in an essay upon Turgenev, in 1884, in which James said: "If Dickens fail to live long, it will be because his figures are particular without being general; because they are individuals without being types;

because we do not feel their continuity with the rest of humanity."

George Moore complained of Dickens, in *Avowals,* that he held to "the vile English tradition that humour is a literate quality." A few years spent among the literary men of France, Moore suggests, would have taught him the value of seriousness. Following the formula of "laughter and tears," upon which the success of so much popular literature has been founded, Dickens pushed sentiment too far and sought, upon occasion, to raise laughter at any cost. Humor is one of the graces of life that retains its full charm only in contact with seriousness. If it is to serve the purpose of relaxation, laughter should arise out of what is in some way serious. To turn all life into a search for relaxation would be to destroy the conditions that render relaxation sweet. Laughter courted too assiduously loses its most endearing quality.

The habit of laughter when indulged in indiscriminately may lead to pointless cruelty. Are we to laugh at Rosa Dartle because of her frustration in love, at Mr. Dick because of his confusion over King Charles' head, and at Miss Mowcher because of her physical deformity? Is a woman to be an object of derision because of her failure to attain marriage? The man who laughs habitually at his fellows may well be disagreeably self-assertive or presumptuous. Despite his great friendship for Traddles, David Copperfield seems nearly always to hold his friend a little in contempt. Similarly his attitude towards Dora appears to be more than a little condescending. Something of this, quite probably, is the penalty exacted of an artist whose profession it is to be humorous.

To turn everything into humor is a way of escaping bitter truth. Those who look for comfort can find it in Dickens because he shows evil as something ridiculous, not something capable of destroying us. We are not afraid of a man like Uriah Heep, and we do not identify ourselves with such weakness as we encounter in Micawber. Fielding and Scott keep their humor in hand and make it serve serious ends. Dickens does not always do so. If we look for perfection in Dickens we shall not find it. And it is well to remember that his excesses would not be what they are without the excessive vitality from which they spring.

CHAPTER X

The Novel of Social Satire

WILLIAM MAKEPEACE THACKERAY

The homage paid to romance by Scott was counterbalanced, as we have seen, by an equally vital concern for everyday reality. It was on his romantic side, however, that he wielded the greatest influence. Among his immediate followers the desire to excite wonder and surprise outweighed all other considerations. *Rookwood*, a romantic story of a highwayman, by William Harrison Ainsworth, is overloaded with such properties of Gothicism as the ancestral curse, the burial vault, poison, an evil prophecy. *The Last Days of Pompeii* is one of a large number of novels in which Edward Bulwer-Lytton demonstrated his versatility in ranging over the favorite romantic themes of his day. He tried his hand at the novel of fashionable life, the historical romance, the philosophical novel, and at various combinations of Gothicism and occultism. The fop, the disillusioned worldling, the gentlemanly criminal, the philosophic searcher after truth—these and many other types are to be encountered in his pages, served up in inflated language and with great pretense of learning.

Scott set forth his romantic stores without subterfuge or apology and with disarming simplicity. Lytton, on the other hand, posing as an elegant man of the world, liked to embellish his writing with philosophical jargon and pseudo-scientific explanations. It was easy for such a writer to fall into the habit of writing down to his readers, of indulging in grandiloquence, and of "faking" in various ways.

Serial publication can be blamed, in part at least, for the tendency of novelists during this period to work not for a cumulative effect but for a piecemeal succession of effects. Dickens, who wrote with his readers definitely in mind, sought a variety of strong effects. He alternated between the droll, the horrific, and the tenderly senti-mental. It was not the representative sequence of events, the normal working of motive, that chiefly interested him. Picturesqueness was dearer to him than plausibility, variety more sought after than verisimilitude. He liked to have his story shuttle back and forth be-tween sinister gloom and openhearted gaiety, between monstrous cruelty and gentle compassionateness, between wild hilarity and sober sentiment.

William Makepeace Thackeray was a journalist before becoming a novelist. For at least ten years before the publication of *Vanity Fair,* in 1848, he was engaged in turning out reviews, accounts of travel, satirical skits, farcical and mock-heroic tales. There were in this early writing a persistently ironical tone and satirical intent. Thackeray was an enemy of pretense and of what he felt to be insincerity and humbuggery. He subjected the artificial and showy romanticism of Lytton to merciless ridicule. He replied to such idealization of roguery as Ainsworth's *Jack Sheppard* by writing *Catherine,* a story of criminals intended to provoke disgust. In *Novels by Eminent Hands* he parodied the styles of several novel-ists of repute, among whom were Lytton, Disraeli, and Lever. He revealed his ability to prick unworthy ideals in *The Book of Snobs,* a series of papers in which snobbishness is considered to be nearly synonymous with affectation and hypocrisy. In this book, as well as in *Vanity Fair,* people are exposed as worshiping hollow and false ideals and missing the best of life while they chase after phantoms.

The realistic temper that seems to have characterized Thackeray from his youth onward was intensified by his experiences and further strengthened by his reaction to the overblown romanticism flourish-ing during his early years. From literature with its shams he turned to life with its shams and thus early came to distrust appearances.

Underneath the heroic mask he saw the careworn face. More to his taste than the ceremonial pomp of courts was the familiar intercourse of friends. In the opening of *Henry Esmond* he complained that history in the past had been too much encumbered with ceremony. The Muse of History had turned away from the vulgar scene to kneel at the feet of kings. It would be better, he thought, to have less of the heroic and more of the familiar.

He might have added that fiction likewise should cease to be stately and declamatory and should take upon itself the easy and confidential manner of the essay or the memoir. That is what happened in his own novels. He did not hold out altogether against the prevailing taste of the time. He was expected to be a storyteller and he made himself one, despite the fact that it was difficult for him to invent the turns and twists of plot that most Victorian novelists seemed to regard as being necessary to the success of a novel. In a letter written while he was engaged upon *The Virginians* he made the following confession: "I hate story-making incidents, surprises, love-making, etc., more and more every day."

Thackeray's best service to the novel was to turn it away from its debased romanticism toward a critical interpretation of reality. It had become confused in purpose; he helped to clarify its aims. It had tried, not very successfully, to compete with poetry; he brought to it rather the contemplative spirit of the essay. It had followed the theater into melodrama; he tried to avoid theatricality and was unusually sparing of drama. In contact with the growing Evangelicalism of the time, prose fiction had lost something of its eighteenth-century nonchalance; Thackeray lightened it with irony and a worldliness of tone unspoiled by pose. It had grown turgid and sensational; he restored lightness of touch to it and taught it the value of restraint. His relationship to his age somewhat resembled that of Jane Austen to hers. He made compromises which she refrained from doing, and he never succeeded so completely in adjusting the various demands of his art. His world was broader and his attitude of mind not so well under control. The struggle between his compassionateness and the sharpness of his vision sometimes stamped his work with inquietude whereas Miss Austen's was notably serene. Nevertheless, as compared with the work of the Romantics of his time, his work was clear in its intention; he wished to turn from the picturesque and restore the critical spirit to the novel. The theme of *Vanity Fair* is in no way striking. It is the old familiar story of the vanity and perishableness of things. Nevertheless, in the wonderfully full and rich treatment given to the subject, in the multitude of lights turned upon it, it becomes a vivid and comprehensive picture of life.

Vanity Fair

Although *Vanity Fair* in book form was called *A Novel without a Hero*, in its first appearance in monthly parts it bore the subtitle *Pen and Pencil Sketches of English Society*. Each of these subtitles suggests that the author's purpose was broad. A *fair* suggests a gathering of people having little in common and coming from widely separated places. The view taken by Thackeray of his subject is that of many people exhibiting in various ways symptoms of vanity and self-deception. What we get from reading such a novel is a sense of experience and of a richly documented commentary upon the human scene. We do not become greatly concerned about the personal fortunes of any of the participants. Even Dobbin's eventual success in winning the lady of his heart does not stir us much. The author did not necessarily intend that it should. He wanted to show us that our lives are made up mainly of vain things. The prize when it is finally won has lost a great measure of its charm. Every life is composed of an infinitude of little things—pleasures and pains that become inextricably mixed. "Which of us is happy in this world? Which of us has his desire? or, having it, is satisfied?" Simple enough questions these, hardly requiring an answer; but when they are put at the close of *Vanity Fair*, they strike us with extraordinary force. There is hardly a scene or a personage or a passage of commentary in the novel that does not help to supply the answer.

In the theme of *Vanity Fair* Thackeray hit upon a subject well suited to the peculiar bent of his mind. To expose the meanness underneath the pomp and parade of the world was to attack at first hand what he had been attacking less directly in books. And for his subject, so characteristically Thackerayan, the author devised a structural scheme admirably well adapted to his material and his purpose. The eminent position of *Vanity Fair* among Thackeray's novels is due in no small measure to the felicity of treatment. *Pendennis* and *The Newcomes,* despite their memorable characters, their great and moving scenes, do not hold together so well as *Vanity Fair.* In them Thackeray had to struggle with the problem of keeping his large mass of material in proper relation to its dramatic center. Being a novel without a hero, *Vanity Fair* did not have to be centered in any one person. This absence of a hero was an advantage of considerable importance to a large-scale novel.

Although Fielding had imposed unity upon the material of *Tom Jones,* he had not succeeded in disposing of all friction between the particular and the general aspects of his work. New disparities and difficulties arose for the romantic novelist. The romantic hero could not be subjected to what was trivial and prosaic. Distinctions had to be made between the polite world and the world of ordinary humanity, between what was conceived in poetic or heroic terms and what was set forth lightly and humorously. Furthermore, the romanticist, being in search of diversity rather than typicality, was more likely than the classical Fielding to include material irrelevant to the main theme. The result was sometimes such an ambiguous mixture of farce, melodrama, comedy, and sentiment as is illustrated by the chaotic *Martin Chuzzlewit.*

It is hardly necessary to say that the absence of a hero could not of itself guarantee the success of any novel. Thackeray had to make up for the deficiency. That such an absence carried with it an absence, for the most part, of the conventionally heroic actions of the main character need not here detain us. Of more importance is the fact that the author escaped the necessity of centering his story about the career of any one person.

The fictional hero as Thackeray knew him was a convention associated with other conventions, such as the villain and the eventual marriage of hero and heroine. By discarding one of these properties the author could thus eliminate much conventional intrigue. To be sure there are love affairs and marriages in *Vanity Fair* but not of the usual sentimental type. George Osborne has to be pushed into his union with Amelia. The marriage of Becky and Rawdon is not for Becky a true love match. Our chief impression of the protracted

Dobbin-Amelia affair is of disenchantment on one side and of selfish blindness tardily awakened on the other. In addition to being different in tone from the conventional treatment of love in early Victorian fiction, these marriages are not given undue prominence in the novel but are simply incidents in a larger pattern of affairs.

In being thus subservient to the central theme they reveal what is most notably original in the structural scheme of the novel: the seemingly effortless adjustment of means to end. Here, for the first time in English fiction, a successful fusion was made of a large and intricate mass of material. No extraneous or arbitrary details were allowed to interfere with the desired general effect. Incidents, characters, and setting were all blended into a harmonious impression of manners, in which no one struggle, however brilliantly depicted, was allowed to usurp the center of the stage or to take on the color of a mere personal adventure. Anything more unlike Dickens' exaggerated emphasis upon separate scenes would be hard to find.

When we look closely into the structure of *Vanity Fair* we find that there are two principal lines of action. One traces the fortunes of Amelia Sedley and involves, in addition to her own family, the Osbornes and her friend Dobbin. The other follows the career of Rebecca Sharp and involves in particular the various branches of the Crawley family. It also brings us into contact with the polite world surrounding Lord Steyne. The Osbornes and the Sedleys show us the world of business vaunting its pride in the full flush of success and suffering the ignominy of defeat. Dobbin and his friends the O'Dowds introduce us to military circles and bring us glimpses of life in India. With the Crawleys we come into contact with country society, and the establishment of Rawdon and Becky in Curzon Street brings us into the whirl of London society. We see something also of Brussels, of the Rhine country, and in the account of Becky during her eclipse we are given a discreet glimpse of the shady side of life on the Continent.

Amelia and Becky, whose careers are intended to balance each other, are complete opposites in character. The former is affectionate, devoted, unworldly, incapable of duplicity, and helpless before the buffetings of fortune. The latter is cold, treacherous, enterprising, and resourceful—caring only for worldly success. The one is a simplehearted creature, a clinging and "tender little parasite." The other is intelligent, tactful, full of address, wonderfully competent in the game of life as she sees it. At the opening of the novel they are young girls just out of school and on the threshold of life. At its close, one is a happy wife and mother, the other a discredited widow, clinging to a modicum of respectability, her son alienated from her. Our first scene is of a family coach being driven up to Miss Pinkerton's academy to take Amelia home, with Becky going along as a visitor. The last time we see them, Amelia is scurrying away on the arm of her son from an accidental encounter with Becky, who is presiding over a stall at a charity bazaar. Meanwhile their paths have crisscrossed a number of times, though not as frequently as the author's method of switching back and forth in his account of them makes it appear. Amelia's fortunes fall as Becky's rise and at about the time Becky falls into disgrace Amelia's situation begins to improve.

Although the portrait of Becky is so superlatively alive that timid little Amelia pales beside her, Thackeray probably intended the two young ladies to balance each other more equally in their power to attract us. According to my somewhat rough calculation, Amelia appears, or is in some way involved, in twenty-three chapters in which Becky does not appear. Becky has a place in twenty-one chapters in which Amelia is not present. There are in addition nineteen chapters in which both appear. To put it in another way, forty-two chapters are devoted in a greater or less degree to recounting the fortunes of Amelia and forty are similarly devoted to Becky. Only four of the total sixty-seven chapters make no reference to either. Becky dominates many of the scenes in which she appears, whereas it is not in the nature of Amelia ever to be spectacular. The type of woman represented by Amelia is less admired in these days of sex equality than it was during the period depicted by Thackeray. Even then, be it noted, it was chiefly the men who admired her. In any case, whatever our opinion of Amelia may be, we must not underestimate her importance in the constitution of *Vanity Fair.* She represents what frequently becomes a preponderant tendency in the eternal feminine as surely as Becky represents a contrary tendency. Amelia is the maternal, possessive woman whose entire life is absorbed by fidelity to the objects of her affection.

As Thackeray conceived his subject, however, both Amelia and Becky, despite their great importance, are essentially functional characters. We are never allowed to feel that their success or failure in a particular situation is a matter of primary importance. We never identify ourselves with either of them but look on at their behavior with cool detachment. Their actions are presented not as isolated moves but in perspective with a mass of related detail. Thus the love affair of George and Amelia is enveloped in reminiscences of school life, in Becky's attempt to entrap Jos, in business failure and bankruptcy proceedings, in parental opposition, and in regimental gossip. Even the reunion of the lovers, after George's wavering, takes place behind closed doors, as it were, with Thackeray reporting that Amelia wept a good deal and thought George the best of men. George felt that he was being generous in marrying a penniless girl. Presented in such a way, the affair interests us in what it suggests but not in any striking features belonging to the situation itself. We are struck by the vanity of the man in marrying to satisfy his good opinion of himself, and of the woman in placing so much value upon a man so little deserving of it.

The practice followed by Thackeray of shifting frequently from one set of characters to another was helpful in preventing any one line of action from acquiring undue prominence. Six chapters at the beginning serve to introduce the two girls and the family circle of Amelia. Then in a series of five chapters Becky is established as a governess and we are introduced to various members of the Crawley family. We then return to Amelia for a couple of chapters, after which we see Becky lose her chance to marry Sir Pitt Crawley, having already secretly married his son. There follows an account of Mr. Sedley's failure, which comes so near to blighting Amelia's hopes of marriage. Next in order is a picture of the rich Miss Crawley in the clutches of a relative eager to secure for her own family as large a share as possible of the old lady's money.

There are altogether as many as twenty such groupings of chapters or single chapters functioning in a similar way. One memorable section of four chapters takes the reader to Brussels just before the Battle of Waterloo, showing the festivity there before the battle and the hush that comes with the fear of defeat. The author's masterly touch in handling general summarizing narrative is well revealed in two chapters dealing with Rawdon and Becky, entitled "How to Live Well on Nothing a Year." The five chapters beginning with Chapter Fifty-one show Becky at the apex of her success. At a party of fashionables one evening she dazzles the guests by her brilliant acting in some charades and is showered with compliments from the most exalted personages. The stage is about to be set for the major climax of the book. But, true to his method, Thackeray does not take advantage of the dramatic impetus arising from this evening of Becky's triumph. On the way home from the party Rawdon is arrested for debt at the instigation of Lord Steyne. Before following him into the sponging house, Thackeray inserts a chapter which goes behind the situation of the moment and explains how Rawdon and Becky have become gradually more estranged, and how Lord Steyne has arranged matters for the greater convenience of carrying on an intrigue by disposing of little Rawdon and Briggs.

The moment finally arrives when Rawdon goes home after his forced detention and finds Becky making merry with Lord Steyne and not at all distressed by her husband's arrest. Here is a moment that calls for drama. The nobleman, accustomed to such situations, has been under the impression that the husband knew of his wife's behavior, accepted it, and shared in the receipts from it. For once in his life he finds himself mistaken. The encounter between the two men has been said to be theatrical, but it is not easy to see how it could have been otherwise. An injured husband must of necessity act with some decision if he is not to appear ridiculous. And for such an audience as Thackeray had it was particularly difficult to present such a scene without forcing the note. It would have been out of the question to be casual or nonchalant with a Victorian audience about a matter of adultery. Thus, having to relinquish his customary casualness of tone, the author was at a disadvantage. To his normal diffidence in the presence of drama there was added hesitancy to deal frankly with a situation regarded by the age as taboo. So we find the affair wrapped up in innuendo and the extent of Becky's guilt left unexplained.

Nevertheless, if we omit a few details in the encounter between the men, there is not much in the scene to complain of. The behavior of Rawdon after the encounter and the manner in which the duel is threatened and averted are beyond praise. Here we have drama without strain or artifice and in perfect keeping with the somewhat somber tone of the narrative. The story flows smoothly on, and the interview between Rawdon and Captain Macmurdo shows how ingenious Thackeray was in restoring it to its normal balance, bringing it back from its fit of heroism to the tone of mundane things.

The last twelve chapters of the novel constitute the longest comparatively unbroken section of the story. It is broken, in fact, by a chapter summarizing the doings of Becky after her husband's break with her. Aside from this interruption, which is made necessary by Becky's reentrance into the story, this portion of the novel is devoted to bringing the story of Dobbin's long courtship of Amelia to a close. As is to be expected, the account of this affair proceeds on a much lower key than had been required for the Lord Steyne episode. What excitement it has is provided by the reappearance of Becky, who shocks Dobbin and Amelia into action by becoming the cause of a quarrel between them. Dobbin's plain speaking has a salutary effect upon Amelia, and Becky hastens the marriage along by producing the letter that disposes once and for all of the ghost of George. For Jos the reappearance of Becky is less fortunate. Years before, through no great merit of his own, he had escaped her. Now he falls into her toils, and in its end the novel thus looks back at its beginning.

It is interesting to compare Thackeray's method with that of sensational novelists like Dickens and Reade, who sought to produce a rapid succession of climaxes and to excite surprise by the variety and intricacies of their situations. It was not for the sake of variety and intricacy that Thackeray shifted his scenes. He sought rather to produce a cumulative impression of vanity in human action and motive by revealing it in all sorts and conditions of men. What others were accustomed to employ for variety he made contribute to uniformity. He did not wish to surprise or to dazzle his reader by brilliant, unlooked-for effects. We are shown the relatives of Miss Crawley, for example, plotting against each other to win her favor while they wait for her to die. Her actual death, however, we learn of only incidentally from a casual reference to her disposal of her property. A novelist in search of variety would probably not have failed to take advantage of the opportunity in such a situation to portray the chagrin of those disappointed in their hopes.

There is probably some connection between this restraint of Thackeray and his deeply ingrained modesty. His letters contain much evidence of self-consciousness and self-distrust. He seems to have been on guard against falling into presumptuousness. Similarly in literature he avoided being spectacular even when it meant sacrificing legitimate climactic effect. He does not want it to appear that he takes himself or his function as an artist too seriously. At the end of his great novel he likens it to a box of puppets such as children use in their games. That is his parting bow to his readers, and there is in it something in the nature of conciliation. As a host he can be gracious and companionable, but he carefully avoids being ostentatious.

The impression that he wished to convey could be best attained, Thackeray probably felt, by examining a large number of people differently situated. If many people could be shown acting from similar motives, there would be a greater sense of authority and universality in their behavior. To suit such a purpose it was better to look intermittently at many people than continuously at a few. The truth that was the author's quarry was a familiar one—a kind of truth to be sought not in extraordinary events but in the gradual revelation of experience. The impressiveness of Thackeray's indictment gains by the fact that it rests not upon a few isolated cases of exceptional individuals but upon the habitual behavior of the rank and file, not upon the happenings of one brief period but upon events covering many years.

Such an extended form of treatment, if it were rendered scenically, would lead to innumerable complications. Characters would have to be moved about even more than they are, and the problem of fitting the incidents into a plausible sequence would require much attention. Thackeray simplified his problem by placing more reliance upon direct narration than was usual, and by organizing his material around a more definite conception, or theme, than was customary in the novel of manners. He abandoned the usual practice of keeping a character or a set of characters continuously in view over a considerable stretch of time, but picked them up and dropped them out of sight as it pleased him.

The idea around which *Vanity Fair* was constructed provided a point of view from which the characters could be observed and their acts judged. It also enabled the author to select the aspects of character and behavior useful to his purpose. One reason why we are not disturbed by the weight of material is the fact that it has been set forth from a restricted point of view and for a specific purpose. Thackeray ranges easily from one incident to another, while appearing to muse over his characters in a long soliloquy, into which the scenes are insinuated without the slightest possible jar. It is as if the subject upon which the author has been meditating suddenly takes form before our eyes. As in the summarizing narrative, the emphasis falls not upon the linking of one incident to another but upon what each incident reveals. The characters and their actions are thus rendered subservient to the general theme. Everything in the novel is controlled from a central motivating point without a sense of struggle or strain between the characters and their actions or between the separate steps of intrigue and the meaning of the whole.

The term *pictorial* as applied to Thackeray's art is perhaps misleading in that it suggests something more objective than is actually the case. Thackeray is far from being an objective writer. It would be almost impossible to detach his created figures from the mass of interpretation and far-ranging commentary with which they are habitually set forth. The refusal of the author to employ a more dramatic form of presentation is essentially a refusal to let his story speak for itself. The characters are not allowed to stand on their own feet. Being limited in function, they are correspondingly limited in opportunity to grow and to occasion surprise. *Vanity Fair* does not open new vistas in the study of character but throws many lights upon familiar vistas. Color and warmth are sacrificed to thematic consistency. We do not find in Thackeray's masterpiece the zest or the richness of Fielding or Scott, nor do we find such complex study of behavior as in Miss Austen's novels. The author does not present his characters as they appear to themselves. His view of them is essentially comic and external.

Becky Sharp is a case in point. Although Mr. E. M. Forster, in *Aspects of the Novel*, has characterized her as being a round rather than a flat character, she is round only in a superficial sense. She bears little if any trace of being modified by her experiences. It is not she who waxes and wanes, as Mr. Forster puts it, so much as her circumstances. There is no essential difference between the young girl who sets her cap for Jos and the accomplished woman who fascinates Lord Steyne. She grows, of course, in assurance and in capacity to excite admiration, but the growth is only in the outward manifestation of traits characteristic of her from the beginning. She is always acting, whether with Miss Crawley, with Lord Steyne, or with anyone who can be of the slightest use to her. The changes in her behavior depend not upon changes in her character or even in her mood, but upon the varying objects of her pursuit.

If we compare her with one of George Eliot's heroines, we see how little there is of a personal nature in her relationship with people. We do not see deeply enough into her to understand much of her attitude to the various people with whom she lives on terms of friendship or intimacy. She worships worldly success and has contempt for simplehearted, loving people like Amelia and Lady Jane. Further than that we know little of what she thinks. She has the contempt of a clever person for Rawdon's stupidity and, one may add, the contempt of an unfeeling person for his devotion to their son. Nevertheless, had circumstances not provided her with more lustrous society, she would probably have gone on finding her husband's company passable enough. What is her attitude toward Lord Steyne? As far as we can see, she has no feeling for him except admiration for his rank and a desire to win his esteem and the advantages which accompany it. She is, in short, a true habitué of Vanity Fair.

All in all, she seems to be not a genuinely round character but a flat one drawn with remarkable skill. She is not, of course, the ordinary type of flat character, consisting of an ever-recurring gesture, a trick of speech, or some other odd quirk of behavior. She does, however, keep showing us the same aspect of herself—an emanation, as it were, of the spirit of the place she dwells in. She is tremendously alive and at the same time in perfect accord with the tone of the novel. The delicacy of the shading given to her portrait is not a shading of individuality but a richly variegated manifestation of that spirit of rivalry and conquest which animates those who seek places of prominence in Vanity Fair.

If Becky had been conceived as a tragic character or as the subject of a psychological portrait, her state of mind at the time of her downfall would be of vital importance to us. Actually we get no clear view of her at this crucial moment. Thackeray looks not at her but at the moral to be drawn from her situation:

What were her thoughts when he left her? She remained for hours after he was gone, the sunshine pouring into the room, and Rebecca sitting alone on the bed's edge. The drawers were all opened and their contents scattered about,—dresses and feathers, scarfs and trinkets, a heap of tumbled vanities lying in a wreck. Her hair was falling over her shoulders; her gown was torn where Rawdon had wrenched the brilliants out of it. She heard him go downstairs a few minutes after he left her, and the door slamming and closing on him. She knew he would never come back. He was gone for ever. Would he kill himself?—she thought—not until after he had met Lord Steyne. She thought of her long past life, and all the dismal incidents of it. Ah, how dreary it seemed, how miserable, lonely and profitless! Should she take laudanum, and end it, too— have done with all hopes, schemes, debts, and triumphs? The French maid found her in this position—sitting in the midst of her miserable ruins with clasped hands and dry eyes. The woman was her accomplice and in Steyne's pay. "Mon Dieu, madame, what has happened?" she asked.

What had happened? Was she guilty or not? She said not; but who could tell what was truth which came from those lips; or if that corrupt heart was in this case pure? All her lies and her schemes, all her selfishness and her wiles, all her wit and genius had come to this bankruptcy. The woman closed the curtains and with some entreaty and show of kindness, persuaded her mistress to lie down on the bed. Then she went below and gathered up the trinkets which had been lying on the floor, since Rebecca dropped them there at her husband's orders, and Lord Steyne went away.

This is undoubtedly an effective tableau, but it is not a profound comment on Becky's conduct, nor does it enable us to see appreciably into her character. Except for the torn dress and scattered finery, she might, in this scene, be almost any figure of a morality intended to typify the bitter fruits of vain ambition.

The tendency of Thackeray to look at his characters from a moral point of view prevented him from making as impartial an examination of their conduct as he otherwise might have done. Belonging to an age which, though worldly, decried worldliness, he was inclined to moralize too much upon the virtue of simple and wholesome living and the vice of worldliness. In the face of a public which preferred to have its novelists either bear lightly upon the seamy side of life or romanticize it as Dickens did, Thackeray felt obliged frequently to take an apologetic tone in regard to his less virtuous characters. As a result of the unfortunate prejudice of the age in favor of virtue, novelists were deterred from an effort to be impartial by the fear that they might seem to be championing vice. Dickens made his position safe by heaping contempt and ridicule upon his evil characters. Thackeray, a more scrupulous realist, failed also to hold the scales even between his good and his bad characters. He did not give us as much of Becky as his mind and his art were capable of. He could not risk the possibility of contaminating his readers.

That he was affected by the conventional prejudices of his time is frequently evident. He censured his characters or commended them as if afraid of being misunderstood. He divided them into fairly distinct classes of sheep and goats. With the exception of Becky, who charms by her brilliance but does not touch us by any trace of softness, his best characters are likely to be those drawn not from a strictly ethical point of view but with a certain detachment, like Major Pendennis and Barnes Newcome. Dobbin is too ideal a character to move us greatly. We may ask ourselves how so intelligent and upright a man could have long been a friend of a shallow cad like George. But Dobbin, the faithful dog in a world of wolves, is

more important as a foil and symbol than as a character. The melt-
ing charm of Amelia may fail today to attract us; we are impatient
with her sentimental devotion to a man whom she ought to have
understood better. But she too is important as a foil—an alleviation
of the hard selfishness disconcertingly characteristic of many of the
female bosoms revealed to us.

In a novel of such large-scale effects the characters are not to be
taken as separate units. They are presented not in isolation but in
conjunction with others, and it is in this way that they must be
seen. They are the threads which together form the whole fabric,
and they gain by the combined effect. They are balanced against
each other in various ways with specific points of contrast. There are
Becky and Amelia to provide the basic contrast. Modest and loyal
Dobbin is put against vain and faithless George. Rawdon Crawley,
coarse and reckless man of the world, has for brother the finicky and
puritanical Pitt. Rawdon's affection for his little son is matched with
Becky's heartlessness. Sometimes the contrast is within an individual,
as in Jos Sedley, a poltroon, who affects the dashing cavalier, and an
awkward, shy booby, who fancies himself a devil among the ladies.

Although Thackeray is a satirist it is not the rational element in
his novels which leaves the most distinct impression. The worldliness
of *Vanity Fair* is tempered by the haze of emotion enveloping it.
The brittle and unfeeling gaiety of these falsehearted people is not
proof against visitations of genuine feeling now and then. Rawdon,
returning to his ancestral home after his father's death, is filled with
recollections of his innocent boyhood. One thinks of Lady Steyne
pitying Becky, who is being snubbed, and asking her to sing. And as
she sings some old religious songs, here, in the heart of Vanity Fair,
Lady Steyne listens in tears:

> She was a child again—and had wandered back through a forty years'
> wilderness to her convent garden. The chapel organ had pealed the same
> tones, the organist, the sister whom she loved best of the community, had
> taught them to her in those early happy days. She was a child once more,
> and the brief period of her happiness bloomed out again for an hour—
> she started when the jarring doors were flung open, and with a loud
> laugh from Lord Steyne, the men of the party entered full of gaiety.
>
> He saw at a glance what had happened in his absence: and was grate-

ful to his wife for once. He went and spoke to her, and called her by her Christian name, so as again to bring blushes to her pale face— . . .

And as a final example of how Thackeray can peer tactfully into secret feelings, let us turn to Amelia when Becky shows her the fateful letter from George:

Who shall analyze those tears, and say whether they were sweet or bitter? Was she most grieved because the idol of her life was tumbled down and shivered at her feet; or indignant that her love had been so despised; or glad because the barrier was removed which modesty had placed between her and a new a real affection? "There is nothing to forbid me now," she thought. "I may love him with all my heart now. Oh, I will, I will, if he will but let me and forgive me." I believe it was this feeling rushed over all the others which agitated that gentle little bosom.

Without going so far as to take a dynamic view of behavior, Thackeray did succeed in giving a certain depth of sensibility and awareness to his characters. He did not ignore the emotional by-products of experience. He did not pretend to know everything, and the humanity and weakness displayed in his commentary cast over his novels a sense of dissatisfaction and doubt somewhat in the nature of a poetic lament. His characters, although not presented as they appear to themselves, do have a dim sense of something in life to be looked for. Life to them is not mere sensation. They live not only in the present but remember the past and are sometimes aware of the changes that time has wrought. At his best Thackeray was an impressionist. A man of sensibility and intelligence, he did not deal in emotion for the sake of emotion or in action for the sake of excitement. Neither did he deal in incidents purely as a means of revealing character. Sometimes he went further and brought to his portraiture a sense of the dreams and frustrations of men.

CHAPTER XI

The Subjective Novel

CHARLOTTE BRONTË

While *Vanity Fair* was still appearing serially the English literary world was treated to another novel destined to make history. By an unknown author, it proved to be a decided sensation, for it had in it the elements of popular appeal and was at the same time substantially different in character from what the reading public was accustomed to. The novel was *Jane Eyre* and its author, who styled herself Currer Bell, was soon to be known to be Charlotte Brontë, the daughter of a Yorkshire clergyman. To make matters more astonishing, Charlotte was found to have two sisters, Emily and Anne, who had also written novels.

Although there was much in *Jane Eyre* and in the mystery surrounding its authorship to excite curiosity and provoke discussion, the actual extent to which it was an innovation was not realized at once. To the readers who greeted its initial appearance its most striking quality was probably the simple and direct intensity of its heroine. With all her exhilarating fervency of spirit, however, Jane was felt to be bold and unladylike. She frankly acknowledged having feelings for a member of the other sex which were not regarded as being proper for young ladies to entertain or at least to acknowledge. Looking at her from the vantage point of the twentieth century, we see that what is most noteworthy about her is not her unconventional frankness. It is rather that, in addition to being a new kind of heroine, she represents a new kind of fictional treatment. In no other novel thus far encountered has the central character been so important. Not only does she stand in the place of the author, but it is through her consciousness that we see the other characters. Moreover, she is rarely if ever an impersonal recorder of what passes before her eyes. What she has to tell she has somehow got into personal relationship with. "I like this day; I like that sky of steel; I like the sternness and the stillness of the world under the frost." Such an outburst from any one of the characters in the novels thus far taken up would be likely to startle the reader. It does not seem strange in *Jane Eyre*, however, for Charlotte Brontë's characters habitually dwell upon such a plane of feeling. They are intensely aware of what surrounds them and colors, or is colored by, their moods. Each thing encountered, be it ever so slight, serves in its own fashion to weigh upon or to lift their spirits. Each thing contributes to their sum total of happiness or distress.

Here then is a new kind of autobiographical novel. Before this time novelists had employed the autobiographical form largely as a technical device. What Moll Flanders had to tell, and Roderick Random, and David Copperfield, was, for the most part, of events in the world outside themselves. Someone else, conveniently stationed, might have served almost equally well. But no one could possibly take the place of Jane Eyre, or of Lucy Snowe in *Villette*, because no one else could see what Jane and Lucy see. The point is simply that they look at things from a personal angle. The real innovation of Charlotte Brontë is that she writes fiction from the point of view of an individual and not from the point of view of society in general. She projects herself without reserve into her leading character and allows her inmost feelings, her secret impulses, to color her narratives. What she has to tell is, in effect, the story of her inner life. With her and her sister Emily the English novel thus comes belatedly to a break with the tradition which has ruled it for more than a century.

According to that tradition the novel was looked upon as being essentially a prose transcript of life. Its method was the method of comedy and its point of view was social, not individual. Its purpose in dealing with the individual was to bring him into harmony with, or to set him against, the requirements of some larger social unit. Love, for example, was a source of family contention or a prelude to marriage, not a manifestation of personality. Sophia Western's refusal to marry Blifil was seen by Fielding as a condition affecting her relation with others, notably with her father; it was only cursorily examined in relation to herself. Much of what I have had to say, in fact, in the course of this study has been concerned with the manner in which individual characters were utilized to serve some purpose exterior to themselves. *Vanity Fair,* as we have seen, excelled in this quality of subordinating the individual to the general survey of manners. Becky Sharp is a striking example of such a character. She presents the somewhat anomalous spectacle of a woman who is finished and brilliant in social demeanor and yet meagerly endowed with temperament. Viewed in relation to her private feelings she is not always clear or easy to distinguish; viewed in relation to a roomful of people whom she wishes to impress she stands out with remarkable vividness.

Although the study of manners had been the dominant concern of the novel, it had of course not been the only one. Richardson had attempted to explore the labyrinths of the Puritan conscience. Sterne had traced the casual deviations of sentiment and humor without regard to the formal regulations of society. Mrs. Radcliffe had sought escape from humdrum in the titillating atmosphere of picturesquely situated old castles and weirdly mysterious occurrences. Scott had done about all that a man could to revive the imaginative outlook of fiction except to enter the inner world of the spirit. No one, in short, had done for the novel what Wordsworth and the other Romantic poets had done for poetry. There was no scarcity of sentiment in fiction and there was romance of a kind, but of ability to cope with inner complexities there had not been much evidence. What Carlotte Brontë termed, in commendation of Balzac, "a subtle perception of the most obscure and secret workings of the mind" had not yet become a serious concern of English novelists.

There is, as one can readily perceive, a gulf between the facile trumpetings of men like Lytton and the inner promptings of the spirit characteristic of true poetic imagination. The passionate heart is reticent. He who would be on easy and familiar terms with life's mysteries may end by rendering them commonplace. Not that any special faculty is requisite to their enjoyment: rather honesty and humility. "Poetry sheds no tears 'such as angels weep,' but natural and human tears; she can boast of no celestial ichor that distinguishes her vital juices from those of prose; the same human blood circulates through the veins of both."

The foregoing statement occurs in the Preface of the *Lyrical Ballads,* in which Wordsworth attacked the craze for Gothicism characteristic of his time. The mind was capable of being excited without the application of gross and violent stimulants, he contended, and the enlargement of such capability might well be the aim of the poet.

What bearing, we may ask, does the condition denounced by Wordsworth have upon Charlotte Brontë? How does she reveal in her work the kind of sensibility that the poet thought ought to be cultivated?

In order to answer these questions let us look for a moment at the three major tendencies in the fiction of the period. These three tendencies, generally speaking, were humorous delineation of character and depiction of manners, sentimental stories of grief and suffering, and romance of the Gothic or the Waverley variety. Lacking both in detachment and in experience of the world, Miss Brontë was not at all equipped to carry on the tradition of the novel of manners. She was an admirer of Thackeray but spoke disparagingly of Miss Austen.

She did make considerable use of the conventional romantic devices. In her early writings, such as has been published as *Legends of Angria,* she was greatly influenced by Byron and Scott. When she came to write for publication, however, she curbed her romantic tendencies. It is perhaps to her credit that she failed to acquit herself well in an aspect of her work in which success would have imperiled what was best in it. It is the artlessness of her melodrama that keeps it from becoming offensive. Obviously her forte was not in conventional romance.

Her place in the tradition of sentiment is not so clear. It would be possible, from one point of view, to call her a sentimentalist. Her novels are about lonely and neglected young women who eventually come into their own. One is reminded of Cinderella or the ugly duckling. The defects of the actual world are rectified in the ideal life of the mind. The scheme of things is remolded nearer to the heart's desire. Deserving heroines are fitted out with suitable mates, sometimes at the expense of plausibility. A happy solution is found for what at a different time and in different hands might well have ended in tragedy.

Despite these limitations, which are only human, there is a noteworthy difference between the novels of Miss Brontë and the conventional sentimental novel. Her feeling is not invented but personal. Wordsworth had said that the feeling developed in a poem should give importance to the situation and not the situation to the feeling. It is in this dominance of feeling over action that *Jane Eyre* and *Villette* show their superiority in sensibility to *The Old Curiosity Shop* and *The Last Days of Pompeii*.

The sentimental novelist set out consciously to be affecting. He put his hero or heroine in a situation designed to provoke sympathy. Charlotte Brontë did not start with such a simple intention. She thought not primarily of the effect she was going to achieve but rather of her subject. Her aim was not simply to provoke sympathy for her heroine but rather to express or to realize her. What she asked of her reader was in reality the more thoroughgoing sympathy of complete understanding. The sentimental novelist did not identify himself with the object for which he was trying to provoke sympathy. He was not in the toils of the pain or pleasure he depicted, and it was easy for him to be superficial or insincere. Miss Brontë, however, did not dally with emotion. She was, like Wordsworth, possessed by her feelings as well as possessing them. She did not flinch from unpleasantness or attempt to prettify her subject. She cut through the evasions and decorums of the sentimentalist.

The very strength and simplicity of her literary impulse helped her to escape the prejudices and preoccupations of her time. She did not attempt, like George Eliot, to solve the problems of existence. She did not attempt to get at the sources of behavior but simply to present it. What is vital in her work will not quickly perish because it deals with life in terms which do not quickly change. In a letter to her publisher she said of *Villette* that she could not write a book handling the topics of the day. Nor could she write a book for its moral. This was not spoken like a true Victorian. It was something new at the time for a novel to have no ulterior purpose. The attempt to express a character or a point of view without *arrière pensée* serves anew to denote her kinship with the Romantic poets, who in their best poems were not obviously didactic. What Jane *is* is the essential thing: her intensity, her truthfulness, her hatred of sham virtue and of apathy. You have to accept her with all her limitations and prejudices. There are no two ways about it. It is not surprising that the author was accused of bad taste and immorality.

If we leave out of account the *juvenilia*, which were not intended for publication, Charlotte Brontë wrote only four novels. Of these, *The Professor*, though the first to be written, was not published until after her death, having been at first refused by the publishers. The material of this novel was used again in *Villette*, where it was handled with much greater effectiveness. The first novel to be published was *Jane Eyre*, after which came *Shirley*. Although *Villette* shows a considerable advance in psychological portraiture and contains more completely drawn characters, I have selected *Jane Eyre* for analysis as being an earlier manifestation of its author's essential qualities. It has probably been more widely read than the others; moreover, it is direct, fresh, unlabored, and very much alive.

Jane Eyre

Turning from *Vanity Fair* to *Jane Eyre* is somewhat like going from a crowded drawing room or a promenade of fashion into a confessional, a kind of secular confessional, so to speak. The irony, detachment, and wit so much in place in a fashionable drawing room are not essential to a confessional, where sincerity and a full heart are more to the purpose. Passionate sincerity Charlotte Brontë unquestionably had, as she did not have the suppleness and ease that come from long familiarity with social intercourse. As befits her situation, the heroine of *Vanity Fair*, if we may call Becky a heroine, touches life at many points while remaining inwardly something of an enigma. Jane Eyre, on the other hand, touches life at few points but reveals herself vividly in each important contact.

There are quite a number of ways in which the two novels differ markedly from each other. One is characterized by reticence, the other by unblushing candor. One sets forth its characters in perspective with their social surroundings; the other shows them in comparative isolation from the world. One deals with the complicated and trivial minutiae of ordinary existence, the other with a fierce longing for life and love, in no way trivial. One is suavely pictorial and undramatic; the other seethes with emotional disturbance and passes through a series of conflicts and dramatic crises. One writer makes a point of avoiding the heroic; the other invests her leading characters with a certain spirited intensity of feeling and undauntedness of courage which are superior to the theatrical heroism of the conventional romantic type.

Jane Eyre is the story of a girl who, having a great craving for affection and love, is condemned by the circumstances of her life to pass her childhood in loneliness and neglect, and to fall in love eventually with a man who proves to be inaccessible to her. It is only after the story has practically run its course that the barrier to her happiness is removed. Viewed simply from the outside, Jane's career was not remarkable. The world would probably have called it commonplace and drab. At the age of ten she quarreled with her aunt and was sent to a charity school, where she was badly clothed, poorly fed, and forced to endure various hardships. After eight years in the school, including two years of teaching, she became a governess at Thornfield Hall, the proprietor of which was Mr. Rochester, a man of strange manners and behavior, and considerably older than Jane. Despite the seeming disparities between them, the two fell greatly in love with each other and Jane was on the point of marrying her master when she discovered that he had already a wife, an insane woman kept in seclusion in an upper chamber of the house. After this harrowing experience the young governess ran away from Thornfield and spent several months with some accidentally discovered cousins: St. John Rivers, a clergyman, and his two sisters. She came near to accepting the entreaty of St. John to marry him and accompany him to India as the wife of a missionary, but she was still in love with Rochester. Fancying one day that she heard him calling to her, she returned to Thornfield Hall, only to discover that it had been destroyed by a fire which had brought blindness and the loss of a hand to Rochester and death to his wife, whom he had tried at his own cost to save. He was now living near by in a state of loneliness and despair, which Jane's return quickly put an end to, there being nothing now to prevent them from marrying.

Stated thus baldly, the plot may appear to be sensational but, aside from the uncanny laughter and the strange appearances of the lunatic wife, there is only one extraordinary episode in the entire novel: the arrested wedding ceremony and its immediate sequel. To these things I should perhaps add the telepathic messages exchanged between the two lovers. If we compare these things to the striking occurrences in a novel by Reade or Collins, we see that *Jane Eyre* is a simple and outwardly quiet story. The excitement with which it is filled is of a different kind from that of the mere sensational novel. It is an excitement derived less from the situation than from the continued turmoil in the feelings of Jane and the volcanic fires that burn in the breast of Rochester.

As for the events themselves, the author failed to make many of them appear plausible. Jane is real enough as a child, but we do not understand why her aunt should have had such a decided antipathy to her. Her young cousins are hardly more than the stock characters of didactic fiction. It is hardly possible that Rochester could have kept his wife confined for so long without exciting more curiosity about her among the neighbors. Here a situation fitting to Gothic fiction was transferred to an atmosphere quite unsuited to it. After leaving Thornfield Jane wandered for days and finally sank exhausted upon the doorstep of unknown relatives, who took her in and treated her kindly. Such a coincidence not only strains the reader's credulity but insults his intelligence. It is a major link in the action which cannot be regarded as casual. It cannot be attributed to an excited state of feelings. There is no way to brush it aside. It causes one to feel that what he is reading is not a serious production but the artless contrivance of a child.

We do not encounter in *Jane Eyre* a world of such solid reality and completeness of detail as is characteristic of the novels of Thackeray or Miss Austen. On the other hand, Charlotte Brontë does not, like Dickens, engage in producing conscious fantasy. The unreality that is frequently characteristic of her world is due to the narrowness of her vision of it. She is limited in experience and in the range of her interests so that she sometimes grasps only a very limited aspect of what she has under survey. So absorbed is she by her particular angle of interest that she ignores many accessory details, proper attention to which would substantiate her work and strengthen its sense of reality. For example, when Rochester visits his maniac wife with those who have been present at his attempt to ally himself to Jane, the woman who has Mrs. Rochester in charge shows no astonishment but acts as if such visits were a common occurrence. It would be more in accordance with the actual situation, however, for her to think that her master has suddenly become as mad as his wife, to betray thus what he has been at such pains to keep secret.

In novels like *Ivanhoe* and *David Copperfield* a degree of improbability does not greatly disturb the reader because of their general atmosphere. In the simpler and more intensely real world of *Jane Eyre*, however, artificial contrivance is more damaging to the illusion. The frustrated love of Jane and Rochester is rendered convincingly and powerfully, but the means used to thwart the two lovers are not altogether credible. The central episode of the novel follows the lines of a mystery story, but the element of mystery is not handled with skill or convincingness. Moreover, it fails to harmonize with the other elements of the novel. In a Gothic romance the situation of a mad wife secretly incarcerated in the upper story of a country house would be utilized for various thrilling effects. In *Jane Eyre*, however, it is first of all a cause of division between the two lovers and only secondarily useful in evoking an atmosphere of dread or terror. As an apparition faintly glimpsed in the nighttime the mad woman is not unimpressive, but grappling with her husband in full daylight and having to be tied to a chair she becomes painfully absurd. Later, when Rochester explains to Jane the circumstances of his marriage to her and their early wedded life, she is made to appear as a rather obvious and impertinent figure of straw.

Such structural imperfections do not spring from a search for technical dexterity. The author pays not too much but too little attention to the more conscious and more mechanical aspects of her art. Although usually sure in her grasp of essentials she is often singularly incompetent in devising a credible framework in which to display her sensibility. Possibly the long indulgence in make-believe in her fanciful *Legends of Angria* and other such writing may have encouraged this tendency to structural naïveté. It can be attributed in part, no doubt, to her subjectivism and her inexperience. Her intense feeling and little knowledge of the world made it easy for her to become absorbed in her personal relation to her material. Jane Eyre once said of herself that in communicating with strong natures she could not rest until she had passed the outworks of conventional reserve and "won a place by their hearts' very hearthstone." So it was with Charlotte Brontë. She was not by nature analytical. It was not her way to search for reality apart from her own personal sense of it. Accordingly it was natural for her to elaborate what was allied to her inner experience and to deal sketchily with what lay outside it. Thus her novels fluctuate between that which gathers strength from its propinquity to the heart and that which arises from a not very alert invention.

There was no dearth of love in English fiction. Practically all novels touched upon it in some fashion or other. It had long been, moreover, a favorite theme of poets and dramatists. But much of what was vital or complex in the depiction of love had evaporated from English literature before the dawn of the eighteenth-century novel. The quest for perfection in love, the language of devotion and adoration, the spiritualization of passion, courtly love, Petrarchan idealism, the subtlety of John Donne—these were all things that belonged to poetry rather than to the novel, and they also belonged to the period before 1700.

By the time of Defoe there had been a reaction against the licentiousness of the Restoration, and the courtly, romantic tradition was also played out. To the average novelist of the eighteenth century, love was a casual manifestation of sensuality without much psychological significance, a source of conflict between parents and children, or a theme for comic collisions, sentimental intrigue, and various sham engagements carried on under the mask of propriety.

It had become, in other words, a social habit rather than a form of personal relationship. Puritanism sometimes gave birth to conflicts between the heart and the conscience, but neither the heart nor the conscience as conceived by Richardson was intensely personal. Clarissa's sense of duty was so much a part of her character that it could almost be called a habit, and the considerations put most prominently forward in the account of her misadventure were very largely prudential. The struggle in her case was not so much between her heart and her conscience as between her honesty and Lovelace's duplicity, or between her sense of fairness and oppressive family authority.

The more romantic novelists like Mrs. Radcliffe and Scott were content, for the most part, to leave the mystery of love a mystery. They set the hearts of their lovesick heroines throbbing violently but did not examine closely into the nature of the throbs. The young men were manly and tenderly devoted; the young women were easily agitated. To the latter, love was an occasion for trembling, blushing, and sometimes swooning, and it was not much else. The frank but superficial animality of the eighteenth century had succumbed to a wave of prudery and timidity.

Love to Dickens meant courtship, and courtship was an occasion for merriment when it was not an occasion for sentiment. Thackeray saw that love was sometimes sacrificed to worldly interest and that it frequently deceived its victims. Among the novelists primarily concerned with the depiction of manners no one was superior to Jane Austen in combining the comedy of courtship with the revelation of character. Her heroines are all different from one another and each one has her characteristic way of behaving to the man who arouses her feelings.

Charlotte Brontë did not follow any of these writers in her treatment of love. She was no sentimental moralist, conventional romanticist, or social satirist. She did not concern herself about the prudential aspects of mating or bother about the proper etiquette of courtship. She did not fill her love stories with dinner parties, balls, and other such social phenomena. The forces that drew her lovers together were not the simply felt attractions operating in the novel of manners; the factors that served to keep them apart were not the accidental misunderstandings of romance or the idiosyncratic frictions of social comedy. The attraction between Rochester and Jane is profound and seemingly inevitable. It arises from traits that lie deep in their natures and is additionally strengthened by peculiarities in their situations.

Jane is far from being a passive heroine. Her love for Rochester is a part of her long struggle for self-realization. The desire to be sheltered and befriended, denied her in her childhood, becomes one of her most marked characteristics. She cannot live without love or kindness, she tells Mrs. Reed, and to Helen Burns she insists that she would submit to having her arm broken to gain some real affection from one she loves. Her departure from Lowood comes as a result of the breaking of ties formed with Miss Temple, the kindly superintendent. At the time of her first encounter with Rochester she is being consumed by a smoldering desire for a greater variety of experience. She is like a piece of dry touchwood, needing only contact with a spark to be ignited. Rochester's masterful wooing, at once tender and teasing, is inexpressibly sweet to her. Greater civility of manner would not necessarily have made him more irresistible to her in her desolate state. It is not his abruptness and occasional harshness that render her uneasy so much as her premonition of disaster and her superstitious fear that such intense happiness as hers cannot last.

Upon Rochester Jane's presence at Thornfield acts like balm on an inflamed wound. She exerts a soothing and healing influence upon his racked mind and stimulates in him a return of the happier and more innocent feelings of his youth. Having long before been saddled with a wife in no way suited to him and subsequently deprived by her insanity of the small amount of satisfaction that such a union might have been made to yield, he has sought relief unsuccessfully in various forms of dissipation. A roving life about Europe has failed to cure his melancholy, and a succession of mistresses —French, Italian, and German—has brought him no real happiness.

Into his restlessness and despair, bred of a repetition of disappointments, the young and eager spirit of Jane brings new life and hope. There is a charming novelty for him in her strange blend of diffidence and assurance. He is pleased to see that she is not disturbed by his occasional displays of ferocity and he finds that, despite her freshness and delicacy, there is nothing frail or fragile in her spirit. How indomitable she is, in fact, he is to learn when he attempts to induce her to leave Thornfield with him. Hard as he tries he cannot conquer her, even though, as he knows, her inclination fights on his side. He cannot, as he says, get at "the savage beautiful creature" that is the inner spirit, the essence, of Jane.

The element of conflict reveals that the stage of the novel has been transferred from the outer to the inner world. It is not so much a conflict *between* persons as *within* them. Rochester's inexplicable behavior while he is courting Jane is eventually seen to have been due to a struggle going on in him between his love and desire and his fear of wronging her. Jane's early struggle against circumstance is largely an invisible one waged not for any material good but for her inward satisfaction. When she is confronted by the necessity of choosing between love and her sense of right, the victory of her conscience is not an easy one. She is tortured by Rochester's tender reminiscences and finds herself in danger of being betrayed by her conscience as well as her feelings. She has only herself to consider, for she has no relatives, as she then believes, to be offended by her action. If she resists such a headlong man, he may be driven to some fatal recklessness. With her "veins running fire" she clings on desperately, however, to her view of what is right and flees from the house. As she passes the door of her master's room her heart fails her momentarily and her hand moves involuntarily toward the latch. Even after she has reached the fields her struggle goes on in a manner which the following passage serves to illustrate:

I thought of him now—in his room—watching the sunrise; hoping I should soon come to say I would stay with him and be his. I longed to be his; I panted to return; it was not too late; I could yet spare him the bitter pang of bereavement. As yet my flight, I was sure, was undiscovered. I could go back and be his comforter—his pride; his redeemer from misery; perhaps from ruin. Oh, that fear of his self-abandonment—far worse than my abandonment—how it goaded me! It was a barbed arrow-head in my breast; it tore me when I tried to extract it; it sickened me when remembrance thrust it further in. Birds began singing in brake and copse: birds were faithful to their mates; birds were emblems of love.

What was I? In the midst of my pain of heart, and frantic effort of principle, I abhorred myself. I had no solace from self-approbation: none even from self-respect. I had injured—wounded—left my master. I was hateful in my own eyes. Still I could not turn, nor retrace one step. God must have led me on. As to my own will or conscience, impassioned grief had trampled one and stifled the other. I was weeping wildly as I walked along my solitary way: fast, fast I went like one delirious. A weakness, beginning inwardly, extending to the limbs, seized me, and I fell: I lay on the ground some minutes, pressing my face to the wet turf. I had some fear—or hope—that here I should die: but I was soon up; crawling forwards on my hands and knees, and then again raised to my feet—as eager and as determined as ever to reach the road.

Nearly everything in *Jane Eyre* is made to contribute to a sense of conflict or frustration. The number of characters is small; there is little that is merely pictorial. We are shown only as much of Mrs. Reed and her children as serves to reveal their cruelty in dealing with Jane. Lowood is presented narrowly, with the heroine at the center of our view of it. At Thornfield again it is the emotional life of the central character that is followed in detail. We see her not so much in her life as a governess as in her growing attachment to Rochester. After her flight from Thornfield she is plunged into a new struggle, in which her exaggerated sense of duty almost leads her to a marriage with St. John Rivers. Rochester, like Jane, is a thwarted character, the reason, in his case, being his unfortunate early marriage.

The setting of the novel is also made to contribute to its sense of conflict. Nature provides a background of calm and storm for the fluctuations of human feeling. When the child Jane is locked in the terrifying loneliness of the red room, she hears the rain beating on the windows and the wind howling through the trees. It is a lovely midsummer night when Rochester and Jane first come to an open avowal of their feelings. A nightingale singing in the wood provides an accompaniment to their duet of love, which is rudely broken into, however, by a sudden rising of wind and rattling peal of thunder. That night the large chestnut tree which has sheltered them is struck by lightning. A month afterwards, on the evening before the day set for her wedding, Jane wanders about outside in a state of anxiety, awaiting the return of Rochester. Filled with fore-boding, she pauses before the chestnut tree, the trunk of which has been split and scarred by the lightning, and addresses it in a man-ner that makes of it a prophetic symbol of the blow soon to divide her from the man she loves.

It is in the depiction of the growth of love, particularly from the woman's point of view, that *Jane Eyre* is perhaps most notably different from earlier English fiction. From the time of her first en-counter with Rochester, before knowing who he is, Jane is reluctant to return to her stagnant life at Thornfield. His presence there has an electrifying effect upon the place for her. Her interest in him im-mediately exceeds that of a servant for her master. His slightest sign of approbation thrills her. She lives from day to day for some visible or audible sign of his presence. His absence fills her with misgiving. Nothing pleases her more than the occasional tête-à-têtes in which they engage. On her return from Gateshead, where she has been to visit Mrs. Reed in her last illness, she walks alone from Millcote, savoring her joy, her heart beating high at the thought of Rochester even though she firmly believes that soon he will be married to Miss Ingram. When he teases her so outrageously about finding a place for her in Ireland, being a real woman and not a manufactured piece of propriety, she casts decorum to the winds and sobs con-vulsively, shaken from head to foot in her acute distress. Finally, after the winter of cruel separation, comes the scene of their reunion, at once tender and sad and triumphant. There is nothing to keep them apart now. Moreover, their situations have changed. She is no longer a dependent and he is now maimed and blind. Such ma-terial matters, however, tend only to strengthen their love and to provide Jane with an opportunity to give herself more completely to the object of her devotion. Her fulfillment has come, and the story can fittingly end.

CHAPTER XII

The Dramatic Novel

EMILY BRONTË

All of the Brontë children who lived to maturity—Charlotte, Patrick Branwell, Emily, and Anne—engaged in writing as one of the games played in their childhood, Charlotte and Emily giving themselves up wholeheartedly to their imaginary world. The habits formed early persisted, and in 1845 Charlotte discovered some poems in Emily's handwriting which she thought were worthy of publication. Emily was now twenty-seven. The result of this discovery was the publication the following year of a small volume of verse by the three sisters at their own expense and purportedly by Currer, Ellis, and Acton Bell, who were, of course, Charlotte, Emily, and Anne respectively. In 1847 there were published *Wuthering Heights,* by Emily, and *Agnes Grey,* by Anne. Although written and accepted for publication earlier than *Jane Eyre,* they did not appear until somewhat later than Charlotte's novel.

Emily, who was two years younger than Charlotte, did not write any more novels. She died late in 1848, when she was only thirty. Branwell had died a few months before her, a drunkard and drug addict. Much had been expected of him when he was young, and his lamentable course was the greatest disappointment that the family had to endure. His behavior, long a source of anxiety to his sisters, left its mark upon *The Tenant of Wildfell Hall,* by Anne, and was probably one of the shaping influences upon the imagination of Emily while she was engaged in fashioning *Wuthering Heights.*

Although *Jane Eyre* was considerable of a novelty when it first appeared, it would be more accurate to say that *Wuthering Heights* was an anachronism. Even with her unconventional lack of decorum and other feminine graces, Jane was recognizably a heroine. Catherine Earnshaw, of Emily's novel, however, must have seemed a wayward creature to occupy the role of heroine, and Heathcliff seems to have filled even Charlotte with misgiving. There are other reasons, as we shall see, why *Wuthering Heights* should have been slow in gaining popularity.

Not a great deal is known of Emily. She was intensely reserved. Only a few of her letters and notes remain, in addition to her novel and poems. Outside the family she did not have any very close friends. We have to depend largely upon Charlotte for information about her, and it is by no means certain that Charlotte thoroughly understood her. She seems to have lived a double life, as it were— the ordinary life of daily family affairs and an inner life which she did not share with anyone. Outwardly she was as undemonstrative as she was inwardly passionate. She is said to have loved the freedom of the moors. There, no doubt, she could have the sense of escaping from the cramped circumstances and confining atmosphere of her life. Quite possibly she ignored or held in contempt many of the conventional opinions of the Parsonage.

Her rebellion, as revealed in *Wuthering Heights,* was none the less powerful because it was largely subconscious. She had much less regard for convention than Charlotte had and was more subjective. *Wuthering Heights* came so completely out of her inner life that it bears little resemblance to the Victorian world to which it was presented. As compared with the polite and respectable world of Dickens and Thackeray it provides us with a view of life that is at once more primitive, more elemental, and more complex.

Wuthering Heights

Although *Wuthering Heights* has been pretty generally accepted as a triumph of the imagination, there has not been the same uniformity of opinion in regard to its merits as a work of art. Something of the frenzy that now and then possesses its two leading characters seems to communicate itself to those who attempt to appraise the novel and prevents them from writing in measured terms about it. One critic[1] sets loose an avalanche of adjectives, of which "stupendous" may serve as an example, and characterizes each act of Heathcliff as being "wrapt in its own infernal glamour, trailing a cloud of supernatural splendour." Another critic[2] would have it that the form of the novel is "as consummate as its subject is sublime," and calls it "the one perfect work of art" among Victorian novels. One of the recent biographers[3] of Charlotte is impatient with her for not having appreciated her sister's genius more thoroughly, and goes on to reveal his own superior appreciation by asserting that although *Wuthering Heights* is among the greatest of novels its "composition and construction are inconceivably awkward." He argues further that since "no single author could have planned a book in so topsy-turvy a manner" Branwell must have written the opening chapters. Yet another writer,[4] after a careful scrutiny of the legal aspects of the novel, says that he was inclined for a time to find the climax of the tragedy in the circumstance that the surviving young people "were to be left destitute." He admits, however, that such an interpretation would be going too far. It would indeed be going too far. Mrs. Dean clearly never had an inkling of such a calamitous turn of events and it was to her, after all, that Emily entrusted the telling of the story. Moreover, it is made perfectly clear by Heathcliff before his death that he is no longer consumed by the desire to destroy the two families.

It is well for us, then, in dealing with a novel that has been so variously commented upon, to avoid farfetched theories and to accept what we are plainly told. As it is, there is enough for the commentator to explain if he can. There is enough mystery in the character of Heathcliff to tax our capacity for strangeness without borrowing trouble by searching for additional hidden meanings.

The title of *Wuthering Heights* is taken from the name of the

---

[1] May Sinclair, *The Three Brontës,* Boston, 1912, p. 245.
[2] David Cecil, *Early Victorian Novelists,* New York, 1935, p. 202.
[3] E. F. Benson, *Charlotte Brontë,* London, 1932, pp. 174, 175.
[4] C. P. S., *The Structure of Wuthering Heights,* London, 1926, p. 18.

dwelling place of the Earnshaw family, in which most of the action of the story occurs. "Wuther," according to the dictionary, means to roar or bluster, and in the opening chapter "wuthering" is said to indicate the atmospheric tumult to which the house was exposed in stormy weather. We may conclude that in giving her novel such a title the author wished to suggest the warring of the elements. She wished to suggest that human passions are not unlike the ceaseless contention going on between the inanimate forces surrounding us, which follow laws of their own, hardly to be understood.

The affinity existing between Catherine Earnshaw and Heathcliff is a product of natural growth and is not amenable to reason. When frustrated, the energy which it has generated is turned into paths of destruction. By marrying Edgar Linton, Catherine thwarts Heathcliff and denies to herself the possibility of a natural outlet for her passion. Kept from union with him in life, her spirit presumably haunts him after her death. There is no peace for her because she is completely herself only in union with the man of whom she has once confessed to Nelly Dean: "He's more myself than I am." Heathcliff, the most completely frustrated character, blames Edgar Linton for robbing him of Catherine, and Hindley Earnshaw for first having made it impossible for him to win her. His frustrated passion bears fruit in hatred which can find relief only in the destruction of everything at all connected with the two men. His wrath thus falls upon their children and also upon his own child, the pitiable offspring of a hated union. It falls even upon Catherine, who in having innocently betrayed him is the cause of his torment.

The struggle suggested in the title, and made manifest in every aspect of the novel, centers in Heathcliff. His feeling for Hareton and for Catherine Linton becomes in time a blend of attraction and repulsion. They are associated in his mind with what he hates and also with what he loves. He cannot dissociate them from his lost Catherine, who looks at him through the eyes of her daughter and to whom Hareton sometimes bears a striking resemblance. There are times too when Hareton, deprived as he has been of a chance for normal growth, seems to Heathcliff a personification of his own youth.

Apart from such minor complexities, Emily Brontë sees how

conflicts arise within the very core of love, which is conceived not as a matter of simple attraction between two persons but as a complex of forces occupying different planes of feeling. One of the most remarkable sections in the novel is that which depicts the conflict growing in the heart of Catherine Earnshaw after she has been introduced to the quieter atmosphere of Thrushcross Grange. She acquires a different set of manners for use with the Lintons, quite without any vulgar intention to deceive. She begins also to look at Heathcliff from a different and more critical point of view. To censure her for planning to marry Linton while she loves Heathcliff is to disregard her inexperience and to fail to recognize how potent such conflicts can be in determining conduct. In any case she might not have married Linton, in spite of her plans, if Heathcliff had remained at home. Furthermore, in first planning her marriage she had hoped to use it as a means of aiding Heathcliff.

Such a way of handling love was revolutionary in English fiction in 1847. It is remarkable that the author was able to depict it so convincingly and with so little attention to the blinding conventions of the period. She was more completely honest and more convincing than Charlotte, who was much more pleasing to their own generation. In what other English novel of the period could such a scene have occurred as the one in which Catherine tries to dissuade Isabella from her fatal infatuation with Heathcliff? Catherine knows that her feeling for Heathcliff is different from her feeling for Linton —a difference which she tries to explain to Mrs. Dean in what seems to be a strange outburst coming from a Victorian heroine:

My great miseries in this world have been Heathcliff's miseries, and I watched and felt each from the beginning: my great thought in living is himself. If all else perished, and *he* remained, I should still continue to be; and if all else remained, and he were annihilated, the universe would turn to a mighty stranger: I should not seem a part of it. My love for Linton is like the foliage in the woods: time will change it, I'm well aware, as winter changes the trees. My love for Heathcliff resembles the eternal rocks beneath: a source of little visible delight, but necessary. Nelly, I *am* Heathcliff! He's always, always in my mind: not as a pleasure, any more than I am always a pleasure to myself, but as my own being.

Those who have looked upon *Wuthering Heights* as being awkward and confused in structure have usually not bothered to consider what other method of construction the author might have elected to follow. Neither have they devoted much attention to the advantages of the method followed or to its suitability to the material of the novel. As a matter of fact, one who reads the novel with ordinary attentiveness to details will find not confusion but a carefully articulated plot. He will find not a surplusage of irrelevant matters but an organically conceived story with a distinct beginning and end, a complete cycle of change, and bearing within its narrow confines an intensity of feeling unapproached in the more sophisticated fiction of the period. The fact that the narrative opens at a point near the end should not occasion any difficulty to readers who are familiar with Conrad or with the technical innovations of recent fiction.

The subject of *Wuthering Heights* as conceived by its author was not suited to autobiographical treatment. Charlotte's best novels were in the nature of confessions, which could be put into the mouth of a character more or less to be identified with the author. What Emily had to tell may well have been intimately connected with her feelings, but she was too reserved to open her heart in a form of confession so little disguised as was her sister's. It is not surprising that, being reticent by nature, she should choose a method of telling her story that would leave her in the background. Besides, like a true artist, she was not content to express merely what she had experienced. She possessed the type of imagination capable of representing in objective terms what she had contemplated and made her own.

An additional reason for the choice of method can be found in the extraordinary nature of the material. On its surface a story of mundane revenge, the novel really has to do with a love that passes beyond ordinary boundaries and results in behavior that seems to be little short of madness. If one pole of the story is fixed in everyday affairs, the other pole takes us into a realm of feeling where not everyone can venture with assurance. What better method can be found to render such strange occurrences credible than to have them related by a person who has witnessed them and who, moreover, is manifestly a sensible, matter-of-fact person, whose obvious disapproval of much that she has to tell is an added guarantee of its authenticity? Lockwood, as intermediary, lends further support to the story. Mrs. Dean, despite her literal-mindedness, might conceivably exaggerate the wonders of which she is, so to speak, the sole custodian. But Lockwood, being a gentleman who belongs to the world of the reader rather than to the narrow circle of the participants, is beyond such suspicion. His curiosity provides Mrs. Dean with a reason for talking. In such a simple way is the authority of the strange tale established. The author has the good sense not to make too much of her difficulties. To have done so would have been to attract more attention to them.

Great artists succeed not by avoiding difficulties but by overcoming them. There are difficulties in the method of *Wuthering Heights.* Mrs. Dean has to remember long stretches of conversation that have taken place years before. She is able to pick her way through a multitude of trivial associations and select what best suits her purpose. She has to supply gaps in her information by various devices and her presence upon some occasions seems intrusive. Catherine and Heathcliff both confide in her, although Heathcliff is by nature secretive.

There are things too in Heathcliff's manipulation of events that seem hardly plausible. Isabella's infatuation fits too neatly into the scheme of revenge. The harrowing marriage of Catherine Linton to young Heathcliff is another circumstance in which the hand of the conspirator is plainly seen. The affair is managed with such diabolical cleverness, however, and the victim of it is so eager to return to her father that, strange as it is, the action is made to seem plausible. We have the horrifying impression of being in a world in which kindness and compassion have suffered a temporary paralysis under the sway of a superior malignant power. It is remarkable, in fact, how well the author overcame her difficulties. Her story carries conviction by the sheer force of its sincerity and simplicity.

The only other character besides Mrs. Dean who might conceivably have acted as narrator was Heathcliff, who was obviously not fitted for the task. Since telling the story by letters would have been practically out of the question for such a situation, the only other obvious method was that of ordinary omniscient authorship. Self-consciousness and lack of experience were probably enough to prevent Emily from adopting the latter method, and there may have been an additional reason. As an omniscient storyteller she would have been put into a position of having to make explanations of things which were better left unexplained. The events of her story needed the authority of dramatic representation, but they were not easily to be elucidated. Mrs. Dean makes no pretense of understanding the meaning of everything that Catherine says about Heathcliff. She is not a person to be much disturbed by what she sees. The desire of Catherine not to be separated from Heathcliff while she is planning to marry Linton is to Mrs. Dean so much folly and nonsense. As a character in whose uncertain hands the fate of the children sometimes hangs, she forms a definite part of the action, but as a narrator she becomes little more than a convention. She and Lockwood both fade into impersonality, and the story thus gains in objectivity. The intrusive personality of the author, so characteristic of most Victorian novels, does not here stand between us and the figures of the drama.

The time covered by *Wuthering Heights* is somewhere near thirty years, of which only certain periods are presented with dramatic continuity. Emphasis is placed upon the time when Heathcliff and the first Catherine reach maturity and upon the corresponding period in the lives of the succeeding generation of characters, when Catherine Linton, Hareton Earnshaw, and Linton Heathcliff provide the triangular situation that in the generation before has been provided by Catherine Earnshaw, Heathcliff, and Edgar Linton.

The novel opens at a point in time somewhat less than a year before the actual close of the story, when Mr. Lockwood, a tenant of Heathcliff, makes a call on his landlord at Wuthering Heights. Notwithstanding his chill reception he returns the following day and makes the acquaintance of a strange but attractive young woman, Heathcliff's daughter-in-law, and of a boorish young man, whom he first assumes to be his host's son but who proves to bear the name Hareton Earnshaw. Having to remain overnight on account of the weather, Lockwood amuses himself before going to sleep by looking through some old books, which contain a fragmentary diary, dating back about a quarter of a century and belonging apparently to a young girl named Catherine Earnshaw. The name is brought particularly to his attention because he has seen the same name scratched on the paint and in some places changed to *Catherine Heathcliff* and *Catherine Linton.* Finally he goes to sleep and has a curious dream, in which it seems to him that a child calling herself Catherine Linton tries to get in through the window. She cries that she has been a waif for twenty years, thus providing us with a time reference that does not extend back as far as the time of the diary. So terrifying is the dream that Lockwood cries out and accidentally arouses his host, whose behavior upon learning about what has happened is so unaccountable that it is enough to raise some suspicion in Lockwood in regard to Heathcliff's sanity.

Certain references in the diary, the recurrence of the name "Catherine" in the dream, the sullen and apathetic behavior of young Mrs. Heathcliff, the viciousness of the dogs, the surliness of the old servant Joseph—these and other circumstances have combined to suggest something sinister about Heathcliff to his tenant, and to link him in some mysterious way with the shadowy Catherine Earnshaw of the diary.

In the three introductory chapters the author accomplishes a number of things. She quickly establishes the atmosphere of her story, for one thing, subjecting us to a series of shocks that prepare us for the cold bath of inhuman cruelty and eeriness to follow. By the device of the dream and the old diary, the curtain is lifted slightly upon earlier stages of the story, and the reader is catapulted into the heart of the mystery without any essential facts being given away. Lockwood is filled with curiosity in regard to his landlord, and Mrs. Dean is provided with a focus for her story. What she has to do is simply to explain the circumstances lying behind the strange state of affairs in Heathcliff's household.

There can be little doubt that the spell cast by *Wuthering Heights* over its reader is in some way connected with the fact that the events come to us, for the most part, through the penumbra of distance. We are never permitted long to forget that we are hearing of events now dead. The narrator may refer passingly to some subsequent period of time, or the thread of narrative may be broken by a colloquy between her and her listener. Eventually Mrs. Dean brings her account up to the present and for a chapter or so the story comes to us directly, with Lockwood making another visit to Heathcliff, this time preparatory to going away. It is probably due to more than mere coincidence that this portion of the novel is comparatively dull and colorless.

How essential the element of time is to the author becomes more evident when we consider how little use she made of the conventional stock in trade of the novel. What we call the elemental quality of her art rests upon her unusual capacity to discard the accumulated weight of tradition—social, moral, religious, literary—which formed the greater part of the ordinary novelist's material. We do not find in *Wuthering Heights* the humor and sentiment of domestic fiction or the system of rewards and punishments characteristic of the Victorian ethic. We do not find the social apparatus of the satirical novel, or the picturesque accouterments of romance. What *is* used is completely assimilated. Heathcliff may be a descendant of the Gothic villain or the Byronic hero, but he fits so perfectly into his peculiar environment that the question of literary affinity does not occur to us. Even the weather is not exploited as it is in *Jane Eyre*. We are aware of it, as people who lived on the moors are sure to have been. But it, like everything else, is reduced to essentials. It marks the passage of time, provides alternations between periods of calm and of storm, and reflects the recurrent cycles of change characteristic of all matter, both animate and inanimate.

The setting of the novel is limited to the two dwelling places, Wuthering Heights and Thrushcross Grange, and the fields which lie around and between them. The nearby village of Gimmerton is a place to which people sometimes go, but the reader is not privileged to accompany them. The characters are limited to the members of the Earnshaw and Linton families and a small number of accessory personages. There are practically no visitors to bring in even a slight stir from the outside world. The doctor is not a talkative fellow, as he would be in a Fielding novel, but a bare functionary.

With so much eliminated or reduced in scale, what remains? Enough, it would seem, for the author's purpose. Time remains, and the absence of distractions enables us the better to see it in the process of functioning. The laws operating in the novel do so on a time dimension. To see them at work to the best advantage, we need to be placed in a position where we can witness a complete cycle of change. Otherwise we should get only a partial view of the resultant phenomena. We need also to be able to look back and forth across the expanse of time. If we were limited to a strictly chronological view we should not have the advantage which comes from foreknowledge. We should lose ourselves in the events of the moment, and our time sense would become less acute. It is only when we look back across the years that the force of time as a factor in our lives becomes fully apparent to us. The aspect of change is kept before us in *Wuthering Heights* by the fact that we never completely forget where we are in relation to the events depicted.

It goes almost without saying that *Wuthering Heights* is one of the most dramatic of English novels. When Mr. Earnshaw takes home a waif from the streets of Liverpool, he unwittingly introduces into his family a source of discord that comes near to destroying it and involving a neighboring family in the ruin. The arrival of Heathcliff causes division between father and son and later between brother and sister. Thence the contagion spreads to the Lintons through the agency of Catherine, whose early death is directly traceable to the conflict set up in her by her brother's degradation of the man she loves.

There is no necessity for the author to seek new and exciting turns of her plot as she proceeds. Her initial situation carries within it all the generative force required. The resentment of Heathcliff at his ill treatment accumulates until it finally breaks out with concentrated fury. Gradually thereafter it spends itself and subsides. After his death peace and tranquillity return to those who are left of the two families. Hareton and the second Catherine are happy young lovers, rambling on the moors, afraid now of nothing. The novel closes on the note of tranquillity when Lockwood visits the graves where the body of Heathcliff lies beside those of his rival Linton and his beloved Catherine:

"I lingered round them, under that benign sky; watched the moths fluttering among the heath and harebells, listened to the soft wind breathing through the grass, and wondered how any one could ever imagine unquiet slumbers for the sleepers in that quiet earth."

There is no intention here to suggest that nature is indifferent to the sufferings of man, as Hardy might have done. The discord, in Emily's view, is not *between* man and nature but *within* nature. Nature is not always in a state of equilibrium. Man, being a part of nature, is subject to disturbance when the forces governing him are thrown out of balance.

Wuthering Heights is a story of terrific conflict. The fury of Heathcliff is like the ungovernable fury of a storm. The feeling aroused in the reader is akin to the sense of powerlessness that one experiences in the presence of unleashed forces of nature. One can only wait for the tumult to subside and hope that not everything in the path of destruction will succumb. As in genuine tragedy, the powers which bring the characters into conflict and collision are powers which, once having been aroused and brought into action, must run their full course before order is restored. They are the expression not simply of chance or of human caprice but of the interweaving of passions and circumstances into an insoluble complex of forces as ruthless in its working as fate.

Death, as we have seen in *David Copperfield*, was frequently brought into Victorian fiction for reasons of sentiment or of sensation. The deaths in *Wuthering Heights*, of which there are several, have, however, a legitimate place in the novel. In a drama of time and of the changes wrought by time, death reminds us that we are subject to the laws of growth and decay. Moreover, the deaths of the more important characters, such as Catherine and Heathcliff, are handled dramatically, not sentimentally or melodramatically. Let us close our discussion by turning to a passage of a quieter kind. The death of Mr. Earnshaw, as related by Mrs. Dean, well illustrates the simplicity of the author and her refusal to adopt the strained, sentimental tone of the average Victorian in dealing with such occasions:

But the hour came, at last, that ended Mr. Earnshaw's troubles on earth. He died quietly in his chair one October evening, seated by the fireside. A high wind blustered round the house, and roared in the chimney: it sounded wild and stormy, yet it was not cold, and we were all together—I, a little removed from the hearth, busy at my knitting, and Joseph reading his Bible near the table (for the servants generally sat in the house then, after their work was done). Miss Cathy had been sick, and that made her still; she leant against her father's knee, and Heathcliff was lying on the floor with his head in her lap. I remember the master, before he fell into a doze, stroking her bonny hair—it pleased him rarely to see her gentle—and saying—"Why canst thou not always be a good lass, Cathy?" And she turned her face up to his, and laughed, and answered, "Why cannot you always be a good man, father?" But as soon as she saw him vexed again, she kissed his hand, and said she would sing him to sleep. She began singing very low, till his fingers dropped from hers, and his head sank on his breast. Then I told her to hush, and not stir, for fear she should wake him. We all kept as mute as mice a full half-hour, and should have done so longer, only Joseph, having finished his chapter, got up and said that he must rouse the master for prayers and bed. He stepped forward, and called him by name, and touched his shoulders; but he would not move, so he took the candle and looked at him. I thought there was something wrong as he set down the light; and seizing the children each by an arm, whispered them to "frame upstairs, and make little din—they might pray alone that evening —he had summut to do."

"I shall bid father good-night first," said Catherine, putting her arms round his neck, before we could hinder her. The poor thing discovered her loss directly—she screamed out—"Oh, he's dead, Heathcliff! he's dead!" And they both set up a heart-breaking cry.

I joined my wail to theirs, loud and bitter; but Joseph asked what we could be thinking of to roar in that way over a saint in heaven. He told me to put on my cloak and run to Gimmerton for the doctor and the parson. I could not guess the use that either would be of, then. However, I went, through wind and rain, and brought one, the doctor, back with me; the other said he would come in the morning. Leaving Joseph to explain matters; I ran to the children's room: their door was ajar, I saw they had never laid down, though it was past midnight; but they were calmer, and did not need me to console them. The little souls were comforting each other with better thoughts than I could have hit on: no parson in the world ever pictured heaven so beautifully as they did, in their innocent talk: and, while I sobbed and listened, I could not help wishing we were all there safe together.

CHAPTER XIII

The Psychological Novel

GEORGE ELIOT

In the work of the Brontës we have seen the point of view of fiction becoming more personal and less conventional. We have seen the novel being turned from its traditional attention to manners to a subjective view of experience. It remained for another woman to explore this newly opened region of feeling with systematic thoroughness and to point out the relation between it and the external world. It was George Eliot who took this additional step, in doing which she extended the frontiers of fictional art as it was then practiced in England. In her hands the novel acquired new and greater resourcefulness in the critical interpretation of experience. The study of character as the product of the dual forces of will and circumstance became one of her most noteworthy themes. She ordinarily took a broad view of conduct and, in examining the motives of her protagonists, attempted to evaluate the relative influence of both internal and external factors.

All novels, of course, have to pay some attention to the whys and wherefores of behavior. It is easy, however, to deal in a general, unspecified way with motives. Love, affection, greed, cowardice, vanity, desire for vengeance, and the like are, in their elementary states, so readily recognizable that they can be represented by very simple acts. It was in such a way that character was ordinarily represented in the novel of manners. The motive of an action was to be discerned in the action itself. Thus the characters of *Vanity Fair* were depicted from an external point of view, each character being so consistent and so decided in what he did that there was not much likelihood of his being misunderstood. The leading characters of *Jane Eyre* and *Wuthering Heights,* on the contrary, were represented from within, without much attention being paid to outside influences. These novels resembled the novel of manners in that motives were taken largely for granted, but they differed in the assumption of an inward starting point for behavior. To put the matter somewhat differently, we can say that the novelist of manners had been accustomed to look at people from the outside without examining closely into the individual shaping of motives. The Brontës, on the contrary, took an inward view of their characters but did not bring them into articulation with the forces of society. They did not study the formation of character as the product of an interaction between two worlds.

It was George Eliot who rendered conscious and particular what had been, for the most part, unconscious and general. She joined the two worlds of inward propensity and visible circumstance and showed them both operating in the lives of her characters. She thus initiated a new type of realism and set in motion a variety of developments, leading in the direction of both the naturalistic and the psychological novel. It may now seem surprising that a step so obviously in order had not been taken earlier. A number of conditions had to be fulfilled, however, before such a change could be effected. A novelist was needed who had enough familiarity with the intellectual outlook of the period to grasp its significance and enough imagination to be capable of projecting such knowledge into the terms of ordinary daily experience. George Eliot possessed such learning and imagination, and, moreover, she had the acumen to recognize that the process of living was a more complex matter than simple acquiescence in a narrow code of conduct.

One must not, of course, forget Balzac and Stendhal, both of whom wrote fiction anticipating the modern novel, about forty years before *Middlemarch* was published. Stendhal was modern in the way in which he individualized his characters, and Balzac combined the painting of social relations with the study of human nature. It was Balzac, according to Edith Wharton, who in joining the psychological novel and the novel of manners produced the modern novel. Neither Balzac nor Stendhal, however, had had any appreciable effect upon English novelists at the time of George Eliot. Not many years afterwards there was to be a marked change of attitude in England toward French fiction, but in respect to George Eliot such influences need hardly be considered.

It had nearly always been a characteristic of English novelists to take their art lightly and easily. The mocking gaiety of Fielding and Sterne had set a fashion that lingered even amid the moral strenuosity of Victorianism. There was nothing very easygoing, however, about George Eliot, even while she was still only Mary Ann Evans and novel writing was something not yet thought of. Life came near to being, for her, a schooling in anxiety. Her early break with the strict evangelical training of her childhood and her subsequent irregular union with George Henry Lewes, whom she could not marry, turned her life into a series of struggles—moral, religious, social—from which she never found peace, unless it was in the rather pathetic marriage to J. W. Cross when she was sixty years of age.

She never found peace, but she did find in her experiences an intensification of the sense of spiritual need. Coming under the influence of such thinkers as John Stuart Mill and Herbert Spencer, she became embued with a deep sense of the necessity of individual effort and saw in life an endless chain of consequences, in which a single act might endanger the permanent well-being of many lives. In her novels she sought to harmonize her sense of human dignity with her sense of human limitations. She sought likewise to show that the need of the individual for expansion and growth had to be brought into harmony with a sense of social responsibility. Conflicts involving relative degrees of good were always arising, for which it was not possible to find a solution by any rule-of-thumb methods. In a world of such endless possibilities for good and evil, spiritual torpor was seen as one of the least pardonable of faults.

Despite the differences between her and other novelists of the time, George Eliot was not a revolutionary either in attitude or in

method. She was more truly a child of her age than was either Charlotte or Emily Brontë, and in her novels, particularly the early ones,
she mirrored much that was characteristic of the Victorian temper
and habit of mind. The sentimental treatment of family life, the
rustic comedy and portrayal of personal idiosyncrasy, the moralizing tendency, the exposure of meanness, the extreme earnestness—
such characteristics were readily appreciated by readers of Dickens,
Thackeray, and Mrs. Gaskell. There was not much to frighten the
timid. The note of revolt was hardly to be perceived. Even the
"philosophy" was doubtless flattering to the self-esteem of the more
"advanced" type of reader. Whatever aversion to novel reading still
remained among the more puritanically inclined must have been
largely dissipated by a writer of such stern morality. Altogether,
George Eliot was an extremely popular novelist.

Nevertheless, although she had so much in common with other
Victorian novelists, she was different from them in at least one
important respect; and this difference caused her eventually to produce an essentially new type of novel. Furthermore, it is the new
trend in her work that is of most concern to us now, whatever it
was that appealed to her first readers. It was only in time that she
came into full command of herself. Readers who prefer *Adam Bede*
or *The Mill on the Floss* to *Middlemarch* probably do so because
there is less in the earlier novels of the author's more deliberate and
reflective manner. Yet it must be granted that it is the reflective
novelist who is the essential George Eliot. What is still somewhat
tentative in *The Mill on the Floss* comes to full realization in the
later novel.

A writer who makes a departure from tradition is not necessarily
aware of the real significance of his step or of the technical adjustments that it may entail. He is likely at first to rely upon the old
methods even though they are inadequate to his purpose. Although
such broad histories as *Pendennis* and *Barchester Towers* were not
suitable models for her treatment of special themes, George Eliot
was influenced by the old loose type of novel. She failed at first
to make a clear distinction between the purpose of such fiction and
her own more particular purpose.

In Adam Bede, for example, her definiteness of theme gave a dramatic center to her story which could not but affect the position of the minor characters. In the older novel a minor character could occupy the center of the stage part of the time without serious offense because he was an admitted part of the spectacle. But such irresponsibility was not suited to Adam Bede, where the issues at stake were all highly serious. Consequently the background should have been managed more strictly with regard to the light which it could be made to throw upon the central situation. In her later novels the author came to recognize this necessity of exercising greater control over her material. In her early novels, however, she allowed her minor characters to assume an importance out of proportion to their dramatic function. Instead of establishing a clear view of the situation of Hetty Sorrel, at the beginning of Adam Bede, she devoted the first sixteen chapters, or approximately a third of the novel, to a leisurely introduction to the various groups of characters.

Such discursiveness produces an impression of clumsiness and leaves the central point at issue somewhat obscure even after a hundred and fifty pages of introduction. Similarly The Mill on the Floss would have gained in dramatic effectiveness if the background of uncles and aunts had been more strictly controlled by its function of contributing to the situation of the heroine and ultimately to her development. A certain amount of vagueness is attributable to the fact that some of the characters have not been handled with sufficient attention to the main purpose of the novel. Is Mrs. Poyser, in Adam Bede, intended to entertain us with her sharp tongue, or is her want of sympathy in dealing with Hetty intended to be a factor in that young lady's fall? Here we have an example of a fundamental difference between the irresponsibility permissible to Dickens and the strict attention to detail necessitated by George Eliot's theory of consequence.

The handling of Mrs. Poyser and Hetty in relation to each other fails to reveal either the detachment or the imagination which the situation requires. The view of Mrs. Poyser is too general and that of Hetty is too narrow. We see the girl from the point of view of the woman, but we do not see the woman from the point of view of the girl. The manner in which Hetty is presented to us serves, in fact, to cut her off from our sympathy. However, if her conduct is to lead to such dire consequences, we need to be given a more inclusive view of the conditions out of which it sprang. For the author to condemn Hetty as she does for the so-called triviality of her emotions and her childish vanity is to take a rather stern view of human nature. It would seem that George Eliot, being herself a strong-minded woman, could not take a lenient view of the butterfly type of femininity.

This failure to be sufficiently objective in dealing with Hetty illustrates the fact that for her kind of character portrayal the author of *Adam Bede* could not follow the traditional methods used in the novel of manners. It was not right for her to employ the old formulas of comedy or sentimentalism. Neither was she justified in seeking thrilling incidents or in dwelling on casual idiosyncrasies. Her purpose was to make a study of human behavior in the light of what she knew about human nature.

In making such a study of conduct, it was necessary for her to show natural causes in operation and to subject individuals to the thwarting force of circumstances. The old-fashioned type of character that was either too good or too bad to succumb to any influence would obviously not be satisfactory for such a purpose. To conceive a character as being inflexibly good or unalterably bad was incompatible with the effort to portray the development of character. The hard and fast distinction between good and bad characters had eventually to be discarded. Moral judgment required that circumstances be considered as well as motives.

In the new type of novel there was a need for leading characters who were more self-conscious and more aware of their surroundings than the novel of manners had required. Minor characters had to be fitted more carefully into the background. The intrusion of the author became less justifiable, because the characters, having ceased to be puppets, needed to have the appearance of being left to themselves. Moreover, it was essential for the author to be a person of broad sympathies and unbiased attitude, able to take a full and understanding view of the circumstances underlying conduct. A new kind of plot became necessary, neither casual nor arbitrary, the determining principle of which was simply the logical demands of the situation and the character.

George Eliot, of course, did not accomplish all these things. She was not free of all prejudice, and she did not know enough about mankind to be always adequate or convincing. She oversimplified the workings of cause and effect, and she overstressed the importance of single happenings. She made behavior too much a matter of the full consciousness and of straining of will. Nevertheless, she took the important step for English novelists of viewing character as a complex of inner and outer relationships. This step was sufficient to produce a great change in the course of the novel. The fact that her knowledge was inadequate did not greatly matter so far as the change of method was affected. It was the new view of character that made necessary the change in the technique of presentation.

Thus, whatever may be her faults, she is historically important. She is memorable less for her execution than for her vigorous grasp of a few significant and far-reaching truths. She has left nothing equal in the perfection of its execution to *Vanity Fair* or *Emma*, but *Vanity Fair* represents the flowering of an old form whereas *Middlemarch* is without distinct prototypes in English fiction except in the author's own earlier work.

The failure to achieve complete control over her medium was a penalty that, under the circumstances, a more gifted writer might well have had to pay. It was as if in her hands the novel suddenly relinquished the irresponsibility of youth and took upon itself the cares and responsibilities of age. It was as if a child had cast aside the carefree garments of his childhood and put on the attire of a man, feeling at first, despite pride in his new estate, a little awkward and constrained. It would take time to learn to wear the new garments easily and unself-consciously. It would take time to recapture the warmhearted spontaneity and grace which had frequently lighted up the earlier time. In short, it was as if the English novel were now entering upon its "awkward age."

Middlemarch

When she wrote *Middlemarch*, George Eliot was a person of considerable consequence, having already published five full-length novels besides the shorter pieces in *Scenes of Clerical Life*. Although the earlier novels had come quickly and easily from her pen, there had been a decided slowing up after *Silas Marner*. *Romola* and *Felix Holt* show the author's method evolving into a more painstaking and systematic kind of realism, based not so much upon reminiscence or upon imitation of established forms but spun more and more completely out of her moral and intellectual consciousness. Despite the danger of such a change leading to artificiality, the change itself was but the logical development of what was implicit in the novels from the beginning. To understand the author to the best advantage it is thus necessary to examine the later work. *Middlemarch* is a more thoroughly satisfactory vehicle for study than any of the early novels because in it the author is more completely herself. Despite their freshness and humor, the early novels are not so completely original. In them the writer is still handicapped by a more or less unconscious clinging to traditional ways. In *Middlemarch* she has worked out her method and has not yet got out of touch with ordinary experience. Observation has not yet been displaced by invention, as it was, in some measure, in *Daniel Deronda*. If there is more artifice in *Middlemarch* than in *Adam Bede*, there is also more art; and there is also a better balance between understanding and sympathy. Weakness is exposed unflinchingly but not unfeelingly, particularly when, as is often the case, it brings suffering to those who are not at fault. The moral problems as here set forth are too complex to be solved by the application of any simple formula. Obligations are shown to be divided, and the desire to do good runs frequently into surprising and unforeseen obstacles. Not everything can be left to the simple functioning of the will. Intelligence and foresight must be brought into play in finding a way that can be made to prevail.

As Thackeray had given to *Vanity Fair* the subtitle *Pen and Pencil Sketches of English Society*, George Eliot likewise enlarged the title of *Middlemarch* by calling it *A Study of Provincial Life*. Although the similarity of titles may suggest a similarity of aims there is, in reality, an important difference. *Vanity Fair* is about society; *Middlemarch* is about individuals. The former subordinates the individual to the general picture of society. What happens to the individual does not greatly matter; we are not primarily concerned about the fortunes of any of the characters. What happens to Dorothea or to Lydgate, however, concerns us greatly. What happens to them, in fact, is symbolic of what happens in some measure to all of us.

Curiously enough, although Thackeray devoted so much attention to society and to the hollowness of the men and women who constituted it, he did not examine into the nature of the workings of society upon the individual. He seems to have assumed that what was wrong with society was simply what was wrong with the individuals who, like so many integers, composed it. He did not take into account, apparently, the fact that the influence between society and the individual was not all exerted in one direction. He did not pay much attention to the fact that the pressure of the group upon the individual might be a factor of greater importance in shaping character than the personal inclinations which he vaguely took for granted. In short, Thackeray did not make it his business to look into the mechanism of society. To him society was not much more than a composite picture cf human nature.

However, if we may say that Thackeray made the mistake of viewing society as a composite individual, there is some justification for saying that George Eliot sometimes fell into the opposite error or seeing in each individual the working of the laws of society. What is true in general of a social organism is by no means necessarily true of each individual therein. Insurance tables may be quite accurate in forecasting the average duration of life of men who have reached fifty, but a *man* of fifty cannot ascertain therefrom how long he himself will live. In reading the novels of George Eliot, one is likely to gain the impression that the characters have been subjected to too rigorous an application of law. In the novel of manners the characters had been granted a certain degree of freedom. Some aspects of behavior were disregarded in the interest of general truth, and, at the same time, general truth was sometimes sacrificed in the interest of individual variation. George Eliot, on the contrary, was inclined to grant her characters too little freedom. She sacrificed individual variation in the interest of general truth. Whereas the older novelists had worked with casually related acts of casually related individuals, being bound only by the need to conform to general truth, the new point of view required the novelist to look explicitly at the continuity of individual behavior. Under such necessity the author of *Middlemarch* sometimes charted the development of character with such precision as to give the impression of a demonstration. It is one of the dangers of philosophical fiction that the intelligence tends to bring the material which it works upon into too complete subjection. It neglects the more imponderable aspects of character and transforms experience into a series of illustrative acts. So controlled, the characters give the impression of performing rather than of living in their own right.

Art like life, however, needs change and growth in order to retain its vitality. In changing the novelist's angle of vision, George Eliot created for herself difficulties that she did not altogether surmount. Nevertheless, it was no small thing to turn the novel away from its preoccupation with comedy and sentiment. Much of what has since been dealt with in fiction is the natural outgrowth of this change of direction and of emphasis. The individual at odds with his environment has been a familiar figure to more than two generations of readers. The theme of *Middlemarch* has now been handled in a great variety of ways. Put briefly, it is simply the problem of individual growth and ambition in the face of adverse social or environmental conditions. It is life attempting to give shape and direction to itself and seeking to accomplish more than mere material satisfaction. It is, in short, one of the most familiar situations in the world, not new to the experience of our time but still highly pertinent. The Rougon-Macquart series of novels, by Émile Zola, which was begun at about the time *Middlemarch* was published, represents an extension of the theme, and Carol Kennicott, of *Main Street*, is an American version of the time-honored motive represented by Dorothea Brooke.

In the novel of manners the characteristic situation had been the clash of opposing personalities. It was a struggle between particu-

lars, but particulars which were intended to typify various aspects
of the general. In *Middlemarch,* however, the struggle is not between particularizations of the general but between the particular
and the general, or between the individual and his surroundings.
For example, the difficulty which arises between Dr. Lydgate and
his wife is not a mere conflict of one person with another. The hostility of Rosamond to her husband's aims is essentially the hostility
of an unenlightened Philistine society to a view of life that it cannot comprehend. Similarly, Dorothea has to struggle against general
indifference or hostility to her aspirations.

The great length of *Middlemarch* is more justifiable than the excessive length of many Victorian novels. An attempt to show the
lives of a number of people reacting one upon the other makes necessary the representation of what is essentially a complex process.
The author wished to deal with ordinary rather than exceptional
situations and to show the process of adjustment under different
conditions. Although the circumstances under which Lydgate bor-
rows money from Bulstrode are not ordinary, the turning of innocence into the appearance of guilt is a common enough happening,
particularly when envy and malice have been aroused.

Middlemarch has sometimes been criticized as not being unified.
The careers of Lydgate and Dorothea are, for the most part, separate and distinct from each other. There is also the story of Fred
Vincy, which is too much like a separate episode. These stories
were intended, of course, to throw light upon the spirit of provincialism in a community in which people devoted themselves to material things and tolerated culture only in the most superficial form.
For such social and intellectual desires as were felt by Dorothea and
Lydgate, the inhabitants of Middlemarch had virtually no understanding or sympathy. Being blind to such aspirations, they were
inclined to assign petty or ignoble motives to what they could not
understand and to waste their energy in shallow personal rivalries.
They distrusted whatever disturbed them or seemed to threaten
their settled way of life.

Considered as a study of provincialism, *Middlemarch* is somewhat analogous to what Zola was beginning to do in France. The
view of life held by the French naturalist would probably have

repelled the English woman, but his aims were much like hers. Both writers were concerned with the struggle between man and his environment. As a picture of a community *Middlemarch* can be compared with *Germinal,* a picture of a mining community. One important difference between the two novels is the fact that Zola makes the swarming mass of laborers the central thing in his novel, whereas George Eliot accentuates a few individuals against the background of community life. The difference of emphasis represents a corresponding difference between the two points of view. One writer sees man as under the control of material forces, while the other wishes to demonstrate the efficacy of the individual will. One pictures the individual as being crushed but destined to rise eventually through the power of united action; the other holds that the individual who remains true to his more enlightened impulses can achieve some measure of success.

Zola, who wishes to depict a representative mining community, can derive unity of impression for his massive document from the descriptions of the mine itself, into which the workers fit like the wheels of a great machine. Accordingly the major and minor characters function in much the same way with respect to the central theme, each one helping to illustrate the devastating power of the social and economic forces at work in the mine mechanism. *Middlemarch,* considered in a similar light, represents the destructive forces of provincial life at work upon the individual. Here the problem is a more complex one, however, than in *Germinal.* The issue is not between man and the machine, but between man in his capacity as an individual and mankind in the mass. The majority of characters, who represent the provincial spirit, are quiescent and resistant to change. Against their passive indifference and unimaginativeness, the aspiring characters have to wage an unceasing battle, as the miners have to struggle against the hardships and privations of their lot. But whereas Zola can show the process permeating his entire community, George Eliot can show her process only in a limited number of individuals. In the case of *Middlemarch* our interest in the community is incidental to our interest in those who are most seriously at odds with community ideals.

We are thus brought back to the point that the unity of impression in *Middlemarch* depends more upon the relationship of the various struggles to the idea of individual development than upon the picture of the community itself. Inasmuch as the problem of adaptation varies somewhat with each individual, the author probably felt that it was desirable to examine the problem with different characters in different circumstances and reflecting different degrees of success and failure. She could hardly avoid being arbitrary in her selection of representative cases. There were advantages to be derived from a broad and inclusive treatment and corresponding difficulties to be surmounted. By shifting the angle of illumination she could bring into view more of the salient features of her theme and give a greater sense of authority to her rendering of it. The multiplication of examples was not in itself a disadvantage. We cannot say that the novel lacks unity simply because it traces the careers of more than one person.

How well these separate threads combine into a unified impression is, however, another matter. Are they all equally convincing, or do they all illustrate different aspects of the same general process? It can hardly be asserted that they do. The position of Bulstrode in the community is not analogous to that of Lydgate or Dorothea. Yet his affairs are presented in too great detail for him to be regarded as a mere accessory to the downward course of Lydgate. Fred Vincy, while occupying a role similar to that of the other leading characters, is not handled with equal conviction. In dealing with this one of her protagonists, the author seems to relax from her customary severity. That such a person as Fred should succeed in a world which defeats Lydgate might be taken as a stroke of irony were it not clear that the author does not so intend it. Young Vincy is meant to represent the average character, being different both from the high idealism of Dorothea and from the more commanding personality of Lydgate. He succeeds, with the help of Mary Garth, because he refuses to enter a profession for which he is not fit. His character, however, is not fully realized. His troubles never command our sympathy as Lydgate's do, but seem, for the most part, petty and a little tiresome.

It is Lydgate and Dorothea who give to *Middlemarch* its most significant passages. In them we are confronted by a new range and

depth of spiritual consciousness. It is Dorothea who best represents
the need of the individual for self-development. She is the character
most definitely in rebellion against the universal apathy of her
surroundings. The society in which she lives does not provide
nourishment for her hunger. It expects her to satisfy herself in
marriage but fails to provide an opportunity for such a marriage
as would be likely to satisfy her. She has faults but the community
is in some degree responsible for her mistakes. A society which
thus hedges its young women in with restrictions, denying them
the opportunity to exercise their faculties, must be held partly to
blame if those who are so restricted grow restless and discontented.

The situation of Dorothea is fraught with peril. Young, ardent,
ignorant, oppressed by yearning for a more exalted life, she has no
one to turn to for sympathetic counsel. Her social life, it seems to
her, is "a labyrinth of petty courses, a walled-in maze of small
paths," which lead to nothing. She will escape from this captivity,
she thinks, by devoting herself to Mr. Casaubon, who will lead her
out of the blindness and narrowness of her lot and share with her
the inspiration of his own great work. So, under the fatal illusion
that he possesses the fervency of spirit which is, in reality, in herself,
she marries him, unaware that he is a narrow, frustrated, bitterly
disappointed man. How far he is from measuring up to her conception of him, she is soon to learn. By her marriage she exchanges one
set of trivial circumstances for another still more galling. She fails
to find in her union the expected inspiration, but she does find a
more formidable bondage than anything she has ever known. She
has to learn to school herself in patience and to guard even against
her natural tenderness for fear of touching inadvertently one of the
exposed nerves of her husband's vanity or self-distrust. She has to
curb her youthfulness out of respect for his age, to tone down her
enthusiasm out of consideration for his weariness. What she has
fondly expected will be the contagion of his spirit becomes instead
a heavy weight upon her own, which, for various reasons, she can
do little to combat. The high hope with which she enters marriage
cannot last even through the honeymoon. "There is hardly any
contact," comments the author, "more depressing to a young ardent

creature than that of a mind in which years full of knowledge seem to have issued in a blank absence of interest or sympathy." It is into such a contact, permanent and binding, that Dorothea is led by the inadequacies of her surroundings and the meanness of her opportunities.

How different George Eliot's art is from that of the earlier novelists is well illustrated by the intricacy of feeling and the complexity of relationship that soon result from this unfortunate marriage. The discovery by Casaubon, who also has illusions, that a beautiful young wife can judge a man, as well as worship him, puts a new aspect upon the bliss that he has promised himself. The advent of Ladislaw leads to a whole series of disturbances. Ladislaw's ebullient youth is a mute reminder to the husband of his age and of his inadequacy as the companion of a young wife. Dorothea's eagerness to see what she considers to be justice done to Ladislaw is easily subject to misinterpretation. Furthermore, the scant respect which he has for the husband makes the young man a dangerous companion for the wife. Already harassed by secret doubts about his ability ever to complete his study of mythology, Casaubon is on the alert for any sign of weakening faith in Dorothea.

Caught in the toils of jealousy and suspicion, he cannot take the slightest act of his wife for what it is. If she is silent, it is a sign that she is rebellious; her liveliness indicates a feeling of superiority; if she is gentle, she is being irritatingly cautious; if she acquiesces in what he says, she is treating him with forbearance. Such touchiness, difficult enough in itself, is soon made more troublesome by an affection of the heart, which renders any kind of shock exceedingly dangerous to him. Dorothea does not fail in the emergency, though at some cost to her peace of mind, particularly when she is called upon by her husband to pledge herself to the continuation of his work after his death—work in which she has now ceased to have faith.

So complete does her subjection become that not even the death of her husband sets her free. She will be looking into his papers for instructions to follow beyond the grave. Fortunately for her, however, she learns of the provision that Casaubon has added to his will. It is the news of this act, reflecting so unjustly upon her, that serves to release her from her bondage. Broken to her casually by Celia, who has her own idea about how to handle "Dodo," it sends her world crashing about her feet. Here we are brought into the very heart of the problem of human relations, as we see her in the process of readjusting herself to a new conception of her departed husband:

> She might have compared her experience at that moment to the vague, alarmed consciousness that her life was taking on a new form, that she was undergoing a metamorphosis in which memory would not adjust itself to the stirring of new organs. Everything was changing its aspect: her husband's conduct, her own duteous feeling toward him, every struggle between them—and yet more, her whole relation to Will Ladislaw. Her world was in a state of convulsive change; the only thing she could say distinctly to herself was, that she must wait and think anew. One change terrified her as if it had been sin; it was a violent shock of repulsion from her departed husband, who had had hidden thoughts, perhaps perverting everything she said and did. Then again she was conscious of another change which also made her tremulous; it was a sudden strange yearning of heart toward Will Ladislaw. It had never before entered her mind that he could, under any circumstances, be her lover; conceive the effect of the sudden revelation that another had thought of him in that light—that perhaps he himself had been conscious of such a possibility—and this with the hurrying, crowding vision of unfitting conditions, and questions not soon to be solved.

The situation of Dorothea represents the dilemma of a woman of sensitive nature struggling against the thwarting influences of an environment that denies to women of her class the opportunity of a full and active life. In the story of Lydgate the problem of individual development is examined under different circumstances. He fails not through lack of opportunity, but through lack of balance and through making an unfortunate marriage. He is young, intelligent, and full of enthusiasm for his work; one would expect him to succeed. Success of the high kind to which he aspires eludes him not because he is wanting in ability but because of the way circumstances turn against him. Events seem to conspire against him; they could not damage him so much, however, had he not by his own weakness made himself vulnerable. It is not simply chance that defeats him but chance in collaboration with character.

What I have referred to as his lack of balance is to be seen in his failure to adjust himself in all things to his surroundings. In that part of his life which is related to his patients' needs he is quick to act intelligently, but in the larger realm of feeling he is sometimes capable of blundering. His impatience of dullness causes him needlessly to offend people at times and thus to arouse resentment against himself. His highborn dislike of narrowness makes it easy for him to slip into an extravagant mode of living, and his unwillingness to face disagreeable necessities betrays him into compromises with his better judgment—compromises that later return to plague him.

Without being so excusable as Dorothea, he makes an unwise marriage. A man of finer perceptions would probably not have chosen as wife a woman of such shallow charm and narrow sympathies as Rosamond. He is under illusions about her, however, and does not see her as she is. It is this marriage, more than anything else, that is responsible for the ultimate failure of Lydgate. The manner in which he is shown sinking gradually under the weight of accumulating difficulties is one of the most memorable features of the novel. Finally, struggling under a cloud of suspicion, without sympathy from his wife, and feeling the smart of an almost universal distrust, he encounters Dorothea, and the drama now rises to its most poignant note. Never has he been so much in need of such an expression of faith in him as Dorothea simply and unreservedly pours forth.

The effort of Bulstrode to live down his past is a different kind of situation from that of Lydgate or of Dorothea. It introduces into *Middlemarch* a theme which had been prominent in some of the earlier novels—that of moral retribution. Bulstrode's problem is not that of adjusting himself to the practical demands of a career, but is a matter of honesty with himself. His failure to take the first step toward moral rehabilitation renders futile all his elaborate measures for bolstering his self-esteem. For such contrition as he exhibits, we can have little pity, but we can sympathize with his wife, who partakes of his humiliation, and with Lydgate, another victim of his fall. The depiction of his state of mind while he is under the fear of exposure is added proof of the author's understanding of mental behavior.

Although such a study of human relations as was made by George Eliot required her to employ a complex method, it did not require her to employ the artificial intricacy of the earlier novel of intrigue. Her novels would have retained their early popularity longer if she had not had a tendency to overdevelopment and to unnecessarily elaborate treatment. We get more of Farebrother and of Feather-stone than is strictly necessary. The complicated past of Bulstrode is reminiscent of the manner of Dickens, although Bulstrode is by no means a Dickensian character. The effect of such complexity, added to the more legitimate complexity of moral causation, leaves the novels sometimes cumbersome and laborious. Moreover, for the author to insist always upon the consequences of behavior is to forget that life can be an adventure as well as a schooling in discipline. A too great sense of responsibility can act as a blight upon life as well as a deepening influence.

Looking at the work of George Eliot in comparison with Thackeray's, we find it lacking in suavity and grace. It is not so perfectly poised and well proportioned as Miss Austen's; nor does it glow with the ardent feeling of the Brontës. It is inferior to the work of Hardy in strength of imagination and to that of James in symmetry and in richness and delicacy of perception. Nevertheless, *Middlemarch* is one of the great English novels, deep in feeling and strong in its grasp of the problems that beset mankind.

CHAPTER XIV

The Comic Spirit

GEORGE MEREDITH

George Meredith as a writer is so strikingly different from George Eliot in mood and in manner of expression that the casual reader may easily fail to recognize the great community of interest existing between them. Far from being grave and methodical, Meredith is characteristically ironical and epigrammatic. His language is supple and effervescent, full of swift turns and surprises, sometimes tangled and confused in an excess of metaphor. Yet the two writers are in some essential respects similar to each other. They both represent liberating trends in the thought of their time. They both criticize society and show a growing alertness to the action of society upon the individual. The characters drawn by each of them are more aware of themselves than the characters of the older novels had been, and they go through a more distinct process of development. Though less grim in his morality than George Eliot, Meredith evinces with her the Victorian tendency to address the reader and to indulge in admonishment and exhortation.

Like George Eliot, too, Meredith is interested in the problem of spiritual autonomy for the individual. His first regular novel, *The Ordeal of Richard Feverel,* deals with the attempt of a father to regulate each stage of his son's development, in the hope that thus he can guard the young man from the blunders of youthful exuberance. This interference, by depriving Richard of the power to act independently, increases the danger which it has been designed to forestall. Eventually it breeds misunderstanding and loss of confidence between father and son and leads to a permanent blighting of the young man's life.

Meredith does not ordinarily take up the struggle between the individual and society in such direct form as it occurs in *Middlemarch*. He prefers to deal with more purely personal relationships in which society figures indirectly or by implication. Society creates artificial situations, which in turn give rise to unnatural forms of behavior. The resultant complexity of impulse and confusion of motive may cause an individual to become involved in a conflict that is at once social and personal.

A favorite theme of Meredith, in this connection, is his belief that a proper functioning together of blood, brain, and spirit is necessary to harmonious development. Right thinking and wholesome feelings are possible only upon a foundation of sound instincts. We are not to look with disdain upon that part of our being which lies embedded in animal instinct. Such thinking recognizes the complex character of human nature and perceives that the individual cannot be treated simply as an isolated unit in society.

It sees man as a link in a chain of natural and spiritual law and insists that we must meet life with a spirit of affirmation and faith, not fretting because of our limitations. Not the least of the lessons we can learn from nature is to accept life gladly on its own terms. Content to follow her reciprocal course of growth and decay, nature stores up in the autumn the seeds of another season's growth. Taking his cue from this example of natural law, Meredith would have us look beyond the limitations of our lot to the larger process of which our lives are a part:

> Teach me to feel myself the tree,
> And not the withered leaf.

We must submit to nature's law, and we must cling to the warmth of passion while we bow to the wisdom of experience. In his poem "Modern Love," Meredith complains that only when passion wanes does wisdom come to our aid, and he contrasts our faltering human speech with the song of the lark in the following lines of "The Lark Ascending":

> Our wisdom speaks from failing blood,
> Our passion is too full in flood,
> We want the key of his wild note
> Of truthful in a tuneful throat.

Here and elsewhere Meredith shows himself to be the champion of a balanced view of life, which mingles intellectuality and feeling and combines the material and the spiritual.

Acceptance, not denial, was Meredith's watchword. It is not by denying the flesh, by sacrificing passion, he thought, that we solve our problems. The instincts are not to be chained down but to be freed from repression and brought into disciplined harmony with the rest of life. Meredith attacked the prejudices that had sprung from a repressive code of behavior and helped to clear the atmosphere of the conspiracy of silence preventing the free discussion of many important topics.

The dilemma of man being pulled in two directions at once, unable to combine the instinctive and the rational, was a problem that haunted Meredith's generation. It had long been a habit of Victorian convention to look with suspicion upon pleasure and the desires of the senses. Consequently, in attempting to redress the balance somewhat in favor of a less purely rational view of life, Meredith was engaged in a work of rehabilitation. It is possible that his interest in the problem of a balanced and disciplined life sprang from a sense of personal need. An advocate of discipline, he remained, on the whole, an undisciplined writer. A champion of naturalness as opposed to artifice, he seems to have been incapable of employing a simple mode of expression. An anatomist of difficult problems of relationship, he failed in his own life, there is evidence for believing, to keep on good terms with his father, with his first wife, and with his son.

Perhaps the novelist himself suffered from lack of balance. A prophet of stability and harmony, he was torn by contradictions, whereas Hardy, by comparison a prophet of discord, was temperamentally at peace. Thus interpreted, the thought of Meredith was nurtured upon anxiety, and his searching studies of uneasy relationships between men, or between men and women, were to some extent the products of deep and disquieting self-knowledge.

There is no occasion to attach great importance to such a hypothesis. Not uncommonly does the artistic process contain some such element of compensation. Let us simply recognize that the human problem as grasped by Meredith was a problem of full and symmetrical development. The Meredithean conflict was not a conflict between greed and altruism, as in the world of Dickens, or between vain display and unpretending honesty of feeling, as in the Thackerayan fable. It was essentially a conflict between nature and some falsification or distortion of nature. Sir Austin Feverel, for example, in attempting to play Providence to his son, became the victim of a delusion. He failed to realize that his great interest in his son was more a matter of pride in his system of education than of genuine feeling for Richard. The issue, we see, was not between saints and sinners but between honest self-knowledge and well-meaning but deluded self-indulgence.

Despite his liberality of thought, Meredith did not approve of the trend toward objectivity characteristic of the fiction of his time. The French naturalists were undertaking to set forth their material in such a way that direct commentary about it was not necessary. They preferred an exact representation of particulars to general discussion and explanation. Maupassant, in his preface to *Pierre et Jean*, in 1887, championed such a method, saying that the novelist who wished to give an exact representation of the spectacle of life should accomplish his purpose not by explanation and analysis but by a careful manipulation of small facts. Such a novelist would conceal his plot and his psychology just as the painter of a portrait would refuse to show the skeleton of his subject.

Meredith did not approve of such a method of representation. In the opening section of *The Egoist*, he said that "the realistic method of a conscientious transcription of all the visible and a repetition of all the audible" was responsible for the production of a vast amount of noise and monotony. One of the perils of civilization, he argued, was its tendency to accumulate an excess of material. It was as if modern progress had transported us into a "land of foghorns," from which escape was to be made not by inquiry into the infinitesimal, in the manner of realism, but by a "broad Alpine survey of the spirit born of our united social intelligence," by which he meant to characterize the spirit that ruled over comedy.

In the opening chapter of *Diana of the Crossways,* Meredith again condemned realism as being an immature form of art devoted to the representation of the material fact, giving "the odor of the roast" but not embracing the whole truth. Two rival kinds of fiction, he said, rose-pink and dirty drab, were engaged in a battle of extremes. By "dirty drab" he meant naturalistic realism, with its emphasis upon squalidness, and by "rose-pink" he was referring to the sentimental type of novel which turned its back upon actuality and sought beguilement in mere prettification. Both forms were to be abhorred. Sentimental "rose-pink," while making a pretense of spirituality, was at bottom as grossly material as realism. By neither of these routes, Meredith believed, could one hope to arrive at a true depiction of reality.

To correct such deformities and guide the novelist in his search for truth, philosophy, in Meredith's view, was what was needed. Philosophy would invest the pantomime of fiction with new force and dignity. Philosophy would teach the sentimentalist respect for nature's fleshly processes, and it would bring animation and shapeliness into the desert tracts of the realist. A philosophical fiction, in short, would perform the valuable service of helping to civilize mankind.

This demand for philosophy in fiction reflects the opposition of Meredith to a mechanistic view of the universe and is another expression of his faith in intelligence as a contributing factor to progress. It corresponds both to his theory of art, as expressed in the *Essay on Comedy and the Uses of the Comic Spirit,* and to his theory of a spiritual order in nature. The comic spirit he considered to be a form of perception, a free and disinterested play of the mind. Being social in character, it enables its possessor to measure himself against the social norm. Its foundation is in common sense rather than in pure intellectuality. Being the product of a balanced set of forces, it acts upon the individual as a balancing agent.

Springing from knowledge tempered by experience, the comic

spirit does not expect too much of men. Let us presume that it expects to find in them the honest self-knowledge and freedom from delusion which are esssential to a civilized society. It does not laugh derisively in the manner of satire, for, being purely perceptual in character, it has no desire to wound. The only lash it wields is the lash it enables its victim to apply to himself. Though essentially corrective in its action as a social agent, it does not spring, in its pure state, from any desire to correct mankind. Its potency in this regard is doubtless heightened by its disinterestedness, for we can bear with more composure the ridicule of those who dislike us than of those who have no cause to find us ridiculous. Disinterested ridicule is likely to be a more truthful form of criticism than that which springs from ulterior motives; in the last analysis, it is only the truth that hurts.

There is no necessary contradiction between this view of the comic spirit and Bergson's contention that the source of laughter resides in mechanical inelasticity of mind or body. Both conceptions emphasize the necessity of an unflagging mental awareness, and both theories also make of comedy a social weapon. The comic spirit, of course, is not to be confused with the comic character or with comedy in general. The comic spirit is, in fact, such a form of balanced perceptiveness as enables its possessor to avoid becoming himself a victim of comedy.

Comedy is most effective, Meredith believes, when it is kept free of sentiment. Sentimental people, he says in the *Essay on Comedy,* dislike comedy because they object to facing the actual world. Comedy frightens them by showing them things about themselves that they wish to ignore. Humorous writing they can endure because it contains an appeal to their feelings. Satire they may find pleasure in because it flatters them into a sense of superiority to the objects under attack.

These distinctions contain the implication that the presence in comedy of a direct appeal to the feelings, either sympathetic or derisive, lessens its value for cultivated men and women and destroys something of its validity as a civilizing force. We laugh at the characters of Dickens, for example, without identifying ourselves with them. Pure comedy, however, does not let us off so easily. It is by nature severe and inflexible, holding up the mirror for us to gaze at our own faults. Meredith believes, in fact, that the ability of a society to appreciate comedy is an index of its state of culture.

British novelists have not in general viewed their material in a purely comic light. They have allowed other considerations to mingle with the comic idea. When we think of Smollett and Sterne and Scott, we are likely to think of humor and sentiment and farce and satire in various degrees and combinations. Although scenes of unadulterated comedy sometimes occur in their novels, the effect in general is mixed. In being thus mixed it reflects the tendency of modern literature to turn away from classical tradition to an increasingly greater realism.

The Egoist

The novel of Meredith that serves to illustrate his comic art most thoroughly is *The Egoist*. Appearing in 1879, two years after the famous lecture upon comedy, to which I have referred, it shows the author consciously engaged in putting into practice his theory of the uses of the comic spirit. Its title in full is *The Egoist: a Comedy in Narrative,* and the extent to which it has been conceived as a comedy is everywhere apparent. It opens with a commentary upon comedy and the comic spirit, and a discussion of the function of comedy in combating the malady of egoism. Its central figure, Sir Willoughby Patterne, is enclosed in a ring of comic irony from which there is no escape. The comic aspect of his pretensions is never for a moment lost sight of. He is conceived of as being attended on his rounds by certain creatures of fantasy, typifying the imps of comedy. They are the hounds of the Comic Muse, so to speak, and have scented Sir Willoughby as their game.

His selection of a comic form of presentation places Meredith in the company of such earlier novelists as Fielding and Jane Austen. Though resembling Fielding in philosophic temper and in the mingling of merriment with underlying seriousness of purpose, he does not allow his imagination to range over such a wide area. Instead of plunging his reader into a crowded world of diverse types and miscellaneous adventures, he withdraws into the secluded atmosphere of a gentleman's estate, from which the hubbub of the world is excluded.

His method is more frankly artificial than Miss Austen's, in whose work there is an effect of greater naturalness than in the kind of drawing-room comedy that has served as a model for *The Egoist*. "Human nature in the drawing-room" Meredith takes to be the proper material of comedy, and he cares less for particulars, either places or people, than Miss Austen. "Credulity is not wooed through the impressionable senses," he proclaims in the opening paragraph of *The Egoist*, and adds: "The Comic Spirit conceives a definite situation for a number of characters, and rejects all accessories in the exclusive pursuit of them and their speech." Accordingly we are not to expect him to devote much attention to the problem of providing his characters with a normal round of daily activity—a matter so expertly managed by Miss Austen. Moreover, as he does not limit himself in the same measure to dramatic presentment, his characters are less free than Miss Austen's from the sense of being interfered with. They do not have the same unstudied air of being left to themselves.

Notwithstanding the marks of similarity between Meredith and Fielding, such as the essay-like introduction and the general attitude of irony, there are other points which remind us of Richardson. The hero of *The Egoist* would make a strange figure beside Tom Jones, whereas he would not be at all out of place in the company of Sir Charles Grandison. In fact, if Sir Willoughby were to be shifted, by some magic, into the role of Sir Charles and presented there without irony, he would make a very creditable showing. The situation of having several young women in love with him would be to his liking, and, although he might not prove to be so competent in the management of affairs as the illustrious Sir Charles, he would take an equal pleasure in his role and would not let any of its magnificence escape him.

It is Richardson, too, rather than Fielding, that Meredith resembles in making his novel an elaborate analysis of a special situation instead of a compendium of materials drawn from varied sources. Just as the whole vast structure of *Clarissa* is controlled by a single spring, so to speak, in the heroine's character, in like manner is *The Egoist* dominated by the single purpose of exhibiting, in the character of a baronet, the damaging effects of egoism. Everything begins and ends with this purpose. There is nothing in the novel that is not in some way tied to it, from the vaguely conceived background of county families to the madcap exploits of young Crossjay. Even Clara Middleton and Laetitia Dale, who rank next to Sir Willoughby in interest and importance, are no exceptions to the rule in occupying positions in the scheme of the narrative distinctly subordinate to that of the hero. They are, in reality, chiefly important as agencies for bringing out to the full and rendering evident the egoism of the central personage.

In general design *The Egoist* bears a closer resemblance to comedy of the stage than to the less closely knit comedy of the novel. In being primarily the exposition of a single character, it resembles a play of Molière; in dealing with a deformity of character and showing a man caught in a trap of his own making, it follows general comic tradition. It is so limited in action and in the number of characters that it creates less of an impression of breadth than is commonly associated with the novel. It is like a product of the stage, too, particularly the comic stage, in the way in which the exposition of character overshadows action and setting.

If we omit the first four chapters, which are preliminary to the main action, the time consumed in *The Egoist* is only a few weeks. These early chapters serve to acquaint the reader quickly with the circumstances of the hero, which, as the world is accustomed to judge of appearances, are in every way fortunate. Willoughby Patterne is young, handsome, rich, the heir of a distinguished name and title. His father being dead, there is no one to stand between him and the full possession of his glories. He is a man of spirit who talks well and knows how to mount a horse. The countryside is at his feet. He has grown up under the adoring eyes of his mother and of two maiden aunts. Laetitia Dale, the daughter of one of his cottagers, worships him. He does not discourage her but accepts her devotion in the name of constancy; it is not clear that the constancy is to be reciprocal.

Whether or not such an excess of felicity in one's circumstances is wholly to be desired is a matter for our consideration. We shall see what Meredith thinks about it. His method is to give Sir Willoughby plenty of rope. He makes him a man of wealth and position, capable of commanding respect, for only in such circumstances is the full and free development of vanity likely to receive encouragement. The fact that the protagonist is a man rather than a woman is probably not an accident. Woman's inferiority of position in the society with which Meredith is dealing makes her a less likely candidate for such a role, particularly when the love relationship is to play a dominant part. Willoughby resides in a country district, not in a city, where his individual importance would of necessity be less. After the death of his mother he is without even her possible restraining influence. His two aunts being incapable of anything but applause in dealing with him, there is no one left to act as the check which perhaps every young male in such a position needs.

One of the first acts recorded of Willoughby is his refusal to admit a needy relative who calls to see him at his express invitation. A lieutenant of Marines, bearing the name of Patterne, has some months before been applauded in the newspapers for a deed of heroism. The story has stirred the pride of young Willoughby, who has sent the hero a complimentary letter containing a check and an invitation to call. It has also led to not a little talk on the part of Willoughby about the deed of valor of his distant cousin in the Marines. When the celebrated lieutenant presents himself at Patterne Hall, however, he proves to be anything but the personable young man whom Willoughby in imagination has pictured to himself. He is not young, and so completely unpresentable is he in appearance that Willoughby cuts him unhesitatingly, making the curt explanation to Miss Durham, who happens to be with him, that he will drop the man a check.

It is to the credit of this young lady—it is one of the few things we know of her—that she is wounded by this act of callousness. Miss Constantia Durham enters the story only to leave it after a brief interval. She is the daughter of a large landowner in another part of the county and is seemingly deluged with suitors. It is this hot pursuit of her more than genuine attachment that stimulates Willoughby to a proposal. Having a passion to excel in every contest he enters, he cannot bear the presence of rival suitors without wishing to carry off the prize. Thus they become engaged. But, a few days before the time set for their wedding, Constantia goes for a visit to an aunt in London—a visit that turns out to be a flight from Willoughby. Suddenly news comes that she has married Captain Oxford.

To save his face in this terrible predicament, Sir Willoughby seeks to create the impression that Constantia's act has been inspired by jealousy of Laetitia. He wishes it to appear that Miss Durham has been his mother's choice for him while his own heart has always inclined to Miss Dale. Accordingly he lets himself be seen with Laetitia by accompanying her to church, and for a time he pays her marked attention. It begins to be gossiped that perhaps he will marry the portionless girl after all. Then he suddenly leaves home, with his cousin Vernon Whitford, on a three years' voyage around the world.

These three years, which are disposed of in as many pages of summary, provide glimpses of Sir Willoughby parading ostentatiously as an English gentleman, more intent upon the stir which he fancies he is creating than upon the world he is visiting. Upon his return to England he greets Laetitia with all his former simulation of ardor. He plays upon her weakness for him, brings new color into her cheeks, fills her with hope, robs her of patience. Then he appears unexpectedly as the fiancé of Miss Clara Middleton, the daughter of a retired clergyman.

Having up to this point presented his material in summary form, Meredith now adopts a more elaborate method, for his novel is to be primarily the story of this engagement. Through it, he exposes the extreme self-centeredness of Willoughby and the plight into which it lands him. It is his unhappy fate to get caught between two mercilessly intelligent women who see through his disguises and tear away every one of the ornamental wrappings with which he has bedecked himself. Aiming high, he falls low, in true comic fashion. He defeats himself by his own devices. As befits comic justice, his victims, Clara and Laetitia, become in turn his judges, and, having exposed their tyrant and rendered him powerless, they are assigned the function of chastising him.

Meredith arranges the stage for an intensive study of the engaged couple by having Dr. Middleton accept an invitation for himself and his daughter to visit at Patterne Hall for a month previous to the wedding. Thus, through no wish of her own, Clara finds herself in oppressively close quarters with her lover and able to observe him with a minuteness that is not to his advantage. Furthermore, she has been pressed into the engagement in a manner that she is inclined instinctively to rebel against. During these remaining days of freedom, which she would like to have to herself, she discovers that she is being drawn into a preliminary stage of vassalage. Already reluctant and quick to take alarm at a threat to her liberty, she is anything but the adoring type of compliant femininity that Sir Willoughby expects in his wife.

In his complete self-absorption, he fails to take into account the likelihood that she may very well have her own desires and inclinations. He expects her, as his wife, to devote herself entirely to his whims, to find her happiness only in studying him, and to pledge herself not to marry after his death. As for Laetitia, whom he strives at the same time to cling to, he prefers for her to remain unmarried so that she may be free, when the occasion arises, to act as governess to his children. This scheme, he fears, may not work, however, for he considers that he may have to bestow her in marriage upon his cousin Vernon Whitford. Otherwise there is danger that Vernon, who has become quite useful as his secretary, may abandon him and go to London. That there is anything odd in this manner of disposing of his friends without consulting them never once occurs to Sir Willoughby.

Finding his importunities more and more oppressive, Clara soon comes to the realization that her lover expects nothing less of her than that she shall worship him. She can no longer hide from herself the fact that there are things about him that are distasteful to her. There is, for example, his unflattering view of scholarship (her father is a scholar) and his offensive manner toward Mr. Whitford, whom her father admires. She has heard, too, a disquieting rumor about his treatment of Miss Dale. His unwillingness to help with the training of Crossjay, the son of Lieutenant Patterne, in the way that she and Vernon believe to be necessary to the boy's future is distressing to her. Gradually her situation becomes more and more disturbing, and she finds herself turning in her mind to Vernon and associating him with the idea of escape. Finally she asks Willoughby to release her. Having sought to make her emulous of Laetitia, he now believes that he has succeeded in making her jealous. To convince her that there is no reason for jealousy, he suggests to her that a marriage should be arranged between Vernon and Laetitia and commissions her to attempt to influence Vernon to that end.

The arrival of Colonel Horace De Craye, a friend of Willoughby, helps at this point to complicate the situation and works ultimately to the advantage of Clara. Unable to get help from her father, to whom her entreaties are only the troublesome signs of feminine skittishness, she takes to flight. After getting as far as the railway station, however, she does not go on, probably because of her encounter with De Craye and her unwillingness to have her flight attributed to his connivance. Willoughby, kept partly in the dark about these proceedings but aware that something is up, begins to be alarmed. He suspects that there is a secret between Clara and his friend Horace.

The refusal of Willoughby to make any concessions to his betrothed produces unfortunate and unforeseen consequences. Clara is driven by her situation to confide, step by step, in Vernon, in Laetitia, and finally even in Mrs. Mountstuart Jenkinson, a lady notable in the district for her wit. Thus the ground is being cut from under him before Sir Willoughby is aware of it, and he is placed at a disadvantage in the negotiations which he institutes to save himself.

Not the least disquieting factor in his situation is the impression, which the harassed suitor acquires gradually, of the air about him being charged with rumors of his danger. Having always lived for the world's opinion, he is now mortally afraid of what the world will say. Moreover, his experience at the hands of Miss Durham has rendered him acutely apprehensive of a second jilting. To make matters worse, it now looks as if he is in danger of losing Clara to his friend Horace De Craye, a man whom he has always treated with negligent condescension.

Fearful of becoming a universal laughingstock, he concocts a scheme whereby his recalcitrant fiancée is to be married to his cousin Vernon, while he himself will wed Laetitia. As the wife of Colonel De Craye, Clara would be an ever-burning source of humiliation to him, but married to a poor recluse like Vernon, she would sink, in Sir Willoughby's estimation, into pitiable obscurity. To be sure of his ground, however, before releasing her, he proposes marriage to Laetitia and, to his stupefaction, she refuses him. A profound change has been taking place in her attitude toward him, of which he has been blissfully unaware. After this unexpected turn of affairs he strives to retain his hold on Clara, but, unfortunately for him, his proposal to Laetitia has been overheard by Crossjay. News of it gets abroad, in more than one version, and spreads, until it must seem to Sir Willoughby that the whole world is aware of it. For a time the action turns into farce, with the victim, in effect, picking his way along the edge of a precipice. Clara being now fully armed against him, he has to humble himself before the once despised Laetitia and implore her to accept him. Having discovered that they love each other, Clara and Vernon plan a union but not under any pressure from Sir Willoughby.

It is a situation typical of comedy for a man to overreach himself. The disaster which the culprit brings down upon his head is likely also to have some special appropriateness to the offense. So it is with Sir Willoughby. A proud man who likes to excite admiration and envy in others, he is punished for his vanity by having to appear as a dupe. With lofty condescension he accepts as his due the finest gifts that a lavish fortune can pour into his lap. He is punished for his presumptuousness by having to fight for a prize that he sees as comparatively valueless. Desirous of making an alliance that will shine in the world's eyes, he actually marries a woman faded in appearance and without wealth or position. The mistress of Patterne Hall should be, of course, a superlative woman, capable of producing superior offspring. As fortune wills it, however, she is frail and anemic and will probably prove to be childless. Clara, whom Sir Willoughby loses, has money and health and beauty; Laetitia, whom he wins, has only brains. And brains, as he will probably learn, can be a troublesome possession in a wife.

To take *The Egoist* as the focus of our study of Meredith is to center our attention upon the more purely analytical aspect of his writing. There is another quality in many of his novels equally deserving of attention—his poetic power—which is overshadowed in *The Egoist* by the study of character. Sir Willoughby, though a magnificently drawn type, is somewhat mechanical as an individual. His portrait bears evidence of having been constructed according to a formula. Notwithstanding the wealth of analysis lavished upon him, he reminds one somewhat of a diagrammatically conceived figure in an early morality play. His name, be it remembered, is Patterne.

As a type he is somewhat different from the old character type found in comedy. He is a psychological type, as it were, a puppet in which the strings of motivation are clearly visible. He is uniformly consistent. We are able to see through him, but in seeing *through* him we cannot be altogether certain that we see *him*. A certain amount of opaqueness in an object will serve to render it more readily visible when light falls upon it. Similarly a certain amount of resistance or confusion in motives is necessary to give to them the color of human experience. It is not necessarily the purpose of the author, however, to make of Sir Willoughby a complete individual. To do so would be to suggest an undercurrent of tragedy and lead to a confusion of issues. An element of ambiguity would be thereby introduced into the novel, and the case against egoism would be weakened by concern for the egoist. In short, Meredith shows that, with all his use of psychological analysis, his purpose remains fundamentally comic.

In any case, he manages to provide in *The Egoist* a legitimate appeal to the feelings. There are several characters to whom our sympathy is drawn—Laetitia, Crossjay, Vernon, and Clara, to name the most important. Clara and Vernon, who are both foils to Sir Willoughby, possess in an eminent degree the sanity and naturalness which are lacking in the central character. Vernon never wastes a moment in acting for effect. His physical prowess is a product of self-discipline, not of the desire to surpass others. His interest in Crossjay is not prompted, like Sir Willoughby's, by selfish motives.

It is Clara Middleton who best displays in this novel the more poetic side of Meredith. She is an excellent example of his instinct for feminine character. Young and sensitive, she always achieves just the right note in her various relationships without ever seeming to strive—with her father, with Vernon, with Crossjay, with Willoughby, and with even the redoubtable Mrs. Mountstuart Jenkinson. It is probably in her meetings with Laetitia that her delicacy of feeling is exhibited to the best advantage. In her comradeship with Crossjay she reveals her delicate imaginativeness, her unspoiled girlish nature, her sunny spirits and freedom from namby-pambiness. When the odds seem to be against her in her battle for freedom, she never loses her courage, and she never resorts to feminine tricks to gain sympathy. Charmingly sweet without being fragile, spontaneously graceful, warmhearted and generous, clear-sighted in love, capable of passion—she possesses a power of attraction in which she far outshines most of her more conventional sisters in Victorian fiction. A novelist who is capable of creating such a character—and Meredith has drawn many fine portraits of women—can be expected to hold a high place in the literature of his period for a considerable time to come.

CHAPTER XV

The Tragic View of Life

THOMAS HARDY

It is not an uncommon occurrence for two writers who reach positions of eminence in the same field at about the same time to become linked together in the public mind, even though the actual ties between them are few or practically nonexistent. Circumstances contrive to make them rivals, and the more eminent they are, the greater is the stir caused by their unintentional but unavoidable rivalry. Their situation is somewhat similar to that of two characters playing leading roles in opposition to each other in a single literary production—like Tom Jones and Blifil or Becky Sharp and Amelia Sedley. It is thus that we sometimes think of Fielding and Richardson, of Dickens and Thackeray, and, to a lesser extent, of George Meredith and Thomas Hardy.

The relationship of Hardy to Meredith is more complex than that of Thackeray to Dickens, and it is not so purely antithetical in character. Between the two later writers, who are both poets as well as novelists, there are numerous points of contrast, to be sure, but also several points of correspondence. Both manifest the usual Victorian tendency to make the novel an organ of moral and social criticism. Both follow the more specific example of George Eliot in building their novels, not around a group of characters in the early Victorian manner, but around an idea, such as serves to give dramatic point and unity to *The Egoist*. Both novelists resemble George Eliot also in taking an intellectual attitude toward life and in devoting themselves to problems of individual adjustment and development. They are both enemies of Philistinism and relentless castigators of self-complacency, conventional piety, and prudery. Each of them, though Hardy to a greater degree, has absorbed enough of the scientific spirit to look upon human law as something enveloped in a larger realm of natural law. Both of them, in short, reveal in their work the ferment of ideas that accompanied the dissolution of the Victorian order in the years between 1860 and 1890. Their novels, along with George Eliot's, reflect an age of spiritual renovation, during which men are casting about in various directions for new sources of inspiration and new formulas of belief.

George Eliot, a compound of rational thinking and religious instinct, seeks a substitute for Christian dogma in a religion of social service. Meredith, whose morality is broader and more imaginative in outlook, seeks not so much to rationalize religion as to spiritualize nature; not to make God human but nature divine. Accordingly, as he conceives it, man's primary duty is not to a problematical life beyond the tomb but to life here and now—a prize of inestimable worth to be cherished in all its varied manifestations of mind, spirit, and sense. Rich in its potentiality, it is not, for all that, a thing to be exploited and despoiled. The possession of it imposes obligations upon the beneficiary. A thing of slow and complex development, it can reach its full growth only in him who learns through courage and love and self-discipline how to know and value it.

Little of this spirit of assent is to be found in Hardy, who is more inclined to protest against the inadequacy of life than to extol its fullness. He finds in nature not a balanced economy but maladjustment, perversity, and frustration. In his novels and poems the earth is not paradise, and life is not a theme for rapture. He quietly remarks of one of his characters that "her experience had been of a kind to teach her, rightly or wrongly, that the doubtful honour of a brief transit through a sorry world hardly called for effusiveness." Instead of sharing in Meredith's faith in the power of intelligence and an untrammeled spirit, he accepts the mechanical interpretation of nature implicit in Darwinian theory. The universe he sees as a place of blind necessity and inexorable law, ruled by a power which takes no account of human aims, and in thus being indifferent to man is, in effect, wantonly cruel:

> O Loveless, Hateless!—past the sense
> Of kindly eyed benevolence,
> To what tune danceth this Immense?

This question, coming at the close of *The Dynasts* and remaining unanswered, because in the author's mind it is unanswerable, suggests upon what ground the tragic outlook of Hardy rests. He is disturbed by the absence of sympathy for human aims that seems to him to be characteristic of the universe. There is a gulf between organic and inorganic matter which leaves man, as it were, an outcast in his own home. Nature is moved by forces foreign to man, although man is himself a product of nature. The absence of any bond of sympathy between parent and child, if we mean by parent the inanimate universe, has the effect of converting the inscrutable power behind the universe into what, as far as man is concerned, is virtually a demon.

We are not to understand from this assertion that Hardy believed in the existence of an actively malign power. There is no question here of evil spirits but rather of an unsentient creation giving birth to sentient creatures. In this circumstance is the source of man's tragic plight. He has been lifted up only to be dashed down. In acquiring consciousness he has acquired dignity, but he has also acquired knowledge of his littleness. The web of consciousness into which he has managed to weave so many brightly colored threads of hope and aspiration has served finally to entangle him in the recognition of his dilemma. In a universe which takes no heed of his projects, he sees himself doomed to be perpetually cheated of his aims and mocked by a superior power, which, though innocent of evil intent, seems to grin maliciously at his fruitless exertions.

Against such pessimism it might be contended that natural phenomena contain many remarkable examples of ministration to man's needs. The adaptation of man to his environment involves innumerable fine adjustments of means to ends. Nature, it would seem, is far from trying to make life hard for man, all her pains being in the opposite direction of seeking to make it easier for him to overcome his obstacles. How else are we to interpret her behavior in equipping him with such intricate machinery of sensibility and action? Is not man's intelligence as well as his senses and his power of motion an extension of his capacity to deal effectively with his surroundings? Looked at in this way, consciousness is not a curse but a gift of the utmost worth. Furthermore, man is not an outcast in a universe that mocks him but the most favored of nature's creatures, enjoying authority upon the earth and looking upon the sun and stars as existing for his advantage and pleasure.

Hardy saw life not in this light but as something predominantly evil. He had a temperamental inclination to the catastrophic. Having been nurtured upon local tradition and superstition, his imagination never lost its penchant for the weird and mysterious. Although he heaped scorn upon the idea of providential intervention in man's affairs, it was not the irrationality of such a belief but the theory of a benign order in nature that drew his ridicule.

The world, as pictured by Hardy, is a place of disaster where sinister powers are at work to thwart man. It is not a place of just punishments or just rewards. Evil turns up repeatedly, but man is not primarily to blame. The evil outside man, in Hardy's view, is greater than the evil in man. Conversely, the good which is within man is greater than the good outside him. The result of such a division is that a conflict arises between the good in man and the evil in nature. Man is too good for the world, which, having fathered him, is blind to his superior qualities and will have none of them.

The characteristic situation of a Hardy novel readily takes the form of drama. It is a struggle between man and his environment. More specifically, it is a struggle between eternal, quiescent, inanimate nature—as symbolized by Egdon Heath, for example—and the aspiring, travailing human spirit. The plea in the final line of *The Dynasts* that Consciousness shall eventually inform the Will of the Universe suggests such a struggle between the impersonal and the personal, with the personal, or at least the conscious, element finally triumphing over the whole.

The rapid growth of scientific knowledge in the latter half of the nineteenth century contributed to a sense of disillusionment, which we find in much of the literature of the period. The study of biology, in particular, brought profound changes in man's estimate of himself and his place in the universe. The scientist explains the world without regard to, or flattery of, human pretensions. He looks upon man not as the chief end of creation, but as a relatively inconsiderable part of a vast quantity of natural phenomena. In seeking to extend his dominion over all existence, he recognizes nothing as being above or beneath his scrutiny. Such an attitude was disturbing to many people, who felt that the most sacred aspects of life were being profaned. The pessimism of Hardy, though it did not originate in shocked piety, was probably strengthened by the support that scientific theory gave to his sense of man's helplessness. Moreover, the unwillingness of some people to face unpleasant truths increased his determination not to flinch in the face of evil.

As has been indicated, Hardy had a pronounced taste for uncommon and mysterious occurrences. He considered that the purpose of fiction was to gratify "the love of the uncommon" and that "a story must be exceptional enough to justify its telling." He introduced extraordinary occurrences freely into his novels, just as if the period of his productivity was not one of growing regard in fiction for an impersonal and objective representation of reality. He worked, it is true, under the handicap of the serial-story convention, with its demand for frequent surprises. Moreover, the later novels, like *Jude the Obscure,* showed an increasing tendency to realism. Yet he was never first and foremost a realist.

How far he was from adopting the doctrines of the realists is revealed by his resistance to what he regarded as the intrusion of the methods of science into the art of storytelling. In an article entitled "The Science of Fiction," appearing in 1891, he condemned the theory put forth by Zola in *Le Roman expérimental* that the writing of fiction could be made to conform to the scientific method. He admitted that art must adjust itself to growing knowledge. To be artistically convincing, a story must present life in terms which were acceptable to our knowledge of reality. Conventions which had ceased to evoke such a sense of reality must be supplanted by a closer following of experience. A more detailed realism in literature was the normal accompaniment, Hardy believed, of expanding knowledge. Yet it was not possible for the novelist to reproduce experience in its entirety. He was obliged to exercise his faculty of selection and to discriminate between what he included and what he excluded. This being the case, it was idle to pretend that the novelist followed a scientific method. The most careful piece of realism was an artificial product, and the novelist could not escape the exercise of art in telling his story. Furthermore, as Hardy pointed out, the observation of externals was not the only function of the novelist. What was apprehended by the mind was more important than what was discerned by the eye and ear. Mental discernment required sympathy as well as understanding. To penetrate below the surface of experience, the observer must have that within himself which enabled him to apprehend significance in what he saw. He was not the mere scientific observer, limiting himself to a particular and specified form of data.

Although Hardy, Meredith, and George Eliot all introduced new currents of thought into fiction, it was Hardy who most completely assimilated his material. There is not a little unresolved matter in the novels of Meredith—ideas which remain simply topics of discussion. George Eliot never for long loses sight of her desire to edify and uplift. Hardy, though no less strong in his convictions, is more inclined to let his novels speak for themselves. Truth for him is not something to be tied up in little parcels of morality or epigram. Thought, in his mind, is more than material for an aphorism. He translates abstract theories into modes of experience and feeling. A poet at heart, not a moralist or a philosopher, he is interested in life in its immediacy. And, whatever his chagrin or despair, he never chills us by indifference. The mere facts of existence assume in his imagination the quality of a spectacle—a dramatic spectacle, as it were, of unequal strife between visible and invisible powers. Meredith, despite a greater warmth of manner, imparts less of an impression of sympathy for his material. Being possessed of a sensibility less one-sided than Meredith's, Hardy can give himself to his puppetry with a wholeheartedness not possible to the more intellectual novelist. His mind being less absorbed in systematization, he can devote the greater share of his attention to the individual aspects of scene and character. Not only does he concentrate thus upon particulars, but he intensifies the process by stripping his action of practically everything that is not relevant to his view of the essential reality. Accordingly it is no accident that his novels, though springing from a different intellectual atmosphere, bring again into English fiction the concentration of dramatic and poetic power which we have hitherto encountered only in *Wuthering Heights*.

The Return of the Native

The character of a work of art depends less upon the materials out of which it is made than upon the use which the imagination of the artist is able to make of the materials. Thus, although a novel similar in subject to *The Return of the Native* might conceivably have been written by George Eliot, who was interested in the problems with which it deals, any such novel would have differed from Hardy's in many important characteristics. George Eliot, for example, would have made Eustacia Vye less of an enigma and Clym Yeobright less fanatical. She might, in accordance with her psychological pretensions, have endeavored to explain the process of change in Clym which led to his momentous decision to give up his career in Paris. She would have found in Eustacia and Wildeve material for her customary condemnation of selfishness. In short, she would have assumed an attitude of greater moral certitude than Hardy maintains and she would have arranged events according to a more orderly and more humanly comprehensible scheme of causation than the obscure pattern of fate which operates in *The Return of the Native*. She would have sought to demonstrate not the helplessness of man before destiny, but his obligation not to contribute to disaster by his own willfulness.

Such a novel, in its rational temper and its insistence upon individual responsibility, would have missed, in all likelihood, the poetry and tragedy of Hardy's story. My reason, indeed, for indulging in the supposition of a different treatment from the one we have is to direct attention to the new turn given by Hardy to the novel. This turn, relatively new in English fiction, was to give poetic value to circumstances that had been more commonly regarded in a moral or a social light. Moreover, it was to bring the novelist face to face with the tragic facts of existence. Hardy was more interested in the eternal verities than in narrow problems of conduct. The prospect of mankind headed toward an unenviable destiny did not arouse in him an impulse to issue warnings or to suggest practical, precautionary measures. His attitude of brooding contemplation, of calm and at the same time embittered pessimism, was something new in English fiction. Hitherto the affinity of the novel in England had been predominantly with comedy. Hardy was fundamentally a writer of tragedy.

In addition to being essentially a tragedy, *The Return of the Native* is a work of great structural beauty and strong imaginative appeal. It is arresting, at the same time, as a piece of literary craftsmanship, as a work of art, and as a commentary upon life. As an example of dramatic art, it may be placed beside *Emma* and *Wuthering Heights,* in each of which productions there is a close knitting together of character and incident. Interior causation and balance between opposing forces serve to produce in the dramatic type of novel a sense of tension and of spontaneous life and movement. In a well-constructed dramatic novel the author seeks to merge all his purposes into one purpose. There should be no tug of war between what is necessary to the characters and what is necessary to the action.

The development of fictional art would seem to be, in fact, largely a matter of bringing into closer union elements which in earlier stages of fiction have been more or less distinct. At one stage of its development, action was the chief element in fiction. Then character came to be considered as relatively more important. In the romantic novel, setting became an atmospheric support to the emotional effect. Jane Austen, an essentially comic artist, blended action and character with remarkable skill but made relatively slight use of setting. For some time yet, setting was to be not much more than an accessory stage property. Scott, it is true, transformed the stiff Gothic landscape into something more genuine and more closely allied with a sense of actual locality. The characters of Charlotte Brontë were presented not only with attention to their surroundings but with attention to their awareness of their surroundings. It was Emily Brontë, however, who lifted setting to the status of an essential dramatic feature. In *Wuthering Heights* the harmony between the characters and the setting is hardly less notable than the harmony between the characters and their actions. The reader gets an impression not simply of a place but of a place and people combined. In *The Return of the Native* there has been a similar merging of character, incident, and setting. No feature of the novel is more important than the use made of Egdon Heath.

Meredith began *The Egoist,* we recall, by disclaiming any intention to employ an appeal to the senses. In *The Return of the Native* an opposite course is followed. Egdon Heath, the setting of the story, is presented in great fullness and with particular care to impress its essential features upon the attention of the reader. It is described as it appears at different hours of the day, in different seasons, and in different kinds of weather. Its varying moods provide an accompaniment to the fluctuations of feeling which grip those living within its boundaries. The deeds which are enacted upon its broad and somber expanse are so closely in harmony with the place itself that the reader is not fully aware of the extent to which he is under its spell. Action and setting are interwoven so skillfully that the two are hardly distinguishable in the total impression.

Environment in *Middlemarch,* though made to function dramatically, is essentially a practical consideration. By providing obstacles of various kinds and checking enterprise, it contributes to human destiny in terms that are generally clear and ponderable. In *The Return of the Native,* however, the adjustment between the characters and their environment is a much more delicate and far-reaching matter. The obstacles that here rise to thwart human hopes have much more complex and more obscure origins. The attractions and repulsions that Egdon breeds in certain of its inhabitants are not to be explained in terms of practical morality or ordinary social phenomena. No one of the central conflicts is precisely a struggle between a character and his environment. Various issues become involved with one another in ways that give rise to trouble.

There are a variety of ways, in fact, in which the setting of wasteland is made to function. It is one of the principal dramatic instruments of the novel in that it inspires the two leading characters with opposite longings and thus helps to bring them into misunderstanding and conflict. Nevertheless, important as it is as an instrument of fate, it must operate indirectly and inwardly upon the characters. The force exerted upon Clym and Eustacia is not something that they can estimate, or control, or even understand. Its insidious influence creeps into their lives, poisoning Eustacia's, she lets herself believe, and filling Clym with nostalgia while he is away from it.

That the heath is to play a role of unusual significance is fairly evident from the time of the initial lifting of the curtain upon the particular afternoon in November with which Hardy begins his story. In a few pages of description and commentary, before any human figures have yet appeared upon the stage to claim our attention, a portion of the heath is set before us at the hour of approaching twilight, when its peculiar impressiveness is said to be most readily perceptible. True to his artistic convictions, the author makes no effort to limit himself to a literal account of externals. Not only does he call attention to those features of the scene that arouse some human response, but he insists, in a general way, upon the susceptibility of man to the influence of natural surroundings. The time may be near, he suggests, when man will find such desolate regions as this in closer harmony with his temper than well-tended vineyards and myrtle gardens. Egdon is not a place, the author remarks, to mock man by putting on a too-smiling countenance:

> It was at present a place perfectly accordant with man's nature—neither ghastly, hateful, nor ugly: neither commonplace, unmeaning, nor tame; but, like man, slighted and enduring; and withal singularly colossal and mysterious in its swarthy monotony. As with some persons who have long lived apart, solitude seemed to look out of its countenance. It had a lonely face, suggesting tragical possibilities.

Much of the most effective use that Hardy makes of his background is veiled in suggestion. The austere stateliness of the heath and its quality of somber mysteriousness are made somehow to communicate themselves to the onward march of the narrative. Being sparsely populated and cut off from the rest of the world, the region serves to isolate the characters and contributes to a sense of dramatic tension. Moreover, the impassivity of Egdon has the effect of reducing the characters to a feeling of helplessness. Such is the effect upon Clym when he learns in detail the circumstances of his mother's death:

> The strangest deeds were possible to his mood, but they were not possible to his situation. Instead of there being before him the pale face of Eustacia, and a masculine shape unknown, there was only the imperturbable countenance of the heath, which, having defied the cataclysmal onsets of centuries, reduced to insignificance by its seamed and antique features the wildest turmoil of a single man.

This unchangeable, indestructible timelessness of Egdon, as it stands waiting through the centuries, is in direct contrast to the fleeting temporality and fragility of its human tenantry. "The great inviolate place," the author states, "had an ancient permanence which the sea cannot claim. Who can say of a particular sea that it is old? Distilled by the sun, kneaded by the moon, it is renewed in a year, in a day, or in an hour. The sea changed, the fields changed, the rivers, the villages, and the people changed, yet Egdon remained." This suggestion of permanence in the midst of incessant change is a basic factor in the dramatic design of the novel. The untamable waste is a symbol of the vast, unexplored, and unfathomable powers of nature, which Hardy sees as being eternally resistant to the efforts of man to bring them into some semblance of cultivation and order.

Closely associated with the heath are the minor characters, the Egdon rustics, who illustrate in their own lives the forces of inertia and resistance to change characteristic of the region. Clym's desire to educate these people receives no encouragement from them; in their opinion he had better mind his business. In addition to commenting upon the action and providing a background of public opinion, somewhat in the manner of a Greek chorus, these minor characters also serve as a foil to the element of tragedy in the novel, and provide an impression of life going on amid the forces of disruption and change. Such a character is Grandfer Cantle, who is always on hand when there is an excuse for merrymaking. Time cannot dampen his spirit or wrest from him his simple, unreasoning pleasure in life. His son Christian is a simpleton, whose folly makes him a fit instrument of tragedy. It is in keeping with the author's irony that far-reaching issues of life and happiness should hang for one fatal evening upon such a slender reed.

Though a profoundly suggestive novelist, Hardy is by no means a vague or haphazard one. On the contrary he is a craftsman of unusual precision and firmness of method. A man of decided opinions, he might have produced novels which were essentially dogmatic statements of his intellectual convictions, had it not been for the transforming power of his imagination. Happily, in his best productions, his sensibility acted as a leavening influence upon his ideas, and his intellectual tenacity gave direction and control to his imaginings. Thus, for all its richness of suggestion and warmth of tone, *The Return of the Native* is marked by extreme simplicity and clarity of design. Following a method of strict economy, the author manages to bring the different factors of his story into close coordination and to achieve a high degree of unity.

The preliminary view of Egdon at the beginning of the novel helps to establish the tone of the narrative and builds up also an impression of people enveloped in their surroundings. From such an impression it is an easy transition for the reader to apprehend that a contest is being waged in which the relationship of these people to the community is an important factor. Almost immediately an atmosphere of tension is created. Underneath the specific clashes of individuals there is a more general impression of tension between the individuals and the community.

Mrs. Yeobright, for example, once having dreamed of doing better things, holds herself aloof from her humble neighbors. After her husband's death she lives so much to herself that she acquires an estranged air. The solitude exhaled from the heath, we are told, had become concentrated in her face. She is a proud, inflexible woman, whose ambition, not having been satisfied in her own life, reasserts itself with redoubled force in her plans for her son. Her desire that he shall rise to a higher social level than Egdon can provide is one of the chief original forces in the novel leading to tragedy.

Each one of the leading characters is in some way associated definitely with the background. Diggory Venn, the reddleman, is in harmony with the heath and its silent, mysterious ways. His lurid

red color, his nomadic way of life, and his never-failing resourcefulness all contribute to an element of picturesqueness in him that goes
well with his surroundings. He represents a romantic convention—
the knight devoted to serving his lady—fitted into the life of the
district and useful as a link between the various characters.

Diggory Venn and Thomasin Yeobright are the only ranking characters who are fully in harmony with their surroundings, and they
are also the only ones finally to achieve happiness. Thomasin, in
keeping with her simplicity, shows no strong feeling either for or
against Egdon. It is not to her, as to Eustacia, a place of "demons
in the air, and malice in every bush and bough." It is home to her
and she is attached to it from long association. An environment
which unsettles stronger natures than hers leaves her undisturbed.
Clym once observes that a storm which brings destruction to the
trees only waves the heather in a light caress. Thomasin is like the
heather, which bends but is not broken.

Damon Wildeve, the landlord of the Quiet Woman, is as much out
of harmony with the heath as his rival Diggory Venn is in harmony
with it. Wildeve is an extreme example of maladjustment. His occupation galls him. Having been brought up for better things, he
looks with scorn upon Egdon and treats the country folk who gather
at his inn with scant courtesy. His manners are not suited to his
surroundings; his union with Thomasin is an ill-assorted one, springing from no genuine feeling for her; his passion for Eustacia would
probably cool if it were not kept alive by jealousy of Yeobright. In
short, Wildeve never succeeds in adapting himself to his circumstances, either personal or practical.

Six characters may be classified as belonging to the main action—
Clym, his mother, Eustacia, Wildeve, Thomasin, and Venn. Each
one of these six characters is at one time or another involved with
two of the others in a triangular relationship, with the result that
there are several strands of narrative closely related to one another
and each one representing an element of conflict.

The earliest of these contests, which has taken place mostly before
the novel opens, consists of the effort of Mrs. Yeobright to prevent
the marriage of Thomasin and Wildeve. Before it gives way finally,
her opposition has been carried to the extreme length of forbidding

the proclamation of the banns announcing the proposed marriage. Based in part upon suspicion that a questionable relationship exists between Wildeve and Eustacia, this action of Mrs. Yeobright prepares us for the more important conflict soon to arise between Clym and his mother in regard to Eustacia.

Closely related to the contest between Mrs. Yeobright and Wildeve is the situation of Thomasin between her two suitors. Although too submissive to fight much on her own account, Thomasin, we have reason to believe, might have married Venn early in the story had she not been afraid of her aunt's opinion. When she is slighted by Wildeve, she goes ahead and lets herself be wed to him in spite of her humiliation, in order to save the famous Yeobright pride.

Another situation, growing out of the preceding one, involves Venn, Wildeve, and Eustacia. Having lost Thomasin, Venn continues to work in her interest by trying to keep her husband away from Eustacia, whom he suspects of being Thomasin's rival. His interference, though well intended, has some unfortunate repercussions. There is, for example, his delivery to Thomasin of the hundred guineas sent by Mrs. Yeobright and intended for both Clym and Thomasin—an error that not only undoes the chance for success of this move for reconciliation but turns it into added cause for estrangement. Another unforeseen result of Venn's meddling is that Wildeve, prevented from visiting Eustacia stealthily, by night, decides to visit her openly, by day. His arrival happening to occur at the same time as the visit of Mrs. Yeobright, there is created a situation which, through the collaboration of human weakness with various blind and incalculable forces, prepares the way for the final catastrophe.

The situation of Wildeve is a one-sided struggle between his romantic longing for Eustacia and the practical reality of his marriage to Thomasin. It is his restless discontent that is responsible for much of the trouble. His intrusion into the affairs of Eustacia makes all the more precarious her chance of happiness with Clym.

This union of Clym and Eustacia provides the novel with its central issue. *The Return of the Native* is essentially the story of the attraction between these two persons who are so much unlike each other in their desires and mental horizons. "Take all the varying hates felt by Eustacia Vye towards the heath," says Hardy, "and translate them into loves, and you have the heart of Clym." It is part of the irony of the situation that the circumstance that has alienated Clym from the kind of life desired by Eustacia is just what first makes him attractive to her. His having resided in Paris is to her a most exciting circumstance; she cannot be expected to divine his attitude of mind toward a place so suggestive of happiness to her.

As a boy Clym has been deeply attached to Egdon. The unsettled state of mind in which he returns home is the product of his having been uprooted and made to live in an altogether different kind of place. Although we are not told much about it, his life in Paris is important in having brought him to his present state of discontent. Being hungry for the very things he would renounce, Eustacia cannot understand or sympathize with his ideas of renunciation. It is natural, perhaps inevitable, that she should be attracted to him. We can hardly blame her. If there is to be any blame it should fall rather upon Clym for his inflexibility in expecting her to adapt her aims to his. Their union is one of tragic incongruity. Knowing from the beginning what each one desires, the reader can see the threatening implications in the circumstances drawing them together.

Clym does not fail to condemn himself for his harsh treatment of Eustacia after her death. But as Hardy conceives the situation the responsibility for what happens is divided between the human agents and the inscrutable forces governing the universe. Consequently rewards and punishments cannot be distributed in the orderly manner of a Dickens novel (the only aspect of his work, one might almost say, in which Dickens was orderly). Thomasin and Diggory are rewarded, to be sure, but their marriage was a concession to the magazine requirement for a happy ending. It was not a part of the novel as originally designed and cannot be regarded as affecting it essentially.

Eustacia's struggle is a matter, not of wavering between two men, but of striving to escape the emptiness and monotony of her lot. She has had to come and live on the heath in circumstances that have prevented her from feeling at home among its people. Temperamentally not in sympathy with the Egdon rustics, she lives to herself, discontented and rebellious, and desiring greatly to be loved. In these circumstances she is attracted to Wildeve and afterwards, more hopefully and more honestly, to Clym. Fate, it would seem, is against her and she fails to attain her desire. Even her moments of happiness are tinged with premonitions of evil. Finally being caught in a dilemma from which there seems to her to be no escape, she ends her life.

Clym suffers from a conflict of loyalties. Whichever way he turns he finds himself at odds with something that claims his allegiance. He strives to retain his mother's confidence, to make Eustacia happy, and to follow his plan of becoming a teacher. One, or even two, of these things might have been attained. The three together are impossible of attainment. When Clym discovers how his quarrel with his mother has ended, he turns in anger upon Eustacia and quarrels with her. Death closes the breach in each instance before there can be a reconciliation. Each of these quarrels, as it happens, starts a fatal train of events, with the result that the well-intentioned hero accuses himself subsequently of having driven both women to their deaths.

Although Hardy is renowned as the novelist of a definite region, known as Wessex, he is not a local colorist. Universal, not local, issues are his concern. Some of his characters may be recognizable as belonging to the district in question, but such identification, if possible, is without particular significance. The creator of Wessex is not the novelist of a period or of a place in the sense of Galsworthy or of Bennett. His novels are never the densely packed social documents exemplified in *Clayhanger* or *The Old Wives' Tale*. One does not receive from *The Return of the Native* an impression of social minutiae. The chief characters, like the characters of *Wuthering Heights*, live in comparative seclusion. They are absorbed, not in the casual happenings of the community, but in their personal desires and predicaments. They dwell, to a large extent, each in a private world of self-communion and are only incidentally members of the social community of Egdon, in which respects they differ markedly from the minor characters.

Thomasin and her suitor appear somewhat as exceptions to this general rule. They are not so completely self-absorbed as are the other main characters, with the result that they seem to belong to the background of the novel almost as much as to its drama. The minor characters, although they serve occasionally as links in the dramatic development, belong primarily to the background. They provide an impression of community life in which they are enclosed and beyond which they have no special interests or needs. Despite their propensity to humor, they are never permitted to usurp the center of the stage or to make a display of their qualities simply in the way of entertainment. What is said or done by them is as carefully calculated for its contribution to the total effect as are the acts of the chief characters. By their quiet acceptance of life and their submission to what fate wills, the minor characters help to create an impression of stability and permanence underneath the tangle and turmoil of those who are in rebellion. Moreover, these characters in the background illustrate the leveling influences at work in nature, against which such ambition as Clym's and Eustacia's is in revolt. Thus it is not the provincialism of these people which primarily interests the author, but their relationship to his dramatic idea. Their essential, timeless humanity is what marks them rather than their accidental differentiations of time or place.

Even in his use of humor Hardy reveals the strictness of his control over his material and the unity of his purpose. The unfailing mirth and gusto of the Egdon rustics act as a balancing agent upon the corrosive despair generated by the central tragic theme. The color and sparkle and warmth that are thus imparted to the narrative cannot be defined simply as comic relief. The tense gloom of the central drama is enveloped, so to speak, in a larger and freer world of rustic comedy. In this sunnier and more relaxed atmosphere, dismay and bewilderment cannot permanently prevail. Men may pass, but mankind remains. Underneath the havoc wrought by individual pride and passion, the unreasoning and indomitable spirit of life persists.

The Return of the Native makes a twofold appeal to our attention. There is the view of life that it embodies and out of which it has been conceived, and there is the process by which its peculiar embodiment has been brought into being. Although the critic is likely to concern himself more specifically with the artistic process, he cannot leave out of account the more fundamental matter of the artist's attitude. The success of any work of art depends both upon the validity of its subject and upon the strength and suitability of its method. Between these two factors there can be no serious cleavage because the latter is but the expression of the former. Technical proficiency cannot of itself ensure a novelist against failure, for dexterity in the handling of material cannot redeem poverty of thought or feeling. In art, as in life, the means cannot justify the end.

At the same time, an artist with the best of subjects and the highest intention cannot triumph over the blighting effects of feeble or inadequate execution. Ultimately success of the highest kind depends not upon worthiness of theme or upon adequacy of presentation, but upon harmonious interaction between the two. Such harmony is abundantly evident in *The Return of the Native*. Characters, action, and setting blend in close union and fuse with the underlying dramatic idea. So nearly perfect is the resultant singleness of effect that, under the spell of the fascinating medium, there ceases, for the ordinary reader, to be any perceptible distinction between the idea of the novel and its incarnation.

It was the artist in Hardy that made such a success possible. In no other novel, except perhaps in *The Mayor of Casterbridge,* did he keep more strictly within the boundaries imposed upon him by his subject. In *Tess,* for example, and in *Jude,* there are times when the author seems to impose his will upon events. Here, however, with the exception of the last book and its contrived marriage, we find events developing naturally from the initial situation and in accordance with what we expect of the characters. Notwithstanding their forcefulness of character, Clym and Eustacia act always in conformity with their natures and, at the same time, according to the requirements of the dramatic theme. What they communicate to us by their words and actions is similar to what is communicated everywhere throughout the novel. By keeping within the limits of his idea and by bringing to bear upon that idea the fertilizing power of his imagination, the author succeeded in producing a novel at once strong in impact and rich in color and suggestion.

How was it possible, it may be asked, to deal so narrowly with
life in dramatic terms and yet retain such wealth of suggestion?
The answer is to be found in the evocative power of the artist's
imagination, in his humor, his fancifulness, and his sympathy with
man and nature. How was it possible, on the other hand, to invest
one's dramatic vehicle with such a wealth of poetry and humor and
yet retain such concentrated fury of conflict? To attempt a full
answer to this question would be to repeat much of what has gone
before. One point of explanation is that the poetry supports the
drama by evoking a mood proper to it. Of still greater significance is
the gift of imagination that enabled Hardy to look at his material
from two different angles and thus to see it as something particular
and also universal. Egdon Heath is a definite country district with
such recognizable features as any such place may be expected to
have. It is also a symbol of vast primitive undercurrents in civilization. Clym and Eustacia are highly individualized persons with such
hopes and anxieties as we everywhere encounter; they are also mankind struggling with destiny. The time that passes from the fifth of
November to the sixth of November a year later is the hurrying
sequence of days, weeks, and months that we all know. Yet there is
another kind of time suggested in the novel—a time so vast in extent that it becomes the timelessness of Egdon. It reduces to insignificance the momentary flicker of a few days or months.

In such a way is the sense of conflict in the situation of the characters enlarged and intensified. Oppositions arise on different planes.
The struggling of Clym and Eustacia is a drama of universal conflict between the will to realize and the will to renounce. Another
basic emotion is typified in the ambition of Mrs. Yeobright for her
son, not to mention her distrust of the woman whom Clym loves.
A still broader aspect of conflict is suggested by the contrast between
the changes wrought by human passion and the resistance to change
so characteristic of the heath. Similar to this contrast is the opposition between the urgency of time as it presses upon Eustacia and
the indifference to time that is manifested by Egdon. It is evident,
in fact, that, however we may choose to regard it, *The Return of the
Native* is dramatic in conception and construction and inexorably
tragic in its outlook upon life.

CHAPTER XVI

The Realistic Novel

Henry James once characterized the novelist as being a lover of the image of life. It is the novelist among literary craftsmen who devotes himself most unreservedly to the creation and projection of life in its greatest variation of scene and character. Even the most romantic of novelists cannot avoid being to a certain extent a realist. He will inevitably be something of a realist because he is obliged to deal with commonly recognizable aspects of experience. Realistic touches are to be found in the most purely fanciful tales. A story in which three bears are depicted as being one large, one medium-sized, and one small, owes part of its success to the skillful use made of a simple and obvious fact about animals, and about people of different ages—a fact which impresses itself readily upon the young reader and which figures prominently in his experience of the world. A storyteller who represents a witch as riding on a broomstick acknowledges, by this token, the logic of a world which requires, for everyone, some visible means of locomotion. A fantasy which turns the normal order upside down, parodies it, or distorts it in whatever fashion, is still tied by its own law to that order which it challenges. Only a mathematician, it has been said, could have invented the system of logic which prevails in *Alice's Adventures in Wonderland* and which contributes so much to its peculiar attractiveness. Such fantasies as *The Invisible Man* and *The First Men in the Moon*, by H. G. Wells, are clearly the products of a scientifically trained mind.

Although they deal with events that could never have taken place, the manner in which they are presented gives to them an air of plausibility. Having adopted his hypothesis in each case, the author is as scrupulous in observing its requirements as if he were engaged in working out an important scientific experiment. Any trifling with the basic assumption, he realizes, would expose the fictitious nature of the situation and destroy the illusion. The romantic world of Sherlock Holmes, to cite another example, must be conceived in terms which are outwardly credible and consistent enough to sustain the logic of the great detective's inferences.

Although this chapter is to be devoted specifically to the topic of realism, it is not because realistic tendencies now appear in the novel for the first time. The reason is that in the work of this period various forces produce a type of fiction more completely realistic than any that we have hitherto encountered. Notwithstanding the strong realistic tendencies in the work of such men as Defoe and Fielding, to name no others, it is hardly too much to assert that whereas up to this time the novel has been incidentally realistic, it now becomes intentionally so. In its earlier stages realism was frequently the result of reaction against the decaying conventions of romance. The picaresque novel, in which the adventures of a rogue were substituted for the more idealistically conceived adventures of a knight, is a case in point, and there are other examples of anti-pastoral, anti-chivalric, and anti-aristocratic novels which illustrate this tendency. Novelists of the eighteenth and early nineteenth centuries did not adopt an attitude of detachment or of scientific impartiality. Even Defoe and Jane Austen were not pure realists, although Miss Austen was close in spirit to the modern realist and Defoe was in some respects similar to the naturalists whom Moore imitated. Fielding, Thackeray, Dickens, and their kin were mocking, cynical, comic, satirical, sentimental, jocular, or what you will; they were never, in their most characteristic moments, bent upon the unadulterated presentation of facts. They took a broad view of mankind without going into a microscopic study of details.

These novelists, in short, were not like trained, impersonal reporters. The conception of the novel that governed their work was philosophical and moral rather than scientific. They frankly adopted many of the formal conventions of classical art and worked with traditional situations and traditional types of character. They regarded themselves as interpreters of reality rather than as students of natural phenomena. The new realists, although generally more skeptical and less inclined to search for final explanations, were themselves men of ideas and some of them were not without a passion for reform. Their beliefs, however, bore a different relationship to their art and functioned differently from the way in which ideas had been utilized in the older novels. In theory at least the naturalist had to relinquish the role of commentator. He had to let his story speak for itself, for its meaning, like the meaning of an experiment, could be understood only in its entirety. The discipline and self-denial required of the novelist under these circumstances led to an enlarged comprehension of the value and usefulness of realistic detail. The novelist became more specifically a realist both because of his attitude and because of the concentration upon particulars and the unity of method demanded by his task. This agreement between the materials used by the novelist and his manner of presentation led to the production of a type of fiction that was *realistic,* one may say, in subject matter, in treatment, and in interpretation of reality. It was this complete subjection of the novelist to an all-embracing formula that distinguished the products of the new school from the realistic novels of an earlier day.

Coming events cast their shadows before, particularly when they are complex events of far-reaching significance. A literary movement of such revolutionary character as naturalism could not come about as an isolated or unheralded phenomenon but only as a consequence of corresponding changes in thought. Indications of such a change can be detected in the work of George Eliot, Meredith, and Hardy. Meredith recognized the limitations imposed upon man by natural law, and the sense of kinship between man and nature figured prominently in the work of Hardy. Although she came too early to feel the full weight of the new movement in thought, George Eliot was closer to it than either Meredith or Hardy. Her work was in some respects an anticipation of the method and spirit of the naturalists. She refused to accept the full consequences of her thought, however, with the result that her interpretation of the conflict between natural and moral forces in the shaping of individual destiny was not altogether clear or convincing.

George Moore and George Gissing, who were both considerably younger than either Hardy or Meredith, came under the influence of the new realistic fiction while they were young enough to respond to it. While he was in Paris, Moore came into contact with the naturalists, and his first efforts in fiction were attempts to imitate the new style of novel. Viewed in its entirety, the work of Gissing is more closely allied to the naturalistic objective than is Moore's. Such novels as *The Unclassed, The Nether World, New Grub Street, The Odd Women,* and *Eve's Ransom,* a lighter tale than the others here mentioned, provide excellent examples of the author's power in the faithful recording of humble and obscure lives passed under the grinding pressure of deprivation and toil. Moore knew less at firsthand than Gissing about the hardships which he set himself to describe. Moreover, the author of *Esther Waters* and *A Mummer's Wife* was a naturalist during only a part of his literary career, and, measured by his full development, not during the most original or the most important part. Nevertheless, it was Moore who gave himself up most unreservedly to the new kind of fiction. Gissing, despite the human quality of his work, never produced anything at once so fully and objectively realized and so charged with feeling as *Esther Waters.*

Unlike the Victorian novelists, the naturalists made an effort to view their material dispassionately. Such an attempt on the part of the artist to eliminate himself from his work, and to express himself only through his subject by the perfection of his execution, was strikingly illustrated in a novel by Gustave Flaubert in 1857. This novel, often regarded as marking the beginning of naturalism, was *Madame Bovary*—a remarkable example of minute observation and painstaking care in the rendering of a highly particularized situation objectively and impersonally. It is a history of the moral downfall and eventual suicide of a pretty but shallow woman who, finding her existence in a small provincial town oppressively dull in comparison with her romantic dreams, longs for a more exalted life. Conceiving his subject with the definiteness of a scientist making an investigation, the author manages, by his treatment, to keep within the limits of his theme without producing the impression of stiffness or arbitrariness likely to characterize a scientific report. The subject under investigation is a type of human weakness illustrated in the character of Emma Bovary and now sometimes, in recognition of the authority of Flaubert's analysis, referred to as Bovaryism. It is the danger, in practical life, of sentimental aspirations and self-delusion in a shallow romantic temperament. The subject requires that the heroine be shown in relation to her provincial surroundings and reacting to them. We need also as readers to be made acquainted with her world and enabled to form an intelligent, independent impression of it. Thus equipped, we can appreciate the nature of Emma's misconceptions and the inadequacy of her understanding of her world. By watching the effect produced upon her by her narrow provincial circumstances, we are able to *see* her. This act of seeing her, which is something different from having her elaborately analyzed for us, is what Flaubert makes possible by his method of presentation.

Although led by his artist's conscience and the requirements of his theme into writing what may be termed a naturalistic novel, Flaubert was not in any narrow sense a naturalist. He was a man of too sensitive and original a mind to tie himself to a school. *Madame Bovary* owes its greatness not to the following of a formula but to the strength and control of imagination which enabled the author to seize upon such details as would endow his characters with life and bring the significant points of his theme into clear relief. A more distinctly naturalistic novel, in which the operation of a formula does begin to be evident, is *Germinie Lacerteux*, by Edmond and Jules de Goncourt. This novel, appearing in 1865, eight years after *Madame Bovary*, bears a preface by the authors, attacking the taste of the public for shallow and sentimental novels and demanding for themselves the privilege to undertake in fiction the work of science and to engage in serious social inquiry. They characterize their novel as a study in "the clinic of Love." There is indeed something clinical in this account of a poor maidservant who passes her life in circumstances of utter drudgery and enslavement to her milieu—the victim of poverty, toil, disease, and her own loving nature. In 1859, not many years before the writing of *Germinie Lacerteux*, Charles Darwin had published *The Origin of Species*—

a book which interpreted all organic life as being essentially a struggle for survival. That is what Germinie's life was, and it was to be one of the chief distinguishing marks of the naturalistic novel that it rendered life essentially as a "struggle for existence."

Naturalism

As naturalism consists essentially in the application to literature of certain scientific concepts and the scientific spirit, it is not possible to trace its earliest manifestations in full detail. The scientific movement of the nineteenth century helped to produce in people generally a scientific habit of mind. The positivism of Auguste Comte, which was so influential in shaping the mental development of George Eliot, was a system of thought founded upon "positive" as opposed to speculative knowledge—knowledge which, in other words, was subject to verification. Darwin's brilliant exposition of the operation of natural causes in the processes of evolution acted as a stimulus to the popular imagination and provided an incentive to look for natural causes in all the phenomena of life.

Such a tendency dominated the thinking of Hippolyte Taine, who applied to the study of culture the method of searching for truth, not through the application of an abstract conception, but through the observation of innumerable small facts. In the introduction to his famous *History of English Literature,* we find him saying that the student of the past must endeavor to reconstruct it in his imagination in order to make up for the want of direct observation so essential to true knowledge. The externals, he claims, are avenues leading to the inner man. "Leave on one side the theory and the mechanism of constitutions, religions and their systems, and try to see men in their workshops, in their offices, in their fields, with their sky and earth, their houses, their dress, cultivation, meals, as you do when, landing in England or Italy, you remark faces and motions, roads and inns, a citizen taking his walk, a workman drinking."

Three sources of influence were conceived by Taine to have contributed to man's development: *race, milieu,* and *moment.* By the factor of race is meant all the traits and tendencies which constitute the chain of interior causation. All physical and social circumstances which affect man from without are to be included in the consideration of his milieu. Nature, for example, in the form of soil, climate, landscape, and navigable waters, has been of tremendous influence in shaping the course of civilization. The term *moment* was used to designate the acquired momentum of any given period, derived from the combination of racial and environmental factors which had produced its dominant spirit. There was much that was artificial and unscientific in this formula, but the assumption that moral and cultural problems could be subjected to such methods of inquiry as were commonly employed in the study of physical phenomena was extremely important in providing a basis for the naturalists.

Coming under the influence of Taine and also of various current works upon physiology and heredity, Émile Zola decided that the new developments in science should be introduced into the novel. Thereupon he set about the task of putting his theory into execution with such remarkable skill and thoroughness that it is now no exaggeration to characterize him as the founder and also the chief representative of the naturalist school in fiction. A man of tremendous energy and strength of purpose, he was able to map out and carry through to completion a vast literary project to depict the life of his time in accordance with his theory of human behavior.

Inspired by Balzac's *Human Comedy,* he conceived the idea of writing a modern human comedy which would picture, as he thought, the physiological man as distinguished from the "metaphysical" or moral man of classical realism. He would show the generic traits and hereditary defects in the members of a family extending for five generations. In addition, he would show the effects of society upon the individual in widely varying types of environment. The general title of the series, which contains twenty novels, is *Les Rougon-Macquart: histoire naturelle et sociale d'une famille sous le Second Empire.* The usual method of the author is to take up in each novel a specific human case and to show in the background a segment of social conditions, or a distinct social or professional class. Thus in going from one novel to another we pass from life in the provinces to artisans in a Parisian suburb, coal miners in northern France, or the world of pleasure centered in Paris. The great range of the series is illustrated by the fact that it includes tradesmen of various kinds, railway workers, peasants, financiers, politicians, artists, soldiers, the clergy, and the medical profession, not to mention others.

In spite of the time required for documentation and the acquiring of firsthand evidence, Zola also wrote numerous critical articles in support of his views. One such article, in which he attempted to expound the principles of experimental fiction and to justify his method, is *Le Roman expérimental*, written several years after he had launched his Rougon-Macquart enterprise. As a specific statement of its author's position, this essay is an important document in the history of the naturalist movement.

Taking his cue from *L'Introduction à la médecine expérimentale*, by Claude Bernard, Zola attempts to apply to the writing of fiction the method advocated for medical investigation. Although his argument is too complicated to be reproduced in its entirety, a few important points may be summarized. The experimental novelist is to guard against preconceptions and look for truth only in natural phenomena. He is to operate upon his human material as a physicist experiments with inanimate matter. One great difficulty in the way of the novelist is that higher organisms have an interior milieu as well as an exterior milieu. This interior milieu is too complexly organized, Zola admits, to yield readily to experimentation. Laws have not yet been formulated for psychological phenomena, with the result that the experimental novel is still under a great handicap. There are, however, the factors of heredity and environment, in the application of which the novelist is considered by Zola to have his great opportunity—to show man struggling with his milieu, modifying it and being, in turn, modified by it.

Let us pause for a moment at this point to note that we have arrived at the heart of the naturalistic formula. The struggle between man and his environment, long a favorite situation of naturalists, must have appealed to them for a number of reasons. It had been popularized by Darwin and given the authority of a ruling principle. The novelist would naturally wish to make use of a theme which occupied men's minds and which, presented in simple terms, could be made to bear the air of scientific authority. It was a situation inherently dramatic and one that could be made to command the reader's sympathy. Universal in character, it could be set forth in a variety of circumstances without necessarily growing stale. It was, in fact, not a new theme but an old theme seen in a new light. Defoe, in *Robinson Crusoe*, dealt with a struggle between man and his surroundings but without specific attention to the effect upon the man—a point which was of primary importance to the naturalist.

The emphasis upon heredity and environment helps us to understand why the naturalist prefers to write about simple people with elementary reactions rather than about complex, highly organized natures. In these simple characters the interaction between the individual and his surroundings can be observed and recorded with greater clarity and precision. Such complex characters as are selected by the naturalist for representation are likely to be people who easily become the victims either of their surroundings or of their own weaknesses.

Returning now to Zola's conception of the experimental novel, we find that the naturalist, being scientific in spirit, is frank in dealing with all aspects of life. There are no subjects which he cannot treat, as there are no phenomena which the scientist does not attempt to explain. Furthermore, such a novelist is under no obligation to condemn his rogues or to look with favor upon his honest men. In fact, he is obliged to treat them all with impartiality. He is no more angry with an evil character than a physician is with a harmful drug or an infectious disease. The novelist, in short, is impersonal. His work is a report which has the merit of exact observation. He does not invent an arbitrary plot or work for a striking denouement. He does not add or detract in the interest of effect but keeps as close to a faithful picture of the course of nature as he can.

Despite his insistence upon the necessity of being impersonal, Zola makes much of the point that the novelist is not a mere observer engaged in making a photograph. He does not simply observe his material but conducts an experiment with it, modifying his phenomena, but not falsifying them, so as to demonstrate the operation of cause and effect. An experiment is based upon an idea, Zola asserts, but the idea is born of an observation. *La cousine Bette*, by Balzac, is given as an example of an experiment in which the ravages made by a man's amorous temperament are shown by placing the man in certain surroundings and exposing him to a series of trials.

It is clear from the outset that what Zola has in mind is something quite different from a true scientific experiment. The scientist does not control the behavior of his subject or determine what its behavior will be. He simply arranges matters so that he can observe specific reactions under specific conditions in sufficient number to enable him to draw the inferences necessary to his chain of scientific reasoning. If the evidence as it accumulates is against his hypothesis, there is nothing he can do but continue his investigation in the hope of new clues, or he must seek a new hypothesis to which his data can be accommodated. In the end he may have to admit failure. The experimental novelist, however, by carrying on his experiment in his head rather than in the unfeeling test tubes of a laboratory, can always be certain of reaching a solution in harmony with his hypothesis. He creates the characters who are to serve as the subject of his experiment; he arranges the conditions under which these characters behave; finally, he determines the nature of their behavior. Whatever impression he may have that his characters act independently of him is an illusion, for their behavior and the idea which it is intended to illustrate are conceived in the same brain in one creative process. In an actual experiment the subject and its reactions are quite independent of the experimenter.

Zola not only overstates his case but fails to conform to it in practice. The "impersonality" which he celebrates is incompatible with art. In an introduction to *Pierre et Jean*, Guy de Maupassant admits that the theory of the whole truth will not stand. A realistic work, no less than a poetic work, has to be composed—has, in other words, to be imagined or observed in accordance with some personal conception. The artist cannot possibly narrate everything. Having to select from a multitude of details, he will inevitably choose that which he regards as necessary to his subject. Life in its entirety contains inexplicable, illogical, and contradictory ingredients. Wishing to present his material so as to make clear its characteristic significance, the artist must compress and eliminate; he must use forethought and skill in composition in order to produce the specific impression of truth that he seeks to portray. Realist or not, he creates a world according to his imagination. Maupassant concludes that a realist in art should call himself an illusionist.

While masquerading as a scientist, Zola is in reality an artist. His fiction is memorable not by reason of its conformity to his theory, for it does not conform, but by the grace of its imaginative power and warmth of feeling, which are not the products of any formula. He ranges from subterranean depths of ugliness and squalor and vice to cloudlands of idealism, ending his career in Utopian dreams of the salvation of mankind. For all his pretense of scientific detachment, he is a passionate champion of truth and justice. Persuading himself that he is a disciple of the scientific materialism of his time, he remains at heart something of a Romantic. Far from being a simple transcription of reality, his work is a subjective product of personal observation and synthesizing imagination. Work which is so broad in scope, so intensely imagined, and so closely tied to its period, has not a little of the quality of an epic—a new kind of sociological epic reflecting the humanitarian and scientific spirit of its age and expressing itself in terms of poetic allegory, with symbols drawn not from a courtly and chivalrous past but from an industrialized and a mechanized present. Thus, the coal mine which serves as the central stage of *Germinal* is conceived as a menacing and devouring beast, which fills Étienne Lantier, a newly arrived worker, with dread:

A doubt troubled him, a fear of the Voreux in the middle of this bare plain, drowned in so thick a night. At every gust the wind seemed to rise, as if blowing from an ever-widening horizon. No dawn whitened the dead sky; only the blast furnaces were aflame, and the coke ovens, spreading a red glow without illuminating the dark unknown. And the Voreux, at the bottom of its hole, in the posture of an evil beast, went on crunching, breathing ever more heavily and slowly, uneasy from its painful digestion of human flesh.

The extent to which art should be an instrument of propaganda, considered theoretically, is a question impossible of solution. It is a shifting, relative matter, which cannot be reduced to fixed or absolute terms. From one angle it is an affair of the writer's purpose; from another it is simply an effect produced in the thing written, regardless of the intention of the writer. The propagandist, we may consider, is a man who devotes himself to means rather than to ends. The goal of one man, however, may be the starting point of another. Moreover, every life must be devoted to the means of achieving some end.

Taking another view of the problem, we may regard it as a matter of detachment or of absorption in the moment. The propagandist in art, we say, is engrossed in the most pressing problems of his time, whereas the pure artist lives in a world of larger horizons and less immediate concerns. Here again the distinction is a relative one. The man who views his world with a certain detachment may turn out in the end to have had the most profound understanding of it and may write what proves to be its most significant "message."

To suggest that art may be an instrument of propaganda is not to say that what is written as propaganda is necessarily art. A man who writes for a limited purpose is likely to have a limited appeal. What is written for the moment may well perish when the moment's need has been satisfied. To devote oneself to the propagation of doctrine is to turn from life to a formalized concept of life. It is as if one were to turn from exploration and discovery to the work of organization and exploitation. By implication at least, it is to confess that the true way of life has been found and that what remains is to make the truth prevail.

There is a close relationship between the naturalistic novel and the novel of social propaganda. Scientific investigation is a quest for truth and also a method of learning how to live. Medical science contributes to the betterment of life through the control and eradication of disease. A study of social problems leads naturally to a search for the means to ameliorate social conditions. Fiction dealing with social problems may contribute to the betterment of life by stimulating the process of social reform. When such a desire becomes the dominant incentive of a novelist, however, it may lead him not to the portrayal of a living reality but to the writing of a sermon, in which a formula operates in place of the writer's imagination and produces not life in its rich diffusion of freshness and energy but a savorless substitute for reality, an oversimplification, prepared according to a recipe. In his later works, written after the completion of the Rougon-Macquart series, Zola yielded more openly to the tendency to use the novel as an instrument of reform through the propagation of ideas. *Fécondité*, an attack upon the declining birth rate in France and a hymn in honor of the principle of fruitfulness and the domestic virtues, is an example of such a tendency—a lesson, Henry James calls it, "chalked . . . on the blackboard of the family sentiment."

GEORGE MOORE

George Moore was born in Ireland in 1852. He was the eldest son of a country gentleman, who lived part of the time on his estate, devoting himself to his family and taking a great interest in racing, and at other times in London, where he served as a member of Parliament. The most marked characteristic of young George during his boyhood seems to have been a disinclination to apply himself seriously to any kind of study. Upon coming of age, his father being now dead, he left Ireland and made his home for several years in Paris. Although the idea of living in a foreign capital must have been in itself a powerful incentive to a young man eager to escape the restraining influences of home, the ostensible reason for this momentous step was the desire to be a painter.

That it was a momentous step can hardly be questioned even though the ambition to be a painter was never realized. The years spent in Paris, coming in his twenties, were of incalculable importance to Moore in their effect upon his artistic development. It was a time of new ideas on art and literature, expressed everywhere in artistic and literary circles with characteristic Gallic vigor and decisiveness. This contact with the clarity and precision of the French mind must have been a particularly valuable experience for one who had been inclined in his youth to drift amiably and somewhat aimlessly, groping his way slowly toward a comprehension of himself and his problems. The sojourn in Paris equipped him with a definite attitude toward a few fundamental aspects of life and art. The tenacity with which he clung to his opinions, once having formed them, together with his eccentricity, probably served to limit his development. Nevertheless, such success as he had would probably have been denied him had it not been for the concentration of power growing out of his narrowness of purpose. Moreover, the Paris experience first imbued him with the impulse toward artistic expression, an impulse which in time became the ruling passion of his life.

This artistic bent of Moore is historically important, for it marks the advent into the English novel of a new development, already beginning to be apparent also in the writing of Henry James. English novelists, as we have seen, were not characteristically artists in a narrow or self-conscious sense. They were accustomed to take their art with a certain large and generous carelessness, gaining thereby in spontaneity but being guilty not infrequently of confused aims and slipshod workmanship. Walter Pater, whose *Marius the Epicurean* was published in 1885, after two of Moore's novels had appeared in print, proved to be an exception, but Pater was not primarily a novelist, and *Marius,* be it noted, was greatly admired by Moore. Fielding, Scott, Dickens, and Thackeray were artists, to be sure, but not in an exclusive or preoccupied sense. Before his financial disaster, Scott did not permit his writing of fiction to interfere greatly with his life as a country gentleman. Jane Austen, an artist to the fingertips, managed to seem quite unconcerned about her role as novelist.

Despite the many differences separating them, Moore and James were alike in recognizing the value of craftsmanship to a novelist. They both found more inspiration in French fiction than in the current work of English novelists, with the result that in their work the English novel was brought into contact with Continental standards and ceased to be a purely English affair. Consequently it began to show a noticeable loss of the English partiality for morality and humor and acquired a tone of greater incisiveness and austerity. This change in temper was due not entirely to the crossing of national boundaries but was also a result of the growing spirit of detachment and skepticism made inevitable by the spread of scientific inquiry.

Any attempt to deal with Moore's entire career would require attention to various strands of influence, classifiable under such headings as aestheticism, impressionism, and symbolism. Analysis of the later novels is made more difficult by the fact that different phases of development became mingled in the same work. One important chain of influence is represented by enthusiasm for Gautier,

Baudelaire, and Mallarmé—an enthusiasm that encouraged Moore to make an ideal of art and to "deify the flesh" in such novels as *The Lake* and *The Brook Kerith.* An admirer of Balzac, he became a convert to naturalism under the influence of Flaubert, the Goncourt brothers, and Zola, retaining at the same time his adoration of beauty. In Pater, in Turgenev, and afterwards in such Irish mystics as Yeats and George W. Russell, Moore found the inspiration for a new metamorphosis leading to the richly atmospheric products of his maturity—such imaginative reconstitutions of the past as are to be found in *The Brook Kerith, A Story-Teller's Holiday,* and *Héloïse and Abélard.* The beginnings of this transformation of the artist can be detected in the delicate simplicity and suggestiveness of *The Lake* and *The Untilled Field.*

When in Paris between 1873 and 1880, Moore became acquainted with a number of Impressionist painters. Afterwards he was always greatly interested in their work and had a particularly high regard for Manet and Degas, both as men and as painters. This interest was reflected in his work as a novelist. Naturalism did not continue to satisfy him artistically because it tended to ignore the differences between art and science. The naturalists paid too little attention to the need of employing the means of suggestion while dealing bluntly in mere physical description. The narration of any fact was useless, Moore wrote in an article on Turgenev, published in *Impressions and Opinions* in 1891, unless it had been "tempered and purified in thought and stamped by thought with a specific value." In another article in the same volume, Zola's mind was likened to a coarsely woven net that allowed live things to escape while capturing only a quantity of debris.

A few years earlier, however, Moore had been an enthusiastic supporter of the new fiction. To attack it for its artistic limitations was not, in any case, to share the hostility of those who attacked it on moral grounds. Against such criticism the author of *A Mummer's Wife* always took the offensive, particularly while smarting under the abuse heaped upon his own early novels. In 1885 he wrote a satirical pamphlet entitled *Literature at Nurse, or Circulating Morals,* in which he likened the circulating libraries to nurseries ruled over by motherly librarians, who, as arbiters of literary taste, sought to exclude from circulation any books dealing honestly and fearlessly with life. There was no more justification, the author contended, for limiting a novelist to the study of a healthy subject than there would be for denying the right of a physician to study a diseased patient.

Literature at Nurse was written in the early stages of a controversy that lasted for a decade or more. When the novels of the new French school were translated and published in England, they met with an eager response but aroused, at the same time, a storm of protests. Newspapers and other self-appointed guardians of the public launched crusades to prevent the spread of the "demoralizing" books. So violent was the uprising that Henry Vizetelly was fined for publishing three of Zola's novels and, after a second trial, was sent to prison for selling novels of Zola, Bourget, and Maupassant. The hostility originated for the most part in the outraged sense of propriety of persons who were shocked by the frank treatment of "unmentionable" topics. The presence of something "improper" in a book made such readers reluctant to admit that there might also be something laudable.

Time was needed for the public to adjust itself to the new point of view. Any radical departure from conventional standards in a popular literary form is certain to bewilder or antagonize a large proportion of readers. The absence from the new novels of conventional tributes to beauty and goodness and innocence, qualities that the most hardheaded Victorian novelists had not failed to treat reverently, must have seemed to many readers like brutal disregard of the noblest things in life. The absence of heartiness and humor was not likely to please those whose tastes had been formed upon the tumultuous high spirits of Dickens. The absence of charm, of chivalry, of the atmosphere of the heroic and the spirit of high adventure, must have been distasteful to those who sought romantic fare in their novel reading. Discussing the French naturalists in "A Note on Realism," first published in 1883, Stevenson said that they worked in a cramped and uncompromising spirit and were too much given to a search for mere technical excellence. They missed the truth for which they searched by forgetting that all representative art must be both realistic and ideal. Although the idealist might be in danger of losing all grip on reality through lack of attention to it, the realist, in his insane pursuit of scientific thoroughness, was in danger of burying his readers under an avalanche of facts not worth learning. To err on the side of realism, and thus to sacrifice beauty and significance, was more in the spirit of his generation, Stevenson considered, "than to sin in quest of the ideal."

Moore's first novel, *A Modern Lover,* published in 1883 and afterwards revised as *Lewis Seymour and Some Women,* was not a very promising beginning. Written, as the author asserted, out of memories of Balzac, Zola, and Goncourt, it is a rather crude account of how an egoistic young painter rises in the world by making compromises with his art and by accepting unfeelingly the sacrifices of various women devoted to his interest. *A Mummer's Wife* (1885) is greatly superior to its predecessor. It traces in naturalistic fashion the downward career of a weak, pleasure-loving woman who abandons her dull, unsympathetic husband to run away with the manager of a traveling theatrical company. Although the central situation is somewhat like that of *Madame Bovary,* the method of representation is more like that of Zola, to whom Moore wrote while he was engaged on the novel that he hoped to put "a dagger into the heart of the sentimental school" and bring about a change in the literature of his country.

Esther Waters

With the publication of *Esther Waters,* in 1894, Moore reached the end of his first period of development. In his next productions, *Celibates* and *Evelyn Innes,* he turned to themes of a more individual character, requiring a less objective type of treatment. Thereafter he was to devote much of his fiction to the analysis of psychological and spiritual problems, while working, at the same time, toward a simplification of method. The desire to simplify the art of prose narrative and recapture for it the air of spontaneous reminiscence and meditation was a cherished ambition of Moore's later years. He wished to catch in his art the intonation of human speech and the charm of a simple, natural idiom; he would restore to storytelling the virtues of an oral tradition which had not had to bear the weight of scientific and aesthetic sophistication.

The simplicity of *Esther Waters* is not, however, the calculated and somewhat artificial simplicity of *The Brook Kerith* or *A Story-Teller's Holiday*. At the same time it is not a merely negative quality but a product of conscious effort. The author refrained from employing complicating factors that would divert attention from the simple and solid virtues of his story. He could have intensified the trials of his heroine and made a greater show of sympathy for her in various forms of protest and lamentation. To have done so, however, would have been to be guilty of the offenses against objectivity characteristic of Victorian fiction.

Although given to speculations of a somewhat freakish and whimsical nature, Moore was not a man of theory. He seems to have cared little for thought that was not in some degree the fruit of his experience. By the time he wrote *Esther Waters* he had become critical of Zola's theories, and he made no effort in this novel to conform to them. Esther's career does not illustrate any particular theory of hereditary or environmental influence. Circumstances sometimes work in her favor, as, for example, the fact that she has such kind and considerate employers as Mrs. Barfield and Miss Rice. Only in its general outline does the novel follow the naturalistic formula. The heroine is an illiterate servant who is driven from home at an early age by a brutal stepfather. Her story is one of struggle against odds to preserve her child's life.

What Moore did was to discard the extreme features of naturalistic usage and refuse to bind himself to the observance of a formula. His novel gained thereby in simplicity and humanity. The theme of struggle for life he transposed into a different emotional key by making it a struggle of the heroine not for herself but for her child. The novel thus gains in compassionateness and is provided with a powerful central impetus.

Esther Waters was written after the author had produced a series of failures—*A Mere Accident, Spring Days, Mike Fletcher,* and *Vain Fortune.* Perhaps under the circumstances Moore found some consolation in Zola's theory that a novelist should curb his imagination and make his novel simply an impersonal report. A conception of fiction writing that removed it from the uncertain realm of personal inspiration and reduced it to ponderable terms had its advantages. It encouraged the novelist to work deliberately as a man conscious of his craft—a course of action pleasing to Moore, who was always a deliberate artist.

The impersonality of *Esther Waters* is evident when it is compared with *Middlemarch* or *The Return of the Native*. It does not appear to have been written to illustrate any particular theory of conduct, or to reveal the working of any set of laws more specific than the forces of love and necessity operating in Esther's life. There is nothing in the novel that we associate with Moore, as we associate the characters of *Middlemarch* with George Eliot's moral philosophy, or the fatality of events in *The Return of the Native* with Hardy's pessimism. Thus the sturdy figure of Esther would seem to have attained an existence apart from her creator in a manner not equaled by the more richly endowed characters of George Eliot and Hardy. In her patient acceptance of suffering and quiet perseverance, Esther represents what Miss Dorothy M. Hoare, in *Some Studies in the Modern Novel*, has characterized as a prose reaction to life, quite different from the poetic reaction of Hardy or the intellectual reaction of George Eliot.

It is one of the weaknesses of mankind to esteem that which is rare and to undervalue that which is common. Prose, being a thing that is common, has come to signify something plain and dull. To be *prosaic*, according to the dictionary, is to be matter-of-fact, tiresome, insipid, flat, unimaginative. The tendency to undervalue a thing, whatever its merit, because it is unpoetical would seem itself to be a product of dullness or lack of discrimination. The mind that reacts readily only to the uncommon is itself dull and insensitive, whereas the alert mind is more readily responsive and is appreciative of the minute shadings or overtones in an experience. Acts of essential beauty and worthiness may go unappreciated by minds that have been deadened by custom. The trivial, so long as it is freakish, arouses more interest than the common virtues without which our civilization would fall.

The function of art is not limited to the celebration of rare and transfigured moments of tragedy or high endeavor. It is no less important for us to recognize the beauty that is likely to pass unnoticed because it makes no pretensions and draws no special attention to itself. Heroism is not an exclusive form of virtue. Even the heroic figure of classical tragedy appeals to us by being close to our common humanity. The difference between one act of heroism and another is more in the circumstances which engender it than in any inherent characteristic. It is with circumstances, however, that we are here concerned. In the past, tragedy was commonly set forth in the panoply of greatness or worldly rank. An admittedly important personage became involved in events of unusual significance, leading to an intensification of feeling. Such an arbitrary method of heightening the effect was theoretically inadmissible to the naturalist, for it would have been a violation of the scientific spirit. To a scientist one fact is of equal significance to another until it is proved to be otherwise. Accordingly, to a naturalist the life of a maidservant is equal in significance to the life of a duchess, and it may provide a better opportunity for the observation of natural phenomena. An honest following of laboratory methods rarely produces spectacular effects, whatever may be the assumptions of the Sunday supplement.

What, then, is a novelist to do who takes for his subject a character whose virtues are, in the world's eyes, of the common and humdrum variety? A Victorian novelist would have been likely to sentimentalize a character like Esther, making her possibly a "flower of the slums," like Gissing's Thyrza. To have poetized her, however, would have been to miss the particular quality in the subject celebrated by Moore. A form of beauty that is common cannot be rendered by the method of turning it into something uncommon. A prose version of life, to succeed on its own ground, must not be adorned with special graces borrowed from poetry.

In keeping with his desire to preserve its homely flavor, Moore was careful not to romanticize his subject either by prettifying or debasing it. For the same reason he deliberately refrained from playing up the dramatic features of his story. Esther, for example, resigns herself after a brief struggle to the second intrusion of William Latch into her life, when she is on the point of becoming the wife of Fred Parsons. Even her seduction is presented as a simple fact without any of the overwrought emotionalism of similar scenes in Victorian fiction. It is treated seriously, as a problem fraught with difficulty and peril for the victim, but in practical rather than in tragic or high moral terms. The account of William's losing fight to accumulate enough money by betting to enable him to go to a drier climate in search of health is another example of the factual, essentially non-dramatic method followed in the novel. The situation is extremely moving but not as the result of any noticeable working up of effect. Emphasis is placed here, as elsewhere, upon the quiet, unostentatious courage and devotion of the heroine.

Having been brought up as a member of the Plymouth Brethren, an austere religious sect, Esther can never get over her feeling that betting and drinking are sinful and wicked. It is her fate, however, to become the wife of a man whose business it is to sell liquor and make bets. The two poles of her life, in fact, are the chapel and the public house, the former of which is represented by Mrs. Barfield and Fred Parsons, and the latter by William, with his life of racing and gambling. Here is material for what might, in a different type of novel, have been developed into a deep personal conflict. Such a development, however, would not have been in keeping with the simple nature of Esther, who, although she cannot approve of her husband's business, is too loyal a wife to make an issue of her dislike. Thus, what might have been a subject for drama is made to contribute to the general effect of stoical resignation characteristic of the heroine's behavior.

For about six years after leaving the hospital, from the time of her harrowing experience with Mrs. Spires, the baby farmer, until she secures employment with Miss Rice, Esther passes through a period of extreme hardship while struggling to support her child. Moore does not spare the reader the harsh details of this experience. At the same time, he does not repress his sympathy and is not over-insistent upon the element of brutality. Not all of Esther's employers are cruel, and there are moments of calm and relaxation for her even during her time of stress. Important as the period is from the naturalist's point of view, the author passes over it quickly, devoting only about one-ninth of the entire space to what in length of time elapsed is equal to one-third of the time consumed by the entire story.

This portion of the novel differs from the rest also in being devoted more exclusively to the heroine. It is to the earlier and later scenes that we owe the background of racing and gambling, which contributes so much to the novel in the way of liveliness and color. In the first twelve chapters we are given a picture of the Barfields and particularly of the servants in this household in which racing is the absorbing concern of nearly everyone. This time of growing happiness for Esther is rudely brought to a close by William's desertion of her and the subsequent discovery of her pregnancy.

Then follows her unhappy return to a home ruled over by a brutal and callous stepfather, her going to the lying-in hospital, and her long struggle against adversity until she finds peace and happiness as the servant of Miss Rice, in a quiet London suburb. It is here that she becomes acquainted with Fred Parsons, whose wife she is prevented from becoming by the accidental reappearance of William, now a prosperous betting man and part owner of a public house.

Esther's feeling for William reasserts itself the more readily because of her devotion to her child's interest, and she becomes his wife. We now find ourselves once more in the atmosphere of racing, not as we have encountered it at Woodview, but as it is reflected in a London public house where betting is carried on illegally and racing is the chief topic of conversation. William, moreover, being a bookmaker, has to spend much of his time at the racecourses. On one memorable occasion he takes Esther and her friend Sarah to see the Derby; the three chapters in which this expedition is described are among the best in the novel. There is the same ring of authenticity in the scenes in the public house, in which the races are discussed and methods of picking a winner are argued over.

Had Dickens been the author of *Esther Waters*, he would probably have made it a special point to expose the evil effects of gambling. He would doubtless have looked for a scapegoat, and William might not have got off so easily as he does with Moore. It is in keeping with the spirit of naturalism that Moore makes no direct attack upon gambling. He recognizes that betting leads to endless trouble and suffering, and he does not fail to show it, but he lets the facts speak for themselves. Gambling, viewed broadly, is not something that can be eradicated by the simple method of attacking the gambler. William, on the whole, is a good man according to his lights. The novelist who remains true to the spirit of naturalism sees that the roots of most problems lie deeper than the surface manifestation with which he deals. One of the weaknesses of the Victorian novel of reform was that it often falsified its subject in the interest of personal drama. In such fiction, the fight between the forces of good and evil was usually presented as a conflict between persons rather than as the operation of impersonal forces envisaged by the naturalist.

In one respect the naturalist may have erred by making too literal an interpretation of scientific theory. Darwin had given currency to the idea of a struggle for survival. But the struggle conceived by Darwin had taken place over a very long period of time. It was simply one aspect of a gradual process by which one species insensibly developed from another. For the novelist to compress into the life of an individual what had been conceived as belonging to the development of species was to produce something quite different from the process of natural selection. It was to make conscious and particular what had been conceived as being unconscious and general, and to make nature an endless war. To depict life as a mere struggle and nothing else was to eliminate normal resiliency and to introduce a sense of oppression not characteristic of ordinary existence. The artist who turned all life into conflict in a rigid application of naturalistic theory was led astray not by following science but by wrongfully applying a scientific theory. He was misled, as people often are, by a phrase.

It is one of the virtues of *Esther Waters* that it creates an impression not simply of conscious effort but of normal impulsive living. In addition, it strikes a balance between sobriety and animation. The background, which is interesting in itself, serves to lighten the atmosphere of the novel and to lessen the tension produced by the central struggle. For all her gravity, Esther is not one to ponder upon her misfortunes, and at the time of her worst trials her great love for her baby upholds her. All in all, her life is not without its elements of satisfaction. In her simple, natural adaptability she blends with her background, seeming at times to sink into it. But her quiet, unobtrusive presence is somehow felt, making William's public house a different place from what it would be without her. She grows upon the reader not by displaying anything unusual or unexpected but by simply being her own stanch, resolute self. Gradually and almost indiscernibly, the shy, awkward girl of twenty becomes the mature, self-possessed woman of thirty-eight, close in spirit and feeling to the cultivated woman whom she serves and who is now more her friend than mistress.

CHAPTER XVII

The Novelist in Search of Perfection

HENRY JAMES

George Moore's endeavor to introduce French methods into the English novel was one of various indications that a tendency to look sympathetically across national boundaries was manifesting itself again in England. For many prominent Victorians, even those to whom literature was a primary concern, the Continental novel seems hardly to have existed. When Dickens crossed the Channel, he took, in addition to his baggage, his English point of view, France being for him, it would appear, not the country of Balzac but rather a place where one might go conveniently in search of recreation. George Eliot, fresh from the writing of *Adam Bede*, noted curtly in her Journal that *Le Père Goriot* was a hateful book, and not long afterwards solemnly expressed the hope that her own novels would be well translated into French so that they might help the French the more effectively "to purify their literary air."

The time was not far distant, however, when such blind and narrowly complacent insularity was to give way to an enthusiastic cosmopolitanism. Arnold Bennett and H. G. Wells wrote for a public that was familiar with many of the novelists of France and Russia. After the First World War the novel, as represented by such writers as Dorothy Richardson, James Joyce, Virginia Woolf, and Aldous Huxley, became increasingly sophisticated. Urbanity, skepticism, and tolerance were characteristic features of the new age, the comfortable provincialism of the Victorians having gone decidedly out of fashion.

A writer who made a unique contribution to this change of temper was Henry James, whose period of productivity, extending over the last quarter of the nineteenth century and the first decade of the twentieth, reached from the time of George Eliot's supremacy to the heyday of Bennett and Wells. Besides literally bridging the gulf between the Victorian era and the day before yesterday, the career of James was expressive in no small way of the growth of a liberal outlook. An American by birth and lifelong associations, he spent nearly all of his life, after he was thirty, in England, seeking in the old world a more mature culture than he could find in America, upon which to nurture his art. Thus, by virtue of his experience, he became a student of contrasting cultures. In America he had looked toward Europe; in Europe he looked at everything from a point of view that remained substantially American. Eventually he was able to look at America with the eyes of a European and at Europe with the eyes of an American.

How could such a person be expressive of his age? How could an American residing in England and writing in a tradition derived largely from France be representative of anything but himself? The answer is that he was a characteristic figure of his literary generation in his growing cosmopolitanism and in his recognition of the complexity and relativity of experience. Eventually he acquired a point of view that was neither American nor European, but an amalgam of both. Similarly his attitude toward life was neither that of a Puritan nor exactly that of a man of the world, but a cross between the two. It was this union of different elements, and of elements more or less in opposition to each other, which gave to the mature work of James its peculiar combination of moral sensitivity and delicate appreciation of the most refined worldliness. The effect produced was somewhat as if a man of the world should be possessed of the qualities of a cloistered devotee, or, conversely, as if a deeply religious man had made a religion of worldliness.

Being an American with a background of New York and New England, having grown up on English and French as well as American literature, an admirer of Balzac and Turgenev, a visitor on many occasions in Italy, a resident of England and frequenter of Paris—such a man could hardly be a provincial. Moreover, there were reasons inherent in his theory of art why James should interest himself in the manners, customs, habits, and forms of civilized living and why his books should bear the marks of a high degree of sophistication. Nevertheless, for all his interest in complex relationships, his novels contain characters who charm us by their simple, ingenuous goodness. The author's experience of the old and new worlds, with their differing degrees of complexity in social relationships, gave him the inspiration for one of his most characteristic themes— problems arising between people of different cultural backgrounds, in which the dissimilarity of point of view was the main factor in creating the predicament. Thus, by virtue of his own background, James became a specialist in tracing the growth of initiation into a more sophisticated or more enlightened point of view—a type of situation that could be given a great variety of turns.

As he grew up in a family which was often on the move and as his father disliked conventionality and conformity, James received a very irregular schooling. There is a passage in *A Small Boy and Others* in which he records that he and the other children were brought up in horror of *conscious* propriety, or of what the elder James called "flagrant" morality. Elsewhere in the same volume, the *conscious* conscience is designated as being "the very home of the literal, the haunt of so many pedantries." The encouragement of the James children to follow their inclinations and to be on their guard against priggishness and formalism of every kind seems to have borne fruit in the case of the future novelist, perhaps the more in that he acquired at an early age an attitude of critical and curious detachment. Subsequently, when he left the United States, in revolt against its commercialism and provinciality, seeking a spiritual home, as it were, in Europe, he was living up to the family tradition of freedom and acting as the individualist son of his individualist father.

Although he had been taken abroad in his infancy, James received his first real experience of Europe during a residence of three years, beginning when he was twelve. Part of this sojourn was spent in Paris, and it was while he was under the spell of that city of such rich and varied appeal that he began to awaken to a sense of what a life devoted to art might mean. The intensity of his impressions during this period is reflected in passages of *A Small Boy and Others*, which glow with memories of more than half a century. One such passage tells of a favorite walk along the streets and quays of Paris, a walk that produced a sense of thickening mystery and mounting emotion as if some curious and important secret were about to be revealed. Sometimes, the author confesses, he would sneak off to take this walk by himself so as to experience to the full the intensity of his adventure. And the message which the "gray-headed, clear-faced" old houses and far-stretching perspectives were all the time uttering might well have been, James suggests: "Art, art, art, don't you see? Learn, little gaping pilgrims, what *that* is!"

The degree to which the little pilgrim did learn this lesson of the Paris streets and shop windows and apply it to the writing of fiction is well attested by the long list of novels and stories, the prefaces to the New York edition of his works, and the several books of criticism which eventually came from his pen. No other novelist has excelled him in joining the critical with the creative faculty, and no critic has ever made a more searching or a more fruitful exploration of the problems confronting the novelist. It was the firmly held conviction of James that art thrived upon discussion and experiment and critical exchange of views. Sometimes he expressed his chagrin that the English-speaking peoples should be so much inclined to take the problems and processes of art as things not to be inquired into; that they should have such "marked collective mistrust of anything like close or analytic appreciation." This failure of the general sensibility he once made the theme of an ironic story, entitled "The Figure in the Carpet," about an artist who wrote for a public that failed to grasp what was his most characteristic intention. The world chattered without comprehending and in the end the secret of the famous man remained unrevealed. The question raised by the story, James suggests in the preface, "can be but whether the very secret of perception hasn't been lost."

Although he developed slowly, James developed steadily and in a manner that was peculiarly his own. There is nothing surprising, accordingly, in the fact that the public failed to keep up with him. Even for the present-day reader, equipped with a knowledge of the artist's whole career, the problem of full appreciation, particularly of the later novels, is not a simple one. Apart from the mannerisms and personal peculiarities of style, there are two general sources of this much advertised difficulty, one being the author's indirectness of method and the other his attitude. This latter barrier to understanding, though not so apparent as the intricacy of method, contributes not a little to the uninitiated reader's difficulties. The resourcefulness of the artist and his flawlessness of craftsmanship are things that yield their beauty to attentive reading, but a point of view that is compounded of various elements may be difficult to grasp. Most of us know what it is to come into contact with an attitude that strikes us as being characteristically French, or English, or American. The point of view displayed in the later novels of James, however, falls into none of these categories, while it reflects something of each. To add to our possible bewilderment, these novels do not seem to belong to a definite period of time. They may seem in some quarters to be a little old-fashioned and sentimental, but no one, for all that, would be likely to put them down as characteristically Victorian. They are the products of one who repeatedly asserted his faith in the importance of art; yet they never breathe the spirit of a narrow aestheticism. They are sophisticated and worldly but never brash and flippant in the post-Victorian manner.

Despite his belief that art thrived best upon a traditional culture, James was no blind follower of tradition. It was never his opinion that the novelist should be limited to any "hard and fast rule of presentation." His definition of the novel was simply that it was a direct and personal impression of life, and he characterized it as being, "under the righ. persuasion, the most independent, most elastic, most prodigious of literary forms."

H. G. Wells considered that the novel should enlighten men and enlarge their sympathies. It should uncover pretenses and uproot impostures and open the way to new and better ways of living. In short, as Wells viewed it, the chief function of the novel should be to perform for civilization a valuable work of elucidation. Whatever advantages there might be in such a utilization of the materials and methods of art, the result attained was not likely to be simply an "impression of life." Virginia Woolf criticized this view of the novel in a pamphlet entitled *Mr. Bennett and Mrs. Brown.* The Edwardian novelists, she contended, were more interested in the material trappings of life than in the thing itself. If they were to write a novel about Mrs. Brown, they would look at things around her rather than at the woman herself—at factories, shops, utopias, decoration, upholstery, but not at human nature. James did not make this mistake, and neither did he confuse the art of fiction with science or sociology. It was no small part of his contribution to the novel, in fact, that he was more scrupulous than most English novelists had been in keeping fiction within the province of art.

Near the end of his life James had the experience of having his work held up to merciless ridicule by Wells in a parody entitled *Boon.* Afterwards the author of *Boon* wrote a letter of apology and explanation to James, a friend of many years, in which he explained his antagonism as being directed against the view that literature was an end rather than a means. In replying, James refused to make any apology for being an artist. He ended his letter by saying: "It is art that *makes* life, makes interest, makes importance, for our consideration and application of these things, and I know of no substitute whatever for the force and beauty of its process. If I were Boon I should say that any pretense of such a substitute is helpless and hopeless humbug; but I wouldn't be Boon for the world."[1]

The novelist, in other words, is not a mere technician engaged in making a transcript of actual happenings. He has to impose some

[1] *The Letters of Henry James*, New York, 1920, Vol. II, p. 490.

form of discipline upon the raw materials of experience. Even when he works from observation, he finds elements which cannot be utilized. What is properly his subject is always related to something else; his problem as an artist is to know where to stop following up these relationships. He must surrender part of his material and must simplify and select. What happens must be right, and its rightness will depend upon the ability of the artist to invoke the right note, to extract the essence of the matter from the trivial and accidental. Art, in short, is a process by which life is transformed and given meaning. It would be an easy process, says James, if the artist could find his simplifications somehow prepared and provided. Since they are not so provided, he must invent them.

To look briefly at the nature of the boundary line separating art from science may be useful at this point. Having to do with life, art has consequently to do with everything—moral, social, or scientific—that affects life. Science contributes to the artist's understanding of reality and provides hints in the matter of technique. It brings new concepts of human relations. Nevertheless, the province of art remains separate and distinct. When knowledge gained from science has become a part of human experience, giving color to man's hopes and fears, it is then such material as belongs directly to the artist. J. B. S. Haldane says, in *Daedalus*, that our poets and artists must be educated in science so that they can interpret the world in the light of our present-day conceptions of it. An artist so educated, it may be added, should write not as the expositor of a theory but with complete freedom of imagination. His enlarged mental horizon should appear in his work indirectly and by implication. *The Way of All Flesh*, by Samuel Butler, is indicative of such a trend. It gives a picture of human relations as seen in the light both of science and of sentiment.

Unlike the painter or the sculptor, the novelist can employ a direct means of communication. He can employ at will narration, description, or exposition—in which respect he is not unlike the historian or the scientist. What makes him different from either of them is his ultimate purpose to produce not an explanation of phenomena but an impression of life.

The scientist is inclined to look beyond the thing with which he is immediately concerned. The problem holding his attention at any given moment will cease to occupy him when it has performed its function of leading him to something else. His attitude of mind is active, whereas that of an artist is, by comparison, contemplative. Art stimulates us without impelling us to action. It calls indeed for a suspension of activity so that we can realize the nature of our impressions. The artist finds pleasure in the world's diversity and devotes himself to savoring the multitudinous echoes that arise from his experience. The scientist, on the contrary, lives for something that is not in his immediate grasp. His interest is not to find pleasure in diversity but to reduce differences in the interest of general law. Strictly as a scientist, he cares for individuals only as they belong to his particular problem or fit into some larger scheme of relationships. Thus Mr. Wells, whose point of view is more nearly scientific than aesthetic, is less interested in his characters as individuals than in the new world order that he would like to see established. The artist, however, looks for life not in institutions or governmental red tape but in the human integer. For him to place institutions above individuals would be to put the cart before the horse. It has been suggested by Virginia Woolf that what is chiefly wrong with Mr. Wells' social order is the inferiority of the Joans and Peters out of whom it has been contrived.

The scientist can accomplish his objective only by keeping within the limitations imposed upon him by the nature of his investigation. Similarly it is important for the artist to know what are the boundaries that encompass him in the performance of his task. He must understand that if he would speak as an artist he must speak through his art. For a novelist to speak as an artist, however, is not a simple matter, particularly if he strives conscientiously to keep strictly within his role. The art of fiction has been developing over a long period, during which time it has become closely affiliated with other literary forms. Moreover, it rests upon a broad base of comparatively artless taletelling, and, as it is generally practiced, liberal use is made of direct modes of communication.

Professor John Dewey[2] makes a distinction between art and science by saying that "science states meanings; art expresses them."

[2] *Art as Experience*, New York, 1934, p. 84.

Science can describe an experience but it cannot supply one. A painter cannot state in words what he expresses in his painting. Similarly a novelist cannot state about his subject what he expresses aesthetically through it.

Closely related to this difference is the fact that the scientific statement of a thing is by its nature general while an aesthetic expression of it is necessarily individual. An explanation of the meaning of grief distinguishes it from other emotional states and is applicable to grief in every possible circumstance. The artist's method of expressing grief, however, is to deal with a particular case. Even a conventional portrayal of such a generalized state as saintliness is to a certain degree individualized, according to Professor Dewey, who aptly observes: "Bliss is not a stencil transferable from one painter's work to that of another, but bears the mark of its individual creator, for it expresses *his* experience as well as that presumed to belong to a saint in general."[3]

James thoroughly appreciated the fact that the novelist must establish the individuality of his characters. We become interested in people by being enabled to share their existence. Only when we know people do their adventures have a meaning for us. A passage from *The Lesson of Balzac* serves admirably to sum up the matter: "There is no such thing in the world as an adventure pure and simple; there is only mine and yours, and his and hers—" An act apart from the conditions that produce it may satisfy the wonder of a child but it cannot contribute much to any deep regard for experience. There must be a fusion of the act with the forces out of which it grows, and there can be no such fusion without both the acting agent and his consciousness of what he does.

The novel as conceived by James is neither an impersonal rendering of life nor a personal autobiography. The author must surrender himself to his subject, but his subject cannot be separated from the point from which it is observed or from the treatment by which it is set forth. To assume that the subject has a reality apart from the work itself is to think of fiction not as an art but as something akin to science, not as an act of expression but as a report upon existent phenomena. It would be well for us to keep this fact in mind when

³ *Ibid.*, p. 92.

we find James being condemned simply on the basis of his treatment without regard to the purpose which the treatment was intended to serve.

That it did serve a purpose can hardly be denied. James was aware that expression in art requires fusion of the various properties. If a work of art is to speak properly as a work of art, the constituent parts must contribute to the whole effect without seeming to be imposed upon the design. In his later novels James achieved a notable fusion of the different elements. Setting, atmosphere, characters, actions, and mental states all merge so well that the reader hardly discerns any shifting of the focus of attention. The very perfection of workmanship adds to the difficulty of analysis.

Similarly, the problem of morality in fiction can be considered properly only in relation with other matters. As the subject cannot be separated from the treatment, so the question of morality is bound up with both. There is no such thing as an intrinsically bad subject. A novelist who takes a low view of life will, in the nature of things, be unlikely to produce an impression of nobility and courage in the life he records. Art deals with life, and in life there are gradations of good and evil, of beauty and ugliness. To look for a specific moral lesson in a work of art is to be literal and inclined to pedantry. One goes to a novel not for guidance in a particular problem but to have his mind opened and his sense of life enlarged and refreshed. The greater the novel the more abundant will be its meaning. Its morality rests ultimately upon the sensibility, truthfulness, and reach of the author's perception.

It has sometimes been assumed of James that his interest in the technique of presentation somehow denoted a corresponding lack of interest in life. He has been pictured by some critics as a coldly formal artist, a sort of ingenious spider engaged in weaving intricate webs. His later novels have been treated by Mr. E. M. Forster[4] as if they are elaborate trifles from which practically all life has been squeezed in a search for pretty and artificial patterns. The characters "remind one of the exquisite deformities who haunted Egyptian art in the reign of Akhnation" and so on. It is interesting to note that the bloodless precisian here postulated regarded Balzac as the

[4] *Aspects of the Novel*, London, 1927, p. 206.

greatest of all novelists and commended in particular the mass and solidity of his representation of social phenomena. "The great difference between the great Frenchman and the eminent others is that, with an imagination of the highest power, an unequalled intensity of vision, he saw his subject in the light of science as well, in the light of the bearing of all its parts on each other, and under pressure of a passion for exactitude, an appetite, the appetite of an ogre, for all the kinds of facts."[5] These do not sound like the words of a man whose chief interest in fiction was a regard for exquisite trifles.

The Ambassadors

It is not easy to select a single novel of James as being the one most deserving of analysis. *The Portrait of a Lady* might reasonably be selected because of its excellence of construction and the fact that it is a comparatively early production. Of the later full-length novels, *The Wings of the Dove*, *The Ambassadors*, and *The Golden Bowl* represent the author at the peak of his development. *The Wings of the Dove* is noteworthy for its delicately drawn and engaging heroine, while *The Golden Bowl* is probably the most subtle of all the novels, the one that is richest in effects and most exquisitely toned. *The Ambassadors* is superior in construction, in the author's opinion, to any of the other novels, and it is simpler in design than *The Golden Bowl*. Those who from lack of familiarity with James find his late method somewhat perplexing at first may console themselves with the assurance that their difficulties would be appreciably less if they had previously read, let us say, *The American*, *Daisy Miller*, *The Portrait of a Lady*, *The Spoils of Poynton*, and *What Maisie Knew*.

The subject of *The Ambassadors* is the adventure of a man during a momentous period of his life. Lambert Strether, the hero, is an American of New England origin, whose home is in Woollett, an important but rather provincial city in Massachusetts. He is a man of intelligence and imagination, who, in spite of his ability, has not achieved a great measure of worldly success. We can detect from various evidences that he stands well in his community, but in his

[5] *Notes on Novelists*, New York, 1916, p. 113.

own eyes he is comparatively a failure. Life in Woollett has not provided him with the opportunity to develop according to his natural bent. There have also been personal circumstances that have worked to his disadvantage.

He has had so little experience of the world that to dine in a public place with a lady before accompanying her to the theater is for him something of an event. Having married early, he "missed the natural time, in Boston, for taking girls to the Museum," and, when his wife died shortly after their marriage, he gave himself up so thoroughly to missing her that upon the death of his son ten years later he accused himself remorsefully of having failed to appreciate the boy. These two deaths and the barren period lying between them have formed a desert space across the middle of his life, cutting him off from his youth and filling him with a sense of deprivation and lost opportunity. The impression of having missed things and been out of it has fastened itself upon him. An early enthusiasm for Europe, kindled by a visit with his young wife and subsequently allowed to slumber through the long years by the force of his double bereavement, begins to stir again almost immediately in Strether under the stimulus of the morning air of Paris:

It hung before him this morning, the vast bright Babylon, like some huge iridescent object, a jewel brilliant and hard, in which parts were not to be discriminated nor differences comfortably marked. It twinkled and trembled and melted together, and what seemed all surface one moment seemed all depth the next. It was a place of which, unmistakably, Chad was fond; wherefore if he, Strether, should like it too much, what on earth, with such a bond, would become of either of them?

At the opening of the story Strether, who is fifty-five years of age, has become engaged to Mrs. Newsome, a widow and a prominent figure in Woollett society. She has a son Chadwick, who has been living for several years in Paris, apparently entangled with a woman. The mother longs for her son to come home, settle down, and take up his rightful place in the family business. His mode of living is loathsome to her, and Strether, knowing her feelings, goes to Paris with the kindly intention of inducing the young man, if he can, to give up whatever it is that holds him and return to the safety and respectability of Woollett.

An ambassadorship to bring home the prodigal son of a wealthy family may appear on the surface to be a trivial matter to engage the interest of a serious novelist. We cannot judge the subject, however, apart from its treatment; moreover, the real subject, as James sees it, is the belated awakening of his hero, the mission to Paris being only a means to that end.

Since Strether is to be the center of interest, some knowledge of his early life is useful to us. Not much of his past is revealed, however, only a little light being thrown upon it here and there. James does not believe in burdening his account with facts. A novelist's first concern is to make his figures live, for which purpose a mere factual record of established data is insufficient. What we do learn of the early life of the hero, of his wife and son and the early pilgrimage to Europe, comes to us in such a manner that we see beyond the facts themselves into the essential man. A larger amount of information might serve to distract our attention from the immediate situation. By limiting his view as he does, James manages to bring into intelligible focus everything necessary to our understanding of Strether's expedition and of its significance to him.

The restricted manner in which the material is presented is not the product of a search for ingenuity but is made necessary by the indirect mode of treatment. Actually the effect sought and achieved is one of naturalness, and in art it is the effect, not the method, that really matters. In *David Copperfield*, Dickens follows a simple plan in handling diverse materials and achieves an effect not of unity and simplicity but of intricate complication. James, on the other hand, employs a complex method of handling carefully selected materials and achieves an effect of unity and harmony. The latter novelist fuses his materials successfully; the former simply ties his together by the device of centering them about a hero. James, moreover, lets his novel speak for itself; for all his wealth of creativeness in detail, Dickens makes various compromises with objectivity.

To read one is to plunge into something abundant and various, and feel the exhilaration of immersion in a flood of sentiment, heartiness, and fun. To read the other is to maintain, by comparison, a certain spirit of detachment, and be, as it were, well bred. James does not engage in verbal pyrotechnics nor does he resort to artful devices in order to dazzle or thrill his reader. He does not indulge in crude or violent manifestations of humor or sentiment. His experience of life does not take the form of facile response to simple or elementary stimuli. There is intense feeling in his work, but it is held in such restraint that he has been falsely accused of coldness and aridity. Actually, in such stories as *The Wings of the Dove, The Golden Bowl,* and "The Altar of the Dead," the emotional tension is all the greater from being held strictly in control.

Feeling, with James, is not a matter of giving way to emotions and turning them loose upon the reader. Such excess would be impossible to him; moreover, it would not be in accord with the requirements of the indirect method of portrayal. Remember that we are dealing with a man who is first of all an artist engaged in projecting an experience of life conceived in its entirety. The emotional response without which a full experience of life is inconceivable must be fused, according to the author's conception of his task, with the process of living of which it is a part. In its deepest and most complex form, as in life, it does not come wholly to the surface, but, hidden though it may be, we feel the tension produced by its silent influence. Feeling as portrayed by James does not fluctuate greatly. Once generated, however, it glows steadily, its strength and persistence being due to the fact that it is not a simple emotional state, but a prolonged and complex process of consciousness, which gathers intensity from the play of forces brought to bear upon it. That the experience of Strether is a highly concentrated one is evident when it is recognized that he is caught in a situation in which two civilizations clash within the area of his consciousness.

In comparison with the more than fifty characters in *David Copperfield,* there are only about a dozen people who figure distinctly in *The Ambassadors.* Of these, only one is presented fully, the others being shown always in relation to him. We know that Waymarsh calls on Miss Barrace and that he later goes about with Mrs. Pocock, but we know about these meetings only in so far as they interest Strether or are brought to his attention. Even Chad and Madame de Vionnet, whose attachment to each other serves to set everything in motion, are never shown together except when they are also with the main character.

Despite this extreme emphasis upon one person, James has a larger purpose than the exhibition of his hero. The coming into contact with a world new to him and full of exciting possibilities constitutes for Strether a dramatic personal adventure, underneath which there lies the contrast of cultures out of which it has grown. It is in this contrast, which is at once international and personal, that the author finds his basic inspiration. Being a novelist and not a historian, he cannot find his subject simply in the general problem of differences between peoples and places. He has to deal with a particular situation and show the cultural condition of specific individuals operating in their lives. This purpose he accomplishes by transporting a few representative inhabitants of a provincial community in New England into the very citadel of cosmopolitanism. Of far greater importance to the novel, however, than the comedy of Sarah and Jim Pocock in Paris is the method by which the opposing standards of the two worlds are made to lead naturally, and with a sense of inevitability, to the dilemma in which Strether finds himself.

Goethe, in conversing with Eckermann about some poems, is reported to have commented upon the great importance of motives to a poet. "Nobody dreams that the true power of a poem consists in the situation—in the *motive*." James had precisely the same opinion when he wrote to Mrs. Humphry Ward that the artist "must have a perception of the interests of his subject." Just as the poet, according to Goethe, could not write merely about his feelings, so the novelist, according to James, could not rely upon his personality to get him through his difficulties. He had to eliminate himself from his work and think only of his situation. *The Ambassadors* serves to illustrate how it was possible for the author thus to give himself up to his subject. He went further than merely to refrain from intruding in the manner of the confiding, commenting, moralizing author. He managed, by his narrative skill, even to eliminate himself to a considerable degree as an impersonal narrator, or to conceal himself as such.

A novelist who employs large blocks of direct information in presenting his material cannot secure an unalloyed effect of drama because such direct statements rest upon the authority of the unseen author. As the artist's purpose is to make his novel appear self-contained, his problem is to find substitute methods for direct presentation. In reading a novel we should be as little aware as possible of the arranging hand of the novelist at work behind the scenes. The story, in other words, should appear to tell itself.

As a means towards this end, information from the outside should be slipped in unostentatiously in the natural course of events. Much of the necessary information can be supplied by the characters themselves, it being part of the artist's business to create plausible occasions for such disclosures. The problem of the novelist in this regard is really a very complex one. It is not simply a matter of disguising the functional nature of a character so that he will not appear obviously in the role of informant. At what point does information thus secured cease to be direct and become indirect presentation? For the author simply to transfer the responsibility of authorship from himself to one of his characters is no solution of his problem. Direct presentation is direct presentation whether it is from the author or from a character. It was for this reason that James did not let Strether tell his own story. He wished to avoid what he called the "terrible fluidity of self-revelation."

The problem here raised is essentially a problem of the point of view from which information is derived. We may consider that the method by which material is presented is indirect when what we learn comes to us in limited particles that are completely revealing only as they combine with other impressions gained from other occasions and other sources of information. Strether, for example, obtains clues from a variety of sources until finally he has come to understand everything. No one thing has taught him what to believe; no one thing could have taught him. Let us assume that Miss Gostrey might have told him a great deal more than she did about what was probably the relationship of Chad and Madame de

Vionnet. The effect upon him would not have been the same as the effect of the method followed. He could not have grasped abstractly what he came to understand by living through. He had to know Madame de Vionnet at first hand and to feel the magnetic quality of her personality. He had to come under the influence of all the things in the Paris atmosphere that helped to prepare him for his reappraisal of the situation. There was no other possible way for Strether to have such an experience but to have his mind made receptive a little here and a little there until he was capable of admitting everything. Similarly the only possible way for the novelist to convey such an impression is by a multitude of little strokes no one of which is very revealing in itself. If what we learn comes to us in such limited particles that its significance is made clear only in combination with many other things, the effect is that of indirectness. It is the method of art, not of science, and it gives us an experience, not an explanation.

Taking the consciousness of Strether as the center of his novel, James manages to present his story as something emanating therefrom. It does not appear to come either from James or from Strether. Nobody *tells* it. It is not a report about something but the thing itself, enacted before our eyes. The author does not, like a stream-of-consciousness novelist, describe the contents of Strether's mind or the flow of his impressions. We have presented to us not a passive and seemingly uncontrolled state of disorder and freakish inconsequence, but an active and discriminating mind engaged diligently in working out the ramifications of a particular problem, the solution of which constitutes for it a definite experience. It is a problem based not upon the operation of any scientifically demonstrable laws, but one involving persons and places and human attitudes and relationships, all of which come together in the mind of the chief actor in such a manner as to form there the substance of his experience in its tangible living embodiment.

Strether is not like the traveling hero of eighteenth-century fiction, who comes into casual contact with various people. The slightest of his relationships is a thread in the main pattern of events, there being no minor issues to distract or mislead the reader. At the same time, the characters who appear before us in such limited roles lose none of their naturalness from being made to appear only in that aspect of their lives which contributes to another person's experience. They are not like the minor characters of *Clarissa*, who are so obviously fragmentary and functional. They have their own individuality and claim to our attention. Yet they do not usurp the center of the stage, even for a moment, as do the parading characters of the old processional type of novel. By blending with the main theme they help to keep our attention upon it, and by throwing light upon the subject they gain additional interest for themselves.

Alfred North Whitehead has commented upon this aspect of harmony between individuality of detail and wholeness of design in art by referring to the interior of a Gothic cathedral. With reference to the sculpture and tracery in the Cathedral of Chartres, he says: "They lead the eye upward to the vaulting above, and they lead the eye onward horizontally to the supreme symbolism of the altar. They claim attention by their beauty of detail. Yet they shun attention by guiding the eye to grasp the significance of the whole. Yet the sculpture and the tracery could not perform this service apart from their supreme individuality, evoking a wealth of feeling in their own right. Each detail claims a permanent existence for its own sake, and then surrenders it for the sake of the whole composition."[6]

At the opening of the novel, Strether has already arrived in England, where it becomes evident very quickly that his contact with the old world is to be for him an adventure. He takes note eagerly of things that are different from life in Woollett, and somewhat queerly it comes over him that he is launched in an adventure that will be quite disconnected from his past. His friend and compatriot Waymarsh, to whom Europe is an uncomfortable ordeal, serves as a reminder of that past by his resistance to all things European. By being so markedly different from Mrs. Newsome, Miss Gostrey also contributes to the sense of contrast. She is an American who has been so long in Europe that she is able to serve as guide and interpreter for her fellow Americans. By the time Strether has accompanied her to the theater and has, on various occasions, explained to her the purpose of his visit, he begins, under

[6] *Adventures of Ideas*, The Macmillan Company, 1933, p. 364.

her influence, to realize that his project may prove to be a less simple one than he has fancied. Afterwards, in Paris, the sense of difference grows until nothing in Chad's situation appears as it has formerly been conceived. Everything eventually takes on a changed aspect for Strether, even Woollett and Mrs. Newsome being no longer the same. The complete reversal of his attitude brings the story to its end.

Each of the characters has his or her situation to be treated, and each one has his or her relation to the leading motive to be made clear. Let us consider how the author utilizes the separate characters in developing his leading motive. Maria Gostrey is not a true dramatic agent, according to her creator, but a *ficelle*, or, in other words, a character devised as an aid to the treatment and not belonging strictly to the subject. In this respect she is like Henrietta Stackpole, of *The Portrait of a Lady*, whom James brackets with her, saying of them that they are "but wheels to the coach," not belonging to the body of the vehicle and not "for a moment accommodated with a seat inside." By the intervention of Miss Gostrey, various matters which would otherwise have to be presented directly can be treated scenically. By being a sympathetic listener to Strether, she provides him with an opportunity to reveal to her, and incidentally to us, his gradually expanding sense of his situation. She also helps along the process of his enlightenment by bringing her familiarity with European ways to bear upon his problem, while she can also divine his American point of view toward it. In addition to the information that she can either give to or extract from Strether, she elicits such revealing admissions from him as his acknowledgment that he cannot give himself up freely to the pleasure of the moment since he is too much dogged by his New England sense of duty. The art of taking things as they come is something that he has not acquired; it is not an art that is much cultivated in Woollett.

There is another and more subtle way in which Miss Gostrey serves the author, simply by being the kind of person she is. It is clear from various implications that she is different from Mrs. Newsome. Strether, to whom an emancipated woman is something of a revelation, cannot but be struck by this difference. Mrs. Newsome, we can be sure, is a managing type of woman, prim, respectable, unyielding. She is capable of sending Strether an ultimatum, of cutting off her correspondence with him abruptly, and of carrying on further negotiations behind his back. She does not budge an inch to meet his changed views, being so narrow and unimaginative that she cannot accept any more lenient view of her son's affair than she has worked out in advance. Miss Gostrey, on the other hand, is none of these things. She knows too much of the world to be easily surprised. She is helpful without being officious and without assuming an air of patronage or protectiveness. She adapts herself readily to every situation, takes things easily, and is always calm and unruffled. She is, in short, everything that is required of her and is in no small way a factor in the amenity of Strether's adventure. It is not surprising that she should fall in love with him. Such a development enables the author to make her position in the novel appear to be more than merely functional. It adds, too, to the richness of the novel and to our understanding of what Strether's experience means to him.

Waymarsh, like Miss Gostrey, is a *ficelle*. He serves as a foil to the hero and as an illustration of the inflexibility of the provincial mind. Since he and Strether are somewhat similarly situated, the contrast between their ways of taking Europe is all the more striking. The experience comes too late, in a way, for both of them, but one can still respond to new impressions and the other cannot. Strether surrenders himself freely to the current flowing about him. His imagination is stimulated and his spirit is given a new lift. One day he pauses before an open-air display of books under the arches of the Odéon. It would have been a privilege, he thinks, to have been young and happy there, if Chad hadn't been too vulgar for his privilege:

He edged along, grazing the tables, with his hands firmly behind him. He wasn't there to dip, to consume—he was there to reconstruct. He wasn't there for his own profit—not, that is, the direct; he was there on some chance of feeling the brush of the wing of the stray spirit of youth. He felt it in fact, he had it beside him; the old arcade indeed, as his inner sense listened, gave out the faint sound, as from far off, of the wild waving of wings.

No such visitation from the past ever stirs in Waymarsh; neither can he bridge the chasm between Milrose and Paris. He remains aloof and suspicious, resentful of Strether's enthusiasm, seeing in such cordiality to Europe, perhaps, an implied snub to the glories of Woollett. This attitude of mute disapproval, of unuttered reproach, on the part of his friend causes Strether to feel that he is being frivolous and that the reproving eyes of Woollett are fastened on him. Waymarsh takes Europe as if it were a doctor's prescription; he makes it as palatable as he can by spending money with American lavishness and by devoting hours to the newspapers, doubtless from America, in the reception room of his bank. Miss Barrace, to whom he is a wonderful specimen of the grand old American, finds amusement in taking him about. She sums him up as follows: "He doesn't understand—not one little scrap. . . . I show him Paris, show him everything, and he never turns a hair. He's like the Indian chief one reads about, who, when he comes up to Washington to see the Great Father, stands wrapped in his blanket and gives no sign. I might be the Great Father—from the way he takes everything." Later Waymarsh softens enough to carry on a flirtation with Mrs. Pocock, and it is an ironic commentary upon the moral code of Woollett that his health improves noticeably while he is thus engaged. He cannot take his pleasures in a carefree spirit, however, for he has a lamentably shamefaced manner of breaking the news to Strether that he is going with the Pococks to Switzerland.

Miss Barrace helps to represent the social world in which Chad is enveloped in Paris. She is at first a baffling person to Strether, not at all like any member of her sex at Woollett. She is both mature and gay, perfectly familiar and freely contradictious. Somehow she makes the occasion of breakfasting with little Bilham seem to be "the most baited, the most gilded of traps." Her conversation with little Bilham gives Strether the impression of being in the presence of other standards and a different scale of relations. Evidently they do not think of things at all as he and Waymarsh do. Later, while Strether gropes his way into an understanding of this different scale of values, he has sometimes the "sense of moving in a maze of mystic closed allusions." It is the particular function of Miss Barrace to give him this impression, and by teaching him that the point of view of Woollett can be amusing she helps him on to grasping the point of view that finds it so.

Little Bilham is an amiable young American who has been made over, to a great extent, by his residence abroad. He has mastered the art of being happy and of taking life as it comes without anxiety or remorse. He seems to Strether to be completely free from prejudice, being unperturbed even by the usual prejudice in favor of a definite occupation. A man of great intelligence, little Bilham represents the reflective attitude, which, according to Miss Gostrey, Americans are so quick to spoil by their wanting so dreadfully to do something. He serves to help along the growth of Strether's understanding and to represent Chad in an amiable light. Strether once tells Maria Gostrey that he never had the benefit of youth at the proper time. Perhaps he sees in his young friend something of what his own life might have been. It is to little Bilham, one day in Gloriani's garden, that he addresses the words containing what the author confesses to be the essence of the novel.

Jim Pocock illustrates the extent to which the culture of Woollett is predominantly a woman's culture. He is glad to have an excuse to accompany his wife to Europe, but he leaves the moral side of their expedition to Sally. He is accustomed, in fact, like a compliant American husband, to leave almost everything to Sally. He takes the worst possible view, somewhat enviously, of Chad's behavior. The vulgarity of his reaction to Paris and to the whole situation strength-ens the determination of Strether to stand by Madame de Vionnet. Will it be an improvement to Chad to send him home if Jim is the result of what long years in Woollett will do for a man?

Sarah Pocock, who takes over Strether's ambassadorship, is a narrow, unimaginative, complacent woman. Accustomed to rule with an iron hand, she will accept nothing less from Strether than his complete submission to her mother's will. His conscientious effort to deal frankly in reporting Chad's situation to Mrs. Newsome has appeared little less than monstrous to the two women, for he seems to them to have succumbed to the very evil that he was expected to counteract. Even a little wildness on his part would be less of an outrage than this open betrayal of Woollett standards. It is his *thinking* as he does that is unpardonable.

Mamie Pocock, a specimen of the wholesome American girl, is the bait by which Mrs. Newsome and Sarah hope to lure Chad away from his European enchantress. It is too much to expect of her, but Strether finds her charming for all that, in spite of her rather flat little voice and her too voluminous clothes. "She was handsome and portly and easy and chatty, soft and sweet and almost disconcertingly reassuring. She was dressed . . . less as a young lady than as an old one—had an old one been supposable to Strether as so committed to vanity; the complexities of her hair missed, moreover, also the looseness of youth; and she had a mature manner of bending a little, as to encourage and reward, while she held neatly together in front of her a pair of strikingly polished hands." Her air of benevolent patronage, of waiting to be congratulated, is in noteworthy contrast to the fluttering shyness of Jeanne de Vionnet. It denotes the indulgent treatment of young people in America and the tribute which is there habitually rendered to pretty girls. The passage in which Strether finds Mamie alone on the balcony, waiting for little Bilham, shows how remarkably discriminating James is in portrayal and how well he can employ a non-scenic method of representation.

Jeanne de Vionnet serves to complicate for Strether the situation which he has to unravel. Feeling about her as he does, he cannot but be shocked when he learns of the manner in which her marriage is being arranged, a form of procedure which Madame de Vionnet assures him is founded on a *vieille sagesse*. Although Woollett doubtless takes a somewhat more romantic view of marriage, it produces such unions as those of Sarah and Jim and of the unhappy Waymarsh. While condemning such a marriage as Jeanne's, Woollett would unquestionably applaud an arrangement bringing together Mamie and Chad.

Gloriani is a symbolic figure in that he helps to represent the cosmopolitan outlook, which is contrasted with the provincial outlook of Woollett. The world in which the celebrated sculptor moves is a place of freedom and intelligence which greatly attracts Strether while it fills him with regret for what he has missed. He feels himself an outsider to such an extent that he once misinterprets an accidental lessening of cordiality in Gloriani as being a recognition by him that the difference between them is too great to be bridged.

Chad Newsome affects Strether to a greater degree and in a more complex manner than is immediately evident. The older man's feelings reach back to memories of his own son and are colored, moreover, by his sense of having missed the privileges of youth. The fact that Chad is no longer the raw young man of Woollett but a polished man of the world, thoroughly considerate but somewhat enigmatic, is a part of the general complexity of Strether's problem. The improvement of the younger man, together with the fact that he fits so easily into his strange and charming surroundings, causes Strether to think better of him for a time than he deserves, to look upon him with a certain dim envy and yearning. The connection with Madame de Vionnet is an added source of luster. Chad, in short, is the spoiled darling of fortune, having in abundance what Strether, with his superior sensibility, has somehow contrived to miss. It is part of the irony of the situation that these things have been largely wasted on young Newsome. He has the good fortune to possess things which he does not greatly value. Strether, on the contrary, has missed things and is intensely appreciative.

It is Madame de Vionnet who best represents to the hero the charm of European culture and who is chiefly responsible for his change of attitude. What he has believed in Woollett about the nature of Chad's entanglement becomes simply grotesque in the light of the actual facts. The fundamental fact, it may be argued in the literal Woollett fashion, is essentially what has been surmised. It is not the same to Strether, however, for the woman in the case is not what he has surmised, and she makes everything different. It is not her social distinction, her going to church, her exquisite taste, her tact, her lucidity, her naturalness together with her seemingly endless variety—it is not any of these things which transforms the situation but all of them together and the fact that, having fallen under her spell, Strether cannot associate the idea of wrong or of ugliness with her.

Contrary to the opinion of Woollett, it is Madame de Vionnet rather than Chad who is destined to be the injured one in their relationship. When Strether visits her for the last time before his departure for America, he sees that she is greatly in fear of being deserted. Having gone to Europe to separate these two, he has become instead a link between them, with the result that he now finds her clinging to him as to a source of safety. Although he does what he can for her, even to telling Chad that he will be a brute to forsake her, it is clearly implied that Chad has begun to tire of the affair and will soon return to Woollett.

The relationship between Strether and Madame de Vionnet becomes in a few brief months something quite different from what it was in the beginning. He establishes himself upon a new footing with her, not connected with his original design. One day spent in the country is indicative of his state of mind, for much of the time is taken up with musings that always return to the woman who has been such a revelation to him. One of the impressions that lingers with him is of her remarkable facility of adapting herself to every occasion. He feels confident that however much one might try her she could always be trusted to find the right tone.

In Woollett, presumably, a woman is everything to a man or she is nothing. There, one is either engaged or not, married or not, in love or not. Thus it was natural for Mrs. Newsome to be disturbed by the evidence of Strether's interest in another woman. But in the more intricate atmosphere of a cosmopolitan society such hard and fast distinctions are inadequate and somewhat crude. They do not include all supposable circumstances in dealing with such a woman as Madame de Vionnet, who, at their last encounter, tells Strether with a hint of regret that they might have been friends. Mrs. Newsome, we can be certain, has employed different and more definite language in "proposing" to him. Miss Gostrey is perhaps less subtle than Madame de Vionnet and certainly more ambiguous than Mrs. Newsome when, in the final scene of the novel, she makes it doubly clear to her visitor that he is welcome to remain with her. If Strether has missed life, as he feels, it would seem to have been due to his own fault. His reflection, made in connection with Madame de Vionnet, seems not to have been inappropriate: "Women were thus endlessly absorbent, and to deal with them was to walk on water."

Nowhere in *The Ambassadors* is the merging of details achieved with greater effectiveness than in the portrayal of Madame de Vionnet. Not only does she belong to her world but her faculty of adaptation is so remarkable that it becomes the quality in her which most fascinates Strether. No element in the novel is more essential to it than the way in which the charm of this woman is exhibited, for she is the living embodiment, as it were, of what is gracious and civilized, just as Mrs. Newsome and her daughter are expressive of an imperfect provincial culture.

Madame de Vionnet is, of course, not merely a symbol. Aesthetic expression, as we have had occasion to note, is necessarily individual. Galsworthy in *The Forsyte Saga* insists rather too openly upon the symbolical aspect of Irene, the wife of Soames Forsyte. She stands for Beauty, we are reminded. So does Madame de Vionnet stand for beauty, if one should care to put it that way, but her creator has made her first of all a vivid individual. Beauty, like virtue, is not a thing to be courted assiduously or self-consciously. One of the characters of *Point Counter Point*, by Mr. Aldous Huxley, is described as seeming "to turn it on, this love of beauty, like an electric light." James is far too sensitive to deal with Madame de Vionnet in such a spirit.

The artist's concern with beauty is not with a pure abstraction but with a condition or state of being of a set of particulars. Whether we consider beauty as a matter of mutual adaptation between the several parts of a thing, as harmony in diversity, as an objectification of the mind's idealizations, or in some other terms, the idea of proportion or of the absence of painful clash is likely to occur to us. Madame de Vionnet is eminently gifted with a sense of what is fitting. Even when her feelings get the better of her and she shows herself as vulgarly troubled "as a maidservant crying for her young man," she retains a sense of proportion, judges herself as a maidservant would not, and recovers quickly from her collapse. Variety without caprice, simplicity, harmony, adaptability—such words cannot in themselves express the secret of Madame de Vionnet's charm. She is not the brilliant, somewhat metallic, woman encountered in Restoration comedy. A truly charming woman, as James doubtless felt, is not an exhibition. His whole conception of art, in fact, was that it should not be too obviously exhibitory. So light is his touch and so supple his method in the presentation of his heroine that it would not be easy to pin her down or to say exactly what she is. It is not easy to say what makes a woman charming. That is one of the reasons why she *is* charming.

Although James has been accused of not being a champion of causes, as an exponent of civilization he was a champion of the cause that includes all others. One of the factors necessary to the preservation and extension of civilization is the destruction of barriers separating man from man, nation from nation, and race from race. Man unfortunately is given to the erecting of new barriers with one hand while tearing down old ones with the other, of substituting new tyrannies for old ones. In its broadest sense, however, civilization works toward the tearing down of all barriers. It is the product of tolerance and considerateness of others, of fidelity and trust among men. It likewise rests upon discrimination, or the ability to separate the relevant from the irrelevant. The civilized person is able to distinguish what is worthy and to cherish it whatever may be its associations. He does not wish, for example, to destroy a cathedral because it may have been produced by an age of superstition and intolerance.

James is preeminently a novelist with a sense of civilization and an interest in the symbols of civilization. His most unsympathetic characters are those traitors to society who betray the ideals of integrity and fidelity upon which civilization rests. His most sympathetic characters are those who reflect in high degree the integrity, sensitiveness, discrimination, magnanimity, and disinterestedness without which a high state of culture would be impossible. Less sympathetic are those who lack the imaginativeness and elasticity of spirit necessary to full appreciation of life in a complex society. It is not lack of sophistication, of course, that James condemns, but lack of openness of mind and of interest in life. Isabel Archer, of *The Portrait of a Lady*, and Milly Theale, of *The Wings of the Dove*, are not particularly sophisticated but they are both notable for their eager interest in life. Strether, aside from his integrity, is a sensitive, discriminating, receptive man who is able to overcome his prejudices. He can separate the relevant from the irrelevant and distinguish what is worthy. Accordingly he does not condemn Madame de Vionnet, whatever he may think of the system which has contributed to her dilemma.

From what has been said about civilization, it should be clear that it represents an effort, however imperfect, of men to live together in harmony. The problem of life is not essentially different from the problem of art, for in each case the materials need to be wrought into some intelligible pattern. Mrs. Ramsey, in Virginia Woolf's novel *To the Lighthouse,* is a sensitive woman who is able to compose the differences of people and bring serenity into their lives. She makes living a work of art, as it were, and she communicates the glow of her own being to those about her. In her different manner, Madame de Vionnet produces a comparable effect upon Strether. Art acts as a spur on man's effort to achieve harmony by presenting fragments of life in which perfection within limits is attained. Madame de Vionnet, by always striking the right tone, represents to Strether the perfection of art. She never fails to display some new evidence of the richness and grace of her spirit. It is no exaggeration to say of her that she is a symbol to the hero of the civilization the discovery of which constitutes his great adventure.

Once being charged with having drawn Miss Birdseye, a character in *The Bostonians,* from an actual person, James replied that he had evolved her entirely from his moral consciousness and proceeded to explain why he had drawn her as he did. Paris, unlike Miss Birdseye, did not have to be created. It was all the more useful to the author by reason of its established traditional association with an advanced stage of culture. As a symbol of things undreamed of in the philosophy of Woollett, it was a likely place for such an adventure as Strether's and a means of making it appear plausible.

It will be noted, however, that James could bend an actual city to his purpose as well as a fictitious character. The Paris of *The Ambassadors* is not the city that a conscientious realist would have described, but only a distillation of atmosphere enveloping the human activity upon which our attention is fixed. There are no extended descriptions, but many little references keep the sense of the city present to us as it is to Strether. The pleasantness of the place, its animated streets, broad vistas, soft spring air, fountains, terraces, alleys—everything, in short, communicates to the hero the sense of breathing a stimulating and refreshing air. The smiling waiter, the taste of the soup, the goodness of the wine, the coarse texture of the napkin, the crunch of the thick-crusted bread—these are things that lift the simple act of dining into a place in the general sense of amenity.

No incident is too trifling to contribute in some way to Strether's adventure. Even a trip to the post office, to send a letter to Madame de Vionnet, arouses in him an impression of close contact with the throbbing life of the city. There are many other people besides himself, he sees, engaged in carrying on a correspondence across the great city. As he looks at them driving their pens at the sand-strewn table, they suggest to him something more fierce, more sinister, and more acute in the national life than he in his innocence has ever known in Woollett. He is "mixed up with the typical tale of Paris." That is what his ambassadorship has brought him to. He has made his choice and taken his stand on the side of Madame de Vionnet. Having dispatched his letter, he is amused at the thought that he, Lambert Strether, has ranged himself "on the side of the fierce, the sinister, the acute." Only one who has read the account of his adventure can appreciate the irony of his position.

CHAPTER XVIII

Realism and the Spirit of Compromise

Arnold Bennett

A story by Henry James entitled "The Next Time" recounts the experience of a talented man of letters who, notwithstanding his great gifts, can never succeed in producing anything that is sufficiently popular to be lucrative. Although he strives to lower his style in order to achieve a popular success, he invariably turns out a masterpiece which pleases the critics but does not attract the general public. Despite repeated failures to win popular acclaim, he continues his efforts in the vain hope that he will succeed the next time.

Such a dilemma is in notable contrast to the career of Arnold Bennett, who stated in his *Journal* in September, 1898, after the publication of his first novel, that he proposed to put aside the serious novel upon which he was then engaged, later to be published as *Anna of the Five Towns,* and to devote himself until the end of the following year to writing the kind of fiction that would sell itself. Although he did not succeed on a large scale immediately, his income was soon £1000 a year and by the end of 1912 he had acquired such a wide literary reputation that his earnings for that year were in the neighborhood of £16,000. He was now able to buy a car and a yacht. Subsequently, until his death in

1931, he could sell for a good price practically every scrap that came from his pen.

Enoch Arnold Bennett was born in 1867 at Hanley, in the region which he reconstructed in his novels as the Five Towns. This region is an industrial district in the north of Staffordshire in which there is centered a great pottery-making industry, the towns in question being Tunstall, Hanley, Burslem, Stoke-upon-Trent, and Longton. In the novels they appear as Turnhill, Hanbridge, Bursley, Knype, and Longshaw, the change of name having been made presumably so as to enable the artist to deal with the typical rather than the merely actual.

The Five Towns are as different in character from Hardy's Wessex as the back streets of Clerkenwell, described in *Riceyman Steps,* are different from the pastoral scenes of *The Woodlanders.* The manufacture of pottery over many centuries has given to these towns a distinctive character. Cut off from the surrounding country, with which they have nothing in common, they are described as lying like an insignificant stain upon the face of Staffordshire. Their architecture is "an architecture of ovens and chimneys" and their atmosphere is black with smoke. They are characterized in *Anna of the Five Towns* in the following grim terms:

> They are mean and forbidding of aspect—sombre, hard-featured, uncouth; and the vaporous poison of their ovens and chimneys has soiled and shrivelled the surrounding country till there is no village lane within a league but what offers a gaunt and ludicrous travesty of rural charms. Nothing could be more prosaic than the huddled, red-brown streets; nothing more seemingly remote from romance. Yet be it said that romance is even here—the romance which, for those who have an eye to perceive it, ever dwells amid the seats of industrial manufacture, softening the coarseness, transfiguring the squalor, of these mighty alchemic operations.[1]

After having been educated in local schools, Bennett read law for a time in his father's office. Then, at the age of twenty-one, he went to London and became a clerk in a solicitor's office. Soon he began to read extensively in the works of the French realists—notably

---

[1] From: *Anna of the Five Towns,* by Arnold Bennett, copyright 1902 by Doubleday and Company, Inc.

Maupassant, the Goncourts, and Huysmans. *A Mummer's Wife,* with its opening scenes in Hanley, may have drawn his attention to the possibility of making literature out of the life of the Five Towns.

In 1893 he became the assistant editor of a periodical for women, in which capacity he had an opportunity to cultivate the faculty of appearing to know a great deal about a great variety of subjects. Later he was its editor from 1896 to 1900, by which latter date he had become the author of *A Man from the North, Journalism for Women,* and a number of serials. He had also written *Anna of the Five Towns,* which was not yet published, and had become a dramatic critic and reviewer. By 1903 he was living in France, where he remained most of the time during the next eight or nine years. After the publication of *The Old Wives' Tale* in 1908 and *Clayhanger* in 1910, and a visit to the United States in 1911, he was a prominent figure in the literary world. Thereafter for many years he held a place in the public mind with other such leading men of letters as Wells, Galsworthy, and Shaw.

Bennett emerged as a novelist at a time when Victorian traditionalism and late-Victorian discontent were giving way before a more adventurous spirit. His escape from provincialism was more than the mere departure of a young man from his native town. To him the Five Towns represented narrowness and boredom and memories of a puritanical upbringing. He belonged to a generation that was in rebellion against the habits of thought of its elders. In *Clayhanger,* as in *The Way of All Flesh,* there is a clash between a father and a son, and in each case the sympathy of the author is with the son. Although he was not the prophet of a new order, Bennett shared the enthusiasm of Wells for progress and was equally hostile to the decaying conventions of Victorian respectability. He turned his back upon the Victorian novel and sought inspiration from the French realists. Being a good man of business, however, he did not seriously challenge basic national prejudices. That he knew how to keep from getting too far in advance of the book-buying public is illustrated by the fact that *The Pretty Lady,* a realistic novel about a courtesan, was published in 1918 without apparently arousing much adverse comment. To be sure, times had changed since the days of Moore's early novels.

Bennett was a self-made man who could hardly conceal his satisfaction at having got on so well. He gave the impression of having found more than normal satisfaction in his escape from the dingy life of the Five Towns. Perhaps one reason why he cultivated so assiduously the air of being a cosmopolite was to prove to himself that he was no longer a provincial. A true man of the world would have taken his role less self-consciously. Underneath his mask of worldliness, in fact, he remained essentially simple in his attitude toward life. His natural if somewhat stereotyped enthusiasm led his friend Wells to say of him that "he was like a child at a fair." D. H. Lawrence, who was less charitably disposed than Wells, referred to Bennett, in a letter to Aldous Huxley, as a "sort of pig in clover."

Being a man of information rather than of ideas or of strong convictions, Bennett did not always succeed in giving a clear sense of direction to his novels. Although they are densely packed with information, the question sometimes obtrudes itself as to what the assemblage of facts is intended to suggest. In *Imperial Palace* we learn a great deal about the running of a large hotel. But what are we to think of the people who keep the machine in order? Are we to regard their lives as squalid, or are we to find romance in the running of such a mechanism, as the author apparently did? The reader of *Middlemarch* or *The Return of the Native* is never long in doubt as to the purport of the story. *Clayhanger,* despite the minuteness and precision of its realistic depiction of surface phenomena, is less clear-cut in its ultimate meaning. The struggle of Edwin Clayhanger against the inimical forces of his environment appears to have been fashioned less from a definite philosophy than from experience and memory and perhaps from imitation. The issue for the hero is neither a defeat nor a victory. It follows not as the logical outcome of a definite course of action but as the product of repeated adjustments to pressures exerted from various directions. The feelings expressed are contradictory, being both disillusioned and romantic, and the point of view of the author is characterized by extreme flexibility. His realism, instead of being ruthless like that of Maupassant, reflects a marked tendency to concession and compromise.

Bennett was like Hardy in being the novelist of a definite locality.

Few English novels are more notable for the richness and accuracy of their local reference than are those of the creator of Wessex. But the novels of Hardy, notwithstanding their superlative rendering of regional characteristics, are not limited to the depicting of life in its provincial aspects. The workings of human destiny are not, in their essentials, greatly affected by superficial variations of manner and custom between different regions. It is not the provincialism of the inhabitants of Wessex that is greatly important but traits of a more universal character. Although the tragedy which engulfs Clym Yeobright springs from his attachment to his native district, the spirit governing his actions is in no sense that of a provincial. Hardy, in short, is a man with a comprehensive view of life who is able to see beyond the world of his immediate representation. Egdon Heath interests him less as a specific tract of land than because of its associations as the localization of human drama.

Hardy bore no resentment against the place of his origin and returned at the age of forty-five to reside in his native Dorset. Bennett, on the other hand, had an extreme dislike of the Five Towns and made a show of being cosmopolitan. Yet of the two novelists it was Bennett who continued to reflect in his later life the marks of his provincial origin. His assumption that life in the provinces was dull and prosaic and that cities like Paris and London were places of glamour and romance was itself the attitude of a provincial. Moreover, there was not a little that was provincial as well as pretentious and unenlightened in his admiration of efficiency and his deliberate pursuit of culture.

Possessed of what was on the whole a materialistic conception of culture, Bennett had not much to offer in place of the provincial world which he condemned. The garish splendors of *Imperial Palace* were a poor substitute. He was neither a very original nor a very profound critic of provincial society. He complained of the narrowness of provincial life, of its mediocrity, its crudity, and its intolerance. He attacked the tyranny of parents and the harshness of the religion that he had known in his youth. But he had no complete view of his problem. Being himself a frank exponent of commercialism in literature, he could not justly attack the commercialism of the Five Towns. He was an avowed admirer of what was practical and efficient, and it was part of his literary creed to find romance in the most ordinary incidents. Apparently unaware of any incon-sistency, he denounced the provinces for their commonplaceness while exalting the commonplace as the true source of beauty and pathos. It is not always clear, in fact, whether his purpose was to celebrate the wonder of life or to decry its vanity.

Similarly he was much given to the practice of describing life as humdrum while repeatedly insisting that nothing in life was hum-drum. This effort to interweave the idea of what is romantic with the idea of what is ordinary becomes at times in his fiction little more than mere juggling with words. It represents the cheap device of substituting labels for reality. Indeed, there is something false as well as immature in thus dwelling on the question of whether life is essentially dull and prosaic or a thing of beauty and mystery. Perhaps the author was trying, in emulation of Wordsworth, to elicit the effect of the marvelous from the familiar. Or perhaps he was endeavoring to imitate the sensitive spirit of the Russian novel-ists whom he so greatly admired. In any case, he exclaimed too much and followed too deliberate a method of stalking his quarry.

Bennett's first novel, *A Man from the North* (1898), is the story of a young man who goes from the Five Towns to London, becomes a solicitor's clerk, and tries unsuccessfully to make himself a writer. Finally disillusioned, he settles down to a commonplace marriage and a life of mediocrity. Aside from the marriage and literary failure of the hero, the situation is similar to that of Bennett during his early years in London. Written under the influence of the French realists, the story is simple and straightforward but is lacking in color and vitality.

The heroine of *Anna of the Five Towns* (1902) is the daughter of a miser. She lives in an atmosphere of narrow Wesleyanism, en-joying few pleasures despite her wealth, and dutifully marries a man whom she does not love. The man to whom she has given her heart, borne down by the disgrace of his father's chicaneries, secretly commits suicide. *Leonora* (1903) reflects an author who has begun to make concessions in the interest of popularity. The central char-acter is a middle-aged woman with grown daughters and a husband who is quite unworthy of her. She finds herself being attracted to another man, whom she eventually marries after her husband has conveniently put himself out of the way. In *Whom God Hath Joined* (1906) we have a realistic account of two divorce suits. Although the characters are somewhat artificial, the situation is handled with power and ingenuity. So much emphasis is placed upon the injurious effects of the publicity given to such trials that the novel has something of the appearance of being a tract against divorce.

Among the concoctions of crime and mystery written by Bennett to sell are *The Grand Babylon Hotel* (1902), *Teresa of Watling Street* (1904), and *The City of Pleasure* (1907), the earliest of the three being an extravagant, somewhat farcical mystery story in which an American millionaire and his daughter, acting as amateur detectives, uncover an international plot. *Buried Alive* (1908) deals with the unusual situation of a celebrated painter who, having a distaste for publicity, exchanges his identity for that of his valet, who has just died. Many amusing complications follow. Other stories of a light, diverting character are *Helen with the High Hand* (1910) and *The Card* (1911). The latter, published in America as *Denry the Audacious*, details the spectacular rise of a man of the Five Towns through shrewdness, audacity, and luck. Although the author appears to be laughing at his characters, he writes in a tone in which admiration is mingled with ridicule.

Clayhanger (1910) and its two sequels, *Hilda Lessways* (1911) and *These Twain* (1916), occupy a high place among Bennett's novels. They give an elaborate account of the development of Edwin Clayhanger, a sensitive young man, and also provide an interesting picture of social evolution in the Five Towns. Hilda Lessways, the heroine of the trilogy, is a less satisfactory character than the hero. Although the author has sought to endow her with the charm of the unexpected and to render her feminine and enigmatic, she not infrequently strikes one reader, at least, as having been made according to a rather mechanical formula. Similarly the incompatibility of husband and wife as recorded in *These Twain* has the air of something manufactured. According to Wells, Bennett was never able to adjust his personality to that of a woman. In 1907 he married Marguerite Soulié, a Frenchwoman, and fourteen years later he and his wife separated. Afterwards he lived with Miss Dorothy Cheston, an actress. Although he seems to have been happy with her in a determined sort of way, his letters to her reveal a certain amount of friction between them. Possibly the exaggerated difficulties of Edwin and Hilda in finding a basis of adjustment are a reflection of the author's personal awkwardness in dealing with women.

Prominent among the later novels of Bennett are *The Pretty Lady* (1918), *Riceyman Steps* (1923), and *Imperial Palace* (1930), the earliest of which recounts the life of a courtesan over a brief period, with scenes of frivolity in London during the excitement of the war. In *Riceyman Steps* we are taken into a dull quarter of London and given a painstaking study of a miserly bookseller. The minute depiction of the drab setting serves to envelop us in an atmosphere of pettiness and comes near to producing the effect of a case report. *Imperial Palace,* in which the various activities of a large hotel are set forth in great detail, provides the author with an opportunity to indulge both his interest in organization and his equally characteristic penchant for the atmosphere of wealth and splendor. The people of the novel are less impressive, however, than the great hotel which they manage with such efficiency.

The Old Wives' Tale

As has been indicated, Bennett was not always successful in fusing his materials. His dramatic idea may be somewhat ambiguous or it may be too slight to bring the materials into effective unity. Thus some episodes may appear to be irrelevant. The impression sometimes gained from *Clayhanger,* for example, is that of historical reconstruction rather than of imaginative evocation. One reason for the superiority of *The Old Wives' Tale* to the other novels is its greater explicitness of theme. The general idea, to be sure, is an old and simple one. Time as the destroyer of youthful grace and beauty has been the theme of innumerable poems, of which one thinks in particular of Villon's *Ballad of Dead Ladies.* The very obviousness of the theme made it suitable for a novelist whose sensibility was limited and whose success was dependent more upon patient accumulation of a mass of material than upon imaginative intensity or subtlety of feeling.

The idea of *The Old Wives' Tale* first came to Bennett, he tells us in his *Journal*, in a Parisian restaurant in 1903, where he saw one evening a stout, middle-aged woman with ridiculous mannerisms arguing with a young and beautiful waitress. The contrast between the two women and the reflection of the novelist that the older one had herself once been young and possibly attractive caused him to think of writing a story about two sisters, one of whom was to live prosaically while the other would become a prostitute. Both would eventually lose the charm of youth, and in old age would live together again, "a nuisance to themselves and to others."

It was not until 1907 that the projected story was actually begun, by which time the original plan had been modified in various ways. While some of these changes were the natural result of slow germination in the author's mind, others were probably due to his unwillingness to go too far in risking the displeasure of his readers. He did not write cruelly in the "tone" of *Ivan Ilyitch*, by Tolstoy, as he had said he would, nor did he make one of the heroines a prostitute. The realism with which the two women are drawn is not ruthless. Instead of being pathetic or repulsive like the woman in the restaurant, they are only mildly and amusingly absurd, and Sophia can be said to maintain her dignity to the end. In fact they are so well provided with dignity, money, and virtue that they constitute for the ordinary reader not so much an exposure of human frailty as a rather flattering representation of human worth. Moreover, their disillusionments are not excessive when measured by those which the heroine of Maupassant's *Une Vie* had to endure.

Although Bennett referred somewhat condescendingly to *Une Vie* in the preface to *The Old Wives' Tale*, he probably owed more of his conception to Maupassant's novel than he would have been willing to admit to himself. Another novel which was less important to him but from which he may have obtained hints for his general situation is Balzac's *La Maison du chat qui pelote*, or *At the Sign of the Cat and Racket* in the English translation. Balzac's novel deals with a draper's shop situated in Paris and owned by Monsieur Guillaume, a man who, like John Baines, is of the old school. His establishment, which is always well stocked, is highly respected and his reputation for commercial honesty and ability is unimpeachable. Like John Baines he has a wife and two daughters. Virginie, the elder, resembles Constance Baines in that she is patient and gentle. Augustine, the younger, though too weak to resist her mother's will in the manner of Sophia, is nevertheless like Sophia in being pretty and graceful and in feeling the emptiness of her life. In the midst of her narrow commercial surroundings, she pines for a life of elegance. She secretly devours two romances discovered in the cupboard of a cook who has been discharged. Sophia finds similar pleasure in reading novels from the Free Library of Bursley.

Joseph Lebas, the chief assistant, occupies a position in the novel similar to that of Samuel Povey in Bennett's novel. He is treated almost as if he were a member of the family and becomes the object of Virginie's secret admiration. Eventually the two marry, live in the old home in the Rue Saint-Denis, and find quiet happiness in managing the family business. They introduce certain changes into the conduct of the establishment and show that, like Mr. Povey, they know how to keep pace with the times. Théodore de Sommervieux, the aristocratic young painter who manages, over the opposition of her parents, to win the hand of Augustine, is similar in some respects to Gerald Scales. Each man is a good-looking and faithless dandy who soon tires of his wife and begins to treat her badly. In each of the two novels the sensible marriage brings happiness and what first appears to be the more romantic union ends in disaster.

La Maison du chat qui pelote is very different from *The Old Wives' Tale* and is only about one tenth as long. It is not likely, however, that so many points of correspondence between them should have arisen from mere coincidence, and there are additional reasons for connecting the two novels. The shop of Monsieur Guillaume is provided with a curious old signboard on which there is a painting of a cat standing on its hind legs and endeavoring to hit a large ball with a racket held in one of its forepaws. It is this signboard which gives the novel its title. The shop of John Baines, on the contrary, as we are specifically told, has no signboard. Once having been blown down in a storm, it is never replaced until after the death of the original proprietor, when Mr. Povey erects a new one. Obviously a novelist would not take over such an easily recognizable detail from another novel without disguising it and adapting it to his particular situation. Here the mere reference to a signboard, taken in conjunction with the other analogous points, is suggestive. Even the title of *The Old Wives' Tale* may have been derived from Balzac's novel. Augustine, after having endured great suffering in her marriage, finally confides her troubles to her parents, for she had reached the point, as the author says, of one who "tries every prescription, and even puts faith in old wives' remedies." This passage may have contained the grain of suggestion which resulted in the choice of title. As first conceived, the projected novel had been called simply *The History of Two Old Women*.

There are a few details in *The Old Wives' Tale* that are reminiscent of *Une Vie*. Sophia, we remember, once sewed some banknotes in the lining of her skirt, following a method for the safekeeping of money that was recommended to Jeanne, the heroine of *Une Vie*, when she was arranging to go to Paris. Fossette has her counterpart in the aged Massacre of the earlier novel. Jeanne's mother spoke constantly of "her" hypertrophy as if it were an ailment that belonged especially to her. It was in such a manner that Constance habitually referred to "*my* sciatica."

Such details, however, are of only minor interest. It was the theme of Maupassant's novel rather than the particular incidents that was useful to Bennett. *The Old Wives' Tale* was conceived, so we are told, as an English *Une Vie*. It was to contain the life histories of two women rather than the single life history of one, but it was to follow the French novel in the essential characteristic that it would show the changes wrought by time. The decision to have two heroines, which seems to have been part of the original plan, provided the author with an opportunity to deal with two contrasting lives—one quiet and respectable and the other of a more picturesque order.

In *Une Vie* the career of the heroine is traced from the time she leaves the convent where she has been educated until she is an old and broken woman. Jeanne de Lamare has a life of almost continual suffering. As a young girl she is quite ignorant of human affairs. She lives in a state of revery and expectancy which at times becomes so intense that she is almost mad with happiness. Tender, innocent, and easily bruised, she soon learns what it is to be robbed of her illusions. She expects to adore her husband but he begins immediately to deceive her; she is deceived too by the servant Rosalie, who has been almost like a sister to her; and she is also betrayed by her friend Gilberte. Even her mother, she discovers by chance from some old letters, has not been the virtuous woman she has always supposed. Her second child does not survive its birth. And through the worst of her trials she is denied the comfort of her religion because of the austerity of the priest, who has a long-standing quarrel with her father.

As is natural in a woman of her temperament who has failed to achieve happiness in marriage, Jeanne centers her affection in her son, and it is at his hands that she receives the cruelest of all her disappointments. He has hardly reached manhood before he gives himself wholly to an unscrupulous prostitute. Thereafter the lonely and grief-stricken mother impoverishes herself in order to pay his debts, while he treats her with complete neglect and the blackest ingratitude.

If *The Old Wives' Tale* is to be regarded as an English *Une Vie*, it is an *Une Vie* with the sting removed. There is little in the English novel to be compared with the progressive accumulation of betrayals and disappointments by which Maupassant's heroine is gradually transformed into a pitiful wreck of her former self. Constance and Sophia Baines, as befits the daughters of a successful Five Towns businessman, are less delicate and vulnerable than the cloistered French girl, whose father is a good-natured but ineffectual aristocrat. The women in Bennett's books, says Wells, "are for the most part good hard Staffordshire ware." They do not break easily. Sophia possesses sufficient strength to rise above the disaster of her marriage and Constance, under her soft exterior, can be unexpectedly determined.

Bennett further lightens the tone of his novel by enabling his two heroines to share between them the sufferings endured by one person in Maupassant's story. Sophia suffers from her marriage and Constance from the ingratitude of her son. The strength of *Une Vie* consists in its concentration upon one character, the ingratitude of the son being all the more terrible because of what has preceded it. Cyril, the son of Constance, is less of a problem, to be sure, than Paul, the son of Jeanne. In addition, Cyril's neglect of his mother is

less devastating in its effect than is the behavior of Paul, because
Constance has reserves of moral strength to sustain her not shared
by Jeanne. She has her position as a respected member of the community and the memory of happiness with a husband who has always cherished her. Similarly, the wedded life of Sophia, so far as
it is revealed to us, is the occasion of far less misery than the prolonged and intense bitterness of Jeanne's union. Then comes success
of a kind in the Pension Frensham, which, though it does not bring
happiness, is at least an alleviation of the suffering that has gone before. In other words, the suffering recorded in *The Old Wives' Tale*
is distributed and balanced in such a manner that it appears almost
casual in comparison with the unbroken accumulation of sorrow
in the life of Jeanne de Lamare.

Inasmuch as Bennett could deal with the material circumstances
of peoples' lives more convincingly than with their thoughts and
feelings, his best work was in the portrayal of simple characters associated with their surroundings. Such characters in *The Old Wives'
Tale* are Mrs. Baines, Constance, and Samuel Povey. We do not have
to penetrate very deeply into them in order to understand them because, in addition to being simple, they are made intelligible by
being closely identified with the spirit of the Five Towns. Samuel,
it is true, reveals after his marriage certain traits that are a little
surprising in one whom we have seen only in the role of faithful ap-
prentice. But his interest in dogs and cigars only marks him as a man
of spirit. It is the kind of thing that adds to the excitement of marriage for Constance without seriously affecting our conception of
the man. His fanatical zeal in the interest of his cousin Daniel is,
however, a different matter. As a revelation of unsuspected depths
of character in a seemingly ordinary person, it reflects, in the author's words, "the vein of greatness which runs through every soul
without exception." It is an example, in short, of the deliberate in-
jection of the heroic into the essentially commonplace.

Judged by her behavior as a young girl, Sophia should be the most
striking character in the novel. She is more intelligent than Constance, more impulsive, and more capable. She fails, however, for
a number of reasons, to measure up to our expectations. Her complexity is not developed sufficiently to render her fully compre-

hensible and she also suffers from being placed in surroundings with which she has nothing in common. Constance, in Bursley, occupying the position of respected wife and mother, retains her identity and her dignity. Sophia, in Paris, unacquainted with the world that she has entered, without friends, and dependent upon the whims of an irresponsible spendthrift, shrivels into comparative insignificance. Instead of being a figure of tragedy, she appears rather as a foolish girl who, after being subjected to numerous indignities by her husband, is finally abandoned by him.

Her failure to fill her role more impressively may be attributed to the fact that the author did not inquire closely into the personal basis of her rebellion. He indicated something of the nature of her dissatisfaction but did not enter completely into her point of view. His main concern was with her career as something to be contrasted with that of her sister. But her career is not of much consequence except as it is realized from her point of view. We know in a general way how Constance feels about her life, but the attitude of Sophia is not equally clear. She is effectually presented as a young girl at home and afterwards as a competent woman of business, but her moments of great emotional crisis are either passed over in silence or are handled somewhat melodramatically. Her childish flirtation and even her defiance of her mother do not prepare us for her elopement. No adequate explanation is given of her theft of money from her aunt—a matter of great psychological importance which appears to have been inserted simply to provide the fugitive with a reason for not returning home after the collapse of her marriage. We are shown only the beginning and the end of her four years of actual marriage, and only a few episodes of the thirty years spent in Paris are related in detail. To compare her with the heroine of *Une Vie* is to perceive that we have only a fragmentary account of this decisive period of her life and only a shadowy impression of the moral forces that animate her.

It is a little surprising that a person of Sophia's temperament should have settled down into the quietly efficient proprietress of a *pension,* or that she should have been content to live so narrowly for so long in a city of so many attractions. In a character of James, such indifference to the charm of one's surroundings would be indicative of a striking lack of sensibility. Bennett doubtless wished to indicate that his heroine had inherited her father's acute business sense and that she was still a provincial from the Five Towns. In addition, he was more interested apparently in such material matters as the public execution at Auxerre, life in Paris during the Siege, and the house of Madame Foucault, than in the moral and emotional nature of Sophia.

Madame Foucault and her friend Laurence are prostitutes of a kind more likely to be encountered in the pages of a theatrically sentimental novel than in any actual quarter of Montmartre. It was such conventional caricatures as Madame Foucault and Chirac, the journalist, that Bennett was pleased to offer as a picture of Parisian life. Probably he believed that his English readers would prefer them to the more sober reality. Not only are they unrepresentative of true French life, but they are too unreal to provide a background with which Sophia can be successfully merged.

The most important single feature of *The Old Wives' Tale* is the impression conveyed of the changes brought about by the passing of the years. These changes are indicated by a variety of devices. One by one the older characters die, except Mr. Critchlow, whose survival gives added emphasis to the passing of the others. There are references to historical events, such as the Civil War in the United States and the Franco-Prussian War. Styles change; the horsecar gives way to the electric car; Dick Povey, who at the age of eleven disturbs the gravity of St. Luke's Square by riding a bone-shaker, becomes as a young man a salesman of motorcars. New methods are introduced into business, such as the Annual Sale with which Samuel Povey defeats the old order. The agitation for federation of the Five Towns, against which Constance casts her vote, is a mark of the changing order, as is also the intrusion into Bursley of a branch of the Midland Clothiers Company.

So that we shall not be insensible to the gradual process of change, the author calls attention to certain moments in the lives of his characters in which they become aware of the flight of time. Numerous such moments serve to mark the stages of the life of Constance. There is the time when she supplants her mother as the mistress of the house and the time, after her husband's death, when the passages between her dwelling and the shop are closed off. Most moving of all such scenes is the meeting of the two sisters after so many years of separation—a meeting that cannot fail to awaken memories of other times. Another moment of intense realization comes to Sophia when she sees her husband lying dead. She has not seen him since he was a young man and now his face is that of one who is painfully and pitiably old. So striking an example is he of the destruction of youth and vigor by the inexorable hand of time that the sight of his withered face fills her with a sense of the vanity of life.

Although Bennett derived a large part of his fictional method from a study of the French realists, he was essentially English in his point of view. Despite his reaction against the Victorian novel, he had more in common with Trollope than with Virginia Woolf or D. H. Lawrence. He dealt with such problems as were familiar themes in Victorian fiction—problems involving marriage, the relation of parents to children, and material affairs of various kinds. Bennett also had something in common with the Victorians in his tendency to mingle romance with realism and in his liking for the exceptional and the bizarre. There are passages in *The Old Wives' Tale* which are faintly reminiscent of Dickens—of a milder and less hilarious Dickens. One thinks of Maggie going out in her new bonnet in search of romance, of Mr. Povey suffering from the toothache, of Miss Chetwynd discoursing about the Reverend Archibald Jones, and of the malevolent Mr. Critchlow. Gerald Scales with his dandiacal charms is similar to the conventional deceiver of Victorian melodrama. There is also an element of the melodramatic in the sudden violent intrusion into the story of Daniel Povey's murder of his wife. And the death of John Baines, coming at a time when Constance and her mother have gone to see a dead elephant, provides a Dickensian note by bringing a touch of the ludicrous into juxtaposition with what is painful and serious.

No other part of *The Old Wives' Tale* is as pleasing as the first book. It is here that the author reveals at its best his skill in the faithful representation of his material. Having as yet not to trouble himself much about his theme, he can give himself up zestfully to presenting his characters in their prim mid-Victorian setting. It is only in the later books that the story takes on a somber tone. Here, before the flight of Sophia, the atmosphere is that of calm content- ment with only minor disturbances. Mr. Baines has been ill for so long that his death makes little change in the family life. But time passes and change occurs. Sophia elopes and Constance and Mr. Povey are married. Mrs. Baines, feeling herself disgraced in the eyes of Bursley, goes to live with her sister at Axe. Her departure is one of the significant moments in which we are made aware of the re- lentlessness of change:

Old houses, in the course of their history, see sad sights, and never for- get them! And ever since, in the solemn physiognomy of the triple house of John Baines at the corner of St. Luke's Square and King Street, have remained the traces of the sight it saw on the morning of the afternoon when Mr. and Mrs. Povey returned from their honeymoon—the sight of Mrs. Baines getting into the waggonette for Axe; Mrs. Baines, encumbered with trunks and parcels, leaving the scene of her struggles and her de- feat, whither she had once come as slim as a wand, to return stout and heavy, and heavy-hearted, to her childhood; content to live with her grandiose sister until such time as she should be ready for burial! The grimy and impassive old house perhaps heard her heart saying: "Only yesterday they were little girls, ever so tiny, and now—" The driving- off of a waggonette can be a dreadful thing.[2]

[2] From: *The Old Wives' Tale*, by Arnold Bennett, copyright 1911 by Doubleday and Company, Inc.

CHAPTER XIX

$\mathcal{T}_{he}\ \mathcal{N}_{ovelist}\ as\ \mathcal{S}_{ocial}\ \mathcal{C}_{ritic}$

JOHN GALSWORTHY

John Galsworthy, the son of a well-to-do solicitor in London, was born in 1867. After going as a student to Harrow and Oxford, he became, in due course, a barrister, but, instead of entering seriously into the practice of law, he was sent by his father on a visit to Canada to look into the affairs of a coal mining company. Not long after the completion of this voyage he went on a long tour to Australia, New Zealand, and the South Seas—the study of maritime law serving as the excuse for the expedition. These travels were followed by a voyage to Russia to inspect mines. In 1897 he appeared as an author, under the pseudonym "John Sinjohn." In 1906, when he was nearly forty, his first book of considerable importance, *The Man of Property*, was published.

In 1905 Galsworthy was married to the former wife of his cousin Arthur Galsworthy. Her first union, which had taken place in 1891, had been for some reason a failure. It may have been her unhappiness that aroused the pity of the future novelist and drew him to her, as Jolyon was drawn to Irene while she was struggling to escape from Soames Forsyte. Although the two are said to have been in love with each other by 1895, it was not until 1902, according to Mr. H. V. Marrot, the novelist's biographer, that the woman in the case formally broke relations with her husband by establishing herself in quarters of her own while he was in South Africa during the Boer War. Even after having waited thus long, the two lovers kept their attachment a secret for nearly three years more, out of consideration for the feelings of Galsworthy's father, whose death in 1904 eventually freed them. They now gave the husband justifiable grounds for instituting divorce proceedings against Mrs. Galsworthy, with the result that when all legal requirements had been satisfied she was able to marry again. There can be little doubt that the experience of living for a period of nine years in such an ambiguous position had a deep and lasting effect upon Galsworthy. In writing *The Man of Property* and *In Chancery,* he was drawing from his own and his wife's experiences. In attacking Victorian conventionality he was writing as one of its victims.

Galsworthy rose to eminence as a novelist and dramatist at a time of great intellectual and social ferment. The first decade of the twentieth century was marked in England by a renewal of earnestness and idealism and a growing humanitarianism. The Boer War, which ended in 1902, had a sobering effect upon the nation, and there were other reasons for the change of temper. A new type of civilization, founded upon scientific theory rather than tradition, was being projected in the minds of intellectuals. Meredith, Hardy, and the French naturalists, as we have seen, had all been critical of what was artificial and stereotyped in nineteenth-century culture. Bernard Shaw found in the drama a means of making the public familiar with ideas drawn from such diverse sources as Ibsen, Nietzsche, Karl Marx, Henry George, and Samuel Butler. H. G. Wells also contributed with great effectiveness to the awakening of public interest in problems of social organization. In novel after novel he set forth his belief that our human society must be rescued from the net of traditionalism in which he saw it as having become entangled. The history of civilization, he believed, had been in large measure a history of confused and misdirected aims. Accordingly it was our duty to emancipate ourselves from long-accepted and long-cherished ways of thinking and create a new mentality. Our only hope for the future was in reeducating ourselves and in reconstructing our society along scientific lines and in accordance with the needs of the entire planet.

Although once characterized by D. H. Lawrence as being, along with Shaw and H. Granville Barker, one of "the rule and measurement mathematical folk," Galsworthy was not primarily a thinker. He did not have the mental audacity of either Shaw or Wells, nor was he like them a champion of science and logic. It was neither cerebral exuberance nor the desire to create a new social order that moved him so much as the humanitarian dislike of inequality and suffering. Whereas it was characteristic of Wells that he should foresee how the use of scientific weapons would affect the conduct of war, it was equally characteristic of Galsworthy that he should be appalled by the destructiveness of modern warfare and should attempt to bring about an agreement outlawing the use of airplanes in war.

Wells, the scientific reconstructionist, created a special type of character expressive of his ideal and qualified by temperament and training to be a citizen of his Utopian state. George Ponderevo, inventor and man of science, in *Tono-Bungay*, is such a character. Seeing England as a place of wasteful and seemingly aimless confusion and social disorganization, he represents in his development the awakening of consciousness to a sense of reality and purposefulness in all life. He is a man of disinterested intelligence who is adventurous and daring, clearheaded, free from prejudices, and quietly efficient. Galsworthy's characters, on the other hand, are not infrequently persons of doubt and indecision who find it difficult to throw off the prejudices of their class.

Though English in his point of view, Galsworthy was influenced, as were Bennett and Conrad, by the Continental novel. He admired Maupassant for the vigor, economy, and clarity of his writing and considered that he himself had learned more about the essentials of style from the Frenchman than from any other writer. He particularly admired Turgenev for the wisdom, breadth, naturalness, and atmosphere of his writing, and Tolstoy for depth of insight and breadth of character drawing. While there is no reason to doubt that these writers exercised considerable influence upon Galsworthy, his work bears no marked resemblance to that of any of his models. His irony lacks the naturalness and pungency of Maupassant's and his use of symbols appears sometimes rather crudely calculated in comparison with that of Turgenev.

To novelists who are also poets, like Hardy or Emily Brontë, says Virginia Woolf, facts appear naturally as symbols, with the result that a character can be at once an individual and a type. A symbolic figure gathers strength by being something more than a symbol. Galsworthy, a man of feeling but of limited imagination, was not essentially a poet. He was a moralist and critic whose primary aim as a writer was not to create a society but to criticize existing society. Much of his writing conveys an impression not of life itself but of an arrangement of life contrived for a special purpose. Intent upon making his meaning evident, he draws attention to the symbolic aspects of his material. Even in his more poetically conceived stories, such as *The Dark Flower* and "The Apple Tree," the atmosphere seems not infrequently to have been imposed upon the story as the result of a conscious and deliberate pursuit of charm. In other words, the author is sometimes lacking in the power to make a successful fusion of the critical and the imaginative and sensuous elements in his art.

In the early writing of Galsworthy it was the critical element that was dominant. Later we find him becoming less satirical and more emotional. Instead of desiring, like Wells, to reconstruct the social order, he wanted to make it more humane. *The Island Pharisees* (1904) is the account of a young Englishman's effort to free himself from the complacency of the class to which he belongs. While returning home from a trip on the Continent, Richard Shelton encounters a young Fleming with a philosophical turn of mind and the rebellious disposition of a vagabond who refuses to bow to the rules of conventional society. Contact with this man has the effect upon Shelton of causing him to take a more critical view of mankind, with the result that he begins to detect the narrow-minded smugness and unconscious hypocrisy that are characteristic of nearly everyone in his social circle. Institutions, says the author, in a preface to the novel, are like worn-out or outgrown garments. While the conditions of our lives continue steadily and imperceptibly to change from hour to hour, the institutions by which our lives are regulated have a tendency to remain unchanged. Most people, unaccustomed to speculation and desirous of being left in comfort, dislike those who insist upon the necessity of introducing changes and taking risks. Shelton by becoming critical makes himself disagreeable to his former friends. Eventually he releases from her engagement the woman whom he has been on the point of marrying.

The Man of Property, later to serve as the beginning section of *The Forsyte Saga*, was published in 1906, and in the same year *The Silver Box*, a play, was produced. Thereafter Galsworthy wrote other plays with so much success that he quickly established his reputation as one of the leading English dramatists of the time. Among the more notable of his dramatic productions are *Strife*, *Justice*, *The Skin Game*, and *Loyalties*. The problem of inequality in the administration of justice serves as the theme of *The Silver Box*. Thefts are committed by two men both of whom are drunk. Although the crimes are similar, the circumstances of the two men are not: one of them is poor and friendless and the other is a member of a rich and powerful family. The poor man is punished by being confined for a month at hard labor, but the man of more fortunate circumstances has only to appear in court and answer a few questions, not altogether accurately. His confession that he has drunk too much champagne causes the presiding magistrate to smile indulgently; the drunkenness of the other man, however, is dealt with seriously as an evidence of unreliability of character. The social chasm here illustrated recurs in a different form in *Strife*, the account of a strike causing much privation and suffering—a strike that might have been averted or brought to an early settlement had it not been for the class feeling and pride of the leaders on the two sides.

Justice has for its theme the inhumanity of the methods by which society protects itself from the criminal. Whatever may be the wishes of those who administer it, the machinery of the law, Galsworthy implies, is such a ponderous and crude mechanism that it cannot be readily adjusted to the requirements of the individual case. The stringency of the marriage laws is a contributing factor in the crime of a young man who alters a check so as to be able to rescue an ill-treated married woman, with whom he has fallen in love, from the brutality of her husband. The penalty exacted by the law for his crime is only a part of the guilty man's punishment. His health is injured by the rigors of prison discipline, and, after having served his sentence, he has yet to face the hostility of society.

Among the early novels of Galsworthy are *The Country House* (1907), *Fraternity* (1909), *The Patrician* (1911), and *The Dark Flower* (1913). *The Country House* is an attack upon the complacency of the landowning class. George Pendyce, the eldest son of a country gentleman, falls in love with a woman who is tied in marriage to another man. About to be involved in a divorce scandal, he finds himself in conflict with his father, a man who clings tenaciously to the traditional views of his class. The woman eventually grows tired of young Pendyce and gives him up, with the result that the problem posed by the author is not worked out to a definite conclusion.

Fraternity has for its theme the problem of the eradication of social barriers. Well-meaning efforts are made by different people to bring the classes together but without appreciable success. One of the characters is an old man who is engaged in writing a book about universal brotherhood while he fails to grasp the actual problems of those who are closest to him. He illustrates the futility of theory without practice. It appears that culture itself has the effect of raising barriers between people by making them too fastidious to endure coarseness or vulgarity. Hilary Dallison and his wife fail in their marriage through an excess of refinement, by which they are prevented from coming to an openhearted understanding of each other. The criticism of caste feeling recurs in *The Patrician*. In this novel, as in *The Man of Property, The Country House, Justice, The Dark Flower, In Chancery,* and *The White Monkey,* a man falls in love with a married woman.

The central character of *The Dark Flower* is the hero of three love episodes occurring at different stages of his life. As a young student, he attracts the wife of his tutor. Seven years later, in his full maturity, he has a more serious affair, which ends this time with the woman's death. Finally in middle age he is attracted to an innocent young girl, whom he manages, before it is too late, to resist. The idea of the novel, it would appear, is that love is a blind and incalculable force which cannot be held in legal or ecclesiastical chains.

The Forsyte Saga

In 1918, twelve years after the publication of *The Man of Property*, Galsworthy decided to continue the history of the Forsytes. Possibly he was moved to emulate Bennett, who had produced the third volume of the *Clayhanger* trilogy in 1916. As a result of this decision, *In Chancery* was published in 1920 and *To Let* in 1921. In 1922 these novels with *The Man of Property* and two short stories, "The Indian Summer of a Forsyte" and "Awakening," were published in a single volume as *The Forsyte Saga*. Afterwards the family chronicle was continued in *The White Monkey* (1924), *The Silver Spoon* (1926), and *Swan Song* (1928). These three novels and two short stories were subsequently published in one volume as *A Modern Comedy*.

The Forsyte Saga is at once a criticism of life and a study of a period. Dealing with three generations of a family, it reflects the decay of the Victorian era and the rise of a new spirit of postwar disillusionment. Although the action extends from 1886 to 1920, between the specific periods of the separate novels there are long intervals left untouched except for incidental and retrospective treatment. The time of each novel is sharply restricted, with the action of *The Man of Property* taking place in 1886–1887, that of *In Chancery* in 1899–1901, and that of *To Let* in 1920. In the second series of novels the record is extended to 1926.

Galsworthy manages to combine personal drama and social history by providing each novel of the series with a specific situation or dramatic center and drawing, at the same time, a picture of the large circle of Forsytes, who, having a strong sense of family ties, take a keen interest in one another's affairs. As commentators upon the action and as representatives of an important class in English society, they help to give an impression of unity to the chronicle and also to express its dominant idea. It is characteristic of the social dissolution of the time that the family sentiment should be seen to weaken in the younger generation of Forsytes. Moreover, in the second series of novels, beginning with *The White Monkey*, a greater proportion of non-Forsyte characters are introduced and the theme of possessiveness is held less steadily in view. The novels of the first series are more effective both as drama and as social criticism.

Of the older generation of Forsytes, Jolyon is distinguished for his daring and for having a certain quality of imagination. James, on the other hand, is timid and conservative in a high degree. Living almost entirely for his family and his possessions, he represents the Forsyte spirit in its purest form. The rivalry that springs up naturally between these two brothers is transmitted to their sons and is transformed into bitter antagonism by the circumstance that young Jolyon comes eventually to love Irene, the wife of Soames. Thus arises a family feud, which, by reaching into the next generation, provides the conflict of *To Let* and leaves its marks upon the novels of the second series.

Irene's discontent and the effort of Soames to please her by having a house built in the country form the central situation of *The Man of Property*. Instead of leading to a reconciliation, the new house brings further estrangement between husband and wife. Bosinney, the architect engaged by Soames, falls in love with Irene and, desiring to build a house worthy of her beauty, he fails to keep its cost within the sum agreed upon. Soames, having more than one cause for grievance, takes legal action against him to recover the excess amount. In the midst of these proceedings Bosinney is killed in an accident while wandering in a London fog, not long after he has learned from Irene that her husband has forcibly reasserted his marital rights over her. His death, in which there is a hint of suicide, leaves Irene in a pitiable state. Since Bosinney has been engaged to June Forsyte, the granddaughter of old Jolyon, this affair adds to the growing rift between Soames and his uncle.

It is Soames again who is the leading figure of *In Chancery*. Irene having left him, he lives apart from her for twelve years, his fortune steadily mounting while his desire to have a family of his own is being frustrated. No longer young and finding himself unable after repeated attempts to recover his wife, he takes steps eventually to divorce her. Eager to be free, she helps to provide the necessary evidence by turning to young Jolyon, who has been acting as the trustee of some money left to her by his father. Thus Soames attains his desire. He is enabled to marry again but at the bitter cost to his pride of seeing the still desired and still desirable Irene become the wife of his cousin Jolyon.

After a lapse of many years we find ourselves in *To Let* in the year 1920, in a world in which time and war have wrought great changes. Jolyon and Irene have a son Jon, who has reached his nineteenth birthday. Soames and his wife Annette have a daughter Fleur, who is only a little younger than Jon. These two young people, who have been brought up in ignorance of the former relationship of Soames and Irene, meet accidentally and fall in love with each other before they know the true nature of the family feud. Twentieth-century London is not Verona, however, and Jon, it must be admitted, is a less impetuous lover than Romeo. When Fleur suggests to him that they can be married in Scotland, he will not act until he has had time to think the matter over. Later, upon having learned from his father the ugly details of his mother's first marriage, he yields to his parents' will in the face of an antipathy so strong and deep-rooted. Soames does what he can to smooth the way for Fleur, but he is helpless, as he has always been, before Irene, who is responsible for Jon's decision. Soames, the man of property and supposed Philistine, acts more creditably at this juncture, in my opinion, than Jolyon and Irene, who are intended to represent an attitude of enlightenment and sympathy. Having made his resolution not to hurt his mother by marrying anyone so distasteful to her as the daughter of Soames, Jon leaves England in order to escape from the oppressiveness of his position. Fleur, in the bitterness of her defeat, accepts another suitor. Her thwarted love will continue, however, to be an element of disturbance through the later novels.

H. G. Wells draws a picture in *Tono-Bungay* of the confusion, sterility, and waste of a competitive commercial society. In science and in the devotion of men to truth he sees the promise of a better civilization. Galsworthy attacks commercialism by drawing a satirical picture of the Forsytes, in whom the sense of ownership is particularly strong. Whereas Wells takes into account the necessity of regulating passion in the interest of a stable society, Galsworthy is more interested in pressing the claims of the individual than in considering the needs of the social order. Like Meredith, he is in revolt against a mechanical or materialistic view of life. Passion is to him a more honorable and valid manifestation of human nature than the stultifying lust of possession. Jolyon, crossing Richmond Park on his way to Irene, sees in the place a symbol of the Forsyte character. Nature there is allowed to go so far and no further. So are the instincts kept in hand among the Forsytes. One who lives for possession, we are told, must first of all possess himself.

The older Forsytes have devoted their lives almost wholly to the amassing and preservation of large fortunes. Their view of life being based upon a sense of property, they do not care particularly for that which cannot be owned. Consequently they take little interest in art, literature, and science. Soames does not care for music. His interest in painting is essentially the interest of a collector with a keen sense of market values. So strong is the sense of ownership in Winifred that she dislikes to lose even such a worthless and troublesome husband as Montague Dartie. Fleur, having inherited the strong possessive instincts of her father, cannot reconcile herself to the loss of Jon.

By being extended to human relations, the sense of ownership is destructive of freedom and equality. Under certain conditions, Galsworthy contends, it reduces marriage to a form of slave owning, from which the only method of escape is the brutal process of divorce. Irene, unhappy at home, allows herself to be persuaded into marriage with Soames without loving him. He has promised her that she shall be free if their marriage is not a success. The victim of his own possessiveness, however, he does not release her, and she finds herself a prisoner in his home, unable to overcome the aversion that he excites in her. Even after having fled from him she still cannot free herself from her marriage so long as her husband refuses to divorce her and gives her no grounds to take such action against him.

Galsworthy's success as a dramatist was due primarily to his skill in constructing effective situations. Having to conform to the exigencies of the theater, where compression and emphasis are necessary, plays can hardly escape being more or less artificial in structure. The novelist, however, working in an ampler medium, can develop his material to an extent and with a degree of naturalness not ordinarily attainable in the theater. Moreover, he cannot rely upon the use of stage scenery and the impersonation of actors to give individuality to his scenes and characters. Thus, while effectively contrived situations are of great importance in the theater, they are less essential in a novel than development and individuality of character.

In a play like *The Silver Box* or *Strife* our main concern is with the situation of the characters rather than with the characters themselves. Their lack of development is not felt as a deficiency because our interest is centered not in them but in the idea expressed by them. In *The Forsyte Saga*, however, the problem of fusing the individual characters with the general idea is a more complex one. Aside from the fact that the characters have more room for development, the theme of possessiveness can be expressed adequately only through characters of some depth and intricacy.

Not having a strong sense of character, Galsworthy tends to rely upon his skill in the construction of situations. He places emphasis upon the typical rather than the individual traits of his characters. Sometimes he fails to bring the particular into complete harmony with the general. Soames' affectionate treatment of his father and sister, for example, is not that of a selfish or insensitive person. His feeling for Irene is not easily distinguishable from the love felt by various non-Forsyte characters. Had he been a typical man of property, he might have consoled himself more easily, one would think, with another woman. There is surely some inconsistency in the fact that this typical Forsyte, who is supposedly blind to the subtle manifestations of the spirit, should, during a great part of his life, be tormented by love for a woman who fails to return his love, and particularly for a woman who typifies the spirit of universal beauty. How are we to interpret his extreme susceptibility to that which, by definition of his type, should leave him indifferent? To say of him, as Jolyon writes to Jon, that Irene was simply in Soames' eyes a piece of property is surely a lame explanation of such singlehearted devotion.

Galsworthy shows himself to be a propagandist by the manner

in which he dwells continually upon the thematic aspects of his material. His characters either illustrate the possessive spirit or, like Bosinney and Irene, represent an attitude of esteem for things of the mind and spirit. Young Jolyon, who stands between the two extremes, is enough of a Forsyte to be able to understand the family temper without sharing it, in which respect he resembles his creator. June is a blend of Forsyte and non-Forsyte traits while Jon, the son of Irene, is essentially a non-Forsyte character.

Bosinney stands for a way of life that is creative and appreciative; accordingly he is indifferent to the material values so dear to the Forsytes. His intrusion into their world has the disturbing effect of something incomprehensible and incalculable by their standards. His death is conceived by the author as a victory over them. Young Jolyon, standing in the mortuary, has a fanciful impression that he sees the Forsytes lying prostrated around the body of the dead man. Notwithstanding his prominent position in the novel, Bosinney fails to leave a clear impression of an individual. The author's presentation of him indirectly as he appears to the Forsytes has had the effect of leaving him somewhat shadowy and incomplete. The separate parts of the man do not form an entirely recognizable whole. His lack of capacity in practical affairs, for example, and his occasional acts of rudeness are details that serve both to disfigure him as a man and to detract from his dignity as a symbol.

Irene, whose marriage to Soames brings the incarnation of lawless beauty into incompatible union with the personification of legal ownership, is so completely a symbol that she is hardly to be judged as an individual. Presented, for the most part, not directly but in her effect upon others, she is intended to be a mysterious figure of magnetic and glamorous charm. To old Jolyon, who is stirred by her loveliness into a state of excitement and expectancy quite unusual for his great age, she looks "like Venus come to life." She makes an easy conquest of Swithin when he takes her on a memorable drive to Robin Hill. Even James, dining alone with her under the mellowing influence of her soft dark eyes and smiling lips, feels her strange seductiveness. Although to Soames, who repels her, she can be hard and cruel, the effect ordinarily produced by her is that of softness and passivity.

Irene is far from being the demure woman of Victorian fiction. In some respects she is an example of the new woman who seeks the liberty to live her own life, like the heroine of Grant Allen's *The Woman Who Did* or of Wells' *Ann Veronica*. Her rebellion appears to be based less upon principle, however, than upon her antipathy to Soames. Once having escaped from him, she settles down into an affectionate wife and mother, content to adorn her home by bending gracefully over flower beds and making soft music at the piano. Only in dealing with the man who has aroused her aversion does her graciousness desert her. It is probably this instinctive shrinking from him, more than anything else, that causes Jon to give up Fleur. Irene tells her son, it is true, to think only of himself. Nevertheless, he acts in accordance with what he knows to be her desire. In thus allowing him to be controlled by her desire, she acts with a possessiveness as strong as that of any Forsyte. She fails, in short, to deal with Jon in the large spirit that she is intended to symbolize. Without appearing to realize it, the author has shifted his position. In *The Man of Property* he is the champion of the rebels against social convention; in *To Let* he is on the side of family ties and the sentiment of motherhood.

One of the important problems in the writing of fiction is that of handling the element of time. The simplification and elimination ordinarily necessary in the construction of a story tend to destroy the processional quality of the narrative. Henry James says in regard to this problem, in the preface to *Roderick Hudson*, that the novelist must balance himself between the necessity of treating his subject adequately and of keeping within the limits of his picture. Time is one of the essential aspects of the subject. It must be accounted for, says James, but it cannot be accounted for satisfactorily by a mere quantity of narrative items. By entering the consciousness of a character, however, the novelist can represent the changes taking place there. In novels like *The Return of the Native*, *The Ambassadors*, and Thomas Mann's *Buddenbrooks* the effect of lapsing time is produced in such a manner. James considered that in *Roderick Hudson* he had allowed his main character to fall to pieces too rapidly and had thus caused him to forfeit some of our sympathy. The reason for the importance of this problem as perceived by

James has been summed up by Herbert Read in the following suggestive passage:

It is a question of creating an *illusion* of duration which shall correspond with an actual *sense* of duration. The illusion can only be effective if the strands of interest which we pick up at the beginning of a story are so woven that they duplicate our consciousness of real events. But consciousness, whether real or induced, is not a simple fact: it is rather a process or state which is only realized upon the completion of some definite rhythm or pattern. In this it differs from awareness, which is an incomplete state of sensibility. We say loosely that we are "conscious" of pain or pleasure, but it would be better to say that we are "aware" of them. We become "conscious" when pain or pleasure is organized into a recognizable unity—when it becomes a sentiment, such as pity or terror. For pity or terror, or love or hate, is a highly organized complex, depending for its duration on its inherent pattern or repetitive rhythm. Still more complex are those organizations of emotions and conscious states which we name personalities, and these too have their dependable rhythm or definite pattern. Now, in order to create personalities and set them in action (which is the object of fiction), it is necessary to repeat, on another plane, an analogous rhythm or pattern.[1]

If we apply to *The Forsyte Saga* the test applied by James to *Roderick Hudson,* we find that many things in Galsworthy's novel either have been developed insufficiently or have been allowed to develop too rapidly. Not infrequently the author is content to state where he ought to present. He shows us that Irene finds Soames detestable, but he does not adequately demonstrate the original basis of her abhorrence. He sets up the Forsytes as people who have become the slaves of their possessive instincts, but he does not indicate the process by which the ownership of property has come to have such a blighting effect upon them. He allows Irene, a paragon of sensibility, to marry a man without love and he also permits Bosinney, another sensitive character, to become engaged to June while caring so little for her that almost immediately afterwards he falls in love with Irene. These things, we grant, could all have happened. The function of the artist was not, however, to ask

---

[1] *The Sense of Glory,* Harcourt, Brace and Company, 1930, pp. 210, 211.

us to take them for granted but to exhibit the process by which they did happen.

The fact is that Galsworthy has not, for the most part, entered sufficiently into the consciousness of his characters to reveal the changes taking place there. We are shown states of emotional disturbance, such as Soames' baffled desire for Irene, his anxiety in regard to Fleur, and Fleur's agitation while she is trying to win Jon. But these things remain somewhat general. Although they are reproductions to a certain extent of mental states, they do not provide a definite pattern of consciousness or enable us to penetrate into the inner springs of character.

Nevertheless, while we may feel that we do not fully understand these people, the author appears to be confident of his own understanding of them. Either directly or through other characters, he tells us unhesitatingly that Fleur instinctively conjugated the verb "to have" with the pronoun "I," that she has a "having" nature, that she is a taker whereas Jon is a giver, and that she has not been bred right. Such ready generalizations are of little use to us in coming to an understanding of the girl. So much insistence upon her possessiveness tends to give us the impression, in fact, that she is being used as an illustration and thus cannot act of her own will. Even her birth is utilized as a device for giving emphasis to the possessiveness of her father, who has to choose between saving his child and risking the loss of his wife.

These things serve to denote the chief weakness of Galsworthy as a novelist. Not only does he insist too much upon his meaning but he employs too direct a method of stating it. As a result his meaning loses some of the suggestive power that we associate with a work of imagination and acquires instead something of the literal quality that we associate with a lecture. Instead of concealing his general intention, he keeps it so steadily in view that we do not feel ourselves in the presence of spontaneous and creative growth. The continual emphasis upon the general aspects of the subject has the effect of limiting the freedom of the individual characters and making them appear cramped and composed. Only those who are not too closely identified with the central thesis give the impression of living freely on their own account. Thus it is not surprising that the best characters in *The Forsyte Saga* are the old men, who are by their nature more or less static. As simple types they can be made to illustrate the general idea of possessiveness without displaying much complexity of feeling. Even so it is not for their interest in property that James and Swithin are memorable but for more amiable and perhaps also more universal qualities of affection and pride. Old Jolyon, who is to some extent a portrait of the author's father, has been drawn with a high degree of understanding and sympathy.

CHAPTER XX

The Impressionistic Novel

JOSEPH CONRAD

The process by which foreign influences were brought to bear upon the English novel, to which both James and Moore had contributed, was continued in a more striking manner in the work of Joseph Conrad. While James was not a British subject by birth, he was of Irish and Scotch ancestry and his language was that shared by all English-speaking peoples. Moreover, the culture under which he was nurtured was largely of English origin. Conrad, on the other hand, whose full name was Teodor Josef Konrad Korzeniowski, was born of Polish parents in the Ukraine, which, at the time of his birth in 1857, was a part of czarish Russia.

As was natural in one whose father had been driven into exile by the Russian authorities, Conrad disliked to have emphasis placed upon the Slavic element in his work. He refused to admit the possibility of Russian influence upon his writing and insisted that he belonged to a racial group that had derived its culture from France and Italy. His early reading, apart from Polish, was, according to his own word, in French and English literature. He characterized himself as being the child of a chivalrous tradition, who had been influenced possibly by French romanticism. It was a product of French romanticism that probably first turned his imagination toward the sea. At the age of eight he read aloud to his father the

336

proofs of Victor Hugo's *Toilers of the Sea,* which the elder Korzeni-owski had been translating into Polish.

Conrad's desire to go to sea must have been partly an outgrowth of his reading. As a boy he probably read translations of the sea stories of Marryat and Cooper, and he was also an enthusiastic reader of books of travel and exploration. The experience of living with his parents in exile and knowing what it was to be under police surveillance doubtless awakened in him a desire to live where it was possible to act freely and openly. Under the circumstances of his early life, the sea must have appeared to him as a symbol of liberty as well as of adventure.

So it was that Conrad left Poland for France in 1874, when he was not quite seventeen, to become for the next three years a seaman, sailing out of Marseilles. Being a maritime country that was friendly to Poland, France was a likely place to attract a Polish boy who was bent on going to sea. It probably did not seem to him to be an altogether foreign country, for there were many Poles living there, and Conrad had spoken French from the time he was a child. Later, after he had become a novelist, he displayed a greater interest in the literature of France than in that of any other country.

The three years spent in France proved to be as adventurous as the youthful seaman could have hoped for. He was drawn into the conspiracy to put Don Carlos, duke of Madrid, upon the throne of Spain, in which adventure he was one of a group of men engaged in smuggling guns into Spain. He had also a somewhat romantic love affair, which ended by his being wounded in a duel. After these experiences he was eager to leave Marseilles; the opportunity to do so came in an English ship in which, after being taken to Constantinople, he finally arrived in England. He was not yet twenty-one and he knew hardly anything of the language of the country that was henceforth to be his home. He now gave himself up seriously to his career of seamanship and within ten years had become the captain of the *Otago.* His professional connection with the sea ended in 1894, from which time until his death in 1924 he devoted himself to writing.

Such a training to become an English novelist was, to say the least, unusual. It was not, of course, a conscious preparation. Conrad did not go to sea with the intention of later turning novelist. His writing in a language that had been learned comparatively late in life could not have been easy for one who was fastidious in matters of detail. Yet the course followed was not without its advantages. It enabled the future novelist to store up during a period of activity a fund of impressions and memories that he could later draw upon. The long hours spent on sailing ships must have strengthened the habit of meditation later to be revealed in the novelist. In addition, the unusual experiences in distant lands and the foreignness of his point of view gave to Conrad as novelist an element of strangeness that heightened his appeal to English and American readers.

The tendency of novelists to seek a precise and scientifically documented type of realism, which had been resisted by James, was no less repugnant to Conrad. Reality was not to be approached, he contended, simply by adherence to the dogmas of realism. Whereas the function of the scientist, he said, was to fit us "for the hazardous enterprise of living," the function of the artist, on the other hand, was not to equip us to meet the practical problems of our lives. The appeal of the artist was described as follows in the preface to *The Nigger of the Narcissus*:

> The changing wisdom of successive generations discards ideas, questions facts, demolishes theories. But the artist appeals to that part of our being which is not dependent on wisdom; to that in us which is a gift and not an acquisition—and, therefore, more permanently enduring. He speaks to our capacity for delight and wonder, to the sense of mystery surrounding our lives; to our sense of pity, and beauty and pain; to the latent feeling of fellowship with all creation—and to the subtle but invincible conviction of solidarity that knits together the loneliness of innumerable hearts . . .[1]

The conviction that we are held together by strong bonds of fellowship occupies an important place in Conrad's thought. The absence of such fellowship serves as the basis of a number of his stories. While we are drawn together, we are also kept apart by forces which, working in opposition to the forces of attraction, cut

[1] From: *The Nigger of the Narcissus*, by Joseph Conrad, copyright 1914 by Doubleday and Company, Inc.
Extracts from *The Nigger of the Narcissus* by permission of Messrs. Heinemann Ltd. and the trustees to the Conrad estate.

us off from the community of mankind. We suffer ostracism, and therein lies our tragedy. Sometimes the barrier is one of race, or it may be the outcome of temperament or of some unfortunate set of circumstances. Flora de Barral, the heroine of *Chance*, after her father has been discovered to be a criminal, is treated with such brutality by persons whom she has believed to be her friends that she acquires the belief that nobody can possibly care for her. This attitude, along with a number of chance occurrences, leads to prolonged misunderstanding between her and Captain Anthony, who endeavors chivalrously to rescue her from her friendless state. Axel Heyst, of *Victory*, who lives to himself on a remote island of the Malay Archipelago, is cut off from mankind by his belief that the world is evil and that all action is harmful. Despite his attitude, he takes upon himself the responsibility of rescuing a girl from a band of disreputable musicians by helping her to escape to his lonely island. There they live, loving each other but unable to break through the barrier of his mistrust of life. Only in her hour of death do they attain the victory of a perfect understanding.

Victory, like *Lord Jim*, is a story based upon the irony of a lost opportunity. Heyst, through the cultivation of aloofness, loses the habit of prompt and ready action, and acquires instead a habit of reflection—"the most pernicious of all the habits formed by civilized man," says Conrad. Consequently, when the forces of evil invade his island retreat, in the persons of three desperadoes, the man of detachment fails to meet the danger with sufficient promptitude, and Lena, the girl, risks her life to save him. Through his lack of faith in life, Heyst loses her, and in losing her he learns from her to trust life, when it is too late.

The inescapable loneliness of the individual is a recurring theme in Conrad's novels. Man, being vulnerable, keeps part of his nature out of sight, shielding it within that part of himself which is capable of resisting the hard blows administered by the hazards of life. Flora de Barral, Lena, Heyst, and Jim, to name no others, have all been injured in one way or another and they all suffer in consequence from a sense of isolation. Their lives are hidden, whereas their greatest need is for fellowship. Whatever the situation of a Conrad story may be, the sense of there being something inscrutable in life is likely to be reflected in it. In "The Secret Sharer" a ship's captain, by concealing a fugitive from justice in his cabin, helps him to escape. The captain's secret has the effect of cutting him off from comradeship with the members of his crew; he even gains the impression that the man whom he is hiding is his secret self. Moreover, the situation of the young man appearing suddenly from the shadowy darkness of the sea and afterwards disappearing into it "to be a fugitive and a vagabond on the earth" is peculiarly Conradian.

The world as seen by Conrad is a place of unending contention between the forces of dissolution and the ideal of brotherhood, between that which makes for disenchantment and that which instills courage and hope. In such a world, in which the powers of disruption prove the need for order and stability, only moral values can be counted upon to last. Duty, loyalty, and courage are virtues necessary to man if he is not to suffer defeat from the forces in league against him. So it is that a sailor is loyal to the unwritten law binding the members of a crew together and to their ship.

Conrad's view of life as something essentially mysterious is well illustrated by a comment made by him in the preface to *The Shadow Line*. In this novel there is a situation of a ship lying becalmed. The sailors are fever-stricken and it seems for a time that, in accordance with the superstitious belief of the chief mate, the ship will never be able to pass the latitude where its former captain lies buried. Is there a possibility that the malice of the dead captain is still being exerted against the ship? The author did not like to have it said of the story, however, that he had been dipping into the supernatural. The supernatural in fiction he considered to be a fabrication of minds incapable of appreciating the true mysteriousness of the world. "The world of the living," he said, "contains enough marvels and mysteries as it is; marvels and mysteries acting upon our emotions and intelligence in ways so inexplicable that it would almost justify the conception of life as an enchanted state."

In order to convey this impression of the elusive and inexplicable character of life, Conrad developed a method of presentation that, while suited to his special purpose, belonged in general to the movement in art now known as impressionism. Although the term *impres-*

sionism belongs more distinctly to painting than to literature, it represents a set of tendencies that has been felt in all the arts. Professor Louis Cazamian[2] has pointed out, in a lecture entitled "The Method of Discontinuity in Modern Art and Literature," that in the latter half of the nineteenth century a discontinuous mode of presentment was sought by an increasing number of artists. This movement was felt not only in painting but in other arts and in literature as well. Music began to be less a matter of the symmetrical arrangement of sounds, and the sculptor began to work for broken surfaces and incomplete contours rather than for rounded and finished outlines. In the thought of William James and Bergson and their disciples, says Cazamian, the mind was no longer regarded as something unified and continuous but was looked upon as being shifting and incalculable—a "complex and discontinuous mass of ever original states." Such a view of the mind tended to bring the traditional conceptions of form into disrepute and to stimulate interest among artists in the direct expression of the inner truth of life.

The theory of the naturalists that the artist should depict everyday life without idealism or moral comment was shared by the impressionist. Zola, however, worked from certain intellectual concepts and arranged his materials deliberately. Similarly *Esther Waters* was constructed with extreme care. The impressionist painter, on the other hand, sought to avoid elaborate composition. He wished to discard intellectual concepts and to paint objects not as he knew them from previously acquired knowledge but as they appeared to him at certain specified moments. What we actually see upon looking at an object depends not upon our knowledge of its structure but upon the amount of light in which it is situated. Outlines of objects seen at a distance may be lost in undefined masses of shadow. The artist, having to represent a three-dimensional scene on a two-dimensional canvas, must take into account the degrees of dark and light intensity in his painting in order to give a sense of depth to it. Forms and colors of objects are not constant but change from hour to hour and even from moment to moment with the character of the light in which they are seen. Thus an impressionist painting is a representation not strictly of an object but of the atmosphere in

[2] *Criticism in the Making*, New York, 1929, pp. 63–80.

which it is placed. Details and outlines are often blurred. The purpose of the artist is to give an impression of the subject in its general characteristics rather than in matters of detail.

Although the technical problems of the painter are different from those of the novelist, the aims of the two are in some respects alike. Conrad, like the impressionist painter, sees his subject as something shifting and somewhat illusory. He presents his material not by direct analysis but as it appears in detached momentary impressions. He devotes himself to the creation of atmosphere, which, as in such stories as *The Nigger of the Narcissus,* "Heart of Darkness," and "The Inn of the Two Witches," contributes to the effect by arousing a mood of strangeness, of apprehension, or of suspicion, through which the events are seen. Likewise, the effort of the novelist to deal with life in isolated and fleeting glimpses is suited to his belief that men's lives are mostly hidden from one another and that the artist searches for truth in moments of vision.

Conrad began his career as a novelist by writing about his experiences at sea and in the East. *Almayer's Folly* (1895) and *An Outcast of the Islands* (1896) deal with some Europeans living in Malaysia and showing in their lives the evil consequences of the tropical environment. *The Nigger of the Narcissus* (1897), one of the best of Conrad's sea stories, is an account of a voyage home from an Eastern port. *Lord Jim* (1900) has its setting in the islands of the Malay Archipelago, and "Youth," a short story published with "Heart of Darkness" and "The End of the Tether" in 1902, deals with a voyage to the East. "Freya of the Seven Isles" (1912) is another notable short story of life in Eastern waters. In addition to *Chance* (1913) and *Victory* (1915), to which reference has been made, other novels deserving of praise are *Nostromo* (1904), *Under Western Eyes* (1911), and *The Arrow of Gold* (1919). One of the best of Conrad's stories giving expression to the demoralizing effect upon a European of life in a tropical environment is "Heart of Darkness."

Lord Jim

Upon our first encounter with him, the central character of *Lord Jim* is making his living as a ship-chandler's water-clerk in an Eastern port. Although he is treated well by his employers, for he is very capable, he never stays long in one place. His restlessness is occasioned by the fact that he is trying to hide from something that he has once done. Whenever he discovers that this episode of his past is known, he leaves his job and goes to another seaport. Eventually he leaves the world of white men altogether and goes to live among the Malays of a jungle village.

Having gone to sea with a boy's romantic desire to perform valorous deeds, Jim found upon actual contact with it that the life of a sailor was barren of adventure; nevertheless, he became enslaved to the life at sea. It so happened that he was made a chief mate before he had ever gone through an experience that tested his real fiber. By being forced to remain in his cabin during a bad storm because of an injury that had made him lame, he missed the opportunity to prove himself. On account of his injury he had to be left in an Eastern port when his ship sailed, with the result that after his recovery he took a place as chief mate on the *Patna,* a rusty old ship chartered to carry eight hundred Moslem pilgrims on a voyage leading into the Red Sea.

This prosaic old steamer with her wheezy engines, her sweating human cargo, and her odious captain, is so different from his dreams of heroic adventure that Jim keeps apart from the other officers. He cannot foresee, of course, that it is in these loathsome conditions, which fill his soul with disdain, that the longed-for chance to distinguish himself is being prepared for him. Suddenly, without warning, the ship strikes something concealed under the water and is so badly damaged that she is believed to be on the point of sinking. As there are not nearly enough lifeboats for the greatly overloaded vessel, any attempt to rescue the passengers would be almost certain to lead to a fatal panic. The officers, with the exception of one who dies in the excitement, desert the supposedly doomed ship, leaving the eight hundred pilgrims and the other members of the crew to perish. Jim refuses at first to join the others in their escape, but finally he jumps, hardly knowing what he is doing until he finds himself in the boat. He would like to go back but there is no going back, and for the remainder of his life he is to be haunted by this irretrievable act of desertion.

The *Patna* does not go down. She is found in her damaged condition by a French gunboat and towed to port. All of the officers who have abandoned their ship manage to escape the official inquiry with the exception of Jim, who, having failed in one emergency, is determined that this time he will not run away. Furthermore, his simple and sensitive nature and his romantic obsession with the idea of heroism render him peculiarly vulnerable to the disgrace of such an inquiry, ending as it does in the loss of his certificate.

Now begins the period of Jim's life in which he tries unsuccessfully to escape from his past. Through Marlow's intervention he is employed in a rice mill. Then he becomes a runner for Egström and Blake, ship chandlers. Later he is with Yucker Brothers in Bankok. Wherever he goes, the story of the *Patna* follows him. Being too proud to live on terms of familiarity with his ignominy, he moves on to another place. His habit of running away from his story causes it, indeed, to become the more widely known against him.

What Jim wants, Marlow finally decides, is not relief but an opportunity to redeem himself. Hardly knowing whether to regard such behavior as a form of heroism or of cowardice and feeling the situation to be hopeless, Marlow consults his friend Stein, a wealthy merchant and learned man, with a special interest, as it happens, in entomology. This consultation marks the beginning of the second and last phase of the hero's rehabilitation.

Through the help of Stein, Jim goes to live in Patusan, a remote settlement of natives where white men are rarely seen. Despite the many dangers surrounding him, he conducts himself with intrepidity and soon wins the respect and confidence of the Malays. He is quick in coming to an understanding of the people and is enterprising in ministering to their needs. Everything that he puts his hand to turns out well. He seems, in fact, to bear a charmed life, and the natives believe him to be gifted with supernatural powers.

Eventually a band of pirates enters Patusan in search of provisions. Acting with characteristic gallantry, Jim allows them to depart safely. They betray him, however, and as a result of their treachery Dain Waris, a chief's son, and others are killed. Thus again fate wills that Jim must lose the confidence of men. They have trusted him and in their eyes he has betrayed them. There is nothing he can do to make them understand him. Nevertheless, he can refuse to fight for himself and in that way perhaps he can conquer his fatal destiny. Thus resolved, he goes unarmed before the father of Dain Waris and stands proud and unflinching while the aged Doramin shoots him through the chest.

Had Conrad so desired, he could have devoted himself to the writing of stirring tales of adventure. He knew how to construct a conventional type of plot and how to handle atmosphere effectively. Ordinarily, however, he was not content merely to tell exciting stories. His interest was centered less in the circumstances of his characters than in the human truth lying underneath. His attention was focused not upon the problem of thrilling the reader but upon the moral value of his situation. It is for this reason that the method followed in *Lord Jim* is not that of straightforward chronology. A simple chronological account of an adventure has the effect of focusing our attention upon the actual occurrences, whereas it is the effect of these occurrences upon the central character that is important. By beginning late in his story and then proceeding retrogressively to an account of the trial and the crucial incident on the *Patna* which has led up to it, Conrad both arouses interest in Jim's situation and explains the cause of his unusual behavior. Thereafter each act of the hero takes on special significance because we see it as a revelation of his striken conscience and of his desire to right himself. The frequent breaks in the narrative and its apparent artlessness prevent us from becoming too much absorbed in the action. The facts of the story cease to be simply facts but become clues to a man's character.

The method followed has the effect of giving to the novel a high degree of unity by making it essentially an elucidation of a problem of character—a problem which, being both obscure and subtle, is difficult to approach openly. Jim's act of deserting the apparently sinking ship is a breach of fidelity that must be expiated. The humiliating experience of the trial and the loss of his certificate serve to cut him off from other men of his world. He cannot free himself from the obsession that he is everywhere an object of scorn. In the inflamed state of his imagination, he must wipe out his disgrace and restore his lost self-confidence. His greatest need is to redeem himself in his own eyes. Even after he has succeeded in becoming the trusted hero of the Malays of Patusan, he is still haunted by the specter of his lost honor. He must go on holding up his end, as he tells Marlow, so as to be assured that nothing can touch him.

The first four chapters of the novel, which are related directly by the author, perform the double function of providing an outline of Jim's career and of leading quickly to the crucial scene on board the *Patna*. They also introduce Marlow, a spectator at the trial, who becomes the narrator at the beginning of the fifth chapter. This change brings an air of informality into the narrative and adds to its naturalness and appearance of authenticity. The device of having the story told by a man who knows Jim and who sympathizes with him provides the author with both a limited point of view and a natural means of commenting upon the action. It also provides a link between Jim and the world from which he has severed himself, and it enables us to see him sympathetically and at close range while he still retains his essential elusiveness and isolation. Marlow is not Conrad, nor is his point of view that of the omniscient narrator. His knowledge is limited, like that of an actual person. He does not know any more than the reader, until near the end, what the ultimate fate of Jim is to be. He is never certain, in spite of the peculiar relationship existing between the two, that he thoroughly understands the young man.

Henry James, as we know, believed that the novelist as narrator should disguise and conceal himself as much as possible. We do not have the impression while reading *The Ambassadors* that someone is intervening between us and the subject. Conrad, on the other hand, by placing Marlow between us and Jim, does not veil or disguise the act of narration but calls particular attention to it. James's use of a reflecting consciousness as a register of the action is different from Conrad's use of Marlow. Ordinarily the characters so used by James, such as Strether in *The Ambassadors* or Maggie and Amerigo in *The Golden Bowl,* are themselves leading participants in the action. By being themselves deeply involved in the matter at hand and by being actively aware of their involvement, they see, and enable us to see, what is important. It is not their function to tell us what we should know but rather to reflect it incidentally. Marlow, on the other hand, has a definite responsibility, in the performance of which he must possess himself of information even if the process of acquiring it appears sometimes artificial. James achieves authenticity by being so subtle and resourceful in his method of representation that we forget the process of authorship. Conrad, following a method somewhat reminiscent of Defoe, achieves an air of authenticity by making the act of narration itself appear plausible.

The method followed in *Lord Jim* is a mixture of simplicity and intricacy. It bears certain resemblances to the indirect method of James and requires that careful attention be paid to the narrative point of view. Marlow, to be sure, is involved in what he has to tell, and he is most successful in dealing with that part of the story in which he is most closely involved. After the inquiry it is he who looks after Jim by finding employment for him in various places. It appears quite fitting that the account of this period should come from the man acting in Jim's behalf. After the hero goes to live in Patusan, however, the two men see each other only at rare intervals. In addition, the necessity of establishing new characters and a new set of conditions in regard to which the narrator is at first wholly ignorant causes the task of narration to become increasingly complex. Thus for a number of reasons these latter scenes are less convincing than the earlier part of the story. Marlow begins to appear as an outsider. The mere problem of providing him with necessary information leads the author to resort to the use of various artificial contrivances.

Jim, it would seem, is an incurable romantic. His case is diagnosed by Stein, the entomologist, who draws a distinction between his behavior and that of a butterfly, a specimen of which he has just been admiring. He says to Marlow:

"We want in so many different ways to be," he began again. "This magnificent butterfly finds a little heap of dirt and sits still on it; but man he will never on his heap of mud keep still. He want to be so, and again he want to be so. . . ." He moved his hand up, then down. . . . "He wants to be a saint, and he wants to be a devil—and every time he shuts his eyes he sees himself as a very fine fellow—so fine as he can never be. . . . In a dream. . . ."

Jim saw himself as a very fine fellow—so fine as he could never be. As a boy he fell into a dream of honor that he followed to the end of his life. It may be that this very dream prompting him to heroic action contributed to his defeat. Had he not lived so much in his thoughts, he might not have failed to take part in the rescue made by the boys of the training ship. Had he taken a more prosaic view of his duty, he might have been equal to the emergency on board the *Patna,* as the officer of the French gunboat would undoubtedly have been. Had it not been for his romantic scruples and the memory of his former failure, he might not have left himself open to the treachery of "Gentleman Brown," a man without honor.

The passage in which Marlow describes his departure from Patusan and his last sight of Jim provides an interesting example of Conrad's impressionism, and it is expressive, at the same time, of the underlying meaning of the novel:

"He was white from head to foot, and remained persistently visible with the stronghold of the night at his back, the sea at his feet, the opportunity by his side—still veiled. What do you say? Was it still veiled? I don't know. For me that white figure in the stillness of coast and sea seemed to stand at the heart of a vast enigma. The twilight was ebbing fast from the sky above his head, the strip of sand had sunk already under his feet, he himself appeared no bigger than a child—then only a speck, a tiny white speck, that seemed to catch all the light left in a darkened world. . . . And, suddenly, I lost him. . . ."[3]

Thus it is that Jim and his shadowy ideal of conduct remain at the end for us elusive and intangible—an impenetrable mystery. There he stands symbolically at the heart of a vast enigma, a tiny speck that catches the light of a darkened world.

[3] This and the preceding quotation from *Lord Jim,* by Joseph Conrad, copyright 1899, reprinted by permission of Doubleday and Company, Inc.

The extracts from *Lord Jim* by permission of Messrs. Wm. Blackwood & Sons and the trustees to the Conrad estate.

SELECTED READING LIST

The following list of novels and stories is intended only as an introductory guide to the more important British novelists from early times to the present day. The major novelists are represented by examples of different aspects of their work.

EARLY PROSE FICTION

JOHN LYLY (1554?–1606). *Euphues, or the Anatomy of Wit,* 1579.

SIR PHILIP SIDNEY (1554–86). *The Countess of Pembroke's Arcadia,* 1590.

THOMAS LODGE (1558?–1625). *Rosalynde, Euphues Golden Legacie,* 1590.

THOMAS NASHE (1567–1601). *The Unfortunate Traveller, or the Life of Jack Wilton,* 1594.

JOHN BUNYAN (1628–88). *The Pilgrim's Progress,* 1678.

MRS. APHRA BEHN (1640–89). *Oroonoko, or the Royal Slave,* 1688.

THE EIGHTEENTH CENTURY

DANIEL DEFOE (1659?–1731). *Robinson Crusoe,* 1719; *Captain Singleton,* 1720; *Moll Flanders,* 1722.

JONATHAN SWIFT (1667–1745). *Gulliver's Travels,* 1726.

SAMUEL RICHARDSON (1689–1761). *Pamela, or Virtue Rewarded,* 1740; *Clarissa,* 1747–8.

HENRY FIELDING (1707–54). *Joseph Andrews,* 1742; *Tom Jones,* 1749.

TOBIAS GEORGE SMOLLETT (1721–71). *Roderick Random,* 1748; *Humphry Clinker,* 1771.

LAURENCE STERNE (1713–68). *Tristram Shandy,* 1759–67; *A Sentimental Journey,* 1768.

ROBERT PALTOCK (1697–1767). *Peter Wilkins,* 1751.

SAMUEL JOHNSON (1709–84). *Rasselas,* 1759.

WILLIAM BECKFORD (1760–1844). *Vathek,* 1787.

OLIVER GOLDSMITH (1728–74). *The Vicar of Wakefield,* 1766.

HENRY MACKENZIE (1745–1831). *The Man of Feeling,* 1771.

FANNY BURNEY (1752–1840). *Evelina,* 1778.

HORACE WALPOLE (1717–97). *The Castle of Otranto,* 1764.

MRS. ANN RADCLIFFE (1764–1823). *The Romance of the Forest,* 1791; *The Mysteries of Udolpho,* 1794.

MATTHEW GREGORY LEWIS (1775–1818). *The Monk,* 1795.

THOMAS DAY (1748–89). *Sandford and Merton,* 1783–89.

MRS. ELIZABETH INCHBALD (1753–1821). *Nature and Art,* 1796.

WILLIAM GODWIN (1756–1836). *Caleb Williams,* 1794.

THE EARLY NINETEENTH CENTURY

MARIA EDGEWORTH (1767–1849). *Castle Rackrent,* 1800; *The Absentee,* 1812.

JANE AUSTEN (1775–1817). *Pride and Prejudice,* 1813; *Emma,* 1816; *Persuasion,* 1818.

SIR WALTER SCOTT (1771–1832). *Guy Mannering,* 1815; *Old Mortality,* 1816; *Ivanhoe,* 1819; *Quentin Durward,* 1823.

JOHN GALT (1779–1839). *The Annals of the Parish,* 1821.

MARY RUSSELL MITFORD (1787–1855). *Our Village,* 1824–32.

MRS. MARY W. SHELLEY (1797–1851). *Frankenstein,* 1818.

WILLIAM HARRISON AINSWORTH (1805–82). *Rookwood,* 1834; *The Tower of London,* 1840.

CAPTAIN FREDERICK MARRYAT (1792–1848). *Peter Simple,* 1834.

THOMAS LOVE PEACOCK (1785–1866). *Nightmare Abbey,* 1818; *Crotchet Castle,* 1831.

BENJAMIN DISRAELI, EARL OF BEACONSFIELD (1804–81). *Coningsby,* 1844; *Sybil,* 1845.

EDWARD BULWER-LYTTON, LORD LYTTON (1803–73). *Paul Clifford,* 1830; *The Last Days of Pompeii,* 1834; *The Haunted and the Haunters,* 1859.

THE VICTORIAN ERA

CHARLES DICKENS (1812–70). *The Pickwick Papers,* 1837; *David Copperfield,* 1850; *A Tale of Two Cities,* 1859; *Great Expectations,* 1861.

WILLIAM MAKEPEACE THACKERAY (1811–63). *Vanity Fair,* 1848; *Pendennis,* 1850; *Henry Esmond,* 1852.

CHARLOTTE BRONTË (1816–55). *Jane Eyre,* 1847; *Villette,* 1853.

EMILY BRONTË (1818–48). *Wuthering Heights,* 1847.

Mrs. Elizabeth Gaskell (1810–65). *Mary Barton,* 1848; *Cranford,* 1853; *Cousin Phillis,* 1865.

Anthony Trollope (1815–82). *The Warden,* 1855; *Barchester Towers,* 1857.

Charles Kingsley (1819–75). *Yeast,* 1851; *Hypatia,* 1853.

Wilkie Collins (1824–89). *The Woman in White,* 1860; *The Moonstone,* 1868.

Charles Reade (1814–84). *It Is Never Too Late to Mend,* 1856; *The Cloister and the Hearth,* 1861.

George Borrow (1803–81). *Lavengro,* 1851.

"George Eliot" (Mary Ann Cross, née Evans; 1819–80). *Adam Bede,* 1859; *Silas Marner,* 1861; *Middlemarch,* 1871–2.

George Meredith (1828–1909). *The Ordeal of Richard Feverel,* 1859; *The Egoist,* 1879; *Diana of the Crossways,* 1885.

Thomas Hardy (1840–1928). *Far from the Madding Crowd,* 1874; *The Return of the Native,* 1878; *The Mayor of Casterbridge,* 1886; *Tess of 'the D'Urbervilles,* 1891; *Jude the Obscure,* 1895.

Mrs. Humphry Ward (1851–1920). *Robert Elsmere,* 1888.

The Close of the Nineteenth Century

George Gissing (1857–1903). *The Unclassed,* 1884; *The Nether World,* 1889; *New Grub Street,* 1891.

George Moore (1852–1933). *Esther Waters,* 1894; *Memoirs of My Dead Life,* 1906; *Héloise and Abélard,* 1921; *Celibate Lives,* 1927.

Walter Pater (1839–94). *Marius the Epicurean,* 1885.

Oscar Wilde (1856–1900). *The Picture of Dorian Gray,* 1891.

Hubert Crackanthorpe (1865–96). *Wreckage,* 1893.

Henry James (1843–1916). *The American,* 1877; *Daisy Miller,* 1878; *The Portrait of a Lady,* 1881; *The Tragic Muse,* 1890; *The Ambassadors,* 1903.

Robert Louis Stevenson (1850–94). *Treasure Island,* 1883; *Dr. Jekyll and Mr. Hyde,* 1886; *Kidnapped,* 1886.

Maurice Hewlett (1861–1923). *Little Novels of Italy,* 1899; *The Fool Errant,* 1905.

Rudyard Kipling (1865–1936). *The Jungle Book,* 1894; *Kim,* 1901.

Samuel Butler (1835–1902). *Erewhon,* 1872; *The Way of All Flesh,* 1903.

William Henry Hudson (1841–1922). *A Crystal Age,* 1887; *Green Mansions,* 1904.

The Early Twentieth Century

Arnold Bennett (1867–1931). *The Old Wives' Tale*, 1908; *Clayhanger*, 1910; *Riceyman Steps*, 1923.

Herbert George Wells (1866–1946). *The Time Machine*, 1895; *Kipps*, 1905; *Tono-Bungay*, 1909; *Mr. Britling Sees It Through*, 1916; *The Undying Fire*, 1919.

John Galsworthy (1867–1933). *The Man of Property*, 1906; *Fraternity*, 1909; *In Chancery*, 1920; *To Let*, 1921.

Joseph Conrad (1857–1924). *The Nigger of the Narcissus*, 1897; *Lord Jim*, 1900; *Youth*, 1902; *Nostromo*, 1904; *The Shadow Line*, 1917.

William Somerset Maugham (1874–   ). *Of Human Bondage*, 1915.

Edward Morgan Forster (1879–   ). *A Room with a View*, 1908; *Howard's End*, 1910; *A Passage to India*, 1924.

David Herbert Lawrence (1885–1930). *Sons and Lovers*, 1913; *The Plumed Serpent*, 1926; *The Man Who Died*, 1931.

May Sinclair (1879?–1946). *Mary Olivier*, 1919; *Mr. Waddington of Wyck*, 1921.

Frank Swinnerton (1884–   ). *Nocturne*, 1917.

Rose Macaulay. *Potterism*, 1920; *Told by an Idiot*, 1923.

"Rebecca West" (Mrs. H. M. Andrews, née Fairfield; 1892–   ). *The Thinking Reed*, 1936.

Max Beerbohm (1872–   ). *Zuleika Dobson*, 1911.

Norman Douglas (1868–   ). *South Wind*, 1917.

Walter de la Mare (1873–   ). *Memoirs of a Midget*, 1921.

Ralph Hale Mottram (1883–   ). *The Spanish Farm*, 1924.

Dorothy M. Richardson (Mrs. Alan Odle). *Pointed Roofs*, 1915; *Backwater*, 1916; *Honeycomb*, 1917.

James Joyce (1882–1941). *A Portrait of the Artist as a Young Man*, 1916; *Ulysses*, 1922.

Mrs. Virginia Woolf (1882–1941). *Jacob's Room*, 1922; *Mrs. Dalloway*, 1925; *To the Lighthouse*, 1927.

Aldous Huxley (1894–   ). *Antic Hay*, 1923; *Point Counter Point*, 1928; *Brave New World*, 1932.

INDEX

Addison, Joseph, 85
Ainsworth, William H., 121, 131; *Jack Sheppard*, 153; *Rookwood*, 152, 350; *The Tower of London*, 350
Allen, Grant, *The Woman Who Did*, 332
Arabian Nights, 132
Aristotle, 18, 50, 52
Austen, Jane, 18, 97–112, 113, 114, 115, 127, 135, 154, 164, 172, 176, 179, 214, 221, 222, 238, 251, 263; *Emma*, 50, 101–112, 113, 128, 144, 203, 238, 350; *Love and Freind-ship*, 98; *Mansfield Park*, 101, 113; *Northanger Abbey*, 99; *Persuasion*, 101, 113, 350; *Pride and Prejudice*, 50, 100, 350; *Sense and Sensibility*, 99

Baker, Ernest A., *The History of the English Novel*, 10
Balzac, Honoré de, 117, 130, 171, 198, 199, 264, 266, 274, 276, 283; *Human Comedy*, 256; *La cousine Bette*, 258; *La Maison du chat qui pelote* (*At the Sign of the Cat and Racket*), 311–312; *Le Père Goriot*, 274
Barker, H. Granville, 322
Baudelaire, Charles, 264
Beckford, William, *Vathek*, 349
Beerbohm, Max, *Zuleika Dobson*, 352
Behn, Mrs. Aphra, 4; *Oroonoko, or The Royal Slave*, 4, 349

Bennett, Enoch Arnold, 274, 275, 303–319, 322; *Anna of the Five Towns*, 303, 304, 305, 308; *Buried Alive*, 309; *The Card* (*Denry the Audacious*), 309; *The City of Pleasure*, 309; *Clayhanger*, 246, 305, 306, 309, 310, 326, 352; *The Grand Babylon Hotel*, 309; *Helen with the High Hand*, 309; *Hilda Lessways*, 309; *Imperial Palace*, 306, 307, 310; *Journal*, 303, 311; *Journalism for Women*, 305; *Leonora*, 308; *A Man from the North*, 305, 308; *The Old Wives' Tale*, 246, 305, 310–319, 352; *The Pretty Lady*, 305, 310; *Riceyman Steps*, 304, 310, 352; *Teresa of Watling Street*, 309; *These Twain*, 309; *Whom God Hath Joined*, 309
Benson, E. F., *Charlotte Brontë*, 186
Bergson, Henri, 149, 220, 341; *Laugh-ter*, 147
Bernard, Claude, *L'Introduction à la médecine expérimentale*, 257
Borrow, George, *Lavengro*, 351
Bourget, Paul, 265
Bradley, A. C., 149
Brontë, Anne (Acton Bell), 184; *Ag-nes Grey*, 184; *The Tenant of Wild-fell Hall*, 184
Brontë, Charlotte (Currer Bell), 19, 169–183, 184, 188, 189, 200, 214, 238; *Jane Eyre*, 142, 169, 170, 173, 174–183, 184, 185, 193, 198, 350;